Housing Economics and Public Policy

T0323549

Housing Economics and Public Policy

Edited by

Tony O'Sullivan

Head of Planning
Communities Scotland

and

Kenneth Gibb

Reader
Department of Urban Studies
University of Glasgow

Essays in honour of Duncan Maclennan

Blackwell
Science

© Blackwell Science Ltd 2003
Blackwell Science Ltd, a Blackwell
Publishing Company
Editorial Offices:
Osney Mead, Oxford OX2 0EL, UK
  Tel: +44 (0)1865 206206
Blackwell Science, Inc., 350 Main Street,
Malden, MA 02148-5018, USA
  Tel: +1 781 388 8250
Iowa State Press, a Blackwell Publishing
Company, 2121 State Avenue, Ames, Iowa
50014-8300, USA
  Tel: +1 515 292 0140
Blackwell Publishing Asia Pty Ltd,
550 Swanston Street, Carlton South,
Victoria 3053, Australia
  Tel: +61 (0)3 9347 0300
Blackwell Wissenschafts Verlag,
Kurfürstendamm 57, 10707 Berlin, Germany
  Tel: +49 (0)30 32 79 060

First published 2003 by Blackwell Science Ltd

Library of Congress
Cataloging-in-Publication Data
is available

ISBN 0-632-06461-7

A catalogue record for this title is available
from the British Library

Set in 10/13 pt Trump Mediaeval
by Sparks Computer Solutions Ltd, Oxford
http://www.sparks.co.uk

For further information on
Blackwell Science, visit our website:
www.blackwell-science.com

Real Estate Issues

Series Managing Editors
Stephen Brown RICS Foundation
John Henneberry Department of Town & Regional Planning, University of Sheffield
James Shilling Department of Real Estate and Urban Land Economics, University of Wisconsin – Madison

Real Estate Issues is a book series presenting the latest thinking into how real estate markets operate. Based upon strong theoretical concepts, it is inclusive in nature, drawing both upon established techniques for real estate market analysis and on those from other academic disciplines. It embraces a comparative approach, allowing best practice to be put forward and tested for its applicability and relevance to the understanding of new situations. It does not impose solutions, but provides a means by which solutions can be found. *Real Estate Issues* does not make any presumptions as to the significance of real estate markets, but presents the real significance of the operation of these markets.

Books in this series

Guy & Henneberry *Development and Developers*
Adams & Watkins *Greenfields, Brownfields and Housing Development*
O'Sullivan & Gibb *Housing Economics and Public Policy*
Couch, Fraser & Percy *Urban Regeneration in Europe*
Stephens *Housing Finance and Owner-occupation*
Brown & Jaffe *Real Estate Investment*
Seabrooke & How *International Real Estate*
Allen & Barlow *Housing in Southern Europe*
Ball *Markets and Institutions in Real Estate and Construction*

RICS **FOUNDATION**

For Amanda, Amy, Gemma, and Angela

Contents

Contributors

Richard Best (Richard.Best@jrf.org.uk)
Director of the Joseph Rowntree Foundation in York and its housing association, the Joseph Rowntree Housing Trust. He was previously Director of the National Federation of Housing Associations and before that Director of the British Churches Housing Trust. He has been involved in housing policy issues for some thirty years, including serving on many government bodies, task forces, Ministerial Sounding Boards, etc. He became an independent life peer in 2001.

Glen Bramley (G.Bramley@riker.eca.ac.uk)
Professor of Planning & Housing at Heriot-Watt University in Edinburgh, where he leads a substantial research programme in housing and urban studies. Recent work is focused particularly on housing need and areas of low demand for housing, flows of funds to local areas, planning for new housing and the impact of planning and infrastructure on city competitiveness. He directs a Centre for Research into Socially Inclusive Services (CRSIS). His publications include *Planning, the Market and Private Housebuilding* (UCL Press 1995), *Equalization Grants and Local Expenditure Needs* (Avebury 1990) and *Analysing Social Policy* (Blackwell 1986), as well as numerous articles in journals such as *Urban Studies, Housing Studies, Environment and Planning, Regional Studies, Policy & Politics.*

David Donnison (D.Donnison@udcf.gla.ac.uk)
Honorary research fellow and professor emeritus in the Department of Urban Studies, University of Glasgow. He was previously Glasgow's professor of Town and Regional Planning and, before that, chair of the Supplementary Benefits Commission and Director of the Centre for Environmental Studies. His latest book is *Policies for a Just Society* (Macmillan 1998), and his more recent writing has dealt mainly with poverty, and the evolution of social policies since World War II.

George Galster (aa3571@wayne.edu)
Clarence Hilberry Professor of Urban Affairs at the College of Urban, Labor, and Metropolitan Affairs, Wayne State University, Detroit, USA. He earned his Ph.D. in Economics from M.I.T. He has published over 100 scholarly articles and book chapters, primarily on the topics of metropolitan housing

markets, racial discrimination and segregation, neighbourhood dynamics, residential reinvestment, community lending and insurance patterns, and urban poverty. He is the co-author of *The Maze of Urban Housing Markets* 1991, and the forthcoming *Why NOT in My Back Yard: Neighbourhood Impacts of Assisted Housing*.

Kenneth Gibb (k.gibb@socsci.gla.ac.uk)
Reader in Housing Economics in the Department of Urban Studies at the University of Glasgow. His research concerns aspects of housing markets and housing policy. In recent years, the main focus has been on housing demand, the economics of social housing and local market analysis. He is the co-author of *Housing Finance in the UK: An Introduction* (Macmillan 1999) and is currently working on a book entitled *The Economics of Housing Policy* for Edward Elgar. Kenneth is on the board of the European Real Estate Society and directs undergraduate teaching in his department.

William Grigsby (grigsby@poboxupenn.edu)
Emeritus professor in City and Regional Planning at the University of Pennsylvania. Professor Grigsby has had a distinguished career research-ing housing markets, urban policy and neighbourhood dynamics. He was the author of *Housing Markets and Public Policy* in 1963 and co-authored *The Dynamics of Neighbourhood Change and Decline* (1987) with Baratz, Galster and Maclennan.

Joseph Gyourko (gyourko@Wharton.upenn.edu)
Martin Bucksbaum Professor of Real Estate and Finance at The Wharton School of the University of Pennsylvania. He also serves as Director of the Zell/Lurie Real Estate Centre at Wharton and Chair of the Real Estate Depart-ment. Professor Gyourko received his BA from Duke University and a Ph.D. in economics from the University of Chicago. His research interests include real estate finance, local public finance, and urban economics. Formerly co-editor of *Real Estate Economics*, Professor Gyourko serves on a number of editorial boards. He is a Trustee Fellow of the Urban Land Institute (ULI), and serves on the Real Estate Roundtable's Research Committee. Professor Gyourko also serves on the board of EII Realty Securities, a real estate mutual fund, and consults on real estate valuation and securities issues.

Stephen Malpezzi (smalpezzi@bus.wisc.edu)
Associate Professor, and Wangard Faculty Scholar, in the University of

Wisconsin-Madison's Department of Real Estate and Urban Land Economics (http://www.bus.wisc.edu/realestate). Dr. Malpezzi's research includes work on economic development, the measurement and determinants of real estate prices, housing demand, and on the effects of economic policies on real estate markets. He is co-author with Richard Green of *A Primer on U.S. Housing Markets and Policy*, published by the American Real Estate and Urban Economics Association.

Geoffrey Meen (g.p.meen@reading.ac.uk)
Professor of Applied Economics in the Department of Economics at The University of Reading and specialises in the use of quantitative techniques in national, regional and urban housing market analysis. He is the author of *Modelling Spatial Housing Markets: Theory, Analysis and Policy* (Kluwer Academic Publishers 2001) as well as contributing to the major academic journals in the field. Geoff is Head of the Department of Economics at Reading University and also Research Director for the University's School of Business.

Tony O'Sullivan (osullivana@communitiesscotland.gov.uk)
Tony O'Sullivan (Ph.D. Economics, Sussex) is Head of Planning for Communities Scotland, a national government agency in Scotland involved in housing investment and community regeneration. He joined the agency in 1989 after holding a lectureship in housing economics at the University of Glasgow for much of the 1980s. He has managed the agency's research activities, including national house condition surveys. He is co-author of *Local Housing System Analysis: A Best Practice Guide* (1998, Scottish Homes, Edinburgh) and has researched in the areas of housing subsidies, fuel poverty and the sale of public housing stock.

John M. Quigley (quigley@econ.Berkeley.edu)
I. Donald Terner Distinguished Professor, and Professor of Economics, at the University of California, Berkeley. His recent research is on the integration of real estate, mortgage, and financial markets, urban labour markets, and public finance. His most recent book, *Homeless in California* (2001, with Raphael & Smolensky, Public Policy of California, San Francisco) evaluates policies to subsidise housing consumption for households with very low incomes.

Mark Stephens (M.Stephens@socsci.gla.ac.uk)
Senior Lecturer in the Department of Urban Studies, University of Glasgow. He specialises in comparative housing policy and in the impact of European Economic and Monetary Union on housing systems. He is co-author of *Housing Policy in Britain and Europe* (UCL Press 1995), co-editor of *European Integration and Housing Policy* (Routledge 1998) and co-author of *Social Market or Safety Net? British Social Rented Housing in a European Context* (Policy Press 2002). He is editor of the *European Journal of Housing Policy* and a member of the Co-ordination Committee of the European Network for Housing Research.

Yong Tu (tuyong@nus.edu.sg)
Assistant Professor in Housing Economics in the Department of Real Estate, School of Design and Environment, at National University of Singapore. Her research concerns aspects of housing markets and housing policy. In recent years, the main focus has been on modelling urban housing demand, price discovery, and Asian housing market analyses.

Christine Whitehead (C.M.E.Whitehead@lse.ac.uk)
Professor in Housing in the Department of Economics, London School of Economics and Director of the Cambridge Centre for Housing and Planning Research, University of Cambridge. Her work in the housing field has ranged from an econometric model of the UK housing system through acting as a member of the government's Housing Policy Review research team. Lately, her research has concentrated on aspects of housing finance and social housing provision as well as on privatisation and the relationship between affordable housing and land use planning. Her latest publications include '*Restructuring Housing Systems*' (York Publishing 2000), which she co-edited with Sarah Monk. She is adviser to the House of Commons Select Committee on Transport, Local Government and Regional Affairs and was awarded the OBE for services to housing.

Nick Williams (n.williams@aberdeen.ac.uk)
Formerly Senior Lecturer in Geography at Aberdeen University, and now a self-employed housing and environmental consultant. His major areas of interest are social rented housing, urban sustainability and environmental aspects of housing. He is co-author of the *Sustainable Housing Design Guide* for Scotland, (The Stationery Office Books, London), and *Greening the Built Environment* published by Earthscan, London. Nick is a committee member

and former chair of Castlehill Housing Association, and is also Policy Convenor of the Scottish Federation of Housing Associations.

Gavin A. Wood (wood@central.murdoch.edu.au)
A senior lecturer in economics at Murdoch University, Australia and deputy director of the Australian Housing and Urban Research Institute's Western Australia centre. His main research area is housing economics. The main focus of his recent work has been the design of microsimulation models of housing markets, agency problems in rental housing and the impact of taxation on housing investment. He has published widely in international academic journals, and is on the International Editorial Advisory Committee of *Urban Studies*.

Preface

This volume honours an urban economics scholar who has bridged long-standing gaps between a number of often quite dissimilar worlds – neoclassical and institutional economics, academia and government, Britain and its neighbouring continents, and the two sides of Hadrian's Wall. By creatively using the knowledge and perspectives of one world to advance discourse in another, Duncan Maclennan has made a singular contribution both to our understanding of urban phenomena and to the design of urban and housing policy. His *Housing Economics* (1982) changed the way in which we think about urban housing markets.

As important as Maclennan's own research and practice have been to the urban economics and housing policy arenas, his research leadership has perhaps been even more influential. In directing Britain's foremost housing research programmes, he developed and implemented a research agenda that has helped to reshape the way in which housing policy questions in Britain are being explored. In carrying out this agenda and through work for OECD, he has brought together housing analysts from different backgrounds and often conflicting ideologies to search for common themes and principles that could be broadly applied.

Maclennan's success in bridging intellectual chasms and crossing the boundaries of academic disciplines has been achieved in part through his wit and warmth but also through the contributions of urban analysts whom he either groomed or influenced. A few of the many persons who have enjoyed and benefited from the collegial settings he has created over the years have chosen to author this book of essays in his honour. These essays do not have a common theme except to the extent that together they reflect the range of Maclennan's interests. Their preparation is also a reflection of the affection and esteem in which the authors hold the person they have chosen to recognise in this fashion.

William Grigsby
University of Pennsylvania
Philadelphia,
May 2002

Acknowledgements

We would like to record our gratitude to a number of people and organisations that helped in the preparation of this book. First drafts of the chapters in this book were presented at a seminar held at the University of Glasgow in November 2001. Communities Scotland provided financial support for this event, which significantly contributed to the quality of the final product. Elizabeth Nicholson gave sterling and stoic support in the organisation and running of this seminar. Gillian Blacklaw provided able secretarial support to the project, and Laure Paterson worked tirelessly on proofing and referencing matters. We received consistent encouragement and support from our commissioning editor at Blackwell's, Madeleine Metcalfe, and constant forbearance and understanding from our families during preparation that was far beyond the limits of reasonable expectation.

As well as providing the substance of this volume, all those who contributed did so with great enthusiasm, and agreed to waive any royalty rights in favour of giving any earnings from sales of the book to Shelter Scotland. We thank them for this generosity.

Tony O'Sullivan
Kenneth Gibb
May 2002

1

Introduction

Tony O'Sullivan & Kenneth Gibb

From its very beginnings as a discipline for the study of society, economists have sought to apply economics to real world issues. While the roots of housing economics can be traced back to the work of the original classical and neoclassical pioneers of economic theory, it did not emerge as a separate and recognised area in its own right until very late in the day. After World War II economists, particularly in Europe, turned their attentions to a number of pressing issues of social policy, leading to the emergence of bodies of work on the economics of poverty, transport, education, and health. Applying the insights of welfare economics and emerging theoretical and practical developments, this work sought to address various efficiency and equity issues as they related to the everyday lives of millions of people as citizens and consumers. Not in the vanguard of this work, interest in housing as a proper area for study in the UK began to develop in a serious way from the 1970s onwards. Duncan Maclennan has from the first been prominent in contributing to and promoting this. The idea behind this book was a wish on the part of many contributors to the field to recognise his contributions.

Perspectives on theory

Housing is a difficult thing to theorise about. An inherently complex commodity, with spatial fixity a defining characteristic, and asset, investment and consumption dimensions to account for, the economics of housing remains a challenge to those who seek equity and efficiency improvements for society to this day. It is a field of inquiry where, in Joan Robinson's terms, thinking in 'theory time' is a poor substitute for recognising the role of real, non-abstract, historical time. Moreover, abstracting from the spatial aspects of housing leads, to quote Maclennan, to a curious form of 'pointless economics'. Good theory necessarily involves jettisoning many of the assumptions usually made in neoclassical economics, rendering the work more difficult and 'messy'.

Early contributions from Maclennan drew on the insights of the Austrian school, and the work of such authors as Hayeck and Von Mises. The insights produced by the Austrians concerning information, knowledge, ignorance and time are central to his work on housing search and choice (Maclennan 1982). For Maclennan, information problems are central features of the housing market, as are spatial externalities, and transactions costs associated with mobility. In such a world, neo-institutional economics (Oliver Williamson 1975, 1985), evolutionary economics and disequilibrium analysis are often the natural modes of analysis to adopt in order better to understand housing phenomena.

Demand for 'housing' in the real world necessarily embodies demand for place, for access to public and private services, and reflects the fact that housing is in part at least a 'positional good' (Hirsch 1976). Maclennan built these factors into his work from the outset, and recognised the implications for the spatial structure of housing markets. Consequently, space and place feature prominently throughout Maclennan's work, both as a key friction for understanding the complexity of housing and its impact on household and market behaviour.

Maclennan has investigated the implications of space at several different housing market scales. An enduring concern has been examining the process of neighbourhood change, within which neighbourhoods are defined as relatively open residential production and consumption spaces. Maclennan has sought throughout his career to apply useful economic models to the problem of interest. One such example at the neighbourhood scale has been his attempt to capture house price change in unimproved properties after nearby properties have received grant aid to improve their fabric, thus measuring the neighbourhood externality (Maclennan 1993b). More generally, in collaboration with American colleagues (Grigsby *et al.* 1987), he helped develop a comprehensive framework for deciphering neighbourhood change.

At the urban or metropolitan scale, Maclennan has both examined spatial aspects explicitly through the early exploration of the concept of housing sub-markets (and the associated concept of 'product groups') and used the urban level of analysis as the implicit or explicit focus for microeconomic models of tenure choice, search and housing choice (often in collaboration with Gavin Wood) (Wood & Maclennan 1982; Maclennan & Wood 1982a). In his 1982 text, Maclennan went a long way to establish a richer conception of housing choice, rooted in real time decision-making, search and bidding behaviour, the active role of institutions and a more appropriate notion of equilibrium initially developed by Frank Hahn, where market equilibrium is based on learning of information by economic actors.

Information, time and space matter as much for supply and its appropriate conceptualisation as they do for demand. Again, Maclennan made it clear from the outset that the reductionist approach of neoclassical theory was particularly inappropriate to many of the tasks at hand. He showed that noise in the market, and uncertainty about the nature and meaning of market 'signals' result in endemic inefficiency and market failure (Maclennan 1982). These insights remain to be built upon.

Defining the product 'housing' is a basic issue in the conceptualisation of housing demand, supply, and the housing 'market'. Equally fundamental is getting an adequate handle on the concept of the 'price' of housing. Over time hedonic analysis has become the approach of choice for most economists, but it has some quite fundamental limitations. These certainly do not invalidate the use of this technique, but they do indicate the need to be careful in its application. Maclennan, who has used the technique frequently in his work, provided an early and cogent summary of these limitations (Maclennan 1977b).

A specific issue relating to the price of housing is that of housing subsidies – their definition, measurement and impacts (not to mention their rationale). Often these take the form of tax concessions. Considerable work in this area has occurred in the last 20 years, following early critique of the efficiency and equity effects of such subsidies (in the UK context see for example Robinson 1981; Maclennan & Wood 1982b; Maclennan & O'Sullivan 1987; O'Sullivan 1984, 1987). Much subsidisation of housing, however, particularly in a European context, has been tied into direct provision through public or social housing. This has raised issues not just about the welfare implications of the pricing of housing, but the comparative efficiency of public versus private provision. On pricing *per se* a considerable literature has developed, to which Maclennan has contributed (Atkinson & King 1980; Grey *et al.* 1981; Ermisch 1984; Hills 1991, 2000; Maclennan 1986b). On the question of public versus private provision, traditionally non-market providers of housing have operated through bureaucratic hierarchies, providing a rich opportunity to apply Coasian transactions costs concepts and insights from the wider work of Oliver Williamson to the specifics of organisational efficiency in public housing. Maclennan contributed to such analysis in the late 1980s in considering the comparative efficiency of different housing providers in the UK (Centre for Housing Research 1989).

While the microeconomics of housing has developed apace over the last two decades, attention has also been given to modelling at the regional and macro scale. At the national scale of analysis, housing in the UK (as elsewhere) was transformed in the 1980s by a process of financial deregulation. Collaborative work by Maclennan with Geoff Meen, John Muellbauer, Mark Stephens and others identified many of the connections between housing and the macro-economy and helped forge a bridge between housing specialists and those macroeconomists coming to the housing sector for the first time. This also helped policy makers who needed to understand the micro-foundations of mortgage market change, housing equity withdrawal, house price volatility and their transmission mechanisms into consumption, indebtedness and the labour market (Maclennan *et al.* 1997).

Policy and practice

Much of the interest in housing economics that has developed over the last two decades has emerged on the back of considerable intervention in housing by central and municipal government. Policy makers of all political hues, especially but not exclusively in Europe, have seen it as desirable if not essential to intervene in, regulate, suspend, replace or compete with various aspects of the housing market. Maclennan has been particularly active in seeking to influence policy, especially, but not exclusively, in a UK context. In doing this, being based at the University of Glasgow for most of his professional working life is not the only link between Maclennan and the classical economists. In his conception of policy there is much to link Maclennan's approach to the classical school.

From the first, any failure to distinguish technical from ideological positions in policy analysis has been rejected as at best sloppy intellectualism and at worst sharp practice. This does not imply however that he has promoted a narrow 'technical' interpretation of the economist's role in policy formulation; on the contrary he has been a constant advocate of a broader 'political economy' interpretation of the role. Moreover, the use of assumptions regarding the operation of housing (and wider economic) systems to progress an argument, where the basis should be the results of applied research, has usually been given short shrift. In this regard, Maclennan has been very aware of the relatively poor base provided for applied research by official statistics and has indeed been a stern critic of government.

In 2001 Maclennan was involved in redesigning the Right to Buy (RTB) in Scotland as an element of what was to become the Housing Act (Scotland)

2001. Starting from an examination of the available evidence he commented:

> 'The RTB has been a source of enduring controversy over the two decades since its introduction. Views on policy proposals can diverge for at least three different reasons. First, individuals or organisations may have different ethical or political views about an issue and facts or evidence may have little relevance in resolving such differences. Secondly, many policy decisions involve changes with complex, long-term effects on the economy and society. Individuals with the same values may reach different conclusions because their model or analysis of impacts differs from each other. Again this requires judgement in choices, but it also requires the participants in a debate to be clear and consistent in their analyses. Finally, even with the same ethical values and analytical approaches, individuals may reach different conclusions if they have different facts or evidence at hand.'

> (Maclennan *et al.* 2000, p. 1)

These views echo those expressed in his 1982 text (which, coincidentally, used the then very new RTB issue to illustrate the point).

Maclennan has consistently rebuked both economists and critics from other disciplines who have sought to interpret or represent the role of the economist in policy discourse as being focused on competitive housing markets, the use of deductive partial or general equilibrium models, or to be unthinkingly centred on Pareto-based social welfare functions. For him,

> '... it is not enough to restrict the role of the political economist to accurately describing market behaviour for policy makers – although such action may be an improvement on proffering advice largely based on deductive reasoning and assumption. Instead, applied economic analysis of policy (or political economy) requires the analysis of a more detailed set of questions. For instance the analyst must enquire as to what are the objectives of government, what role housing policy plays in attaining such objectives, who actually makes housing policy, what economic and political constraints restrict action, what advice and information exists and what model of the housing system is used by policy makers? These questions are not to be viewed as minor concerns for applied economists. Economists may deduce conditions for optimality or second best conditions for the design of housing policies *ad infinitum* but unless they understand how economic analysis and research is absorbed and transformed by the policy

process they run the risk of having their work, at best, ignored or, at worst, misused.'

(Maclennan 1982, p. 142)

Policy influence, then, must start from an understanding of the institutional, administrative and legal contexts from which policies emerge. Ethical positions on policy issues are acceptable (indeed unavoidable) but should be explicit and honest. Value judgement should not be dressed up as technical issue, and ignorance on empirical matters of importance must be acknowledged and must constitute the soil to be tilled by the applied researcher. This view of the policy role is demanding above all else of honesty, and for this reason is brutally demanding in application.

While Maclennan has been clear from the start of his career that governments can quite legitimately hold to non-Paretian objectives, he has also been steadfast that these objectives must be capable of clear operational interpretation. This in Maclennan's eyes is perhaps the key part of the bargain policy makers have to deliver, for the policy-making process to have any hope of working to the benefit of the citizen – the impact on whom always remains the focus of Maclennan's work. In his writings but even more so in direct dealings with senior government administrators, ministers and politicians, he has delivered this message in an uncompromising way. Given this, other issues can be largely worked around – recognising there is plenty to be so worked.

For a start, the structure of government and the distribution of policy responsibility across different tiers and geographies of government make the achievement of coherent policy intrinsically difficult. Joined-up government is a popular current slogan, but also a desideratum recommended by Maclennan over 20 years ago – with due recognition of the inertia built into the existing system, and the consequent need for an institutional economics perspective on the problem. Writing in the UK policy context he noted:

'[The] complex organisational model for housing policy in Britain would not necessarily be inadequate if some centrally determined operational principles for policy existed such as market pricing or income/wealth related subsidy systems. But where policy, as in Britain, lacks a central organising principle then the distribution of subsidy reflects neither house type nor household characteristics but is an outcome of chance, history and in particular of tenure selected. Thus, whilst it has been argued that housing market intervention may be rational and required, it is difficult to believe that the present system could not be improved or it may even

be that the imperfect market system that the policy is designed to circum-
vent would perform more effectively as an agent of allocation and redistribution. However it is probably not possible to answer this question in the
UK because, as in most fields of policy in the country, there is often more
concern with the level than the quality of public expenditure.'

(Maclennan 1982, p. 167)

In his 1982 text, he categorised housing policy into a number of different
types of successively greater generality. These were:

- Removing specific market failures through taxation, subsidisation, or
  regulatory action

- Replacing fundamentally unfixable market with administered allocation
  mechanisms

- Using housing as primary vehicle for achieving non-allocational ends,
  such as income redistribution, or regional growth.

His subsequent work has demonstrated that simple or pat conclusions on
the relative attractiveness of state versus market-based policy solutions,
while endemic in policy debate, invariably miss the point. In local markets,
for example, it is not clear that public monopoly provision would be in any
way superior to a private sector version. In a sense the policy question of
interest to Maclennan has always been not whether housing (and regional
economic) outcomes can be optimised by state intervention or forbearance,
but whether, working in a real world context, market failure or state failure
constitute the least bad means to achieve clearly articulated ends. To answer
this question, he made an early plea for what has come to be widely referred
to as 'evidence based policy'.

Starting in his 1982 text, Maclennan made a point that has continually re-
curred in his work: that there is a need for a co-ordinated provision of market
and non-market information to drive market allocation decisions, and to
inform public action. The absence of this information base resourced (if not
necessarily discharged) as a function of government has, he has argued, led
to poor investment planning in the private as well as the public sector. In a
public policy context, the consequences are as follows:

'In this context for policy formulation, there are two alternatives at least
for formulating strategies. First, ministers ... will listen to the arguments
of pressure groups and interested parties. Power, in this case, not to the

people, but to the groups with organisation and capital to present the most convincing (not the best) case. Alternatively, ministers with an inner circle of policy advisors may form a view as to what is appropriate policy. These views may be based either simply on ideologies or on a limited or even partially researched view of the housing system.'

(Maclennan 1982, pp. 168-9)

Part of the problem as he saw it was the absence of appropriate training for those engaged in policy making and implementation, from the strategic to matters of detailed operation. He certainly demonstrated the personal courage of this conviction, in one instance telling an audience of around 500 not-for-profit housing practitioners that in his opinion they couldn't strategically plan their way out of a paper bag! More constructively, his view has been expressed as follows:

'It must be of some concern within central government that many officials responsible for policy have no initial familiarity with housing and that, within the British Civil Service, transfer often follows mature acquisition of insight. Similar comments ... apply within local authorities and the lack of formal training within public housing management is now the cause of some concern ...'

(Maclennan 1982, p. 168)

This in part has led to the establishment of major programmes of housing training at Glasgow University from the early 1980s onwards, integrating theory, policy and practice. These covered both the needs of housing management and development practitioners through to the tutelage of civil servants and local authority officials at a postgraduate level.

Maclennan was heavily critical of policy reflected in key pieces of housing legislation in the late 1970s and early 1980s (Maclennan 1982). He saw it as a professional responsibility on him and fellow economists to present government with usable models, methods and material that can improve the quality of public policy. His subsequent career has been geared to the dispensation of this responsibility at the national and international level. His success in this regard is perhaps best reflected in the pivotal design role he played in the development of the Housing Scotland Act 2001, which gave him the opportunity, albeit in a purely Scottish context, to influence the structure of the Right to Buy, of which he was so critical in 1982.

Contributions to this book

The contributors to this volume have all had the opportunity and pleasure of working with Duncan Maclennan at some time in their careers. Each of the chapters picks up on an area of interest to him over the last 20 years. Collectively, these chapters cover much of the landscape of housing economics and housing policy.

Urban housing models

The chapter by Kenneth Gibb assesses the different types of urban housing models that have been developed. Gibb considers the role the 'standard' access-space approach has played as the starting point for analysis of urban housing in much of the literature. The chapter makes a case for more extensive use of filtering research in the future investigation of urban housing systems. It also looks at the latest generation of urban simulation models, in particular those associated with Anas and Arnott, and presents a simplified metropolitan model of Greater Glasgow developed by Gibb, Meen & Mackay (2000).

More fundamentally however, Gibb argues that the evolution of these different types of model has failed to address many of the concerns voiced by Maclennan (and subsequently reiterated e.g. Maclennan & Gibb 1994). It is not that these models fail to give useful insights, but that by and large their strengths and weaknesses remain as profiled two decades ago. While filtering models perhaps as noted have a greater potential for providing insights than they have so far delivered, the whole field would benefit from new thinking. The future development of spatial models of the housing market will need to incorporate adjustment and disequilibrium on both sides of the market, information imperfections, reflect the importance of real time and process in market evolution, and capture the key role of housing market institutions in a way that can be sensibly operationalised. This is a formidable challenge.

Segmentation, adjustment and disequilibrium

Urban housing markets are generally thought of as segmented in one or more dimensions. This can be in product group terms, or in terms of quality hierarchies, where the key distinction is made in order to classify the market into sub-markets involving dwellings that are more or less substitutable as far as consumers are concerned. In her chapter, Yong Tu provides an analysis of the causes and consequences of housing market segmentation. Using the well-known conceptualisation of housing as a composite commodity, she defines sub-markets in terms of underlying attribute prices. A given attribute has a constant hedonic price within a sub-market but across sub-markets it will vary. One important implication of the analysis of segmentation Yong Tu provides is that disequilibrium is likely to be the norm. She examines the properties of such disequilibrium in the housing market.

Turning to the thorny problem of identifying housing sub-markets in practice, Yong Tu evaluates the main alternative methods and concludes that there is nothing that intrinsically distinguishes one as superior to another. Of more significance, her analysis suggests that urban house price indices should be constructed at sub-market level, and is again strongly persuasive that disequilibrium should be explicitly factored into analysis of urban housing. Yong Tu also argues that a disaggregated framework is the proper basis for analysing the local neighbourhood impacts of urban and housing policies.

Transactions costs

John Quigley's chapter deals with the question of transactions costs and their significance for the housing market. Apart from the costs of search, consumers must deal with legal negotiations and bargain with other parties. In addition, because choice is infrequent and information or knowledge of the housing market decays, costs linked to uncertainty and expectations are important (if inherently difficult to measure). His chapter sets out a taxonomy of these costs and reviews the empirical literature on their individual magnitudes. He reports, for example, that the average costs of negotiating and legal transactions in the US housing market vary from 6% to 12 % of house value. However, these costs may be relatively small in comparison to moving and psychic (adjustment) costs. Quigley presents a simple model based on consumers making move/stay decisions by comparing the discounted utility gains forgone by not moving with the discounted transactions costs that a move will incur. This, he suggests, gives an alternative basis for measuring the magnitude of transaction costs facing households to deriving this information through survey work.

Quigley also considers whether transactions costs in the housing market involve significant costs for the wider economy, and whether policies can be developed to lessen any such costs. Although Quigley acknowledges some limited theoretical support for Oswald's contention that reduced owner-occupier mobility is the source of higher associated unemployment among homeowners in different OECD countries (Oswald 1997b, 1999) (where debt constraints, such as negative equity, effectively act as arbitrarily high transactions costs inhibiting mobility), he finds no credible empirical evidence that home ownership causes high unemployment. Quigley argues that government should act to reduce transactions costs in the housing market, however, facilitating flows of information, and in the development of standards that can make transactions simpler.

Hedonic pricing models

Stephen Malpezzi reviews research on one of the most important tools in housing economics: hedonic price models. There is a voluminous literature concerned with house price index construction and a smaller field of work examining the underlying demand for individual attributes. In his chapter, Malpezzi provides a clear exposition of the fundamental conceptual and empirical issues often ignored when undertaking applied work in this area. In particular, he considers the functional form problem (there is no obvious *a priori* functional form to adopt and the one chosen is usually on the basis of convenience alone). Malpezzi reviews the econometric issues associated with identification, mis-specification, non-robustness of co-efficients, non-linearity and disequilibrium tendencies.

Malpezzi provides an overview of the main applications of hedonic analysis in housing and identifies areas that would repay further study. He draws on Maclennan's (1977b) work to suggest, given the continuing dependence of housing economics on this class of model, that hedonic models should *de minimis* possess three features: their use in any specific application should have a firm theoretical basis; their specification should be complete and if not the practical consequences should be fully explored; and, perhaps most critically, the design of a pricing model should be fit for its intended purpose. These recommendations are pertinent to a literature that is too often consumed by a sterile battle between protagonists of different index schools, the performance of which are not always strictly comparable.

Housing in the macroeconomy

In his chapter, Geoff Meen surveys the relationship between housing markets and the macro-economy. Meen organises his review around five themes: the relationship between house prices and consumer expenditure; the effect of housing on the labour market nationally and regionally; national differences in housing markets and their consequences for EMU; the contribution of housing to economic cycles; and possible links between housing and the spatial concentration of business start-ups.

He calls into question the feasibility of house price prediction, house price being the key variable linking housing to the macroeconomy, and moves on to investigate the implications of unpredictability and to suggest a different basis for housing market analysis starting from the bottom up, recognising that local markets cannot be treated as if they are all effectively the same. Meen examines the scope for using complexity theory as a basis for simulating local housing markets, characterised by heterogeneous agents, non-linear outcomes (such as 'tipping') and multiple equilibria (including prolonged disequilibria). Meen argues that tipping and thresholds are important processes underpinning neighbourhood housing market change from decline through normalcy to gentrification. While arguing that the reductionist neo-classical models may well be inappropriate for many aspects of housing economics research, however, he does point out that they continue to have relevance under specific circumstances and that 'a slavish attitude to any approach is rarely likely to be optimal'.

Taxation, subsidies and housing markets

Gavin Wood examines taxation as one of a set of frictions that impact on the efficiency of housing market outcomes, as well as having important distributional consequences. His chapter demonstrates the regressive and often counter-intuitive effects of housing taxation. He then uses tax arbitrage models to analyse tenure choice. His literature review and subsequent analysis of the distributional incidence of taxation on housing shows that, while the user cost effects of housing taxation may be well known, the systematic variations in landlord user costs associated with differential tax treatment are less well known or studied despite their importance for rental investment. In the discussion of tax-induced efficiency distortions, Wood makes a case for rental housing supply segmentation arising from 'clientèle effects'. Furthermore, there are 'lock-in' effects associated with this segmentation because capital gains taxation is rarely levied on an accruals basis.

Wood goes on to review the literature on the size of the welfare loss associated with taxation expenditures for home ownership, assessing the proposition that tax-induced housing investment (often in second-hand housing) may have crowded out industrial or 'productive' capital. He finds the evidence to be conflicting, suggesting that housing investment generates both positive and negative externalities in the wider economy.

The economics of social housing

In her chapter, Christine Whitehead applies economic principles to another question of considerable policy importance: what is the rationale for social housing? Whitehead concentrates on three issues: the efficiency rationale for government intervention, the role of housing as a method of redistribution, and the insights that economic theory can provide into appropriate governance structures for housing provision and management.

Whitehead shows that housing is subject to a significant number of market failures, and that their impact is, on the balance of evidence available, probably large enough to matter; but that it is far less obvious that social investment in housing will necessarily solve the problems these failures create. The political case for the provision of social housing has usually been made in terms of the efficacy of housing as a direct means of redistribution. Whitehead shows that the relative merits of income versus supply subsidies for achieving distributional objectives are less obvious in the case of housing than many assume, and that the most appropriate way to achieve distributional objectives comes down to empirical answers to questions regarding the relative importance of market failures in the context of specific economies and housing markets.

Moreover, the possibility of state failure must also be factored into any analysis of the appropriate response to market failure, or assessment of the form of intervention needed to achieve an agreed distributional objective. What is required in a housing context is a proper evaluation of governance issues. As Whitehead notes, in reality, any governance system is imperfect. It is therefore a matter of analysing the different attributes of market, regulatory and administrative systems in particular social, political and market contexts to determine the least-cost approach. Whitehead concludes in the UK context at least that in the future there should be less emphasis on social housing *per se* and more on managing markets, ensuring adequate investment and enabling different types of providers (public, non-profit and private) to compete on cost and quality.

Neighbourhood dynamics

In his chapter, George Galster considers the notion of 'neighbourhood' from an economic perspective. Defining neighbourhoods as bundles of spatially-based attributes (including such things as class profile, tax/public service levels, demographic profile and the political activity characteristics of residents as well as property-based characteristics), Galster shows that

neighbourhoods have a number of important features. These are that attributes vary in their durability and ability to be priced, that they are valued
in a relativistic (cross-neighbourhood) way by consumers and that the spatially-based attributes comprising neighbourhood can change by the very
act of consuming them. Galster shows the implication of these features to
be that the costs and benefits associated with consuming a neighbourhood
largely originate externally to the consumer in question.

Galster presents neighbourhoods as dynamic and subject to constant change,
and at the same time highly risky for potential consumers and investors.
He conceives urban neighbourhoods as being situated within a broader
segmented housing market, with change at the neighbourhood level driven
fundamentally by external shocks transmitted across the market. Once initiated by such a shock, within-neighbourhood micro processes that can be
represented through complexity models embodying non-linear threshold
effects ensue. Galster argues the intrinsic nature of neighbourhoods is such
that they are not likely to produce socially efficient outcomes. Moreover,
because neighbourhoods are valued in a relativistic way, poorly conceived
policy might have zero sum effects. On the other hand he points out careful
targeting can be highly effective in assisting neighbourhoods on the cusp of
catastrophic decline.

Home ownership and constraints to tenure choice

Joe Gyourko looks at the determinants of access to owner occupation in the
US. Until quite recently, permanent income and the relative cost of owning
versus renting were thought to be the dominant factors. Gyourko reviews
recent theoretical and empirical work that shows it is net worth and asset
price that drives the transition from renting to owning. This view of the
world implies that attempts to improve access to owner occupation through
policies aimed at reducing payment to income ratios are misconceived.
Leaving aside the question of whether such an objective is in fact appropriate, Gyourko shows that reducing the required down-payment on purchase
should be considered the more effective policy instrument.

Gyourko goes on to consider the implications of this new view for explaining racial differences in US home ownership rates, and finds that these can
be eliminated once household wealth is properly controlled for. Properly
controlling for wealth in this context means allowing for racial differences
in intergenerational wealth transfers between parents and children, as well
as accounting for a household's own net worth. Because of these differences
in wealth, black households are far less likely than their white counterparts

to apply for a mortgage, and Gyourko reports evidence that shows this is far more significant than discrimination in the mortgage market in explaining ownership differentials.

Gyourko also considers trends in the affordability of ownership in the US since the 1970s. Rather positive conclusions on this can be derived from a prominent national interest rate-based index measuring housing costs to the median income household purchasing the median home. In contrast, he presents evidence showing that affordability conditions have varied across the income distribution, with low-income households having fared badly. This finding reinforces the significance of Gyourko's conclusions regarding the relevant budget constraint facing households who are seeking to become owner-occupiers.

Planning regulation and housing supply

In his chapter, Glen Bramley discusses housing supply. While supply is clearly of central importance to housing economics and the operation of housing markets (as well as more generally), Bramley points out that it typically receives much less attention than demand, and suggests this might derive from the difficulty of applying deductive modelling to this subject.

Bramley reviews past economic research on new housing supply, and discusses the operation of land use regulation in Britain, which he contrasts with systems in other countries. While land use regulation is likely to affect the supply of land for new housing development, land and house prices and housing densities, the scale of these effects and their welfare interpretation is not certain. Bramley concentrates on the measurement issues and employs a panel model to analyse the impact of the amount and type of available land on new housing supply and house prices in England. The data are organised spatially on the basis of 90 'zones' constructed as simple aggregations of local authority districts and Bramley builds a straightforward supply and demand system, on the basis of which he concludes the price elasticity of new build supply is low in Britain, and may be getting lower.

Bramley also finds low land price elasticities and draws a number of conclusions of policy significance from his model. These include that land availability through planning is a strong driver of development, that greater land supply reduces house prices to a modest extent only, and that emphasis through the planning system on residential development on urban and recycled land carries a significant output penalty.

Housing planning

In his chapter, Tony O'Sullivan looks at local housing planning in the UK. There has long been a presumption in the UK that such planning is necessary (and the chapter by Galster supports this conclusion), and that municipal government is the appropriate agency to carry it out. Having considered the case for such planning, O'Sullivan looks at what it is expected to achieve, and compares this with what it has actually delivered. Housing planning and the related land use planning that occur in the UK are shown to be almost entirely devoid of economic content.

O'Sullivan details the areas where it is reasonable to expect economics to play a role in housing planning as conceived in the UK and contrasts this with the economic tools actually available. However, he points out that even with better tools a major gap between requirements and reality might be expected to remain unless incentives structures between and within levels of government are adjusted. He concludes that housing planning *per se* is needed, and that the American apathy towards such planning is not a better approach. However, the emphasis should be on the process of planning, and plans produced should be seen as contingent on unknown and currently unknowable future events.

The Right to Buy

The final three chapters in this book look explicitly at different aspects of the relationship between research and academics on the one hand, and government and policy development on the other. The chapter by Williams looks at the Right to Buy in the UK, a policy under which local authorities have been required to sell rental stock at a substantial discount to market value. Right to Buy has been the most significant and contentious housing policy in the UK in the last 20 years. Williams shows that between the introduction of the Right to Buy in 1980 and the end of the century there was little connection between research and policy development. It was introduced to increase owner occupation, pure and simple, not to address any specific equity or efficiency issues in the UK housing system. Key restrictions on sale under Right to Buy were adopted at the outset on the basis of skilful political lobbying, not hard evidence of a problem to be addressed. Meanwhile, subsequent evidence on the negative and unintended effects of Right to Buy was largely ignored.

Academic (and housing professional) reaction to Right to Buy was largely hostile, and Williams argues this too was at least in part ideological rather than evidence-based. While much research has now been done, key research into the local effects of Right to Buy, called for as early as 1981, still remains to be undertaken. Williams considers recent developments in Scotland where the establishment of the Scottish Parliament in 1999, with housing as a devolved function, have provided an opportunity for more rational arrangements for the Right to Buy to be established. In 2001 a Housing Act was passed that significantly amended the terms under which Right to Buy can be exercised in Scotland. He shows how these amendments were based for the first time on serious examination of the available research evidence. Whether or not the revisions to Right to Buy lead to better efficiency and equity outcomes in the Scottish context remains to be seen. The more general light Williams' chapter throws on the relationship between academics and policy makers also raises many interesting questions.

The political economy of housing research

Donnison and Stephens address some of these questions in their chapter. They consider the scale and scope of housing research undertaken over time, in the context of changes in the political and academic environments for such research. In doing this, they are able to identify some of the main factors responsible for shaping the evolution of housing research in Britain. They situate housing research clearly in the time-specific cultural, political and economic circumstances of the countries in which it takes place, but argue that over time academics have faced increasing competition as a source of knowledge for policy makers, and greater difficulty in disseminating their findings to the wider public. Reminding academic colleagues 'who think of themselves as analysts of housing problems and policies, that they are applied social scientists for whom their own profession is also a proper subject for study', Donnison and Stephens argue 'the comparative advantages remaining to academics are their opportunities – and obligations – to gain a broad understanding of the workings of their society, and to speak uncensored truth to power and to the public at large'.

Policy and academia

The final chapter comes at the relationship between academics and policy makers from a completely different direction. For Best, the issue is one of how to maximise the relevance and impact of research findings on policy development. He acknowledges the tensions that exist between academics and policy makers, but sees them as in something of a symbiotic relationship. Sometimes academics take a direct and active part in the development of policy, even to the extent of taking up active political roles. Best outlines the pros and cons of these situations, and considers some of the personal qualities needed to make this transition successfully. He goes on to discuss how research undertaken by those who do not wish to take an active political role feeds into policy development and sees this as being determined by four factors: who pays for the research (and what their motive is); how it is presented; the timing of research findings; and the persistence with which they are presented to policy makers. Best makes the case that the skills needed to bring research to bear on policy making are not the same as those necessary to do the research in the first place, and raises the question of strategic alliances with intermediate agencies that specialise in driving research into policy development. As such agencies are thin on the ground, he suggests an alternative might be to promote the development of specialist units within universities to carry out the task.

Recurrent themes and key issues for the future

The contributions to this book cover a very broad range of issues in theory, policy and practice. In terms of the contributions Maclennan has made to housing and urban economics, one can identify a number of common themes that recur across chapters.

One relates to the fitness-for-purpose that models of housing markets exhibit. Malpezzi points out that fitness-for-purpose is a fundamental criterion in deciding which method to use in the construction of a house price index. Simple frictionless neoclassical models are neither right nor wrong, and to try and categorise them as such would be to miss the point. For some purposes, as Gibb, Galster, and Quigley show, they are extremely valuable. But for much housing market analysis there is a need to accept that many of the assumptions made in the development of such models actually dispense with the real problems of interest. The chapters by Yong Tu and Quigley, Galster, Meen and Bramley, in different ways, testify to this.

A second relates to the issue of state versus market failure, and choice of the 'least worst' policy option in any given context. The chapter by Whitehead deals explicitly with this issue, but in essence, this is an issue underlying the chapters by O'Sullivan, Galster and Meen. If neighbourhoods are socially inefficient and there is a concern with the local equity effects of housing consumption and production, what should be done about it? Is there a case for state-led planning, or will the outcome be no better, or even worse than

that which the market will deliver? In practice of course there is no definitive answer to this and the issue must be considered on a case-by-case basis
– another instance of being aware of fitness-for-purpose.

A third relates to the issue of evidence-based policy. The chapters by Wood,
Gyourko and Williams show that in the absence of sound evidence policy
positions can be irrelevant to the problem they are attempting to address, or
generate unintended and unwanted distributional and/or efficiency effects.
Developing evidence-based policy is often no simple matter, however, as the
chapter by Bramley shows.

A fourth concerns the more general issues that the chapters by Williams,
Donnison and Stephens, and Best throw up in terms of the appropriate relationship between academia and policy makers. There is a constant tension
between the world of politics and the world of the academy. Should research
be the handmaiden of policy, or the guardian of the public interest? Can it
be both? In practice, there must be times when academia speaks truth to
power, and times when power returns the compliment. Again, the relationship between policy-making and research must in any specific situation be
one that is fit for the given purpose – but we must all be aware of the rules of
the game being played.

The individual chapters in this book also show how housing economics has
developed over the last two decades. An important complementary question
to ask is how it might develop in the years to come. Our crystal ball is as clear
or as foggy as the next person's with an interest in the field, but we offer the
following thoughts and hopes on the matter.

As with any applied area, data and access to it is of fundamental importance
to housing economics. In the last 20 years there have been remarkable leaps
in computing power and ease of use for even the most demanding econometric and mathematical software. With some important exceptions, this has
not always been accompanied by improvements in the quality of housing
market data sets. This is partly the result of commercial confidentiality but
it is also a consequence of data providers failing to recognise the policy and
practical relevance of better information. In Britain, the pursuit of evidence-
based policy is becoming reflected in more open access to public data, in
recognition of the greater need for good empirical information at local levels
and in an increasing amount of longitudinal data collection. However, even
in 2001, the Census was carried out without any question on household
incomes or resources. Our hope for the future is that technological developments in statistical and GIS software will marry with increased access to improved data in the UK – but this is unlikely to happen evenly or smoothly.

We suspect that space will become more rather than less important in both theory and policy terms. While an increasing amount of research in theoretical housing economics is attempting to allow for space in a meaningful way at different levels of aggregation, it is also becoming increasingly clear that housing analysis has to cohere *across* levels of aggregation (Meen 2001). An integrated framework of analysis from the level of urban neighbourhoods, through sub-markets and segmented housing markets to an adequate representation of regional and ultimately national housing markets is a long way off, but a prize for which more people are reaching. Galster sketches elements of it in his chapter, and Meen is actively working on aspects of this agenda, but as we say, it will be the work of many years and many hands to achieve.

One reason why it is likely to come is an increasing awareness, certainly in the UK context, that policies developed to operate at different spatial levels can inadvertently work against, even neutralise one another, or alternatively greatly enhance each other's chances of succeeding. Maclennan points out that '[ignoring] geography has a long tradition in British policy making' and that '[for] most of the period since 1980, until the last few years, economic policy was constructed as if the economy existed on the head of a pin' (Maclennan 2002, p. 1). But Britain, in common with a number of other advanced European economies, is beginning to accept the idea of 'territorial management' as a legitimate, indeed inescapable policy objective. Community regeneration policies (for reasons Galster and Meen elucidate) cannot work without an explicit spatial dimension:

> 'There are also major gains to be had from setting community level initiatives in a better-understood geography of wider systems, for instance in a city-regional framework. More often than not a failure to do this means that policies concentrate on local physical actions and facilities rather than convincingly connecting regeneration activities to wider labour markets, transport systems and the environment; but if they are to succeed long term [these are] precisely the wider system connections that have to be made.'
>
> (Maclennan 2002, p. 7)

And of course both local and city level policy has to connect in some meaningful way with national and international developments.

> 'We need a new framework of policy thinking and development which marries the impact of top down external forces and events with the creative and recursive effects which clearly push from the bottom up.'
>
> (Maclennan 2002, p. 6)

With a continued growth in understanding by policy makers of the significance of space, not at one, but at many levels simultaneously, there will be increasing demands for models and theory to provide an evidence-base for policy work.

And this last requirement is the final big pointer towards the future. While academic independence must never be taken lightly, the trend to evidence-based policy will gather steam, and hopefully create a positive dynamic between the academic and policy-making worlds. As new benchmarks are set in the evidence-base of specific policies, greater demands will be placed on research to furnish the needed information. More sophisticated policy positions will increase the demand for more sophisticated and realistic representations of housing markets. The meaning of 'fitness for purpose' is shifting in policy terms, and with it the goalposts for what is acceptable as a representation of housing markets will shift also.

2

Urban Housing Models

Kenneth Gibb

Introduction

The fact that different approaches to modelling housing markets exist probably reflects the complexity of the commodity 'housing'. Olsen (1968 p. 612) took this complexity as motivation to develop a competitive model consistent with the standard microeconomic paradigm and not restricted by the 'idiosyncratic concepts used by housing specialists'. Initially, spatial models of the housing market focused on long run equilibrium explanations of the impact of commuting on residential markets for space (Alonso 1964). Other research de-emphasised the spatial aspects of housing in favour of attention to its durability and dynamics, emphasising the effects of 'filtering'; the process by which a dwelling's attributes and occupants change over the property's lifetime (Arnott, Davidson & Pines 1983; Grigsby *et al*. 1987). The importance of heterogeneity has been reflected in work concerned with the creation of price indices, and the study of sub-markets. In these areas, the 'hedonic' approach has been of central importance.

The purpose of this chapter will be to consider and assess different classes of urban housing model; in particular, neoclassical spatial models and the more heterogeneous filtering tradition. Both literatures have included important contributions from Duncan Maclennan (Maclennan 1982; Grigsby *et al*. 1987). These different ways of analysing the urban housing market have provided controversy and insight alike; yet they are rarely considered as classes of model or explanation of housing phenomena.

The chapter also assesses progress in the development of computer-based simulation models of urban housing markets. Maclennan has constantly emphasised the potential importance of such models and their relevance to housing planning and policy assessment if developed with sound micro foundations capable of reflecting market processes (e.g. Maclennan 1986a; Maclennan & Gibb 1994). As they have developed, these models have often embodied elements of either or both of the main classes of model considered in this chapter but additionally they have sought to provide frameworks to test policies, scenarios and the consequences of system shocks. This is an area in which there has undoubtedly been significant progress in the last 20 years (Ingram 1979; Anas & Arnott 1991, 1993a, b, c, 1994, 1997).

Urban residential trade-off models

There is a considerable literature regarding the monocentric residential model or 'new urban economics' (Alonso 1964; Mills 1967, 1972; Muth 1969, 1985; Evans 1973; Solow 1973; Wheaton 1974; Quigley 1979; Fujita 1987; Straszheim 1987; Wheaton & DiPasquale 1996; McDonald 1997; Anas, Arnott & Small 1998) and I do not intend to revisit it extensively. Rather, in this section, I focus on a limited number of central conceptual and empirical issues that arise from this modelling approach.

Maclennan (1982) argued that the (access-space) model 'represents the real starting point for an analysis of local urban housing markets. The model is currently the dominant paradigm of urban economic research in North America and it is thus important to show its uses, merits and demerits' (p. 7). Appraisal of urban economics and urban real estate texts (e.g. Wheaton & DiPasquale 1996; McDonald 1997) shows that this remains the case 20 years on.

The basic trade-off

The essence of the model (following Henderson 1985) is that within a simpli-fied model of urban land use, utility maximising households offset employ-ment accessibility to a central workplace and retail location (measured in monetary and time commuting costs) against the consumption of residential land (or housing) space. The model generates a long-term spatial structure for household distribution that can be empirically tested. It can be analysed in terms of comparative statics and has been extended in a number of ways to increase the realism of the basic structure (e.g. with polycentric rather than monocentric economic activity locations).

In the basic model, the modelled city structure is assumed to be a flat and featureless plain where all employment is located in the 'Central Business District' (CBD) and, with the assumption of no congestion, commuting takes the same unit of time (t) to travel a given distance in any direction. Households in such a world are assumed to maximise utility subject to an income and a time constraint, consuming three generalised goods: the city's own traded good (x), the city's imported good (z) and housing services (h). Only the price of the latter varies across urban space. Housing is viewed as a consumption good with a locational amenity. The only amenity choice is leisure consumption, which is a direct function of commuting time to the CBD. In this world, the 'rental on housing implicitly prices both housing services and access, or leisure consumption' (Henderson 1985, p. 3). Thus, the unit price of housing p(u), at distance (u) from the CBD, varies spatially as leisure varies and leisure is the time T left after working and commuting. The representative consumer has leisure consumption e(u) at distance u from the CBD equal to:

$$e(u) = T - t(u) \tag{2.1}$$

The formal maximisation problem is:

$$\text{Maximise } V(u) = V'(x, z, h(u), e(u)) \tag{2.2}$$

subject to:

$$Y - p_x x - p_z z - p(u)h(u) = 0 \tag{2.3}$$

and

$$T - e(u) - t(u) = 0 \tag{2.4}$$

where V(u) is utility at location (u) and Y is household income. If this is maximised with respect to e(u) and location u, the following first order conditions are obtained:

$$\partial V'/\partial e(u) - \gamma = 0 \tag{2.5}$$

and

$$-\lambda h(u)[\partial p(u)]/\partial u - \gamma t = 0 \tag{2.6}$$

where the multipliers γ and λ are the marginal utilities, respectively, of leisure and income. The consumer's optimal location is found by solving out for γ.

$$h(u)\partial p(u)/\partial u = \partial V'/\partial e(u)t/\lambda = p_e(u)t \tag{2.7}$$

where $p_e(u)$ is the monetised value of the marginal utility of leisure. At this optimal location, any move farther away from the CBD leads to a loss of leisure. The value of this loss is the marginal monetised value of leisure, $p_e(u)$, times the loss in leisure, $-t$. The optimal location conditions state that lost leisure is exactly offset by reduced housing costs such that utility is unchanged and welfare cannot be improved by moving.

On the supply side, it is typically argued that the housing production function consists of two inputs, land and a composite housing structure capital input, and that the latter is perfectly elastic with respect to location. In elaboration beyond the simplest version of the model (where density is fixed), density varies and this operates through the elasticity of substitution between these factors. At high residential densities, near the CBD, non-land is substituted for land but this intensity declines as production moves out into the suburbs. In a competitive land market, land rents are bid up nearer the CBD such that different land users will bid for land in different locations according to the trade-off that keeps them on the same iso-utility or iso-profit function, creating a land rent gradient for the city as a whole. In equilibrium, price-taking households are at a tangency between the land rent gradient and their best (lowest) 'bid-rent' or marginal willingness-to-pay curve. Once income differentiation is included in the framework, and provided that higher income groups display an income elasticity of housing space demand that is greater than their price elasticity of commuting costs, then higher income groups will tend to locate towards the suburbs.

Quigley (1979) summarises the outcomes of the basic model succinctly thus:

> 'the principal conclusions of the monocentric model are: (1) residential densities decline with distance from the central place; (2) densities decline at a decreasing rate; (3) house prices decline with distance; (4) the land price gradient is steeper than the housing price gradient; (5) households with higher incomes locate further from the central place.' (p. 39)

Qualitative comparative statics associated with the model depend primarily on whether the city is assumed to be 'open' or 'closed' (Smith, Rosen & Fallis 1988). In the open set-up, there is an exogenous level of utility associated with living outwith the city. Should utility fall below a certain level, there will be outward migration and house prices will fall to restore equilibrium. In a closed city, population is given, while the level of utility is endogenous. McDonald (1997) runs through a series of comparative static exercises utilising a model based on Fujita's contribution (1987). A decrease in the agricultural bid rent is demonstrated to decrease all bid rents, expand the city radius, increase average occupied household space and decrease population density within the old boundaries of the city at all distances. Increased population is shown to expand the CBD (to accommodate increased employment), increase equilibrium land rents, expand city size, increase population density and reduce average household space consumption.

Extensions, evidence and criticisms

There have been many extensions proposed to the basic model. These have been aimed at relaxing certain assumptions in order to provide more richness or realism into the framework, or, alternatively, to try to take better account of empirical regularities at odds with the basic tenets of the model. Straszheim reviews many of these extensions, judging them valuable, though bought at the cost of 'added complexity in modelling location and investment equilibria over time' (Straszheim 1987, p. 730). Muth (1985) also highlights this loss of tractability.

Anas, Arnott & Small (1998) assess the access-space model in a broader historical context (see also Maclennan 1982) and ask what it can tell us about the long-term trends of urban change. They consider the conclusions drawn from the monocentric model against the changing patterns of centralisation and decentralisation, and clustering and dispersal of economic activities evident in modern cities, the phenomena of suburbanisation and the emergence of 'edge cities' (polycentric employment and activity nodes). The basic model cannot explain polycentrism (although Fujita's 1987 framework incorporates both sub-centres and the labour market). However, it may shed some light on suburbanisation.

Population density gradients have empirically declined over time in cities across a wide range of economic conditions. While this may be consistent with rising incomes and falling transport costs, Anas *et al.* (1998) note that commuting impacts more in lost leisure time for higher income groups. However, it has been difficult to isolate and fully specify transport costs. Evidence suggests that within many cities the employment density gradient is larger than that for population but has been falling faster than the population gradient, and this can be construed to weakly support the hypothesis that jobs have been following people. Other possible explanations of decentralisation take us further away from the basic model. These include 'flight from blight', racial discrimination, negative neighbourhood externalities created by poor areas, and Tiebout mechanisms (Anas *et al.* 1998, p. 1439).

I have already covered a number of the typical criticisms of this class of models. These in sum relate to: the need for restrictive assumptions to deliver tractable results and comparative statics; consequent incapacity to deal with durability, dynamics and short-run market behaviour; and difficulty in dealing with certain patterns of evolution of real world cities, particularly with respect to decentralisation and polycentrism. In response, it may be argued that the inability of such models to deal with short-run dynamics reflects the fact that they seek to provide a general equilibrium account of long-run trends in urban land use and market outcomes – although they do not provide an altogether satisfactory account here either. A more fundamental criticism relates to the underlying and enduring relevance of this class of model. In other words, does it adequately address the important questions about urban housing markets (Maclennan 1982; Straszheim 1987); is it fit-for-purpose?

Urban housing market choices do not only rely on workplace accessibility and locational amenity but also reflect choices to do with neighbourhoods, housing product differentiation, the pervasive role of the state in the land market, urban transport structures and local fiscal bundles. The insights provided by search and bidding models, models that account for durability and product differentiation and by game theory approaches may be at least if not more important than highly reductionist spatial competition models in understanding housing processes. The slow adjustment, inherent lags and disequilibria tendencies of housing markets articulated by Whitehead & Odling-Smee (1975) present a very different (European?) conceptualisation of the housing market. Maclennan & Gibb (1994) suggest that the pervasiveness of policy impacts and the influence of history that play a central role in real urban housing systems cannot be adequately addressed within the access-space framework.

One can also question whether the urban level is the appropriate scale for analysis as compared with lower levels such as the neighbourhood (Grigsby *et al.* 1987). A long-run urban-scale equilibrium construction with no role for the state or these other features simply misses too many of the key dimensions of housing markets. In the next section, I consider one of these dimensions: the dynamics of the existing housing stock at intra-urban levels through filtering processes.

Filtering in urban housing markets

Filtering models, with their focus on process and dynamics, and the relationship between new, rehabilitated and existing second-hand stock, are often far removed from the long-run equilibrium outcomes of the new urban economics (although see Olsen 1968, which I discuss below). This type of model has often been the basis for applied economic work and, of course, has a central and controversial place in housing policy debates. In this section, I briefly review the development, differentiation and assessment of filtering processes and models and point to their continuing relevance (the earlier literature is reviewed in Maclennan 1982, pp. 22–35).

Homer Hoyt (1939) provided the first study that might be labelled 'filtering'. Triggered by growing incomes and a preference for newness among high-income groups, Hoyt suggested that wealthier households would move out to newly developing suburbs. The formerly occupied neighbourhoods would in turn be replaced by the next socio-economic group, setting off a series of vacancies and moves down a price-income and sub-market hierarchy (Maclennan 1982).

Apart from the strong implicit and explicit assumptions in this stylised model, addressed by Maclennan and responded to by a series of authors such as Grigsby (1963), there were also important policy ramifications. The filtering process in the form presented suggested that promoting private market development of housing for high-income households could improve housing quality for all households throughout the housing system and implied that there was a case for subsidising such new development. Lowry (1960) argues that urban housing policy has been 'haunted' by the implications of this approach (p. 362).

The crude or laissez-faire filtering model has been comprehensively criticised (Robinson 1979; Maclennan 1982; Quigley 1998). First, it is often not well defined (Lowry 1960). Second, it rests on assumptions that can be challenged empirically, for instance about the distribution of income and the location of income growth, as well as assumptions about the behaviour of non-moving households (Maclennan 1982). Third, as Lowry puts it, the 'effectiveness of filtering as a means of raising housing standards hinges on the speed of value-decline relative to quality-decline' (1960 p. 364). If depreciation occurs more quickly than unit prices fall (as much evidence suggests) then the beneficial filtering process cannot occur. Fourth, as Quigley (1998) indicates, supply behaviour is endogenous. The filtering of dwellings, therefore, will not just depend on incomes and preferences on the demand side and on physical depreciation on the supply side but also on the regulatory environment and cost structures faced by suppliers and the heterogeneous demands of real households (p. xiv). Fifth, from a policy point of view, Maclennan emphasises there may be ethical concerns about the subsidy targeting implied by the model. It may exacerbate decentralisation, and the filtering may take a very long time to work through the system (especially given the impacts of trading-down within the system).

Grigsby (1963) proposed a different interpretation of the filtering concept. His concern was with filtering as an outcome, and he sought to develop a better understanding of the empirical relationships between the stock of houses, households and moving decisions. Grigsby developed a matrix model where household moves are observed across housing quality or price ranges. As the market matrix evolves over time, households move around the system and this in turn has reinforcing effects, shifting the income mix and the average value of entire neighbourhoods. Using this approach, the study of wider dynamics becomes possible, for example, the knock-on effects, spillovers and backwashes that affect housing neighbourhoods after exogenous shocks take place or when, for instance, regeneration or rehabilitation takes place (Maclennan (1982) presents a nice summary of the Grigsby approach).

From a very different perspective, Olsen (1968) addresses filtering through his competitive model, which utilises the device of an unobservable unit of housing 'service'. Olsen argues that filtering represents changes in the quantity of housing stock, such that filtering up (down) can only take place if the quantity of housing stock has increased (decreased). Filtering is a process by which the quantity of housing service yielded by a dwelling adjusts to the pattern of demand as a result of competitive profit incentives (pp. 615–16). For Olsen, filtering is an essential market mechanism that allows profit-maximising housing producers to adjust supply and maintenance behaviour in order to move the competitive market toward equilibrium in terms of the price per unit of housing service.

In fact, use of the filtering approach has been hampered by a lack of clarity in how the concept should be defined. Grigsby *et al.* (1987, Chapter 4) identify ten different approaches to filtering in urban housing markets:

> 'Depending on the definition, filtering is either a process or set of outcomes and, if the latter, could involve, in differing combinations, change or no change in: occupancy, occupants' incomes, value or rent of dwelling units, price per housing units or neighbourhood environs ... It is not surprising that the literature is replete with controversy over whether filtering occurs or works.' (p.109)

Galster & Rothenberg (1991) also distinguish between different forms of filtering, which they consider within a quality-differentiated housing sub-market framework. First, when relative prices fall in a given sub-market, some households previously in lower quality sub-markets may now be willing and able to trade up to the now cheaper higher quality strata. This can be called *price filtering*. Second, falling relative prices within a sub-market will also encourage some owners to change the quality of their dwelling to improve its rate of return, known as *dwelling filtering*. Third, if the converted dwellings are spatially concentrated, households in such neighbourhoods may *passively filter* as a result of the spatial externality on the overall dwelling bundle value. Fourth, beyond the short run, these price-induced changes will lead to knock-on *filtering-like dynamics* in related sub-markets through changes to prices, household moves and quality conversions.

We can see elements of the filtering approach in many urban housing models (Sweeney 1974; de Leeuw & Struyck 1975; Ingram 1979; Anas & Arnott 1991; Rothenberg *et al.* 1991; McDonald 1997). Discussion of these processes continues (Somerville & Holmes 2001). The inherent value of the concept of filtering, both as process and outcome, makes it an important tool for urban housing market research. However the true potential of the concept remains to be fully realised.

Simulation models of urban housing

One approach taken to capture more of the richness and interdependence of real housing markets has been the development of computer simulation models. They use parameter values for equations based on a mix of econometrics, good practice and judgement, to build more or less sophisticated urban housing models. These can in turn be used to model policy changes, and provide insights on housing market dynamics. These models can and have been widely criticised for their limitations (e.g. Maclennan 1986a; Gibb 1989) but recent developments, both in terms of the quality of the economic modelling they embody and computing power, have greatly improved their usefulness. There are still problems with this type of model, but their practical relevance and continued improvement suggest that they will become increasingly valuable.

Modelling developments

Simulation models of the housing market provide a framework in which it is possible to consider the dynamic short-run path of market processes. The original 1970s and 1980s models, American in origin, were extensively used to forecast the effects of introducing housing allowance programmes and other tax reforms (early versions were reviewed by Ingram 1979). The two urban simulation models associated with this period were the UI (Urban Institute) model (De Leeuw & Struyck 1975) and the National Bureau (NBER-HUDS) model (Kain & Agpar 1985). Both models sought to allocate households to dwellings, while incorporating an explicit supply side. The UI model, for instance, consists of households, differentiated by age and race, which are allocated intertemporally to dwelling types across six residential zones (with differentiated workplace accessibility, and rents). Supply is set to maximise profits and households maximise utility such that the different actors search for equilibrium outcomes in the markets for existing dwellings and new build. The UI model embodied certain filtering processes.

Attempts to allow choice and maximising behaviour within an (eventually) equilibrating framework can be seen through all of the successive models of this class. Smith, Rosen & Fallis (1988) argue that this type of model involves too much of a black box approach, where model parameters are not econometrically-defined but:

> 'simply chosen to ensure realistic model outcomes (and) are often ad hoc rather than based on economic behaviour.' (p. 39)

However, parameter estimates are likely to come from econometric work undertaken in other studies. Furthermore, it can be argued that these models have a different purpose and should be assessed in terms of their capacity to aid planning, forecasting, and policy development.

Anas and Arnott, in a series of papers, have gone a long way to provide more secure theoretical foundations for urban housing simulation models. Anas & Arnott (1991) develop a robust dynamic discrete choice equilibrium model of the housing market that allocates different types of consumers to different housing types, clears the market and has an integrated supply side (including investors operating with perfect foresight). It is specifically designed to be useful for simulations and policy experiments.

Anas & Arnott (1993c) further extend their work by developing and testing a housing market simulation model for Chicago. The key choices in the model concern the household's choice of location, house type, quality and tenure status. The model demonstrates the feedback and second-round effects of specific policies on different parts of the housing quality hierarchy (and consequently on different income groups). In their 1994 paper, Anas & Arnott go on to test their model in four other US cities, examining the impact of housing allowances and construction subsidies. They find that targeted demand-side allowances are more effective for the targeted groups than construction subsidies. This work is extended in 1997 by looking at the welfare effects of taxes and allowances on low-income households and the landlords providing their housing.

Meen's (1999a) paper has applied and extended urban-level discrete choice modelling of housing in a UK context, through the development of a model of the London and South East housing market. Meen starts from the argument that declining demand for public housing reflects, among other things, cumulative processes of decline as the least advantaged are left behind in the process of economic change and relocation. His work suggests that non-housing social and neighbourhood factors need to be employed to capture, among other things, spatial externalities, and highlights three modelling implications. Population patterns vary within the region of study, implying different rates of new household formation and housing requirements. Second, the factors that drive household relocation include income changes, local social ties, the desire for a better neighbourhood, larger houses and changes in personal circumstances. Third, in-migration at the regional level must be specified and modelled.

Case study: the Glasgow citywide model of housing demand

Recent work in Scotland has built on Meen's study (and other work carried out on the South East of England (Meen & Andrew 1999)). A simulation model has been developed to forecast social housing demand in Greater Glasgow, where Glasgow is partitioned into three parts (North and South of the City and its suburbs). This model explicitly involves a tenure choice between social renting and owner-occupation (private renting is treated as part of the non-owning sector and subsumed within the analysis for forecasting purposes). The study (Gibb, Meen & Mackay, 2000) was designed to provide demand estimates for social housing under a range of assumptions about migration, neighbourhood and income change, taking full account of the economic choices of households, and the drivers of housing demand.

Housing demand in each of the areas comes from three sources: migration into and out of the overall Glasgow area, new household formation, and moves *among* the three Glasgow areas of the *existing* population by tenure and by housing type. Each process is modelled. The existing residents housing choice model suggested that mobility decisions are based on demographics and income, and that tenure and locational choices are a function of neighbourhood quality, incomes, costs and the previous location of households. The supply side is modelled more mechanistically. For each sector, current supply is the sum of last period's supply plus new investment by the construction sector, plus net transfers into the sector (which could be negative), minus demolitions and also minus long-term vacancies that reduce the effective stock. The model clears the market through supply adjustment (which essentially assumes that real house prices are constant).

The model was estimated and then applied using a 1996 base, and projects forward to 2009 for the City of Glasgow and its suburbs (termed 'outwith' in the tables). Table 2.1 summarises the proportionate changes in demand, provides a combined total for the City of Glasgow and makes a correction for private rented housing, in order to calculate social rented demand. The estimates presented show the difference between the 1996 figures and the 2009 projections, *in the absence of intervention.*[1] The numbers suggest that owning households in Glasgow will increase from 115 000 to just below 150 000. In the same period renting households (social and private) will fall from 155 000 to just over 130 000. In the suburbs, owning households will grow from more than 262 000 in 1996 to more than 346 000 in 2009. Suburban renters will decline from slightly more than 176 000 to a little more than 144 000.

Table 2.1 suggests that social housing demand will fall in Glasgow by 18.1% of the 1996 level. At the same time, owner occupation in the City will increase by 30.2%. This reflects an overall increase in households in Glasgow of 3.7% from 1996 to 2009. For the area outwith Glasgow, social housing demand will fall by 19.1%. Owner-occupied demand in the *outwith* area will rise by 30.9%. Overall, households in the area outwith the City will increase by 11.2%.

Scenario simulations

A scenario simulation alters the parameter value of one of the driver variables in the system so that one can trace the longer-term impact of the change by contrasting the outcome with the estimates reported above.

Table 2.1 Base housing demand change 1996–2009.

Tenure and location	Absolute change (number of households)	Percentage change in households
Glasgow owning	+34 681	+30.2
Glasgow social renting	−25 667	−18.1
Outwith owning	+81 104	+30.9
Outwith social renting	−32 135	−19.1

Two scenarios are briefly reported:

- an improvement in neighbourhood quality in Glasgow relative to its suburbs

- an increase in incomes within the wider Glasgow housing system.

Neighbourhood quality is proxied in the model through a geographically-based deprivation index. In scenario one, the deprivation scores of Glasgow relative to its suburbs are changed to mimic a change in the relative quality of the City's neighbourhoods. By examining the deviation from the base estimate benchmark it is possible to assess how tenure and location choices would shift as a consequence.

Table 2.2 compares the original 2009 estimates with those of the model assuming a 5% improvement in the deprivation scores of the City. The simulated percentage change is a large one but the message is clear. Improving neighbourhood quality in this way should lead to a significant increase in owner-occupation, primarily from owners moving into the City from the suburbs. However, some suburban renters would seek to move into owner-occupation within Glasgow as well.

In scenario two, the assumed income change affects all of Greater Glasgow. This is more plausible than assuming that only the administrative jurisdiction of the City would benefit from income changes. We increase average incomes after 2002 by 10% and compare the new housing demand configuration that occurs with the original estimate for 2009. Table 2.3 indicates that increased incomes would increase demand for owning in Glasgow and in the suburbs. Renting demand falls substantially in both Glasgow and its suburbs. Income effects would appear to play their usual role of increasing owner-occupation but, in addition to reducing rental demand, Glasgow households are using their higher incomes to purchase wider afield, reflecting supply constraints in Glasgow.

Table 2.2 Simulation impact of 5% improvement in Glasgow's deprivation scores in terms of overall households by tenure.

Location and tenure	2009 [central] (1)	5% improvement in score (2)	Deviation (2–1)
Glasgow social renters	116508	108805	−7703
Glasgow owners	149607	175325	25718
Outwith social renters	136380	132599	−3781
Outwith owners	346334	333390	−12944

Table 2.3 Simulation impact of 10% increase in incomes after 2002.

Location and tenure	2009 [central] (1)	10% increase in incomes (2)	Deviation (2–1)
Glasgow social renters	116 508	108 480	−8 028
Glasgow owners	149 607	153 320	3 713
Outwith social renters	136 380	126 355	−10 025
Outwith owners	346 334	362 790	16 456

The Citywide model is the first serious attempt in the UK to build a simulation forecasting model of the entire housing system for a metropolitan area, explicitly including the social rented sector. In many ways, it is much less developed than the Anas & Arnott model for Chicago but it does incorporate several desirable features of such models – in particular a defensible multi-level discrete choice model of housing choice, and the use of well-determined models of regional migration.

There are also important weaknesses with the model as it stands. The supply side is under-developed. There is only an implicit residual role for the private rented sector, and there is no explicit modelling of transition probabilities for household change (such as the transition from a pensioner couple to a single pensioner household). The crude spatial nature of the model must also be acknowledged. Notwithstanding these limitations, the results show the potential of this class of model to support city level planning and policy development.

Conclusions

In conclusion, I return to the issue of the comparative strengths of the different approaches to urban housing market modelling before considering the wider theme of future developments in urban housing market research.

The trade-off model of new urban economics raises three fundamental problems as an approach seeking to explain housing market behaviour. First of all this type of model is highly reductionist, and relies on the concept of unobservable housing services and other simplifications to make it tractable. In doing this, such models remove many of the important elements or aspects of the urban housing system of interest (e.g. the role of the housing stock, its history, the role of the state, the possibility of intra-urban housing submarkets, or any focus on adjustment and disequilibrium). Second, even on its own terms, this type of model has difficulty coping with certain empirical regularities one might expect it to explain, such as suburbanisation and the development of edge cities. Third, by excluding all other dimensions except the spatial, this class of model removes from the field alternative conceptual starting points such as search and bidding, bargaining, imperfect competition, housing market segmentation and product differentiation.

However, there are important and enduring contributions that access-space models have made. First of all they make explicit the link between housing and transport within urban systems. If one rejects the mechanics of the access-space model that does not mean that one can afford to neglect transport and other land use issues. Second, they are clearly correct in emphasising employment and general accessibility factors as important drivers of housing demand. Third, these models do provide a well-defined benchmark long-run spatial equilibrium position, from which deviations and different trajectories can be considered and explained.

Filtering models as a class have the potential to provide considerable insights once we accept the importance of housing market segmentation, sub-markets and neighbourhood structures. However, for several decades their use has been hamstrung by definitional problems and by earlier policy baggage. Recent work by Galster & Rothenberg (1991) has been valuable in addressing these problems. Filtering models provide a very different set of modelling tools for housing market analysts. The ideas of household and dwelling succession and change, depreciation, upgrading and market dynamics are immensely useful for applied economic analysis of housing and neighbourhoods.

Simulation models embody elements of both trade-off and filtering models, and are built for very practical purposes. They have been shown to be potentially useful tools for policy development and planning purposes. However, these models are only as good as the economic and econometric foundations they are built on and neither the access-space nor the filtering frameworks provide the basis for a comprehensive urban housing model. This should not be surprising. Filtering and access-space models are designed to address both different and specific types of questions and represent different methodological forms of explanation.

Maclennan & Gibb (1994) proposed a forward direction for UK housing economics. If one wishes to understand urban housing markets, then modelling disequilibrium processes and accounting for the role of key institutions will be at least as important as seeking to define equilibrium outcomes. In understanding markets for urban housing, it is important to have a clear conceptual and empirical understanding of the system under investigation:

'It is critical to understand its *evolution*. A modelling of the *heuristics* of behaviour in the context of *limited* information is required. And it is critical to understand the *institutions* which emerge, adapt and dissolve as the system unfolds' (1994 p. 4, original emphasis).

The challenge for the future development of spatial models of the housing market is to incorporate these features in a rigorous but relevant model that can be sensibly operationalised and disseminated. The recent work by Geoff Meen and colleagues is a possible way ahead (Meen 1999a, 2001; Meen *et al.* 2001; and see the chapter by Meen in this volume). Here, the focus is on the explanation of movement of households, tenure change and the growth and decline of urban areas. Important themes include the processes of cumulative causation, exclusion and the factors that shape intra-urban housing choices by existing households. This work is at an early stage but it is suggestive of a promising way forward for UK and wider housing market research.

Acknowledgements

These are due to Steve Malpezzi, Tony O'Sullivan and George Galster for comments on an earlier draft. The chapter also benefited from the comments made by participants at the University of Glasgow workshop for the book, held in November 2001.

Note

(1) In other words, in the absence of any response by planners in terms of land release as a result of observed demand levels or change thereof.

3

Segmentation, Adjustment and Disequilibrium

Yong Tu

Introduction

Housing is a complex commodity. Of special interest here is how this complexity creates housing market segmentation and the market consequences of segmentation, which I discuss in the next section. I move on from this to discuss the equilibrium and disequilibrium properties of a segmented housing market, and then the issues involved in empirical identification of housing sub-markets. I conclude with a discussion of the wider implications for the study of housing economics of rejecting equilibrium as a starting point in modelling the housing market.

The causes and consequences of housing market segmentation

Housing as a complex commodity can be considered in terms of three dimensions (see the discussion in Galster 1996): spatial immobility, durability and heterogeneity. Spatial immobility implies that characteristics associated with a location are inherent in the bundle of attributes of a dwelling found at that location. These locational attributes include the socio-economic status of the neighbourhood, its physical conditions, as well as wider notions of accessibility to any desired destinations, in terms of jobs, relatives and friends, private goods or public facilities. Combined, all of these attributes contribute to differences in housing quality and housing prices across locations.

Housing is also durable, and typically has a relatively high purchase price involving the need for extensive mortgage borrowing. It is also common for dwellings to experience long run price appreciation. The investment aspect of owning a home, therefore, is likely to make housing a principal personal sector financial asset. This also means that the housing market shares certain characteristics with the capital asset market (Maclennan 1982). On the supply side, a dwelling is modifiable. The quality of a housing unit can be either improved through modification or reduced in value through depreciation over time at any location. Modified dwelling units form an important source of housing supply in any housing market.

Heterogeneity of dwellings' physical characteristics refers to the intrinsic variation found across housing types, sizes, ages, building materials, exterior or interior structures, and architecture designs, as well as different forms of land leasing. Heterogeneity generates variation in housing quality and house prices within a location, providing a homebuyer with a variety of dwelling choice alternatives. The multidimensional heterogeneity of an urban housing market gives rise to its likely segmentation. An urban housing stock that is immobile, durable yet capable of modification, and heterogeneous, can be thought of as being segmented into a series of interrelated but distinctive housing product groups (Maclennan *et al.* 1987). The dwellings within each product group are more substitutable than the dwellings between the product groups and the degree of substitutability varies from group to group.

At the same time, homebuyers are also heterogeneous. Past studies of housing choice behaviour (Quigley 1982b; Tu & Goldfinch 1996) show that would-be homebuyer preferences are determined and differentiated by, amongst other things, income levels, employment status and occupation, household composition, and previous housing experiences. A would-be homebuyer is likely to be interested in dwellings contained within only a few closely substitutable housing product groups. These product groups are likely to be spatially separated, implying the prospective buyer may only have imperfect knowledge regarding the pattern of spatially-dispersed dwelling units offered by sellers.

Because housing is also one of the most expensive consumption and investment goods purchased by a household, it may be expected, for any would-be homebuyer, that the consideration given to (and evaluation involved in) purchasing a dwelling will be relatively intense. Search activity is required to inform the process of housing choice decision-making (Clark 1982a), which incurs both time and money costs. Maclennan (1982) points out that the housing purchase process involves a would-be homebuyer typically having not only to search and evaluate dispersed housing offers but also to search in order to secure home loan finance. It also requires bidding if there is more than one potential buyer for a dwelling unit (abstracting from the institutional details of house purchase in individual countries). Therefore, housing search may have three outcomes.

First, a buyer finds the desired dwelling from a particular product group and is happy with the offer price. The transaction happens if there are no other competitors on the demand side.[1]

Second, the dwelling units offered by the product group are not acceptable to the potential buyer. A housing mismatch arises. Due to the slow adjustment of housing supply, to find the desired dwelling, the potential buyer has to either continue searching among other groups or adjust their housing preference.[2] Such mismatch creates high transaction costs for both buyers and sellers. For the buyers, it will create higher search costs and search time. For the sellers, they have to pay all the costs associated with retaining the dwelling unit. Market trade friction may therefore arise and force the seller to lower the offer price as a trade-off against an anticipated lower transaction cost.

Third, where multiple potential buyers are interested in one dwelling unit, this gives rise to another form of housing mismatch. The bidding competition will eventually drive up the transaction price. In the absence of instantaneous housing supply adjustment, would-be homebuyers' chances of obtaining desired housing attributes depend on ability and willingness to pay for them, as well as the ability to successfully negotiate the bid in the market (Wood & Maclennan 1982). The buyer who can afford the highest price will get the unit. This buyer may particularly be interested in certain attributes associated with the dwelling – for example, a dwelling close to good schools – and consequently be willing to pay a higher premium to obtain this housing attribute, increasing the locational attribute price among certain product groups. Differences across housing product groups in the price of a particular housing attribute (also defined as hedonic price or implicit price; see DiPasquale & Wheaton 1996; Dale-Johnston 1982) give rise to topographically-based housing sub-markets.

A topographically-based housing sub-market consists of a cluster of housing product groups that may or may not have a contiguous geographical boundary. The price of an individual housing attribute has no statistically significant differences within these product groups, but does have significant differences across housing product groups belonging to different topographically-based sub-markets. This definition is supported by the empirical findings of Schnare & Struyk (1976), Goodman (1981), Maclennan *et al.* (1987), Goodman & Thibodeau (1998) and Bourassa *et al.* (1999). The theoretical discussions given by Tu (1997) and Maclennan & Tu (1996) also suggest that the spatial patterns of topographically-based housing sub-markets may change over time.

A different approach to sub-market definition is that of quality-based housing sub-markets, as defined by Rothenberg *et al.* (1991). A quality-based housing sub-market consists of a sub-set of dwellings in an urban housing market. The dwellings in the group, though different, are viewed by demanders and suppliers as producing a similar level of quality. Thus, the urban housing stock as a whole can be considered as arrayed along a single quality dimension, across which exists a spectrum of sub-markets ranged from the highest to the lowest quality levels. Under this definition, dwellings within a sub-market are more highly substitutable than the dwellings between the sub-markets.[3]

A hybrid housing sub-market approach was proposed by Tu (1997). Here, the urban housing sub-market structure is conceived as a nested framework. Within the structure, the market is divided into topographically-based sub-markets, and inside each topographical sub-market, the dwellings are grouped into different sectoral housing sub-markets defined by dwelling type. A similar approach was taken in Straszheim (1974) and, more recently, by Goodman & Thibodeau (1998).

Maclennan (1982) points out that there are good reasons to believe that, due to the existence of housing sub-markets, disequilibrium characterises the urban housing market and may be pervasive. First, disequilibrium appears in the form of mismatch between demand and supply, and continuously purposive housing search creates housing sub-market trade frictions, ensuring that the housing market cannot clear its excess demands or supplies instantly.

Second, the impacts of mismatch on market disequilibrium are reinforced by the slow adjustment of housing supply. Changes in demand for the dwellings in a sub-market occur more quickly than changes in supply. Therefore disequilibrium is likely to be persistent.

These intrinsic disequilibrium features associated with an urban housing market suggest that any theory that hopes to provide a robust explanation of urban housing market dynamics or that seeks to provide a framework for evaluating housing policies must take the features of housing market disequilibrium into account. The conventional concept of neoclassical market equilibrium is particularly inappropriate in the urban housing market because factors such as transactions costs (including search costs) and market trade frictions are of more than usual importance. Economic models of urban housing will yield satisfactory prediction of real world phenomena only if they take such factors into consideration (Whitehead & Odling-Smee 1975).

A model of housing market disequilibrium

This section draws on the preceding review and provides a theoretical framework from which housing sub-market equilibrium and disequilibrium properties are derived. The framework is a hybrid model of housing sub-market structure and represents a modification and an extension of Tu (1997).

Consider an urban owner-occupied housing market, and assume that this market is divided into two topographically-based housing sub-markets (T_i-Submkt, i=1,2). Within each topographically-based housing sub-market, there are two quality-based housing sub-markets (Q_{ij}-Submkt, i = 1,2 and j = 1,2). In each quality-based housing sub-market, the dwellings not only share the same spatial characteristics (for example, neighbourhood and public amenities) but are also highly substitutable. The housing economics literature provides evidence with respect to a would-be homebuyer's housing choice behaviour.

First, housing search is a requirement and search costs limit a would-be homebuyer to seek housing in selected topographical areas (Wood & Maclennan 1982).

Second, a would-be homebuyer's housing preference, for example, the desire to live close to friends or workplace, may confine him or her to certain topographical areas (Tu & Goldfinch 1996).

Third, financial affordability constraints may also restrict opportunities to choose a dwelling located in certain expensive areas (Tu & Goldfinch 1996).

Therefore it appears that a would-be homebuyer often examines housing in a few limited areas, and housing choice decision-making processes start from a favoured area. Within this area, as a rational buyer, the potential purchaser will continue to search across dwelling units, with particular attention paid to those dwellings satisfying housing quality requirements. For this would-be homebuyer, the dwellings of interest form one quality-based housing sub-market because the purchaser evaluates those dwellings that are highly substitutable (providing approximately the same level of housing quality). The searching process stops if and when a dwelling unit from the area can be found that can generate the maximum household utility. Otherwise, the supply constraints will drive the potential purchaser to switch to another favoured area to keep searching (which I shall call *re-choice*). Supply constraints mean that housing supply does not respond to demand changes instantaneously, due to the slow adjustment of housing stock in the area and the lack of vacant land in built-up areas.

The hybrid model of housing sub-market structure presented in this section reflects this housing choice decision-making process. In an urban area, a well-defined hybrid housing sub-market structure may assist the prospective homebuyer to gather more housing information and hence to reduce market trade frictions. It may also aid housing suppliers to identify development opportunities from the demand–supply gaps within each sub-market.

The operational process of this urban housing market is a dynamic matching process between the would-be homebuyers and the sellers (see Fig. 3.1). In the figure, 'T-choice' and 'Q-choice' refer respectively to the choice between topographically-based housing sub-markets and between quality-based sub-markets.

The current state of an urban housing market is a group of k points in a three-dimensional space Γ^k,

$$\Gamma^k = X^k \otimes Y^k \otimes Z^k$$

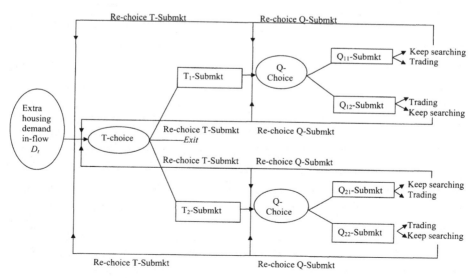

Fig. 3.1   Urban housing sub-market operational system.

where k is the number of housing sub-markets. X and Y are the non-negative real axes. Z is the positive real axis. For example, in Fig. 3.1, there are 6 housing sub-markets (k = 6). The current state of the housing market at any time point can be represented as a matrix W(t) illustrating the 6 points in the space Γ^k.

$$W(t) = \begin{bmatrix} w_{10}(t) \\ w_{20}(t) \\ w_{11}(t) \\ w_{12}(t) \\ w_{21}(t) \\ w_{22}(t) \end{bmatrix} = \begin{bmatrix} d_{10}(t) & s_{10}(t) & p_{10}(t) \\ d_{20}(t) & s_{20}(t) & p_{20}(t) \\ d_{11}(t) & s_{11}(t) & p_{11}(t) \\ d_{12}(t) & s_{12}(t) & p_{12}(t) \\ d_{21}(t) & s_{21}(t) & p_{21}(t) \\ d_{22}(t) & s_{22}(t) & p_{22}(t) \end{bmatrix}$$

In the matrix, w_{ij}, $i = 1,2$ and $j = 0,1,2$, indicates the current situation of either a respective topographically-based sub-market (for $j = 0$) or a quality-based sub-market (for $j = 1,2$). Each situation is determined by three sub-market variables: the number of housing units demanded (d), the number of housing units supplied (s) and the price (p). Each variable is, in turn, defined on the axes of X, Y and Z. As long as the urban housing market is not in equilibrium, this group of 6 points $(W(t))$ moves in the defined space. Mathematically, the dynamic process can be expressed as:

$$\frac{d(d_{ij}(t))}{dt} = a_{ij}(t,W(t)) - b_{ij}(t,W(t)) \tag{3.1}$$

$$\frac{d(s_{ij}(t))}{dt} = c_{ij}(t,W(t)) - b_{ij}(t,W(t)) \tag{3.2}$$

$$\frac{d(p_{ij}(t))}{dt} = \chi_{ij} \times (d_{ij}(t) - s_{ij}(t)) \tag{3.3}$$

where $i = 1,2$, $j = 0,1,2$. a, c and b are the extra housing demand, supply inflows to the respective sub-market, and the number of dwellings transacted at time t. Obviously, at the level of the topographically-based sub-market, a_{i0}, c_{i0}, b_{i0}, d_{i0} and s_{i0} are the sum of the respective variables at the level of quality-based sub-markets nested in the relevant topographically-based sub-market. χ is a coefficient reflecting changes to the sub-market house prices in response to the difference between sub-market demand and supply. Changes to sub-market housing demand, supply and price, at any time t, are determined by the urban housing market situation (W(t)) as indicated in equations (3.1)–(3.3).

The necessary and sufficient conditions for an urban housing market achieving equilibrium are:

$$d_{ij}(t) = s_{ij}(t)$$

(3.4)

$$a_{ij}(t) = b_{ij}(t) = c_{ij}(t) \text{ where } i = 1, 2 \text{ and } j = 0, 1, 2$$

(3.5)

The above equilibrium conditions are defined as the stock-flow market equilibrium (Weibull 1983, 1984). Three important implications can be drawn from the stock-flow equilibrium conditions.

First, equations (3.3) and (3.4) imply that, when the housing market achieves stock-flow equilibrium (equilibrium at both topographically-based sub-markets and quality-based sub-markets), there is no price movement in each sub-market.

Second, even in the equilibrium, there exists unsatisfied demand (home-buyers keep searching) as well as unsold dwelling units (some sellers search for a suitable buyer) in any of the housing sub-markets (equation 3.5). This phenomenon is a result of housing sub-market trade friction (TF) measured by equation (3.6).

Third, the stock-flow equilibrium in each of the quality-based housing sub-markets is a necessary, but not sufficient condition for the stock-flow equilibrium in each of the topographically-based housing sub-markets.

$$TF_{ij} = \frac{\min(d_{ij}(t), s_{ij}(t))}{b_{ij}(t)} \text{ where } i = 1, 2 \text{ and } j = 0, 1, 2$$

(3.6)

A bigger value of TF implies a higher level of trade friction. The reciprocal of TF is interpreted as the housing sub-market transaction velocity (β). The seller's average waiting time (q) in each sub-market can therefore be defined by equation (3.7).

$$q_{ij}(t) = \frac{s_{ij}(t)}{b_{ij}(t)} = \frac{s_{ij}(t)}{\beta_{ij} \times \min(d_{ij}(t), s_{ij}(t))}$$

(3.7)

To derive the short-run and long-run housing sub-market equilibrium/disequilibrium properties, four assumptions are needed.

Assumption 1

An urban housing market is assumed to be a free market. There is no regulated price control and changes in sub-market housing demand and supply are the only cause of house price fluctuations.

Assumption 2

The market is assumed to be in a stable socio-economic environment. Therefore, the extra housing demand inflow in to the housing market at any time t (D_t) is time-invariant.

Assumption 3

New additions to or deletions from the housing market are not considered. The only source of supply is via turnover in the second-hand housing market, and the turnover rate (ε) is a constant indicating a fraction of the occupied dwellings, that is, the difference between the sub-market dwelling stock (δ) and the number of dwellings on sale in the sub-market. To simplify the discussion, it is assumed that, at any time, there is only one consumer group in the market sharing the same housing preference distribution. Therefore, the subscript denoting an individual buyer is dropped from equations (3.8)–(3.11). These equations indicate a measurement of the choice probability of an individual buyer in choosing a housing unit from a sub-market. Given the hybrid housing sub-market structure (see Fig. 3.1), a nested multinomial logit model is used here to measure the probabilities (McFadden 1978).

$$Pr_{j/i}(t) = \frac{\exp(\alpha_1 \times p_{ij}(t) + \alpha_2 \times q_{ij}(t) + \alpha_3 \times X_{ij})}{\sum_j \exp(\alpha_1 \times p_{ij}(t) + \alpha_2 \times q_{ij}(t) + \alpha_3 \times X_{ij})} \quad \text{where } i, j = 1, 2 \tag{3.8}$$

$$Pr_{i0}(t) = \frac{\exp(\lambda \times Y_{i0} + (1-\sigma) \times I_i)}{\sum_i \exp(\lambda \times Y_{i0} + (1-\sigma) \times I_i) + 1} \quad \text{where } i = 1, 2 \tag{3.9}$$

$$Pr_{00}(t) = \frac{1}{\sum_i \exp(\lambda \times Y_{i0} + (1-\sigma) \times I_i) + 1} \tag{3.10}$$

$$I_i = \ln\left(\sum_j \exp(\alpha_1 \times p_{ij}(t) + \alpha_2 \times q_{ij}(t) + \alpha_3 \times X_{ij})\right) \quad \text{where } i = 1, 2 \tag{3.11}$$

where $(1-\sigma)$ is the coefficient of the inclusive value representing a buyer's preference for the nested quality-based sub-market as a whole, X and Y are a vector of variables that may influence a would-be homebuyer's housing choice (X indicates physical dwelling conditions, Y indicates dwelling re-lated spatial attributes), α_1 and α_2 are negative. Pr_{00} indicates the probability of quitting the urban housing market after searching. Pr_{i0} indicates the prob-ability of entering a topographically-based sub-market while $Pr_{j/i}$ indicates the probability of entering a quality-based sub-market after entering the respective topographical sub-market.

After a would-be homebuyer (a housing searcher) enters a quality-based sub-market at any time t, he or she either finds a dwelling and a housing transaction occurs, or he/she has to leave the sub-market, to adjust his/her preference and to make a re-choice between the topographical sub-markets or the quality-based sub-markets (Fig. 3.1).

Assumption 4

In each quality-based sub-market, the re-choice rate (γ_{ij}^{k}) is a constant indi-cating the fraction of housing searchers in the jth quality-based sub-market nested in the ith topographically-based sub-market who join the re-choice flow after searching in the respective quality-based sub-market, where $k = 2$ indicates that the would-be homebuyer makes a re-choice between the topographical sub-markets and $k = 1$ indicates that the would-be homebuyer makes a re-choice between the quality-based sub-markets.

Based on the above four assumptions and equation (3.7) that defines the housing sub-market trade friction, the dynamics of urban housing sub-mar-kets (a, b, and c) can be specified (as equations 3.12–3.17). In each quality-based sub-market:

$$a_{ij}(t, W(t)) =$$

$$[(D + \sum_{v,\omega=1,2}\gamma_{v,\omega}^{2} \times d_{v,\omega}(t)) \times Pr_{i}(t) + \sum_{\omega=1,2}\gamma_{i,\omega}^{1} \times d_{i,\omega}(t)] \times Pr_{j/i}(t) - (\gamma_{ij}^{1} + \gamma_{ij}^{2}) \times d_{ij}(t) \quad (3.12)$$

$$b_{ij}(t,W(t)) = \beta_{ij} \times \min(d_{ij}(t), s_{ij}(t)) \quad (3.13)$$

$$c_{ij}(t,W(t)) = \varepsilon_{ij} \times (\delta_{ij} - s_{ij}(t)) \quad (3.14)$$

where $i, j = 1, 2$.

In each topographically-based sub-market:

$$a_{i,0}(t, W(t)) = \sum_{j=1,2} a_{ij}(t, W(t)) \tag{3.15}$$

$$b_{i,0}(t, W(t)) = \sum_{j=1,2} b_{ij}(t, W(t)) \tag{3.16}$$

$$c_{i,0}(t, W(t)) = \sum_{j=1,2} c_{ij}(t, W(t)) \tag{3.17}$$

Substituting equations (3.12)–(3.17) into the stock-flow equilibrium conditions (see equations 3.4 and 3.5), a unique stock-flow market equilibrium position is obtained (equations 3.19–3.23) for this hybrid urban housing submarket system (Fig. 3.1), if equation (3.18) is satisfied. The superscript '*' used in the following equation denotes equilibrium and 't' is dropped from the equations. The mathematical derivation of equilibrium is given in Tu (1997).

$$D > \sum_{i,j} \varepsilon_{ij} \times [\delta_{ij} - s_{ij}^{\cdot}(t)] \text{ where } i, j = 1, 2. \tag{3.18}$$

Equation (3.18) means that the pre-condition for a hybrid housing sub-market system achieving its stock-flow equilibrium requires that the total extra housing demand is bigger than the total extra housing supply in the housing market. The housing market is, therefore, demand-driven. The stock-flow equilibrium is then achieved if the following equations are met (equations 3.19–3.23).

$$d_{ij}^{\cdot} = s_{ij}^{\cdot} = \frac{\varepsilon_{ij} \times \delta_{ij}}{\beta_{ij} + \varepsilon_{ij}} \tag{3.19}$$

$$q_{ij}^{\cdot} = \frac{1}{\beta_{ij}} = TF_{ij} = \min(d_{ij}^{\cdot}, s_{ij}^{\cdot}) \tag{3.20}$$

$$p_{ij}^{\cdot} = -\frac{\alpha_2}{\alpha_1} \times q_{ij}^{\cdot} - \frac{\alpha_3}{\alpha_1} \times X_{ij}^{\cdot} - \frac{\lambda}{\alpha_1 \times (1-\sigma)} \times Y_{i0}^{\cdot} + \frac{1}{\alpha_1} \times \ln(\text{Pr}_{j/i}^{\cdot}) + \frac{1}{\alpha_1 \times (1-\sigma)} \times \ln(\frac{\text{Pr}_{i0}^{\cdot}}{\text{Pr}_{00}^{\cdot}}) \tag{3.21}$$

and

$$\text{Pr}_{j/i}^{\cdot} = \frac{\varepsilon_{ij} \times (\delta_{ij} - s_{ij}^{\cdot}) + (\gamma_{ij}^1 + \gamma_{ij}^2) \times d_{ij}^{\cdot}}{\sum_j [\varepsilon_{ij} \times (\delta_{ij} - s_{ij}^{\cdot}) + (\gamma_{ij}^1 + \gamma_{ij}^2) \times d_{ij}^{\cdot}]} \tag{3.22}$$

$$\frac{\text{Pr}_{i0}^{\cdot}}{\text{Pr}_{00}^{\cdot}} = \frac{\sum_j \gamma_{ij}^2 \times d_{ij}^{\cdot} + \sum_j \varepsilon_{ij} \times (\delta_{ij} - s_{ij}^{\cdot})}{D - \sum_{i,j} \varepsilon_{ij} \times (\delta_{ij} - s_{ij}^{\cdot})} \tag{3.23}$$

where $i, j = 1, 2$.

A set of static and dynamic equilibrium and disequilibrium properties in an urban housing market can be derived from the above equilibrium equations.

Static equilibrium properties

First, the sub-market equilibrium housing price is determined by four factors (equation 3.21).

(1) The price is positively related to the bundle of attributes associated with a dwelling.

(2) The price is positively related to a homebuyer's preference for each housing attribute in a sub-market. In equations (3.8) and (3.9), α_3 and λ indicate a would-be homebuyer's preference for a housing attribute.

(3) The price is negatively related to the seller's average selling time in a sub-market. Therefore the sub-market housing price is negatively related to the level of housing sub-market trade friction (see equations 3.6 and 3.7).

(4) On the right-hand side of equations (3.22) and (3.23), the numerator is the sum of extra sub-market housing supply and the total number of housing searchers who join the re-choice flow in the respective sub-market. A large sum at equilibrium implies that the sub-market has a higher trade friction. Therefore the right-hand side of equations (3.22) and (3.23) indicates the relative trade friction of a sub-market to the average. Bringing equations (3.22) and (3.23) together with equation (3.21), it can be concluded that a sub-market with a relatively high level of market trade friction in an urban housing market will have a lower level sub-market housing price at equilibrium, given other factors remaining the same.

Second, increasing the housing demand inflow to an urban housing market will generally increase house prices in each sub-market (bringing equation 3.23 into equation 3.21). Any socio-economic factor that may change the demand inflow will have significant impacts on sub-market house prices.

Third, equilibrium sub-market housing demand and supply are positively related to the sub-market housing stock and the sub-market turnover rate, but negatively related to the sub-market transaction velocity. A faster trans-action velocity defined by β_{ij} in equation (3.13) can reduce the numbers of those searching in the sub-market, giving rise to a lower level of equilibrium sub-market demand and supply. Higher β_{ij} means that, at any time, a larger proportion of buyers can find a matched dwelling unit if supply exceeds demand, or a larger proportion of sellers can find a matched buyer, provided that supply is less than demand. In other words, the market trade friction is lower (equation 3.20), which leads to a lower level equilibrium house price (equation 3.21).

Dynamic disequilibrium properties

Dynamic sub-market disequilibrium properties can be derived from a com-puter simulation based on equations (3.18)–(3.23). The details of the simula-tion are given in Tu (1997). These dynamic properties illustrate the feature of housing sub-market dynamic stock-flow equilibrium stability. Stability analysis is an important part of equilibrium theory: many economic theories depend on the comparative statics of equilibrium. However, equilibrium properties make sense only if the underlying equilibrium system is stable.

Four types of stability can be defined in terms of degree. *Global stability* means that the market price can converge to equilibrium from any disequi-librium position. *Neighbourhood stability* means that the market price can only converge to equilibrium from a disequilibrium position located in the neighbourhood of an equilibrium position. *Bounded instability* is a mixture of stability and instability. Herein, market price follows an oscillatory move-ment around its equilibrium after it leaves an equilibrium position but still lies within the neighbourhood of the equilibrium. *Instability* means that the market will never return to equilibrium after once leaving its equilibrium position.

Computer simulations reveal that an urban housing market stock-flow equilibrium can take the form of a neighbourhood equilibrium, bounded instability or instability depending on the levels of substitutability between sub-markets. A highly segmented housing sub-market structure (or a low level of housing substitutability between sub-markets), which is determined by significant differences in housing quality and housing attributes between sub-markets, will have a higher level of stability. The reason for this is that a highly segmented housing sub-market structure results in significantly different choice probabilities for a would-be homebuyer within the sub-mar-kets (equations 3.8–3.11). If a would-be homebuyer could not find a satisfac-tory dwelling in a sub-market, he/she would have less chance to re-enter other sub-markets and maintain housing search due to the high degree of segmentation. The average searching time for each would-be buyer is therefore shortened, which reduces the sub-market trade friction. The market, therefore, takes a shorter time to get back to equilibrium.

The study of urban housing sub-market structure and its equilibrium properties is an important dimension of the analysis of urban housing markets and also provides a solid framework to understand the links between an urban housing market and the other sectors of an urban economy. However, sub-market models can only be used in the analysis of housing and the urban economy if the market is carefully divided into sub-markets that are likely to show a discrete attribute price structure (Palm 1978). The next section introduces the key problem of sub-market identification.

Urban housing sub-market identification

Although dividing the urban housing market into sub-markets raises numerous theoretical and methodological questions (Palm 1978), Goodman & Thibodeau (1998) point out that urban housing sub-market identification has typically been performed on an ad hoc basis. A significant difficulty with the ad hoc procedure for identifying sub-markets is that one cannot be confident that the resulting sub-markets are identified in an optimal way (Bourassa *et al.* 1999). The result is, to some extent, determined by the grouping methodology adopted. However, there are three criteria to apply in identifying urban housing sub-markets (adapted from Cliff *et al.* 1975):

(1) Simplicity – a solution with few sub-markets is superior to a solution with many sub-markets.

(2) Similarity – the housing attributes associated with a dwelling should be as similar as possible within a sub-market. In other words, the dwellings in a sub-market should have a high degree of homogeneity (or substitutability), while the dwellings in different sub-markets should be subjected to a higher degree of heterogeneity.

(3) Compactness – dwellings located in contiguous areas should be more likely to be grouped into one sub-market than dwellings in more distant areas.

A variety of housing sub-market grouping methodologies have been developed to identify either topographically-based housing sub-markets or quality-based housing sub-markets (Rothenberg *et al.* 1991; Watkins 1998).

Almost all these methodologies, albeit different, are derived from the hedonic housing price model (this model is discussed in detail in the chapter
by Stephen Malpezzi).

The major limitation of using the hedonic price model is the lack of a solid
theoretical basis for the identification and the measurement of the associated housing attributes and the choice of functional form. The results obtained using the hedonic approach therefore may not be optimal or unique.
In practice, the identification of neighbourhood amenities has usually been
based on considerations of data availability, and measurement based on the
convenience of dealing with the data at hand, particularly for qualitative
variables.

Halvorsen & Pollakowski (1981) argue that economic theory does not suggest an appropriate functional form for hedonic price functions. But it is
possible to develop a general functional form that incorporates all types of
functional forms of possible interest as special cases. They suggest using the
Box-Cox flexible functional form for hedonic analysis and measuring the
best performance with a goodness-of-fit test.

The major criticism of Halvorsen & Pollakowski's method is that the advantage of adopting Box-Cox functional form is purchased at the expense
of other important goals in hedonic analysis. Cassel & Mendelsohn (1985)
point out that using the Box-Cox functional form may be problematic in several respects. First, the large number of coefficients estimated with the Box-
Cox functional form reduces the accuracy of any single coefficient, resulting
in a poorer measurement of hedonic price. Second, the Box-Cox functional
form is not suited to any dataset containing negative numbers. Third, the
Box-Cox functional form may be inappropriate for predicting house prices.
Fourth, the non-linear transformation used in the Box-Cox functional form
results in complex estimates of elasticities, that are often too cumbersome
to calculate.

Despite criticism, the hedonic price model has proved the most popular
method employed in housing sub-market identification.

Identifying topographically-based housing sub-markets generally takes two
steps. First, the housing market is divided into market segments on the assumption that the dwellings within a segment are more homogeneous than
the dwellings between segments. Typically, researchers have formed market
segments based on prior expectations related to municipal boundaries, census tracts, school districts or racial divisions. In many cases, there has been
no basis on which to assume that the dwellings are homogeneous in the areas

employed, and thus the resulting sub-market identification may have been neither optimal nor unique. To solve this problem, Bourassa *et al.* (1999) propose a more systematic method to form market segments. They first apply principal component analysis to a large dataset to extract a set of principal factors from a group of housing-related attributes. Then the factor scores are calculated for each dwelling and are used in cluster analysis to form homogeneous dwelling groups (that is, market segments). Although this methodology provides a comprehensive procedure for constructing housing market segments, the disadvantage is that dwellings that are located far apart may be grouped into one market segment, resulting in the final sub-market identification possessing a lack of compactness. This difficulty presents a research challenge to develop a more powerful grouping method that more effectively tackles the spatial aspects of housing market segmentation.

Second, once market segments are identified, a hedonic price function is estimated for each segment to analyse hedonic house prices disparities across them. A housing segment becomes a housing sub-market if its hedonic prices are statistically significantly different from the ones in the rest of the housing segments (Goodman & Thibodeau 1998). Statistical tests – for example, a Chow test, a weighted standard error test or an F-test – can be used to test if there are any significant differences in the hedonic house prices between segments (see Schnare & Struyk 1976, and the review by Watkins 1998). Segments demonstrating no significant differences in the hedonic prices are merged into a new segment, for which the hedonic function is then re-estimated.

The procedure used in identifying quality-based housing sub-markets is usually based on the method proposed by Rothenberg *et al.* (1991). Again, dwellings within a sub-market are more substitutable than dwellings between sub-markets. Substitutability implies a functional 'nearness' for consumers and builders. The gradations of substitutability are given by utility differences perceived by a household, which provides the theoretical basis for defining a single-dimensional index of the quality of housing services provided by a dwelling unit. Empirically, it takes two steps to divide an urban housing market into quality-based housing sub-markets.

First, a hedonic function is applied to the sample to obtain the hedonic price for each dwelling-related attribute. A housing quality index for a specific housing unit can then be operationally defined as the value of that unit calculated through the estimated hedonic function.

Second, the dwellings are arrayed according to their quality index, and then the array is subdivided to form quality-based housing sub-markets. The disadvantage of this method is that households differ markedly in their taste for housing. Different households are likely to disagree about the pattern of substitutability. Therefore, no quality index would be unanimously valid for any two households.

Housing sub-market identification has important ramifications for housing market analysis. First, Watkins (1998) argues that the clear evidence of housing sub-market existence from a large range of studies implies that failure of housing economists to adopt the housing sub-market as a central concept in housing market analysis may lead to spurious conclusions. Second, a well-defined urban housing sub-market structure is particularly important for applying the hedonic technique to property valuation (Adair, Berry & McGreal 1996; Watkins 1998), in the construction of property indices (Berry, Chung & Waddell 1995), for housing market planning (Jones & Watkins 1999) and in the evaluation of urban policy initiatives.

However, there is, in fact, nothing intrinsic to the notion of a housing sub-market that leads one to conclude that the use of any of the methodologies discussed is superior to the others. Each methodology requires assumptions about, for example, how market segments or housing quality are defined, perceived and agreed upon by participants in a housing market. The dynamic features of housing sub-market structure also suggest that it may be necessary to re-classify or re-identify housing sub-markets after a certain time period, for example, every 3–5 years.

Conclusions

Heterogeneity, locational fixity and durability underpin the distinctive nature of the housing commodity, and, together with heterogeneous housing demand, imply that the urban housing market should be considered as segmented. Housing sub-markets are likely to exist, but there will be linkages between them. Any changes in the demand, supply and price within a sub-market may lead to changes to demand, supply and price in the remaining sub-markets, but the impacts will be stronger in those that are closer substitutes to the sub-market initiating the change. Therefore, changes beginning in one sub-market will generate repercussions in others, and in time these may re-establish the original interrelationship between the sub-markets (Rothenberg *et al.* 1991). Disequilibrium characterises an urban housing market.

The urban housing sub-market concept lays a foundation upon which theories of the urban housing market as well as the links between an urban housing market and other urban sectors should be constructed. For example, the existence and the different dynamic patterns of urban housing sub-markets suggest that disaggregate urban house price indices at sub-market level should be constructed. The disequilibrium property inherent to an urban housing sub-market model suggests that any successful economic analysis of an urban housing market should take disequilibrium issues into consideration. Failure to do so may result in a biased understanding of the urban housing market and its processes.

The sub-market approach also provides important potential insights into the impacts of urban policy or housing policy. Many urban or housing policies are aimed at having localised impacts; for example, neighbourhood urban regeneration programmes are aimed at improving the neighbourhood economy, which may have impacts on the housing sub-market in which the neighbourhood is located. The urban housing sub-market model suggests that these impacts can then be transmitted to the rest of the market.

Notes

(1) The same outcome would occur in a multiple bidding auction where the purchaser's initial offer price exceeds all potential competitors.
(2) Search burdens are exacerbated by the slow adjustment of housing supply in response to any demand changes. Housing supply comes from three sources: existing dwellings for sale, newly modified dwellings for sale in response to market demand and newly constructed housing units. The supply from any of these sources will not be able to respond to demand changes instantaneously. Slow turnover in the second-hand housing stock (partially related to high transaction costs) together with lagged new housing completions from either modification or new construction imply that the demand can change more rapidly than supply (Wood & Maclennan 1982; Rothenberg *et al.* 1991).
(3) A similar definition can be found, for example, in Grigsby *et al.* (1987), while Allen *et al.* (1995) and Bajic (1985) define housing sub-markets in relation to different dwelling types and dwelling structures.

4

Transactions Costs
and Housing Markets

John M. Quigley

Introduction

The durability, fixity, and heterogeneity of dwellings imply that transactions costs are significant in the housing market. Certainly, relative to financial markets and to the markets for most consumer goods, housing transactions require costly search to uncover the prices and attributes of commodities. Transactions may require complex negotiation with financial institutions as well as bargaining among housing market participants. Moreover, active choice in the housing market is infrequent, so participants may find housing market options and choices more uncertain than those in other markets. In particular, bargaining itself may be costly to households given its infrequent occurrence.

Duncan Maclennan's well-known 1982 book, a treatise and a widely used text (Maclennan 1982), recognises the importance of these features of the housing market. Indeed, the expanded framework offered in Chapter 3 of that book stands in stark contrast to that offered in conventional economic texts of the time. It is fair to say that one of the enduring contributions of the book is its emphasis on dynamic processes in the market for housing and the need to recognise these processes both in applied research and in economic policy. This paper provides a review of the most important sources of transactions costs in the housing market and an assessment of the magnitude of these deviations from the simple model of frictionless competition by fully informed actors.

In the second section, below, I explore a taxonomy of costs associated with transactions in the housing market. These transactions costs are, of course, specific to the market institutions of Britain and North America, and most of the quantitative evidence presented on costs comes from the US. The third section presents a simple theoretical exercise to investigate the magnitude of transactions costs relative to housing consumption measured in terms of rent or housing values. The final section considers some selected implications of the analysis.

A taxonomy

As emphasised by Maclennan (1982, pp. 59–75), 'the' housing market is really not a single neoclassical exchange market, but is rather a set of overlapping sub-markets differentiated by tenure, location, size and quality. There are markets in which the capital good, housing, is exchanged, and there are other markets in which the consumption good, housing services, is exchanged. The impediments that inhibit the adjustment of the market to a neoclassical equilibrium can be summarised in five broad categories: search costs, legal and administrative costs, adjustment costs, financial costs, and the costs of uncertainty. Each can be expressed in terms of identifiable components. Some of these components are quite hard to measure and quantify, but are nevertheless significant.

Search costs

The heterogeneity of housing and its unique spatial component suggest that it is costly to identify available dwellings. The essence of housing market choice is the trade-off among size, quality, and locational considerations, together with price. Identifying and evaluating these attributes typically involves the physical inspection of dwellings at disparate locations. Some of these inspections can be made simply by driving past a property, and others can be made by examining photographs or newspaper advertisements. These are the inspections that lead to the elimination of properties from consideration. Any property that is a 'serious' candidate for choice will no doubt be the object of physical inspection by a potential renter or purchaser. There is little survey evidence on the number of dwellings inspected by households before making residential choices. Clark (1993) reports on studies of Canadian and US housing markets that document that a third of all homebuyers and half of all renters consider only one alternative. Clark's own research (1982b) found that recent homebuyers in Los Angeles searched for less than a month, within an area of about a three-mile radius, and looked at 15 houses. Survey evidence from Glasgow suggested that renters spent between 7 and 19 days searching and that a large fraction accepted the first available unit (Wood & Maclennan 1982).

In addition, some information is available on the time spent searching by low-income renters. This information, the average number of days spent searching for rental accommodations, was gathered as a part of the Experimental Housing Allowance Program (EHAP) in the US (Weinberg *et al.* 1981). In the two markets in which the experiment was conducted, the median household spent 61 days searching (in Pittsburgh), with a standard deviation of 19 days, and 37 days searching (in Phoenix), with a standard deviation of 18 days. If households spent merely five hours a week searching during these time intervals, they would have devoted the equivalent of between one half and one full work-week to searching for housing. This is a substantial expenditure of effort.

For renters, there are rather limited opportunities to employ brokers to reduce search costs. For home purchasers, whose other transactions costs are higher (see below), there is every reason to expect that the time devoted to search will be greater. However, for institutional reasons, there is more scope for the substitution of the services of brokers or other middlemen to assist in the search process. By custom in the US, brokerage commissions are split between buyer and seller brokers. On a given transaction, the buyer's broker commission may be 3% of the selling price of a dwelling. DiPasquale & Wheaton (1996) assert that aggregate realtor (or estate agency) fees for housing transactions range from 3% to 6% in the US. A recent paper by Wood (1996) documents the regulated real estate commissions in Australian states. Average commissions range from 2% to over 8%, and commissions are proportionately smaller on more expensive houses.

Technology has already begun to reduce some of these costs for homeowners. Online services (see, for example, homegain.com) provide richer opportunities to observe the qualitative and quantitative aspects of housing alternatives, at least in comparison with multiple listing services. It may be possible to 'view' a large fraction of available housing alternatives using web-based technology in the near future. This has the potential to reduce buyers' search costs, at least in markets characterised by multiple listing services rather than a tradition of exclusive listings by individual brokers.

Despite this potential, search costs in the housing market will remain high. Technology may help to eliminate inappropriate alternatives from consideration, but ultimately serious contenders will require physical inspection.

Legal and administrative costs

Legal and administrative costs are considerably different for consumers who choose to be renters rather than owners. Rental contracts may specify the payment of security deposits, key fees, and other costs. These may amount to a couple of months' rent, but under typical contracts (Jaffe 1996), these fees are returned (sometimes with interest) at the time of lease termination. However, these fees may contribute to a cash flow problem, especially for low-income renters.

For home purchasers, the legal and administrative fees due at the time the contract is executed may be far larger. In many jurisdictions, *ad valorem* taxes are levied at the time of title transfer. These transaction taxes are widespread in continental Europe. Stamp duties, a form of *ad valorem* transfer fee, are levied in Australia as well as the UK and in many jurisdictions in the US.

In some jurisdictions in the US and the UK, lawyers are present at conveyance, and substantial legal fees are incurred. Recording and conveyance fees are levied by local governments. In the US, most lenders require a new title search at the time a transaction is completed, often involving substantial legal costs. Finally, there may be costs associated with opening or transferring accounts for public utilities and local services. Together these transactions costs for home purchase may reach several per cent of the value of the house. DiPasquale & Wheaton (1996) estimate that closing costs are 1–3% of the purchase price.

Work by Chambers & Simonson (1989) suggested that the aggregate transactions costs of homeownership amount to 6–10% of house value. Cunningham & Hendershott (1984) argue that the value is roughly 12% of house value. Malatesta & Hess (1986) report survey evidence: average homeowner transactions costs were 12% of house values based upon a sample of 100 movers. These costs are quite substantial.

Adjustment costs

The adjustment costs of moving include both out-of-pocket and psychic costs. Out-of-pocket costs include the costs of moving possessions and, perhaps, the value of furnishings rendered unusable after the move. For low-income renters, estimates are available from EHAP. For Pittsburgh households, median out-of-pocket moving costs were 12% of one month's income; for Phoenix households, the median was 3% of a month's income (Weinberg *et al.* 1981, Table 1; and Friedman & Weinberg 1981, Table 1).

These estimates seem quite low. However, they refer to the intra-metropolitan moving costs of low-income renters. Presumably, short distance moves are cheaper than long distance moves, and poor households have fewer possessions. In contrast, it is reported by Allied Moving Company that the average cost of an interstate household move in the US was $9000 in 1998, roughly two and a half times monthly income.

The psychic costs of moving to a different residence are much harder to ascertain. Presumably, these psychic costs are larger for long distance moves than for short distance moves. In principle, the psychic and transactions costs are revealed by the maximum amount that a household of static socio-economic characteristics is willing to pay to continue residence in its current dwelling. An early paper by Dynarski (1986) drew attention to this concept. Papers by Venti & Wise (1984) and by Bartik *et al.* (1992) provide estimates of this willingness to pay. Both estimates are derived from EHAP data. Thus, they are likely to be underestimates of the willingness-to-pay of middle-income households, especially owners.

The estimates are quite large indeed. The Venti & Wise methodology suggests that the average household in the EHAP sample would require a 14% increase in utility to make moving to another location as attractive as staying. The income equivalent is about $60 a month for these low-income households – or roughly 50% of their monthly rental repayments. The methodology employed by Bartik *et al.* suggests that the average low-income household in Phoenix (Pittsburgh) has moving costs, out-of-pocket plus psychic costs, of 25% (14%) of income. Households with longer periods of tenure have total moving costs that are larger still. Households whose heads are ten years older than the average have moving costs, out-of-pocket plus psychic costs, that are estimated to be 34% of income in Phoenix and 24% in Pittsburgh. The estimates of moving costs are yet higher for minority households, presumably reflecting their higher search costs.

Expectations and uncertainties

Household uncertainty and expectations about the future can increase the transactions costs of moving. Expectations of declines in interest rates make homeowner mobility more expensive today if there are any costs to contracting (Quigley 2002), even with variable rate mortgages. Expectations of falling house prices make homeowner mobility cheaper today (Chan 2001). Expectations about tax changes affect the *ex ante* user cost of capital, and this affects the mobility decisions of households and their homeownership propensities (Rosen *et al.* 1984). There are many similar instances in which uncertainty and expectations affect *ex ante* transactions costs and ultimately residential mobility. Quantitative estimates are hard to come by.

Financing costs

Beyond the transactions costs of negotiating and recording contracts, securing title, and so forth, there may be purely financial costs associated with housing market transactions, and these costs may be quite large for some homeowners. For owner-occupants with fixed rate mortgage contracts, increases in market interest rates may increase the value of the mortgage contract itself. When rates increase, the right to make monthly payments at the contract interest rate may have quite a large present discounted value. Unless mortgages are completely assumable, this value would be completely dissipated by moving to another residence. This factor alone can greatly increase the transaction costs of changing residences. It has been reported that the incidence of homeowner mobility declines substantially when interest rates rise (Quigley 1987, 2002), and homeowners are more likely to invest in renovations and home improvements as an alternative to incurring large transactions costs (Potepan 1989). Declines in house prices increase the costs of mobility that would force households to realise capital losses on their homes (Stein 1993; Chan 2001). Transactions in a declining market are less numerous due to loss aversion by sellers (Genesove & Mayer 2001). This also drives up search costs.

Other institutional aspects of the market for mortgage finance may increase the transactions costs of home purchase for some households or may shut households out of the market for owner-occupied housing entirely. For example, the inability to borrow against human capital interacts with the mechanics of the level payment mortgage to make it impossible for some younger households to enter the homeownership market at all, even though the actuarial risk of default is low (see the chapter by Gyourko in this volume).

A simple model of transactions costs

As suggested in the previous section, the extent of transactions costs in the housing market is large, and the sources of transactions costs are myriad. There is some survey evidence on the magnitude of these costs, at least for some households. But this evidence is noticeably incomplete. A full enumeration of the magnitude of these costs, especially as they affect different kinds of households, would be a formidable undertaking.

A simple model may help provide a benchmark for the magnitudes involved. For illustration, suppose the utility function of consumers is Cobb-Douglas in housing (H) and other goods (X). The unit price of housing is P_H; the price of the numeraire is set to unity. Thus,

$$U = H^\alpha X^{1-\alpha} = H^\alpha (Y - P_H H)^{1-\alpha} \tag{4.1}$$

where Y is household income and α is a parameter. This implies a demand function for housing

$$P_H H = R = \alpha Y \tag{4.2}$$

where, in equilibrium, the household spends a fixed fraction of its income on rent (R). Now consider a household observed to be consuming H_O or paying R_O in rent with income Y_O. (In general this rent payment need not be the equilibrium expenditure, αY_O.) The income (Y^*) required to make the household as well-off as if it incurred the transactions costs associated with moving to consume its preferred housing bundle H^*, is the solution to

$$H_O^\alpha (Y^* - P_H H_O)^{1-\alpha} = H^{*\alpha} (Y_O - P_H H^*)^{1-\alpha} \tag{4.3}$$

In terms of rent,

$$Y^* = \left(\frac{R^*}{R_O}\right)^{\alpha/(1-\alpha)} [Y_O - R^*] + R_O \tag{4.4}$$

Thus, the income equivalent is

$$\tilde{Y} = Y^* - Y_O = \left(\frac{\alpha Y_O}{R_O}\right)^{\alpha/(1-\alpha)} (1-\alpha)Y_O + R_O - Y_O \tag{4.5}$$

Clearly, if the household is consuming its desired equilibrium level of housing services (i.e., if $R_O = \alpha Y_O$), the right-hand side of (4.5) is zero. If the household is not consuming its desired equilibrium level of housing services, this is because the transactions costs in the housing market for this household are larger than the income equivalent of the gain in utility from changing dwellings. Thus, the income equivalent, $\tilde{Y}$, is a lower bound estimate of the transactions costs incurred in the housing market. For households with transactions costs lower than $\tilde{Y}$, housing market adjustment will occur. For households who do not make market adjustments, $\tilde{Y}$ must be less than the costs they would incur by being active participants in the market.

If the demand function for housing is known, say $P_H = D(H,Y)$, but not the utility function, then the difference in consumer surplus provides an approximation to the income equivalent

$$\tilde{Y} \approx \int_{H_O}^{H^*} D(H,Y)\,dR + R_O - R^* \qquad (4.6)$$

For example, if the demand curve for housing services is log-linear,

$$\log H \ = \ \log Z + \alpha \log P + \beta \log Y \qquad (4.7)$$

then substitution into (4.6) yields

$$\tilde{Y} \approx \int_{H_O}^{H^*} \left(\frac{H}{ZY^\beta}\right)^{1/\alpha} dH - R^* + R_O \qquad (4.8)$$

or, in terms of rent

$$\tilde{Y} \approx \left(\frac{\alpha}{\alpha+1}\right)\left(R^* - R_O^{(\alpha+1)/\alpha}\,R^{*-1/\alpha}\right) - R^* + R_O \qquad (4.9)$$

Again, $\tilde{Y}$ is a lower bound estimate of the transactions costs associated with housing market transactions.

Of course, the model sketched out above is deceptively simple. In particular, it abstracts from issues of dynamic adjustments, as households' demands for housing change over time and over the life cycle. Any calculations based on it are certainly very crude.[1] Housing is a vector of attributes, not a scalar, and these attributes are priced jointly in some hedonic framework. The demand for these attributes varies for households of different characteristics (see Malpezzi's chapter in this volume). Estimation of such a model would not be straightforward. But the essential point, that discounted transactions costs in the housing market are at least as large as the discounted utility gains forgone by consumers' inertia, is an alternative to cumbersome surveys in quantifying these costs.

Some policy implications

The magnitude of transactions costs in the housing market raises at least two issues: first, the effect of large transactions costs on the rest of the economy; and second, the set of policies that might reduce these costs.

It has been argued that the transactions costs inherent in home ownership affect the macro-economy by leading to increases in unemployment rates.

In particular, A. J. Oswald (1997a, 1999) has argued that homeowners are less mobile than renters and are less willing to move to areas of job growth when they become unemployed. This is true, he argues, precisely because the transactions costs of the housing market are large for owners, relative to renters. Apparently, the only evidence offered in support of the proposition is a series of cross-tabulations and bivariate relationships. Across OECD countries, across US states and European regions, the simple correlation between homeownership rates and unemployment is positive.

Recently, the proposition has received some theoretical support. More precisely, logically consistent models have been developed which possess this property. For example, Haavio & Kauppi (2001) have developed an intertemporal multi-region model with stochastic business cycles in which owner-occupied and rental housing markets are imbedded. With permanent boom-and-bust towns, or with random uncorrelated cycles, owners suffer no capital losses and owner occupation is just as efficient as renting (in which case all capital effects are borne by absentee landlords). However, with any persistence in business cycles, some homeowners suffer repeated capital losses. With exogenous borrowing constraints, these households are unable to move to booming regions where employment opportunities are expanding. Stochastic capital losses represent a kind of transaction cost that arises from debt constraints, not risk aversion.

The general hypothesis that homeownership rates and unemployment rates are correlated has been investigated more systematically for the United States by Green & Hendershott (2001a). The authors investigate state level unemployment and homeownership rates. They abstract from fixed effects by analysing first differences between 1970 and 1990. When the bivariate relationship is tested, weighting by population, any simple correlation vanishes (in fact, the estimated coefficient is negative).

In a series of regressions using age-specific measures of homeownership and unemployment, the coefficients of homeownership are again generally insignificant. Green & Hendershott (2001b) compare the magnitude of the estimated effects for household heads and for secondary workers. They do find differences, leading them to conclude that 'tenure seems to influence labour decisions of those for whom the transaction cost of owning is large relative to the cost of not finding a job immediately'.

Of course, households are not randomly assigned to the category of owner or renter, and this has important implications for the interpretation of these results. As documented earlier, the transactions costs of homeownership are much larger than the transactions costs of renting, and many of these are fixed costs incurred at the time of the move. Presumably, households take this factor into account in choosing between homeownership and rental status. Thus, the observed and unobserved factors that cause households to expect to be long-term residents affect the probability that an 'otherwise identical' household will choose home ownership over rental status. This selectivity bias surely leads to an overestimate of the effect of the transactions costs of homeownership on unemployment in the results reported by Green & Hendershott.[2]

Thus, it does not appear that the transactions costs associated with the housing market are of much consequence to the functioning of the labour market. At least, there is no credible evidence that the institution of homeownership 'causes' higher unemployment levels in the economy.

This does not mean, however, that there is no cause for concern about the extent of transactions costs in the housing market. Many of these costs are incurred simply as a waste of resources (e.g., time spent searching). Others represent fees to market intermediaries (and thus appear as national income), but the resources may be better employed elsewhere. Government can assist in improving this allocation of resources. It can play an active role in facilitating flows of information and public goods. Government can also provide a forum for the development of standards that can make transactions simpler. The well-functioning homeownership market in regions where solicitors and lawyers are not active participants suggests that standardisation can reduce legal fees. Online property records can be extremely useful in many planning and financial activities of local government. However, these online records would also provide an external benefit to housing market participants by making title search instantaneous. Higher levels of government can efficiently finance this external benefit.

Property referrals for renters could economise on search costs for demanders and vacancy costs for suppliers. Some of these cost reductions will arise naturally as cheap information technology proliferates. But if these technologies are compartmentalised in parts of the market, through exclusive listings of various kinds, the advantage of cheaper information will not be fully realised. Governments and professional organisations can help in the production of these public goods.

Acknowledgements

This chapter benefited from the comments of Christine Whitehead, Geoff Meen, and Gavin Wood, and from the assistance of Tracy Gordon.

Notes

(1) One simple example: consider a five-year time horizon, a household of $40 000 income, and a structure of preferences in which households spend 25% of their income on housing in equilibrium. If we observed a household spending 30% of its income on housing, we could conclude (from equation 4.6, above) that the transactions costs in the housing market for that household were at least 10% of its monthly housing expenditures.

(2) This is clearly recognised by the authors. Indeed, a more recent analysis by the authors (Green & Hendershott 2001b) attempts explicitly to address this selectivity issue.

5

Hedonic Pricing Models: a Selective and Applied Review

Stephen Malpezzi

Introduction

Twenty-five years ago, a few years before his *Housing Economics*, Professor Duncan Maclennan published a seminal paper entitled 'Some Thoughts on the Nature and Purpose of House Price Studies'. The two publications were well-timed: hedonic price modelling was in the process of moving from a cutting-edge empirical curiosity to a standard method of price index construction that has been used in literally thousands of studies since.[1] In those two publications and in Maclennan's subsequent work, several important themes recur:

- the need to put hedonic models on a firm theoretical footing, including, but not limited to, consideration of the consequences of disequilibrium;

- whether common specifications are complete, or reasonably so; including, but not limited to, questions of omitted variables, functional form, and the proper definition of a market; and the implications for our work of inevitably imperfect specifications; and

- that the design of the pricing model should fit the purpose at hand.

In this chapter I selectively review the hedonic price literature (and, briefly, some other related models) with a focus on these questions. Theory will be discussed; but my orientation is more towards the applied economist estimating these models, rather than specialised theorists. In particular, several other recent surveys such as Follain & Jimenez (1985a) and Sheppard (1999) have discussed certain theoretical and econometric issues which I will discuss only briefly below; readers are referred to those excellent reviews, which I aim to complement rather than compete with.

What is a hedonic price index?

The method of hedonic equations is one way that expenditures on housing can be decomposed into measurable prices and quantities, so that rents for different dwellings or for identical dwellings in different places can be predicted and compared. At its simplest, a hedonic equation is a regression of expenditures (rents or values) on housing characteristics. The independent variables represent the individual characteristics of the dwelling, and the regression coefficients may be transformed into estimates of the implicit prices of these characteristics.

The fundamental hedonic equation

Hedonic regressions are basically regressions of rent or house value against characteristics of the unit that determine that rent or value. The hedonic regression assumes that one knows the determinants of a unit's rent:

$$R = f(S, N, L, C, T) \tag{5.1}$$

where

R = rent (substitute V, value, if estimating hedonic price indices for, say, homeowners using sales data);

S = structural characteristics;

N = neighbourhood characteristics;

L = location within the market;

C = contract conditions or characteristics, such as whether utilities are included in rent; and

T = the time rent or value is observed.

In this chapter, I will refer to a hedonic model more or less along these lines as a 'single equation' model or the 'first stage' of a 'two-stage' model. Two-stage models attempt to go beyond the initial estimation of a hedonic price surface, and in the second stage recover structural supply and demand parameters for individual housing characteristics.

Collapsing the vectors S, N, L and C into a larger vector X for the moment purely for notational convenience, and adopting a common (but sometimes criticised, see below) semi-logarithmic functional form, (5.1) can be re-written compactly as:

$$R = e^{x\beta\epsilon} \tag{5.2}$$

so that

$$\ln R = X\beta + \epsilon \tag{5.3}$$

and we estimate:

$$\ln R = Xb + e \tag{5.4}$$

where β and ϵ are of course the unknown true parameters, and b and e are actual estimates.

Now, by properties of logarithms, the predicted rent of a unit can be computed as $R = e^{xb}$; the price of an individual attribute, X_1, at a given level of X_1, given the level of the *other* m-1 attributes, $X_{i\neq1}$, can be calculated in dollars or pounds as:

$$P = e^{xb} \tag{5.5}$$

Notice that with such a logarithmic specification, the dollars or pound price of X_1, or any other single characteristic, varies with the level of X_1, as well as with the level of other X_i. Prices are non-linear, an important point to which I return below.

'Second-stage' hedonic models: recovering structural parameters

Much of the hedonic literature focuses on the basic hedonic relationship discussed in the preceding paragraphs. However, as papers discussed below by Rosen and others make clear, the hedonic equation discussed above is a reduced form. Under certain maintained hypotheses hedonic equations also admit of a structural interpretation: for example, if the supply of each and all characteristics is perfectly elastic, hedonic coefficients reveal demand for characteristics. But in most real-world contexts such a stringent maintained hypothesis is untenable. A number of papers attempt to recover structural parameters of demand and supply; or at least the demand for characteristics.

Specifically, because dollar or pound prices vary within a sample, if the level of characteristics also varies, one can make use of this variation to estimate price elasticities for individual coefficients. For example, one specification that has been used in a number of papers is to presume a linear demand model in the second stage, after a first-stage logarithmic hedonic. It is not uncommon to place prices of each characteristic on the left-hand side, i.e., to assume an inverse demand relation, and to then estimate an equation for each characteristic, of the form:

$$P_{1i} = D_i\alpha_1 + S_i\gamma_1 + \mu_{1i} \qquad\qquad (5.6)$$
$$P_{2i} = D_i\alpha_2 + S_i\gamma_2 + \mu_{2i}$$
$$\vdots$$
$$P_{mi} = D_i\alpha_m + S_i\gamma_m + \mu_{mi}$$

where $P_{1i} = e^{Xb}$ as before. Note that the money price of each of the m characteristics will vary from one observation to the next (will vary with i) because of the property of joint determination of prices discussed above. Armed with this variation in price, demand estimation can proceed.

Papers such as Follain & Jimenez (1985b) and Witte, Sumka & Erekson (1979) present estimates of the demand for housing characteristics from such models. Vectors D and S represent exogenous demand and supply shifters, such as income, or input costs (typically land). Often supply is assumed elastic, so that only demand shifters, like household income or family size, that are more readily available, are included. Thus, a prototypical dataset for the first stage would include household level data on some dependent variable like rent or sales price; and on the characteristics S, N, L and C. The prototypical dataset for the second stage would add information on household/unit level demand and supply shifters. Sometimes neighbourhood-level data are appended to household level data.[2]

A point now well understood by most experienced practitioners, but only occasionally discussed in the literature, is just how central a role functional form plays in the set-up for most two-stage demand for characteristics models. Consider that if the first-stage hedonic regression were linear, there would be no variation in characteristic prices within the sample, and hence no second-stage system to estimate. In fact, it is the *difference* between hedonic functional forms, and second-stage demand functional forms, that makes such systems potentially estimable. This point was made clearly by Nelson's (1982a) insightful critique of Witte, Sumka & Erekson's (1979) otherwise exemplary early study. Witte *et al.* (WSE) estimated logarithmic hedonic *and* logarithmic demand functions; Nelson showed that these were not in fact estimable, and Nelson suggests that the fact that WSE did obtain numerical estimates was, paradoxically, due to rounding error. On the other hand, models that involve (say) logarithmic first-stage hedonic equations and linear second stage demand equations may be estimable (though subject to remaining problems discussed below).

Repeat sales models

In this chapter, the focus is on hedonic pricing models. In order to place this class of models in context, consider briefly another pricing model, namely repeat sales models, which are in fact related to hedonic price indices in a certain way.[3]

Repeat sales indices are estimated by analysing data where all units have sold at least twice. Such data allow us to annualise the percentage growth in sales prices over time.[4] These are time series indices in their pure form. They do not provide information on the value of individual house characteristics or on price levels. They have the advantage of being based on actual transactions prices, and in principle allow us to sidestep the problem of omitted variable bias.

One way to understand the key features of the repeat sales index is to start by reconsidering the hedonic model. Consider a simple semi-log hedonic equation:

$$\ln P = X\beta + \beta_1 T_1 + \beta_2 T_2 + \beta_3 T_3 + \beta_4 T_4 \tag{5.7}$$

where P is the value or rent for the unit, and where the vector X includes all the relevant characters, including a constant term; and the time dummies T_i represent periods that follow the initial base case period.[5]

The vector X represents a list of housing and neighbourhood characteristics that would enter a hedonic equation. The vector T is a series of dummy variables representing the time periods under consideration. These could be months, quarters, or years, depending upon the type of data at hand.

Consider a house 'A' that sells in periods 2 and 4 (period 0 is the base year). In period 2:

$$\ln P^A_2 = X\beta + \beta_1 T_1 + \beta_2 T_2 + \beta_3 T_3 + \beta_4 T_4 \tag{5.8}$$

$$= X\beta + \beta_2 T_2$$

since T_1, T_3, and $T_4 = 0$. And of course, by similar reasoning, in period 4:

$$\ln P^A_4 = X\beta + \beta_4 T_4 \tag{5.9}$$

Then, by subtraction:

$$\ln P^A_4 - \ln P^A_2 = X\beta + \beta_4 T_4 - X\beta - \beta_2 T_2 \tag{5.10}$$

$$= \beta_4 T_4 - \beta_2 T_2$$

This is for a representative housing unit that sells twice. Given a sample of such units, we want, in effect, the 'average' β_4 and β_2. Recall that regression is, in effect, estimating a series of *conditional means*. Clearly, by subtraction the characteristics vector drops out, as do the dummy variables for periods in which no transaction takes place. Green & Malpezzi (2001) illustrate with sample data.

Another possible refinement is to consider the fact that the variance of these housing prices will generally increase over time. In today's econometric parlance, such prices are not *stationary*. Case & Shiller (1987) suggest a refinement to the Bailey, Muth and Nourse model to mitigate such problems. The model just described is used as a first stage, and the residuals from this first stage model are used to construct weights that can be used to correct for heteroskedasticity using generalised least squares.

Repeat sales indices are currently much discussed in the literature because they have a number of advantages. First, no information is required on the characteristics of the unit (other than that an individual unit has not significantly changed its characteristics between sales). Second, the method can be used on datasets that are potentially widely available, at least in the US, and collected in a timely manner, with great geographic detail, but which do not have detailed housing characteristics. For example, Case and Shiller's original work used data collected by the Society of Real Estate Appraisers. Much of the current US research in this area has been undertaken by Fannie Mae and Freddie Mac, which have the advantage of large datasets with price data from a huge number of transactions nationwide.

The repeat sales method has a number of shortcomings as well.[6] First, while raw data have been widely available in the US, data are often harder to come by in other countries, including Britain. Second, even at its best, the method only yields estimates of price *changes*. No information on price levels, or place-to-place price index, is derivable from the repeat sales method. Of course, the repeat sales method can be combined with some other method; i.e., to update earlier estimates of price levels constructed using some other method. Also, because only a few units transact twice over a given time period, the repeat sales method utilises only a fraction of potential information on the housing market.

Other potential issues with repeat sales include the following. Units that transact frequently may be systematically different from units representative of the stock as a whole. How big a problem this selection bias is depends partly on the purpose of the index. It certainly would be less of a problem if the purpose of the index were to track the prices of units available on the market.

The method also implicitly assumes that there is no change in the quality or quantity of housing services produced by the unit between periods. Of course, this assumption is always violated to some degree. Those who construct these indices spend a lot of time weeding out units that have been upgraded using, for example, collateral data on building permits, or the limited structural information that may exist in the dataset in use. The method also assumes that the coefficients on the underlying hedonic model remain constant: this is what allows the house characteristics to drop out of the model. But this assumption may also be questioned. For example, as families have become smaller, so too has the value of bedrooms, holding all else equal. Thus the hedonic coefficient for bedrooms in 1990 was almost certainly different from the coefficient in 1960, regardless of the particular market.[7]

The roots of hedonic price models

In essence, the hedonic relation arises because of heterogeneity. The model postulates a market containing a heterogeneous housing stock, which can only be modified at some cost, and heterogeneous consumers, some of whom put different valuations on a given bundle of characteristics ('house') than others. A full history of hedonic pricing models would be another paper, at least, but it is worthwhile to identify the roots of this approach, and point out some of the classics of the literature here.

Two oft-cited classic papers are those by Kelvin Lancaster (1966) and Sherwin Rosen (1974).[8] Focusing on the demand side of the market, Lancaster developed a sophisticated branch of microeconomic theory in which utility is generated, not by goods *per se*, but by *characteristics* of the goods. The applicability to housing is direct and obvious. I'm happy to be home, not so much to be in anything called a 'house', but to be in a warm dry place, with a quiet space for a comfortable chair, a functioning toilet or a hot bath should I require them, and some other rooms in the house to store stacks of papers or noisy children.[9] Thus, many hedonic studies cite Lancaster's work, and justifiably so, for providing microeconomic foundations for analysing utility-generating characteristics. Lancaster developed this theory using the tools of 'activity analysis', and did not limit his discussion to housing, but applied the concept to topics as diverse as financial assets, the labour/leisure trade-off, and the demand for money. Perhaps Lancaster's main contribution was to put centre stage the still-slippery question of what exactly is the 'good' housing, and how is it related to more fundamental characteristics?

Rosen's (1974) article is the other oft-cited classic reference. Like Lancaster, Rosen focuses on characteristics, but has less to say about their utility-bearing nature and more about how suppliers and consumers interact within a framework of bids and offers for characteristics. Furthermore, while he did not much discuss functional form explicitly, Rosen's model naturally leads to a non-linear hedonic price structure. Many two-stage characteristic demand models, in particular, cite Rosen as their theoretical foundation, although Rosen had little to say about how the estimation of such structural parameters might be carried out.

Of course, there were other early theoretical papers that contributed to the development of this literature. One might point to Sir John Hicks' (1939, 1960) elaboration of a 'composite commodity', and to Fisher & Shell's (1971) related 'repackaging hypothesis', anticipating other early work by Triplett (1974) among others.

As regards the actual estimation of hedonic price models, the study most often cited as the pioneer was not a housing application at all, but a hedonic price index for automobiles developed by A. T. Court (1939). A later, but still early and influential automobile application was by Griliches (1961). Recently, Goodman (1998) and Colwell & Dilmore (1999) have filled in more of this history, telling us more about Court's early work as well as even earlier efforts by Wallace (1926) and Haas (1922). I have seen less discussion of which two-stage study has pride of place; Witte *et al.* (1979) and Awan *et al.* (1982) certainly helped get the ball rolling.

Conceptual issues in hedonic modelling

In this section, I discuss briefly some matters of underlying theoretical importance in hedonic modelling. The discussion is short because the issues have been so well discussed in two recent surveys, by Follain & Jimenez (1985a), and Sheppard (1999), as well as in several of the other papers cited in the next few paragraphs.

Two identification problems

The identification problem – disentangling supply and demand, when faced with data only from their interaction – has bedevilled applied econometrics for years. In addition to the 'usual' identification problem, two-stage hedonic analysis of the demand for characteristics faces an additional potential problem. The problem stems from the nonlinearity of the price structure. In garden-variety supply and demand models, individual consumers (and, often, suppliers) are *price-takers*, i.e., the price of the good is exogenous and the consumer chooses a quantity conditional on the reigning price. In non-linear hedonic models, whether a simple logarithmic model or a more flexible form, prices and quantities are correlated by construction; in effect, consumers choose *both* a quantity of some characteristic and, implicitly, its price. The problem has been well analysed by Blomquist & Worley (1982) and Diamond & Smith (1985), and in the Follain & Jimenez (1985a) and Sheppard (1999) surveys; the reader is referred to their more discursive treatment. Suffice it to say that a number of studies have tried to tackle the problems using well-established techniques like instrumental variables. The problem, as ever, is in finding good instruments.

Equilibrium or disequilibrium models?

Another ubiquitous feature of housing markets is that their extremely costly adjustment processes make the usual simplifying assumptions that markets are in equilibrium when observed less tenable. In fact, the disequilibrium nature of the housing market is a recurring theme in Maclennan (1982) and in many of his other papers. What are the consequences of this disequilibrium, and what can be done about it?

Several possible approaches to issues arising from disequilibrium are possible. In addition to the examples included here, see also the chapter by Yong Tu in this volume. One possible approach to the problem of disequilibrium is to estimate hedonic price functions using only observations in or near equilibrium. For example, a switching regression approach could be used, following generally the econometric methods described in, for example, Bowden (1978). Such approaches have been applied generally to the housing market, notably by Fair & Jaffee (1972); but their models are generally studies of the determinants of housing starts, not models of housing prices. An example of a later disequilibrium hedonic model is Anas & Eum (1984).

Several difficulties must be overcome to implement such a switching regression model. First, it is necessary to specify the nature of the process that distinguishes equilibrium from disequilibrium observations; in a typical cross-section hedonic sample it is not always obvious how this would be done. Second, depending on the purpose of the hedonic index, successfully estimated equilibrium prices may or may not be what it is needed. For example, if one were constructing place-to-place price indices to study, say, the cost of living or to set appropriate levels of housing subsidies, presumably one would wish the index to reflect actual prices paid in the market, whether in or out of equilibrium.

An alternative approach is to focus, not on the effects of disequilibrium on the construction of the price index, but rather on the amount of disequilibrium in a given sub-market or period, and the adjustment process back to equilibrium. Examples of studies that illustrate the principles include Abraham & Hendershott (1996), Dreiman & Follain (2000), and Malpezzi (1999), each of which studies prices over time. While different in important details, each of these studies essentially proceeds in three steps. First, estimate a time series price index.[10] Second, find some way of differentiating equilibrium prices; in these studies, prices were considered near equilibrium if price *changes* in the next period were near zero. With this subset of equilibrium prices, estimate their fundamental determinants, e.g. based on income, recent growth, supply conditions, etc. Now for each period we have the price and index actually realised, and an estimate of the equilibrium price; thus we have an estimate of disequilibrium as well. The third and final phase of these studies is to study the determinants of the disequilibrium, including in these time-series studies the nature of the time path back to equilibrium, once the market has been 'shocked out'.

Specification issues

In this section, I discuss a number of practical issues such as which variables or functional form to use, and how to define the geography of a market. But first, one should note an overarching reason why decisions on these matters so often seem ad hoc. It is unfortunate, but the answer to 'what *does* theory tell us about specification of hedonic models?' is, in brief, 'not much'. Papers like Lancaster (1966) and Rosen (1974) elegantly present models of housing characteristics without having much to say about just what those characteristics are, or how exactly they are related to price.

Choice of dependent variable

Firstly, the choice of dependent variable is about choosing rent, or value, of the housing unit. Confusion sometimes reigns because of sloppy terminology, especially among real estate professionals, but also sometimes among housing economists. The term 'housing price' is often used loosely as a synonym for 'housing value', when of course it is a true 'price' only under special conditions. But the usage is so entrenched by now that even housing economists generally rely on context to keep the meaning clear.

Of course it is well known that house rents and house values are related, though only in special cases proportionately so; papers such as Ambrose and Nourse (1993) and Phillips (1988) explore systematic variations in the relationship, or 'capitalisation rate'. Papers that focus on rents must wrestle with problems stemming from the fact that different units have different lease terms or contract conditions. One notable example is the inclusion, or exclusion, of utility payments in rent. One common procedure is to obtain data on such utility charges for units where they are not included, and to add these charges to contract rent to 'gross it up', so that rents in the sample are for comparable services. Lump sum payments (deposits or 'key money') can be annualised with an assumed capitalisation rate, and added to rent as in Malpezzi's (1998) study of key money paid for Cairo rent controlled units. Another is to use contract rent as the dependent variable, but to add dummy variables to the right-hand side to indicate units with various utilities *included* in rent, so that the estimated coefficients 'dummy out' the price of utilities, leaving a rental index net of utilities.

When estimating a hedonic regression on values, several other measurement issues emerge. A number of studies use owner or tenant estimates of the value of the unit. This gives rise to concern over the accuracy of such self-reported appraisals. Several papers have examined the issue with US data, such as Kain & Quigley (1972b), Follain & Malpezzi (1981b), and Goodman & Ittner (1992). As yet I have found few non-US studies addressing the issue. Early studies such as Kain & Quigley and Follain & Malpezzi suggested that while the *variances* of owner assessments are high, *biases* are modest; given enough data, hedonic models based on owner assessments would be reasonably reliable. But Goodman and Ittner's recent study finds larger biases, and suggests more caution.

Recent sales 'prices' (house values from observed recent transactions) have some obvious advantages as dependent variables. Recent transactions data may present less potential bias, and greater potential precision, than occupants' or owners' self-assessments. But recent sales are not necessarily a random draw from the total housing stock. If the purpose is to index the market of available units, this may not be of great concern, but if the purpose is to index the total stock, we must concern ourselves with possible selection bias. Several papers such as Gatzlaff & Haurin (1997) have tested the presence of such biases. Test statistics often reject the null, but so far most studies have found the magnitude of the bias to be modest.

Some datasets, like the American Housing Survey, truncate housing values; values over $300 000 are reported simply as 'over $300 000'. Such dependent variable truncation can cause significant bias in results. Maddala (1983) presents some econometric techniques that attempt to attenuate the effects of such bias, when truncation is an issue.

Selection of independent variables

There are literally hundreds of potential housing characteristics that could be included on the right-hand side. Butler (1982) and Ozanne and Malpezzi (1985) show that, unfortunately, coefficient estimates are not robust with respect to omitted variables. But interestingly, the same correlation between omitted and included variables that biases individual coefficient estimates can and often does help improve prediction from a 'sparse' model. This suggests that hedonic applications that rely on overall predictions – like place-to-place price indices, or cost-benefit analysis of housing subsidies – can proceed apace, even while papers that rely on interpretation of individual coefficients must be interpreted more cautiously.

While theory is not much of a guide, experience from many studies suggests that, whatever the purpose, a full dataset would include the following:

- rooms, in the aggregate, and by type (bedrooms, bathrooms, etc.)

- floor area of the unit

- structure type (single family, attached or detached, if multi-family the number of units in the structure, number of floors)

- type of heating and cooling systems

- age of the unit

- other structural features, such as presence of basements, fireplaces, garages, etc.

- major categories of structural materials, and quality of finish

- neighbourhood variables, perhaps an overall neighbourhood rating, quality of schools, socio-economic characteristics of the neighbourhood

- distance to the central business district, and perhaps to sub-centres of employment; access to shopping, schools and other important amenities

- characteristics of the tenant that affect prices: length of tenure (especially for renters), whether utilities are included in rent; and possibly racial or ethnic characteristics (if these are hypothesised to affect the price per unit of housing services faced by the occupant)

- date of data collection (especially if the data are collected over a period of months or years).

However, this list, while still incomplete, is also general. Hocking (1976), Amemiya (1980) and Leamer (1978) are among useful guides to the actual selection of variables.

Functional form in general

There is no strong theoretical basis for choosing any specific functional form for a hedonic regression (see Halvorsen & Pollakowski (1981) and Rosen (1974)). Follain & Malpezzi (1980b), for example, tested a linear functional form as well as a log-linear (also known as semi-log) specification. But they found the log-linear form had a number of advantages over the linear form, detailed below.

The log-linear form is written:

$$\ln R = \beta_0 + S\beta_1 + N\beta_2 + L\beta_3 + C\beta_4 + \varepsilon \tag{5.11}$$

where $\ln R$ is the natural log of imputed rent, S, N, L and C are structural, neighbourhood, locational, and contract characteristics of the dwelling,[11] and β_i and ε are the hedonic regression coefficients and error term, respectively.

The log-linear form has five things to recommend it. First, the semi-log model allows for variation in the dollar value of a particular characteristic so that the price of one component depends in part on the house's other characteristics. For example, with the linear model, the value added by a third bathroom to a one-bedroom house is the same as it adds to a five-bedroom house. This seems unlikely[12]. The semi-log model allows the value added to vary proportionally with the size and quality of the home.

Second, the coefficients of a semi-log model have a simple and appealing interpretation. The coefficient can be interpreted as approximately the percentage change in the rent or value given a unit change in the independent variable. For example, if the coefficient of a variable representing central air conditioning is 0.219, then adding it to a structure adds about 22% to its value or its rent. (Actually, the percentage interpretation is an approximation, and it is not necessarily accurate for dummy variables. Halvorsen & Palmquist (1980) show that a much better approximation of the percentage change is given by $e^b - 1$, where b is the estimated coefficient and e is the base of natural logarithms. So a better approximation is that central air conditioning will add $\exp(0.219) - 1 = 24\%$.)

Third, the semi-log form often mitigates the common statistical problem known as heteroskedasticity, or changing variance of the error term. Fourth, semi-log models are computationally simple, and so well suited to examples. The one hazard endemic to the semi-log form is that the anti-log of the predicted log house price does not give an unbiased estimate of predicted price. This can, however, be fixed with an adjustment (see Goldberger 1968). Last, it is possible to build specification flexibility into the right-hand side, using dummy (or indicator) variables, splines and the like (of which more shortly). This allows a fair amount of flexibility in estimation, even with the semi-log form.

However, some authors have recommended more flexible forms than the semi-log. One common flexible form is the translog functional form, suggested by Christensen *et al.* (1973):

$$\ln R = \beta_0 + \sum_m \beta_m \ln X_m + \frac{1}{2}\sum_m \sum_n \gamma_{mm} \ln X_m \ln X_n \tag{5.12}$$

where $\ln R$ again represents the log of rent (value can be substituted), and there are m characteristics denoted X. Examples of the translog form can be found in Capozza *et al.* (1996, 1997).

There is an even more general and flexible class of functions, within which linear, logarithmic and translog functions are subsumed; these flexible forms are carefully analysed by Box and Cox (1964), and applied to hedonic prices by Halvorsen and Pollakowski (1981):

$$R^\theta = \beta_0 + \sum_m \beta_m X_m^\lambda + \frac{1}{2} \sum_m \sum_n \gamma_{mn} X_m^\lambda X_n^\lambda \qquad (5.13)$$

Such a form is quite flexible, with parameters θ and λ limiting the functional form.[13] For example, when θ and λ are both 1 and γ_{mn} are all identically zero, the Box-Cox form becomes a simple linear model. When θ and λ approach zero and γ_{mn} are all identically zero, the Box-Cox form becomes a logarithmic model. When θ and λ approach zero and but some γ_{mn} are nonzero, the Box-Cox form becomes the translogarithmic model.

This is a good place to reiterate the special role functional form plays in two-stage structural models of characteristics demand and supply. I have already noted this important fact: it is functional form – indeed, differences in functional form between stages – that makes the system of demand (or supply and demand) functions potentially estimable. Thus it is particularly problematic that theory yields little guidance to the functional form of the hedonic relationship, and only tenuous guidance to the functional form for second-stage estimation of the demand for characteristics.

Functional form and independent variables

If data permit it, judicious use of dummy or indicator variables for independent variables can be useful. For example, entering a variable for the number of total rooms in (say) a semi-logarithmic hedonic regression constrains the percentage increase in value from a one-unit addition to a 3-room unit to be the same as the percentage increase in value from a one-unit addition to a 6-room unit. If degrees of freedom permit it, at least the most common values can be coded as dummy variables, imparting more flexibility to the form. Malpezzi *et al.* (1980) provide additional details, e.g. how to code combinations of dummies and continuous variables. See also the classic review by Harold Watts (1964), and Suits (1984). The special topic of how to interpret dummy variables when the dependent variable is logarithmic is treated in Halvorsen & Palmquist (1980) and Kennedy (1981).

Of course dummy or indicator variables are not the only method that can be used to incorporate flexibility on the right-hand side. Continuous variables can be entered in quadratic (or cubic or even higher power) form; in fact, as much flexibility as needed can be readily constructed using piecewise spline techniques (Suits *et al.* 1978).

Market and sub-market definition

The definition and testing of sub-markets is an important recurring theme in Maclennan's work. Housing markets are local and diverse, and hedonic price estimation requires careful consideration of sub-markets (see the chapter in this volume by Yong Tu).

Sub-market assumptions in hedonic models can be roughly categorised as follows. The first category comprises papers that define a market as an entire nation, or at least a large region, or perhaps a state. Linneman (1981) and Struyk (1980) fall into the category of national hedonic models, and Mills & Simenauer (1996) present a regional model. The second category, including much of my own work such as Malpezzi *et al.*(1980) and Follain & Malpezzi (1980a), adopts the metropolitan area as the unit of analysis. Metropolitan areas are usually thought of as labour markets, more or less, and it is certainly appealing to consider housing markets and labour markets as roughly coincident. The third category, including many of Maclennan's own studies as well as papers such as Straszheim (1975), Gabriel (1984), Grigsby *et al.* (1987), Rothenberg *et al.* (1991), Maclennan & Tu (1996), and Bourassa *et al.* (1999), examines sub-markets below the metropolitan level. These may be segmented by location (central city/suburb), or by housing quality level, or by race or income level.

Studies that obtain large datasets and test for the existence of sub-markets, usually by segmenting the sample and performing F-tests for equality of hedonic coefficients across sub-samples, generally find them: the F-tests usually reject the null. Ohta & Griliches (1975) suggest a more conservative method that focuses on changes in the standard error of the regression, in effect on how well the segmented model predicts.

Hedonic modelling: the current position

Single-equation models, or structural models?

Taken together, the problems discussed above – especially the identification problems, imperfect specifications, and the general non-robustness of coefficient estimates – suggest that reliable two-stage structural estimation of the demand for characteristics is difficult. Qualitatively, that is the judgement we reached in the World Bank's housing demand research project, after investing significant resources attempting to develop characteristic demand models that would improve low-cost housing project design (Follain & Jimenez 1985b; Gross 1986; Mayo & Gross 1987).

That does not mean that there is no hope for developing useful models somewhat along these lines. Models of aggregate housing demand work well enough, despite undoubted problems (see Mayo 1981; Olsen 1987; Whitehead 1999). King (1975) presents an 'in-between' model where housing is broken down into three categories – space, quality and location. Possibly further work along these lines would be fruitful.

Hedonic specification: art or science?

Generally, there is art as well as science in model specification: choice of variables, functional form, and definition of sub-market. Whenever sample sizes are small, and especially if the application will involve some prediction out of sample (as with, say, pricing rent-controlled or subsidised units), it is often best to stick to a simple parsimonious specification, possibly using the metropolitan area as market definition. But if samples are large and well-drawn, and especially if the focus of the hedonic model is a single metropolitan area, more flexible forms, and more careful attention to the delineation of sub-markets, will generally pay off.

It is somewhat surprising that the literature applying formal specification tests, such as those of Hausman (1978), is modest, since specification is such an issue in hedonic analysis. Burgess & Harmon (1982) is an interesting example that could be replicated further.

Examples of applications

While there are many important and interesting theoretical issues related to hedonic models, some of which have been discussed above, our main interest ultimately is in understanding real-world housing markets, and hence in applications. Space precludes an exhaustive review, but here I mention some examples. I list a few representative applications mainly by topic; note also that while I know the US literature best and cite it heavily, hedonic models are now truly universally applied. As previously cited work by Maclennan (1982) and Ball (1973) make clear, there is of course a long-standing, large and growing literature focused on the United Kingdom, as well as the rest of

Europe and of North America; but in fact hedonic models have been applied in every permanently inhabited region of the globe.[14]

One of the first, and still most important, uses of hedonic models is to make general improvements in housing price indices, whether time series, place-to-place, or panel data price indices. Follain & Ozanne (1979), Chowhan & Prud'homme (2000), Englund, Quigley & Redfearn (1998), Follain & Malpezzi (1980b), Hoffman & Kurz (2002), Moulton (1995), Malpezzi, Chun & Green (1998) and Tiwari & Hasegawa (2000) are among many examples of studies that basically aim to improve the precision of housing price benchmarks. Some hedonic studies have been undertaken to construct special-purpose housing price indices, for example to improve the measurement of poverty thresholds (Short *et al.* 1999).

Hedonic prices have also been examined within cities. In addition to the sub-market tests already discussed, many tests of the 'standard urban model' of Alonso, Muth and Mills have been carried out. The standard model predicts a generally declining pattern of prices with distance from the centre of the city. Competing models based on localised amenities, and models with multiple centres, have other predictions. Adair *et al.* (2000), Follain & Malpezzi (1981c), Mozolin (1994), Soderberg & Janssen (2001) are examples of studies that examine intra-urban variation in the price of housing using hedonic models. Perhaps unsurprisingly, results for the 'standard model' are mixed; while there are some broad tendencies for house prices to fall with distance from CBD, amenities and sub-centres generally play an important role as well (also, see the discussion and further references contained in the chapter by Gibb in this volume).

Hedonic models have also been used to develop measures of environmental quality. One common approach is to examine whether house prices increase when near environmental 'goods', or fall when near 'bads'. Examples of this literature include Cheshire & Sheppard (1995), Freeman (1979), Boyle & Kiel (2001), Des Rosiers & Theriault (1996), Din, Hoesli & Bender (2001) and Garrod & Willis (1992 a, b).

Many other interesting studies have been undertaken that focus on interpretations of individual coefficients. One must always be cautious in interpreting individual coefficients in light of the specification issues discussed above. With this *caveat*, a number of studies have examined racial, ethnic and socio-economic differences in housing prices. Kain & Quigley (1972a), Follain & Malpezzi (1981a), Chambers (1992), Galster (1992), Nelson (1982b) and Vandell (1995) are among many contributions to this strand of literature. Other studies have used hedonic age coefficients to measure depreciation, such as Malpezzi *et al.* (1987), Clapp & Giaccotto (1998b), Goodman & Thibodeau (1995), and Shilling *et al.* (1991).

Hedonic prices have been applied to market-rate units and then used to price subsidised or publicly provided units, in order to calculate the costs and benefits of different housing subsidy programmes. Olsen & Barton (1983), Buchel & Hoesli (1995), De Borger (1986), Quigley (1982a), Satsangi (1991), Turner (1997), Gibb & MacKay (2001) and Willis & Cameron (1993) are representative examples. Closely related are studies that undertake regulatory cost benefit, including rent control; for example, Olsen (1972), Malpezzi (1998) and Willis & Nicholson (1991).

Another important use of hedonic models is the appraisal of individual housing units. Appraisers and other property market professionals increasingly use hedonic models. They can be used to improve professional practice of appraisers and chartered surveyors (Dubin 1998), or for undertaking mass appraisal for property taxation and other public purposes; see Berry & Bednarz (1975), Lusht (1976), and Pace & Gilley (1990).

Hedonic models are also used to examine the capitalisation of a wide range of amenities, as well as costs. One of the earliest literatures along these lines developed to study whether differential local tax rates were capitalised into house prices, following the model of Tiebout (1956), as extended by Oates (1981). After several false starts, papers by Edel & Sclar (1974) and King (1977) clarified the need to include measures of public services as well as taxes paid, and pointed out some important details of the correct functional form for such tests. Many subsequent studies have found such capitalisation, on both the benefit and tax side; Zodrow (1983) provides a convenient review.

Lastly, despite the problems discussed above, many studies have tried to recover demand parameters (and sometimes supply and demand parameters) for individual housing characteristics, or groups of characteristics. Studies here include those by Awan *et al.*(1982), Pasha & Butts (1996), Witte *et al.* (1979) and Kaufman & Quigley (1987).

Concluding thoughts

A lot of cutting-edge work on conceptual issues relating to hedonics is still being done. Theoretical work continues apace to develop the foundations of hedonic models, and in particular to attempt to address some of the issues I have noted with two-stage structural models. In addition to the literature cited above, on this see, for example, Rouwendal (1992) and Epple (1987).

An alternative way to think about hedonic models is a two-stage process of a different sort: samples used for hedonic estimation are not necessarily random draws from the population of houses, but are selected samples (especially when transactions-driven databases are used). Ermisch *et al.*(1996), Jud & Seaks (1994) and Clapp *et al.* (1991) are examples of studies addressing selection issues.

In terms of functional form, one of the cutting-edge areas is to eschew parametric forms altogether. Semiparametric and nonparametric approaches can be found in Anglin & Ramazan (1996), Mason & Quigley (1996), Meese & Wallace (1991) and Pace (1993). Another approach is to use Bayesian restrictions on hedonic estimates, as outlined in Gilley & Pace (1995) and Knight *et al.* (1992). But perhaps one of the most exciting areas for extending hedonic models is making use of the spatial structure of the data, using the emerging technology of geographic information systems and spatial autocorrelation. Among other recent contributions in this area, see Can (1992), Dubin (1992), Pace & Gilley (1997), Basu & Thibodeau (1998), Gillen *et al.* (2001), and Thibodeau (2002). Thibodeau (2002), for example, finds a roughly 20% improvement in the fit of hedonic models using these techniques. Especially in applications regarding mass appraisal, these techniques are extremely promising.

However, there is also no end of applications that might not be thought of as cutting edge technically, that have not been done, but that are potentially terribly useful. Many of these are extensions of the studies listed in the previous section. Many housing programmes and policies have yet to be submitted to rigorous cost-benefit analysis. Improving systems of mass appraisal remains important; for example, Russia is embarking on the development of a valuation system for all property in the entire country.

While I have already cited individual hedonic studies from every continent, there is clearly scope for more and better international comparisons of housing prices. Recently there has been resurgence in cross-country comparisons, partly driven by the United Nations Centre for Human Settlements' Housing and Urban Development Indicators project.[15] Angel (2000) and Malpezzi & Mayo (1997) present data and comparisons, but these are generally based on simple median house prices from selected cities; more careful analysis, including estimating inter-country hedonic models, remains to be done.[16] An issue of fundamental importance to future hedonic work is the collection of more and better data for hedonic estimation (as well as other kinds of housing analyses). For example, good benchmark data in many countries are still needed. Guides to improved housing data collection include Malpezzi & Mayo (1994) and Malpezzi (2000).

Lastly, while housing is the bulk of every country's real estate, and in fact typically over half a country's tangible capital, hedonic models have rarely been applied to other forms of real estate. Hedonic applications to commercial real estate will be of interest for their own sake; and the functional interdependence of residential and non-residential real estate is often under-appreciated by those of us focused on housing.

Over the past three decades, hedonic estimation has clearly matured from a new technology to become the standard way economists deal with housing heterogeneity. Duncan Maclennan's own work in this area, and the work of his colleagues and students, has helped push out these frontiers. Building on this progress, many exciting applications and innovations in hedonic technique undoubtedly lie ahead.

I am grateful to the editors and to fellow contributors to this volume for constructive comments on a previous version. Opinions in this chapter are those of the author, and do not reflect the views of any other individual, or institution.

Notes

(1) In drafting this highly selective review, I have benefited from many previous studies, only some of which are listed below. Even the list of other surveys is incomplete. In my own early work, I greatly benefited from Ball's (1973) classic review of early literature. Among many recent reviews, see especially Follain & Jimenez (1985a) and Sheppard (1999).

(2) Some hedonic studies use aggregate data, e.g. average levels of variables over, say, census tracts; but these have gone out of favour, partly because of aggregation bias (as discussed in Ball 1973) and partly because household/property level data have become more readily available.

(3) The classic reference on repeat sales is Bailey *et al.* (1963); while there were early applications such as Nourse (1963), they were greatly popularised by several papers by Case & Shiller (e.g. 1987, 1989). Wang & Zorn (1997) provide a thorough review. There are also hybrid models that combine information from both hedonic and repeat sales estimates; see, for example, Case & Quigley (1991) and Quigley (1995). Green & Malpezzi (2001) presents further discussion of these as well as of simpler 'models' such as simple medians of transactions, and Laspeyres, Paasche and Divisia time series indices, and the very important user cost model of price determination.

(4) Actually, as we will see later in this section, with large samples regression techniques are used, but it amounts to the same thing.

(5)   For notational simplicity we suppress error terms. Careful consideration of house-specific errors and their 'drift' over time is a hallmark of Case & Shiller's (1987) treatment.

(6)   In addition to the references on repeat sales above, see Gatzlaff & Haurin (1997) and Gatzlaff, Green & Ling (1998). I also recommend the excellent review of repeat sales issues contained in Wang & Zorn (1997).

(7)   *Hybrid* indices combine elements of two or more methods into one index. Such methods seek to take advantage of the strengths while minimising the weakness of the constituent indices. These could be time series, cross-section, or both. I have already alluded to hybrid models that combine hedonic and repeat sales methods. The essence of most hybrid models is to 'stack' repeat sales and hedonic models, and then to estimate the two models imposing a constraint that estimated price changes over time are equal in both models. Such methods have the advantage of making use of all available information (see Case & Quigley 1991; Quigley 1995; or Hill *et al.* 1999, for good examples of hybrid indices). Knight *et al.* (1995) use seemingly unrelated regressions as a way to get more efficient coefficient estimates than the coefficient estimates obtained by OLS, but this procedure requires tedious matching of similar observations across years.

(8)   Interestingly, a casual perusal through stacks of papers suggests that UK scholars more often cite Lancaster as their fundamental reference, and US authors more readily cite Rosen. Of course, both papers are often cited by writers from any country. See also Lancaster's later elaboration of his ideas in Lancaster (1971).

(9)   My stepsons view the problem somewhat differently, of course; in their childhood they certainly saw their rooms as refuges from noisy parents.

(10)   Abraham and Hendershott and Follain use repeat sales indices, while Malpezzi combines hedonic and repeat sales indices. But whether hedonic or repeat sales indices are adopted, the general approach is the same.

(11)   Without loss of generality, we've written one of each, when there will usually be several; or if you like, consider each (S, N, L, and C) as a *vector*.

(12)   In fact, if housing units could, via some *Star Trek*-inspired machinery, be instantly and costlessly re-formed, then such costless repackaging would imply a linear structure of prices, where the dollar or pound price of each characteristic was simply added up, much as one would add different items in a shopping basket full of groceries at the checkout to obtain their final price (Fisher & Shell 1971; Triplett 1974). It is ultimately the cost of adjustment that gives rise to the nonlinearities that are observed empirically in housing prices.

(13)   As Halvorsen and Pollakowski point out, additional flexibility could be built in by allowing λ_m to vary with each independent variable; for computational convenience and degrees of freedom, all the hedonic applications Halvorsen and Pollakowski cite, and all those I am familiar with, constrain λ to be the same across all independent variables.

(14)   I have yet to find a hedonic study of Antarctica, but that's about the only region as yet unstudied.

(15)   Initially the indicators project was a joint World Bank–UNCHS research programme, but the World Bank has effectively ceased research in housing and urban development in recent years. See the symposium in *Netherlands Journal of Housing Research* (e.g. Angel, Mayo & Stephens 1993, Maclennan & Gibb, 1993, and Priemus 1992) for critical reviews of the project. See also Flood (1997).

(16)   General discussion of cross-country comparisons include Malpezzi (1990), Annez and Wheaton (1984), Malpezzi and Mayo (1987), Maclennan and Gibb (1993), Harsman and Quigley (1991), Strassman (1991), and Boelhouwer and van der Heijden (1993).

6

Housing, Random Walks, Complexity and the Macroeconomy

Geoffrey Meen

'The dominant theoretical framework for microeconomic analysis of housing markets is the standard, contemporary Walrasian synthesis of the neoclassical framework. In that synthesis the behaviour of consumers and producers, and the institutions of the market itself, are modelled in an extremely reductionist framework of assumptions. Consumers and producers are assumed to be fully informed and fully rational and the system is usually regarded as competitive. Goods are assumed to be relatively simple and, in the main, either transportable to the market or capable of full, believed descriptions within the marketplace. The market itself, in which fully informed trading takes place, is essentially a single point in space which adjusts or clears in the market trading period. These reductionist assumptions, which can be relaxed, are unsurprising because the essential purpose of the theory is to show how well-functioning markets clear and how such markets interact to generate a general competitive equilibrium in an economy.

'Although the insights of the standard neoclassical model are very important, it is clear that economic phenomena such as mis-information, commodity variety, space, time, and the nature of the market itself are all victims of the abstraction process.' (Maclennan & Tu 1996).

Introduction

The quotation above illustrates two of the concerns that run through Duncan Maclennan's writings: first, a dissatisfaction with conventional reductionist models that dominate mainstream housing micro and macroeconomic analysis, and second, a concern that housing markets are not aggregate, national entities, but consist of a series of interconnected local sub-markets, each of which may behave in a different way. Nevertheless, Maclennan's work recognises that housing markets have important macroeconomic consequences (see Maclennan *et al.* 1997, 1998b). It is the relationship between housing and the macroeconomy that is the subject of this chapter and the extent to which traditional forms of analysis have proved to be the most appropriate vehicle.

In the late eighties, when a boom in UK house prices coincided with a boom in the macroeconomy as a whole, the relationship between housing and the macroeconomy became an important research topic. However, although our understanding of the interactions has improved considerably since then, it is still arguable whether this knowledge has helped us in macro policy terms since house prices themselves are difficult to predict. Forecasting of house price movements, for example, has been just as poor as ever with a failure to capture important turning points, particularly during the nineties. Therefore, a major theme of this chapter is to assess where we stand at the moment and to indicate the limitations of housing research at the aggregate level.

Indeed, is accurate prediction ever possible from housing models? In line with the quotation, do we need to move on from reductionist models; do we need to recognise more fully the aggregation problems implicit in macro models if local markets are the more appropriate spatial scale of analysis; is prediction impossible because housing has increasingly become like any other financial asset, whose price follows a random walk? Do bubbles exist and imply that the coefficients of housing models are unstable? More speculatively, from a totally different perspective, do ideas from complexity analysis currently in vogue in economics imply that the future of housing markets is unpredictable? If so, then knowledge that housing affects the macroeconomy is of limited value to policy makers because they cannot forecast the state of the housing market at any stage over the cycle.

The chapter is divided into two substantive sections. The first reviews the state of play on the relationship between housing and the macroeconomy and identifies the key variables. Unsurprisingly, house prices play a central role, but other housing market variables such as construction have a smaller impact. The second section is devoted to what is now known about the determinants of housing markets at the macroeconomic level and, particularly, their predictability. The question of the adequacy of the standard neoclassical paradigm arises in this context and the need to take into account spatial structure. We suggest that standard, aggregate analysis, based on representative agent models, has to be treated with considerable caution in today's climate of increasing heterogeneity and, at the very least, macro analysis has to be supplemented with careful micro analysis.

The relationship between housing and the macroeconomy

The literature in recent years has identified a number of potential ways in which housing markets affect the macroeconomy. These affect both the demand and supply sides of the economy. Among the most important, which are discussed in turn, are:[1]

- the relationship between house prices and consumers' expenditure;

- the effect of housing on wages, migration, and labour markets in general. The transmission mechanisms operate in a number of ways, although house prices (both at national and regional levels) and the owner occupation rate have been suggested as particularly critical. Through labour markets, housing affects the regional dispersion of economic activity as well as the national aggregate;

- the influence of international differences in European housing markets on monetary union;

- the contribution of housing activity to economic cycles; and

- the links between housing and the spatial concentration of business start-ups.

Housing and consumers' expenditure

In the UK, interest in the relationship between housing and the macro-economy began in the second half of the eighties with the observation of a correlation between changes in house prices and a boom in consumers' expenditure. Between 1986 and 1988, consumption grew in excess of 5% in each year – well above the economy's productive capacity – whereas real house price growth averaged 13% per annum over the period. In policy terms, these movements are highly inflationary. However, although few researchers have doubted that a correlation exists between the two variables and the relationship appears to have continued through the nineties, considerable controversy still surrounds causality.

Muellbauer (1990) was the first to argue that a causal relationship exists between house price growth and excessive growth in consumers' expenditure in the liberalised mortgage market conditions of that time. Some other countries, notably Scandinavia and the Netherlands, appear to have found similar evidence, but there has always been a contradiction between macro-economic time-series evidence and microeconomic findings.

All forecasting institutions, including the Treasury, failed to predict the eighties consumption boom, leading to an over-relaxation of monetary policy at that time (see Meen 1996). House price booms had, of course, taken place before in the early and late seventies, but no corresponding boom had occurred in consumption. However, the difference between the periods was the liberalisation of mortgage markets in the early eighties. Under the rationed conditions of the seventies, an increase in house prices could not be translated into higher consumption through borrowing. But the removal of rationing enabled households to borrow against the accumulated equity in their houses to finance consumption. Furthermore, liberalisation of credit markets increases the sensitivity of housing markets and, indirectly, consumption to changes in interest rates. Equity withdrawal – the propensity to borrow on mortgage more than is required to finance the purchase of a home – rose dramatically in the late eighties, reaching almost 7% of household income in 1988. Similarly, Boelhouwer (2000) reports that, in the Netherlands, rapidly increasing house prices have been responsible for sharply increasing consumers' expenditure in 1999 through the same route of equity withdrawal.

But, although equity withdrawal began to re-emerge in the UK in the late nineties, the volume has not approached that in the late eighties. Furthermore, equity withdrawal disappeared altogether in the early nineties as house prices collapsed. Negative equity replaced equity withdrawal and Henley (1998) has argued, reasonably, that negative equity lowered labour mobility in the nineties.

However, the boom in consumption of the second half of the eighties has also been attributed to other causes. King (1990) argues that, instead, the boom represented a re-assessment of permanent income. Since the demand for housing, and hence house prices, would also be affected by the revision to expectations, the correlation between consumption and house prices may represent a proxy effect. In terms of policy, which explanation (if either) is true is important. The explanation in terms of a wealth effect might suggest tax measures explicitly targeted at the housing market to prevent price booms – a measure that would be irrelevant if expectations were the true causal mechanism.

As Hort (1997) points out, macroeconomic and microeconomic data yield conflicting evidence. On microeconomic data, both Attanasio & Weber (1994) and Miles (1997) do not support explanations of the consumption boom in terms of house price changes. But on macroeconomic data, Muell-bauer & Murphy (1990) find significant effects in the UK. Berg (1994), Berg & Bergstrom (1995) and Koskela & Viren (1992) find that in the Scandinavian countries, which have experienced house price movements similar to the UK, there are significant effects. In the USA, Case *et al.* (2001) have found significant housing wealth effects in a panel study across the US states and over fourteen countries. Overall, however, the inconsistency between micro and macro results remains a puzzle.

Housing and labour markets

In principle, the effects of housing on labour markets are straightforward. However, compared with the last sub-section, which was concerned with aggregate *demand*, any effects on the labour market affect primarily aggregate *supply*. Therefore the influences on the economy are more likely to be permanent than transitory.

First, since housing costs are a component of consumer prices, a direct effect on wage pressures is likely and is relatively uncontroversial. Bover *et al.* (1989), Blackaby & Manning (1992), and more recently Cameron & Muellbauer (2000) all find house prices to be important in determining wage claims. Furthermore, the last of these studies shows that prices have a permanent effect on the level of unemployment. At a more local level, housing constraints and high housing costs are the central element of the key worker shortages facing South East England (see Monk 2000a).

Second, regional variations in house prices may have an impact on migration patterns, and thus on regional unemployment rates. As such they contribute to the North/South divide. It has been argued that high house prices in southern England act as a barrier to mobility as workers seek to move from high unemployment northern areas to low unemployment southern regions. This effect is likely to have been particularly important in the late eighties when the ratio of house prices in the South East relative to the North reached record levels (see Meen 2001, chapter 2). At the time of writing, recent increases in house prices, concentrated in the South, have again exacerbated the divide.

There is, however, some doubt as to the quantitative impact of relative house prices on migration patterns. The earliest work on migration in the UK (a series of papers by Hughes & McCormick 1981, 1985, 1987, 1990, 2000) was concerned primarily with the effect of *tenure* on migration rather than house prices. But in terms of house prices, Hughes & McCormick indicate that the effect of relative house prices on out-migration rates is negligible and the influence on destination choice is only small (Hughes & McCormick 1990, p. 103), although they note that the estimates are obtained for members of the labour force and the retired may have a higher propensity to migrate from the South East to take advantage of accrued capital gains.

But Hughes & McCormick's findings are by no means universally accepted and Thomas (1993), for example, suggests that, after standardisation for the moving motivation is made, relative house prices have a strong effect on destination choice. On balance, however, as Gordon (1990) argues, it is unlikely that housing price variables alone can account for low rates of migration in the UK, particularly among manual workers (who have lower rates of owner occupation). Cameron & Muellbauer (2000) also find that relative house prices primarily affect the wages of non-manual workers.

Housing and monetary union

Maclennan has been among those who have argued strongly that differences in housing conditions and institutions across Europe raise problems for monetary union (see Maclennan *et al.* 1998b).

Considerable differences in housing volatility still exist across Europe, both in terms of house prices and construction activity (see Stephens 2000 and Ball & Wood 1999), despite the presence of a common monetary policy since the beginning of 1999 for most European Union members. At the time of writing, only the UK, Sweden and Denmark have opted out. The most important differences in housing structures across Europe concern:

- variations in owner occupation rates;

- differences in mortgage debt as a percentage of GDP; and

- the fact that in some countries mortgage debt is primarily at fixed rates but in others debt is mainly variable rate.[2]

In the UK it is sometimes argued that owner-occupier rates are high and this is certainly the case compared with Germany and France. The owner occupancy rate in Britain stands at 69%, but only approximately 40% and 55% in Germany and France respectively. But this is relatively modest compared with Ireland and Spain at around 80% and Greece and Italy at approximately 75%. However, high owner occupancy rates are not necessarily correlated with high levels of outstanding debt. The ratio of outstanding mortgage loans to GDP stood at 57% in 1995 in the UK, only exceeded in Europe by the Netherlands at 60% and Denmark at 65%. But of the high owner occupancy countries, the debt ratio was only 27% in Ireland, 22% in Spain, and 6% in Greece and in Italy (Stephens 2000). Clearly a high degree of development in financial markets is not a necessary condition for high levels of owner occupation. Therefore, in low debt countries, variations in interest rates are not critical despite high owner occupancy rates.

But, even at high debt ratios, variations in market interest rates would not be significant for the macroeconomy if the majority of mortgage debt were at fixed rates. Around 70% of mortgage debt is variable rate in the UK, but only 10% in the Netherlands, 20% in France and 40% in Germany. Although it is certainly not the case that housing conditions are uniform across the rest of Europe, the United Kingdom has experienced a special combination of circumstances – high owner occupation rates, high debt levels and high proportions of variable rate debt. In these circumstances, it would be unsurprising to find that (i) activity in mainland Europe is less elastic in response to changes in interest rates[3] and (ii) the same level of interest rates may not be suitable to all European countries.

Housing construction, growth and economic cycles

The previous sections emphasised the interactions between house prices and the macroeconomy. Far less research has been conducted on the effects of new housing construction, although housing pressure groups have long argued that one of the reasons for increasing housing investment is the positive benefits to GDP and employment (see, for example, Clapham 1996). But housing construction, potentially, plays a number of roles in the national economy. In addition to adding to aggregate demand, perhaps, the two key contributions are:

- as a factor of production; and

- as a contributor to cycles in the economy.

As a factor of production, in principle, housing has three effects:

(1)   directly by increasing the capital stock;

(2)   by affecting the rate of technical progress: for example, well-housed workers and children are more productive and educational standards rise; and

(3) by either crowding-in or crowding-out other parts of the capital stock, i.e. extra housing may reduce business investment and, therefore, output growth in the economy.

Nearly all empirical work has concerned the effects on demand and crowding-out. But since new housing construction is only a small part of the economy, its direct impact is limited. New construction annually comprises only approximately 1% of the housing stock and private and public housing investment totalled only 2% of Total Final Expenditure in 1999. As an example, Meen *et al.* (2001) use an econometric model to simulate the economic effects of reducing new housing construction by 25% per annum over a 10-year period. Although precise numbers from econometric models are always subject to margins of error, certain points stood out.

- Though cutting housing production would reduce demand and GDP in the first few years, through standard multiplier effects, even the initial effects are modest.

- Crowding-out causes any effects to die away over time. Although employment in the construction industry falls substantially, in the long run, there is little effect on unemployment in the economy as a whole. Employment in other industries expands.

But these conclusions may be misleading because they treat housing in the same manner as any other consumption good, ignoring the importance of housing as a capital good. In other words, they omit points (1) and (2) above. In general, standard analysis of housing and the macroeconomy ignores any induced enhancements to productivity or technical progress. In the current stage of knowledge, we simply do not know whether they are significant or not.

Even if additional housing construction has limited long-run effects on the national economy, housing is one of the most volatile sectors of the economy and, clearly, volatility causes problems for the design of macroeconomic policy. Neither is the volatility of new housing confined to the UK. Ball & Wood (1999), for example, discuss both long-run trends and volatility over a wide range of countries, covering data from the nineteenth century onwards. They suggest that, since the 1970s, fluctuations in housing investment have added to instability in the world economy.

Meen (2000) explores the reasons for this volatility in UK housing markets and suggests that monetary policy, designed with general inflation targets in mind, in some circumstances is inconsistent with stability in housing, if housing is inelastic in supply. Policy exacerbates fluctuations in housing.

Housing and business start-ups

Although the previous sub-section has suggested that housing may crowd out business investment, an alternative line of thought has suggested that, in fact, the two are positively related. First, Black *et al.* (1996) suggest that house values are important in providing collateral for the start-up of new businesses, although the view is challenged by Cressy (1996).

Second, although the determinants of industrial location are multi-faceted, surveys suggest that the availability of skilled labour is one of the more important factors determining industrial firm location. But skilled labour is attracted to areas of better housing. Therefore, both firms and the skilled workforce tend to be co-located. It appears that innovating industry is attracted to highly qualified labour, which, in turn, is attracted by high-quality living conditions, typically in the home counties of South East England. Furthermore, Keeble & Walker (1994) show that the key variable determining new firm formation is the rate of population growth. They argue that population growth incorporates both demand influences (through the provision of local markets) and supply effects. Increases in population raise the pool of potential entrepreneurs, which, they argue, is stimulated by residential preferences.

Furthermore, South East England has a high rate of new firm formation compared with other regions, particularly in the innovative, high growth industries. This performance appears to be related to the disproportionate presence of highly skilled technical, managerial and professional groups in the South East from whom potential entrepreneurs principally emerge. Since these entrepreneurs start new firms close to where they live, areas of strong economic growth, high-quality environments and amenities tend to be self-reinforcing (see Barkham 1992).

Are house prices predictable?

The previous section illustrates that, in terms of the relationship between housing and the macroeconomy, prices are the most important influence. New construction has a more limited (although possibly understated) effect. Although other aggregate housing indicators are regularly reported – notably housing transactions, arrears and possessions – their influence on the macroeconomy is rarely discussed. A possible exception is mortgage advances, but again the main effect is generally taken to be through house prices.

It is, however, worth noting that models of house prices have had a chequered career in the UK in terms of prediction. The key issue in this section is to examine whether standard models based on the neoclassical paradigm have proved adequate or whether we have to go down other routes as might be suggested by the opening quotation. In order to understand the problems, we need to examine both the methods that are currently typically used and to ask whether house prices are intrinsically unpredictable. Clearly, if house prices are unpredictable, then knowledge of the relationship between prices and the macroeconomy is of limited value to policy.

House price to income ratios

By far the most common method of analysis used in the UK to predict future house price movements is a simple rule-of-thumb related to the ratio of house prices to household income. The rule-of-thumb states that if the current ratio is above the long-run average (usually assumed to be constant), future prices will fall and *vice versa*. No theory lies behind the 'analysis', which can be highly misleading. Figure 6.1, at first sight, seems to suggest that a constant ratio has existed since the early seventies. The ratio rises in boom periods and falls in the slumps. Two recent events, however, illustrate the difficulties. First, the UK economy began to recover from a slump, with GDP increasing from 1993; based on the ratio, commentators predicted that house prices would also begin to recover. In fact, the ratio fell further with prices not rising until the end of 1996. The fall in the ratio over this period can be seen in Fig. 6.1. Second, although the period 1998–2000 has been considered a boom period in terms of house prices, the ratio of prices to incomes has risen modestly compared with some previous booms. The question is why prices are not even higher than we currently observe, particularly given the very low levels of mortgage interest rates.

Therefore, although there may appear to be some simple long-run ratio, if we look in more detail, the ratio has been far from constant in the long run. Those who made predictions on the basis of this ratio have made serious errors, particularly since 1990.

A number of issues that arise in house price modelling and prediction undermine simple house price to income ratio analysis. Although such ratios have the advantage of simplicity and are readily explainable to a wider audience,[4] they are seriously misleading.

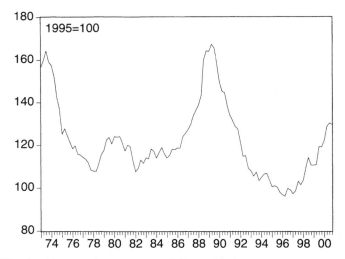

Fig. 6.1   UK ratio of house prices to personal disposable income.

A theoretical framework

Although all theoretical and empirical research on housing demand and house prices stresses the importance of income, few studies imply that income is the *sole* determinant. However, there is an increasing consensus as to the most appropriate modelling approach to house prices. In line with the opening quotation, the consensus is almost entirely neoclassical. Although there have certainly been cries that this is an inappropriate framework, in practice it is dominant.

Empirical models of house prices are generally derived as representative agent models, where households maximise utility subject to a lifetime budget constraint. From this approach, equation (6.1) can be derived as the basic house price relationship underlying most modern work.

$$g(t) = R(t)/[(1-\theta)i(t) - \pi + \delta - \dot{g}^e/g(t)] \qquad (6.1)$$

where:

$g(t)$ = real purchase price of dwellings

$R(t)$ = real imputed rental

θ = household marginal tax rate

$i(t)$ = market interest rate

δ   = depreciation rate on housing

π   = general inflation rate

(.)   = time derivative

$\dot{g}^e/g(t)$ = expected real capital gain.

Equation (6.1) implies that the return on housing, represented by the imputed rental plus any capital gain on housing net of depreciation, equals the post-tax return on alternative assets. In principle, data permitting, we could simply use equation (6.1) as our predictor of house price movements. But note:

(1) income has no role in this specification;

(2) it treats housing in exactly the same way as any financial asset;

(3) there are no lags in the specification; the market is fully efficient and prices react immediately to, say, changes in interest rates; and

(4) in practice, with the exception of Meese & Wallace (1994), no empirical model estimates equation (6.1) directly.

Equation (6.1) could be seen as the most extreme version of the neoclassical model. In practice, empirical models in the UK (and in the US) pay only lip-service to equation (6.1). This is partly due to data deficiencies – we cannot measure $R(t)$ directly – and partly due to rather sloppy analysis. In the UK, a more typical example looks like equation (6.2), into which the expected determinants of $R(t)$ are substituted. Notice that income now reappears in the specification, but (6.2) only bears a loose relationship to the underlying theory. Almost all empirical specifications can be justified by the inclusion of different variables in (6.3).[5]

$$\ln(g) = f(\ln(RY), \ln(W), \ln(HH), \ln(H), \ln[(1-\theta)i + \delta - \pi - \dot{g}^e/g]) \tag{6.2}$$

$$R(t) = h(RY(t), W(t), HH(t), H(t)) \tag{6.3}$$

where:

RY   = real personal disposable income

W   = real wealth

HH   = number of households

H   = housing stock

In (6.2) a number of factors, in addition to income, affect prices – real interest rates, taxation, demographics, the supply of housing, wealth and expectations. If any of these variables change, house price to income ratios will be inadequate as a predictor.

Efficiency and random walks in housing

Life-cycle models under rational expectations imply that house prices follow a random walk. In this framework, housing behaves in the same way as a financial asset that denies many of the distinguishing characteristics of housing. As such, prices are efficient and unpredictable, because lagged values of no variable have an influence on current house price movements. Clearly, if this is a true representation of price movements, this causes considerable problems for macroeconomic policy.

However almost all evidence suggests that housing markets are neither efficient nor can be adequately characterised as a random walk (see, for example, the surveys of US evidence by Gatzlaff & Tirtiroglu 1995 and Cho 1996). Internationally, the most comprehensive set of efficiency tests have been conducted by Englund and Ioannides (1997). Following the approach for the USA of Case & Shiller (1989, 1990), the basic equation is given by (6.4):

$$\Delta \ln(g_t) = \alpha + \sum_{j=1}^{n} \beta_j \Delta \ln(g_{t-j}) + \varepsilon_t \tag{6.4}$$

where:

g_t = real house prices at time (t)

ε_t = error term

Δ = first difference operator

$\ln$ = natural logarithm of the variable

If housing markets are fully efficient, then no autocorrelation in price inflation is expected, $(\beta_j) = 0$, for all (j) so that house prices follow a random walk. Englund and Ioannides, estimating a panel model across 15 countries, find that real house price inflation exhibits short-run positive autocorrelation and longer-term mean reversion. Furthermore house prices are predictable by lagged income growth and real interest rates.

An alternative approach is to test for the presence of significant lagged variables in equations such as (6.2). In an efficient market, prices should respond immediately to changes in the determinants so that lags should have no effect. In European studies, tests have generally been conducted in the context of error correction models. Without exception, lags are found to be important and, indeed, prices appear to adjust fairly slowly to equilibrium following any shock. Using rather different methods, similar results are found for the USA. DiPasquale & Wheaton (1994) and Mankiw & Weil (1989) find support for the view that housing markets are not fully efficient.

If housing markets are not efficient, then what are the key differences from financial markets that can account for the presence of lagged adjustment? There appear to be two main factors: first, the presence of transactions costs which are much larger than, say, for shares (see the chapter in this volume by Quigley) and, second, the presence of credit market constraints. Whereas it may be reasonable to assume that large institutions operating in financial markets face perfect credit markets, young first-time buyers entering the owner-occupier market do not. Because of adverse selection, for example, they face downpayment constraints (see Haurin *et al.* 1997). This has two implications. First, prices become more volatile and regional diversity becomes more pronounced. Second, the presence of 'hurdles' means that households remain for long periods of time 'off their demand curves'. When the hurdles are overcome, housing adjustment is more lumpy than in the presence of perfect capital markets. Again this adds to volatility in the housing market.

In summary, there are good reasons why simply applying the standard neoclassical life-cycle model to housing is inadequate. At the very least, transactions costs and credit markets have to become a fundamental part of the analysis. Lagged adjustment is to be expected in an extended framework implying that, in principle, house price movements should be partly predictable. We cannot appeal to random walks as an explanation of our failure to predict adequately future house price movements.

However, there are a number of other reasons that impinge upon our ability to predict price changes. One of the most important is the fact that the neoclassical model is based on a single representative agent. No consideration is given to the aggregation conditions involved in moving to the macro level. As I show in the next section, this issue has become very important in recent years, where agents have become increasingly heterogeneous.

Aggregation and structural change in the housing market

Models based on equation (6.2), incorporating lags, have performed poorly during the nineties. As an example, Fig. 6.2 shows the post-sample errors of the house price equation estimated in Meen (1990). The record is hardly distinguished with consistent over-prediction of the outcome for price changes after 1990.

It has been suggested that housing markets are so volatile and difficult to predict that variable parameter methods are necessary to model house prices. Methods of estimation have been imported from the financial econometrics literature. But volatility in itself does not necessarily imply non-constant parameters. Volatility may simply arise from high elasticities with constant parameters. In fact, the empirical evidence (Meen 2001 Chapter 6) suggests that house prices are particularly sensitive to changes in interest rates and incomes.[6] But variable parameter methods *may* be necessary if the coefficients are not constant over time (see Hall *et al.* 1997; Brown *et al.* 1997). This might be the case if bubbles occur regularly.[7] In fact, I would argue that the parameters of house price equations are no more unstable than many macroeconomic time-series; supposed instability is sometimes used as an excuse for inadequate theoretical specification and detailed analysis of the micro structure of markets.

In the UK there appear to have been only two major structural changes corresponding to explicit policy initiatives. The first took place in the mid-eighties in response to financial deregulation. For *aggregate* housing market

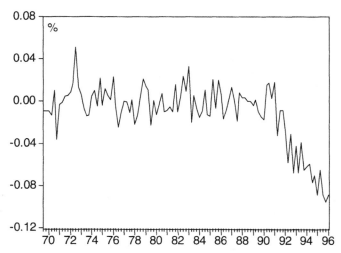

Fig. 6.2 House price prediction errors. Source: Meen and Andrew (1998).

analysis, its main impact was that house prices became more sensitive to changes in interest rates (see Meen 1996). However, if allowance is made for this change, there is little evidence that the remaining coefficients of house price equations altered significantly. The second, in the early nineties, has proved more difficult to model. The extent of the problem was shown by the errors in Fig. 6.2.

The two most likely explanations of the breakdown in the relationship concern (i) changes to housing market risk in a new low inflation environment and (ii) the effect of structural labour market changes. Meen & Andrew (1998) argue that the latter was probably the more important, leading to a form of aggregation bias discussed in more detail below. It highlights the need to supplement macroeconomic analysis with detailed analysis of underlying microeconomic movements. However, it also suggests that variable parameter modelling is a rather poor substitute for looking at the fundamental causes of change, particularly if the interest is in policy implications.

Neoclassical models are based on the analysis of representative agents. Aggregate models are then constructed by simply summing individual functions. But the conditions under which this is a valid procedure are strict; *either* all agents must be identical in their behaviour (homogeneous) – characterised by all the coefficients of the individual agent functions being identical[8] – *or* movements in the regressors in the functions must be the same over time. For example, everyone's income must grow at the same rate over time. More recent research by Hall *et al.* (1999) modifies the condition to one in which the regressors follow common stochastic trends.

Similar conditions exist in terms of spatial aggregation and reflect Maclennan's concern with the importance of local housing markets. For modelling at the national level to be valid, all sub-national markets must behave in the same way or economic conditions within those spatial markets must be identical. Clearly these conditions are rarely likely to hold. It is easy to think of cases in which the individual agent aggregation conditions will not hold.

First, the parameters of housing demand functions (and hence price equations) are likely to vary by demographic group. For example, the income and price elasticities of housing demand by young, first-time buyers are unlikely to be identical to those who are retired. Second, Holmans (1996) shows that, during the nineties, there was a strong shift in demand by the 20–25 age group away from owner occupation towards the private rented sector. Meen (2001) suggests that this was associated with a fall in relative real income growth by young households compared with older age groups, i.e. a violation of the second aggregation condition through a change in the income distribution.

A priori we might expect that these changes would lead to an over-prediction of house price growth in the nineties by 'traditional' models, consistent with Fig. 6.2.

Similarly, the failure of national models in the nineties reflects differences in behaviour at the regional level. Meen (1999b) shows that there are non-random differences in the coefficients of regional house price equations; typically the south of the country is more sensitive to national economic stimuli (particularly interest rate changes) than the north of the country. I speculate in that paper that these differences reflect variations in debt gearing around the country.[9] The recent continuing low levels of interest rates, therefore, confer particular benefits to the South, contributing to the increasing regional dispersion in house prices. Furthermore economic growth has varied considerably across the regions in the nineties; although the slump hit the South hard compared with earlier recessions, growth since the mid-nineties has also been concentrated on the South.

In conclusion, in the modern environment, characterised by increasing dispersion, prediction and policy analysis at the macro level have to be backed up with careful microanalysis. Heterogeneity matters and is, typically, not adequately captured in simple representative agent models.

Complexity and housing markets

Ideas developed from complexity are becoming increasingly important in economics but, although regional scientists have incorporated the techniques into their models of city structures, the impact of complexity on empirical housing models has, so far, been small. However, one of the implications of complex systems is that events are typically unpredictable, although for very different reasons from those employed in random walk models.

Complex systems are those with a very large number of interacting parts where the interactions are non-linear and the behaviour of the system as a whole cannot be understood simply from a consideration of the constituent elements. A central feature of complexity is self-organisation. Seemingly individual action generates beautiful, complex and ordered patterns of behaviour at an aggregate level.

However, modelling housing behaviour using complexity is fundamentally different from traditional neoclassical econometric models; in conventional models, all agents are homogeneous and random errors are considered a nuisance. By contrast, the properties of modern agent-based computation models, often used to apply economic principles to complexity, are dependent on stochastic distributions, stressing the heterogeneity between agents. The driving forces and structures, therefore, are very different from the neoclassical paradigm. Multiple equilibria are the norm; furthermore, although equilibria may exist, they may not be achievable or may be unstable. Lastly, although equilibria may be obtainable asymptotically, the system may remain out of equilibrium for very long periods of time. The dynamics are typically more interesting than any long-run equilibrium.

This is a highly attractive approach, particularly for modelling local housing markets where interactions between agents are strong, but such models have important aggregate properties. From our point of view, a key feature of these models is that they exhibit 'tipping' or thresholds that makes prediction in these markets extremely difficult. Complexity suggests that housing markets may organise themselves into a state 'on the edge of chaos'. In this case small random shocks to individual agents may generate completely different patterns of spatial (and aggregate) housing demand. The system may *appear* to be in equilibrium for many years (and over this range is predictable), but what we are, in fact, observing is a drawn-out disequilibrium state, which suddenly tips very quickly to a new state through a series of random events that are unpredictable. Using a totally different framework from the random walk model, which assumes complete rationality and individual homogeneity, prices become unpredictable in a world of bounded rationality and heterogeneous agents. Models of this form are not just an intellectual curiosity; work by Galster *et al.* (2000) suggests that thresholds are an important feature of local housing markets and might be used to explain why, for example, local hot-spots emerge, which can co-exist with poorer areas (see also the chapter by Galster in this volume).

Forecasts for local housing markets are becoming increasingly common in this country, but complexity suggests that the foundations on which they are based can be insecure. However the implications for *aggregate* housing market forecasts are not yet entirely clear. Disequilibrium states can persist for long periods and, given path dependency and lock-in, there is some basis for prediction. However, we should not be surprised when highly non-linear behaviour occurs and traditional aggregate, neoclassical-based relationships break down.

Conclusions

Analysis of the interactions between housing and the macroeconomy has come a long way over the last 15 years. Theoretical and empirical evidence has been provided for both the demand and supply sides of the economy; the former has concentrated primarily on consumers' expenditure, whereas the latter has centred on wage formation, migration and unemployment. Work has been conducted at both the national and regional levels.

In this work, house prices play the central role, although the impact of new construction in the economy is a neglected field. Therefore, in macroeconomic policy terms, an understanding of the determinants of price movements is central. In this chapter, I have suggested that house price analysis is currently conducted in two frameworks. First by using rules-of-thumb based on simple house price to income ratios; such analysis is highly misleading and should be treated with a great deal of caution. Second, most modern academic work is based on neoclassical models set in a life-cycle framework. Although I have been critical of some aspects of this paradigm, one should not lose sight of the valuable insights into the working of the housing market that the approach has generated. It is likely to remain the dominant paradigm.

However, it is right to be concerned with the *uncritical* use of the neoclassical model. In particular, I have highlighted two issues that are important in the current environment: (i) the use of representative agent models in a world of increasing dispersion both over household types and space; this leads to problems of aggregation; and (ii) the fact that there are alternative approaches, which yield insights that the neoclassical model cannot; models of complex systems lead to highly non-linear behaviour, multiple equilibria and outcomes that are typified by long-lasting disequilibria. Although, in the current state of knowledge, one cannot conclude that complexity approaches are always more appropriate than neoclassical analysis, there are instances when they are more likely to be appropriate.

Finally, the warnings of Maclennan and Tu in the opening quotation are valid. It is clear that the reductionist approach of the standard neoclassical model is not always the most appropriate to housing analysis, although in many cases it will be. But we need to be aware of the very different implications that arise at both micro and macro levels from adopting a different approach. A slavish following of one approach is rarely likely to be optimal.

Notes

(1) Planning also has a key influence on both national and regional economies, but planning is discussed elsewhere in this volume (in the chapter by Bramley).
(2) Planning systems also vary across Europe but these are not discussed.

(3) Note, however, that even this is controversial. Britton & Whitley (1997) estimate simple IS/LM models for different European economies and find no evidence that the IS curve is more elastic with respect to interest rates in the UK.

(4) House price trends attract a huge amount of media attention. The virtues of price to income ratios are clearly important in this context.

(5) A high degree of variation in the regressors also appears in the quantitative US literature; see, for example, DiPasquale and Wheaton (1994), Abraham and Hendershott (1996), Malpezzi (1999).

(6) Note that this is one of the reasons that forecasting is so difficult. Small errors in income or interest rate forecasts generate large errors in house price forecasts.

(7) There are dangers in assuming that because bubbles exist in financial markets they automatically occur in housing markets. The parallels are not exact; for example, housing bubbles may be ameliorated by credit market constraints. Bubbles may, and at times probably do, exist but there are alternative explanations for price movements that look like bubbles. Although not discussed in detail here, credit multipliers generate similar behaviour. Furthermore, under complexity, increasing returns and 'herd' behaviour can generate outcomes that mimic bubbles. One needs to be wary of assuming that strong volatility in prices necessarily signals the presence of bubbles. Forming appropriate tests is far from straightforward. Tests for the existence of time-varying parameters in conventional house price equations are far from adequate.

(8) Pesaran and Smith (1995) show that the parameters of aggregate functions are inconsistent except under coefficient homogeneity.

(9) Note that debt gearing also affects the volatility of house prices and credit multiplier models can be used to explain the strong cycles in house prices (see Meen 2001).

7

Taxation, Subsidies and Housing Markets

Gavin A. Wood

Introduction

One of the most important influences on my academic work in housing economics has been the idea that various frictions such as space, information asymmetries, regulation and fiscal measures can impede the operation of efficient housing market processes. Segmentation of housing markets can be a by-product of these frictions. That this idea has been so influential is in large part due to collaboration with Duncan Maclennan over a period that is approaching 25 years. In this chapter I investigate the role of taxation as a fiscal intervention that impacts on housing market processes. The literature on the distributional and allocative impacts of taxation is reviewed. The role taxation plays as one possible cause of housing market segmentation is a particular focus of the chapter (see also the chapter by Yong Tu in this volume). My own recently completed empirical work on this subject is summarised, and used to highlight the possible role of clientele effects as a source of segmentation in private rental markets.[1]

An interesting aspect of taxation measures and housing is that such measures are rarely viewed as an explicit component of housing programmes designed to further housing policy goals[2] (Rosen 1985; Bourassa & Grigsby 2000). Typically the direct and indirect tax base and schedule of tax rates are framed with broader fiscal policy goals in mind. Their impacts on the price of housing in different tenures, or the price paid by households with different incomes, is a relatively less important influence in this regard. Yet the budgetary impacts of 'official' housing policy can be overwhelmed by taxation measures (Yates & Flood 1987). Their significance in housing policy debates is in large part due to the widely held view that the taxation of housing is the source of distortions and inequity. As a result of tax measures:

- the price that must be paid in the owner-occupied housing market for a given bundle of housing services will vary inversely with the income of the purchaser;

- the price paid by homeowners will typically fall as they age; and

- the cost of supplying rental housing is inversely related to the income of the landlord.

In the next section I explore the distributional issues that arise as a result of these distortions. Evidence from micro data is presented to show that low-income home purchasers with a correspondingly low net worth are particularly disadvantaged. A more novel finding is that taxation of landlords can result in the concentration of marginal (high cost) investors in low-income rental housing. Thus the low-income tenants of affordable rental housing end up paying rents that are high relative to the capital values of the property they occupy.

I then analyse the impacts of tax measures on tenure choice using tax arbitrage models. It is shown that when agency costs (the costs of managing landlord–tenant relationships) are taken into account, home ownership has a relative after-tax cost advantage over renting for most housing consumers. Renting is only financially advantageous to low-income individuals, but this is typically restricted to high value segments of the market that are not affordable; because marginal landlords are concentrated in low-income rental housing, such higher value housing is financially unattractive to low-income households unless targeted subsidies overcome homeownership's relative cost advantage in this segment of the housing stock.

The next section turns to questions of efficiency. The early literature concentrated on how homeowners benefit from tax subsidies that are the source of static deadweight welfare losses. Since Laidler's (1969) seminal contribution there have been numerous attempts to measure such losses. However, there is a parallel literature that recognises that the housing sector as a whole is tax advantaged (Vandell 2000). Thus over-investment in housing is encouraged, and economy-wide productivity losses can ensue unless offset by positive externalities.[3] I review this literature and discuss other potential sources of inefficiency, such as tax clientele effects and lock-in effects, which are less well known but can be important sources of housing market segmentation. A concluding section offers some comments on policy implications.

Distributional issues

Vertical and horizontal equity in owner-occupied housing markets

OECD countries have a long tradition of extending tax preferences to owner-occupied housing (Wood 1988b). Among the English-speaking OECD countries there is an increasingly uniform tax treatment. Australia, Canada, New Zealand and the United Kingdom exempt imputed rental income and capital gains from taxable income, but do not permit deduction of mortgage interest and real estate taxes from taxable income (Bourassa & Grigsby 2000). The USA grants very favourable tax treatment because it not only exempts imputed rental income, it also permits deduction of mortgage interest and real estate taxes.[4]

Why do these tax arrangements raise equity concerns? The main reasons are that they generate a non-neutral intra-tenure and inter-tenure tax treatment of households, with the consequence that the price paid for a given bundle of housing services is a function of the occupants' incomes, and the tenure in which the housing services are consumed.[5] I focus in this section on distributional concerns that arise because of variation in the price paid for owner-occupied housing.

To assist analysis I begin by describing an intra-tenure neutral tax treatment of owner-occupied housing. It would treat income from imputed rents and capital gains in a symmetric fashion; it would permit the deduction of all operating expenses, including interest and real estate taxes, from imputed rents; and it would permit the deduction of capital improvement and transaction costs from taxable capital gains. To demonstrate formally the tax neutral properties of these provisions, consider an owner-occupier who has acquired housing capital (q).[6] It is assumed that the owner-occupier's holding period (T) is exogenous; house prices and rents appreciate at the constant uniform rate π_h;[7] the constant rate of general inflation (π) may differ. The present value of the stream of after-tax returns (V) is given by:

$$V = (m - p(0)q) + (p(T)q - m)e^{-kT} + \int_0^T \tau \pi_h p(0) q e^{\delta t} +$$

$$\int_0^T (1-\tau)[r(t)q - \upsilon p(t)q - im] \times e^{-kt} dt \tag{7.1}$$

where p(0) is the asset price of housing in year zero, m is mortgage debt that is not amortised, τ is the marginal income tax rate, r(t)q is gross imputed rent, υ is operating cost (including real estate taxes) as a fraction of asset price and i is the market rate of interest at which investors can borrow or lend. The parameter k is the owner-occupier's discount rate, and $\delta = \pi_h - k$.[8]

In competitive markets the present value function can be set equal to zero. Evaluating the integrals, and factoring q and m we obtain two sufficient conditions:

$$1 - \frac{(1-\tau)i}{k} = 0 \qquad (7.2)$$

$$\frac{(1-\tau)[r(0)-\upsilon p(0)] - \tau\pi_h p(0)}{\delta} + p(0) = 0 \qquad (7.3)$$

Combining equations (7.2) and (7.3) we find that

$$R = \frac{r(0)}{p(0)} = i + \upsilon - \pi_h \qquad (7.4)$$

The right-hand side of equation (7.4) represents the after-tax annual costs of the homeowner, or his/her user cost of housing capital. It is a measure of the effective price that is paid by a homeowner, including the after-tax cost of equity capital.[9] The neutrality of this simple expression is evident. The price paid by the homeowner is independent of its marginal income tax rate and the chosen loan-value ratio.

Consider now the typical tax treatment of owner-occupied housing in English-speaking OECD countries.[10] The present value function can now be defined as:

$$V = (m - p(0)q) + (p(T)q - m)e^{-kT} + \int_0^T [r(t)q - \upsilon p(t)q - im] \times e^{-kt}dt \qquad (7.5)$$

Repeating the steps described in equations (7.2) and (7.3) we obtain:

$$R = (1-\tau)i + \tau i\alpha + \upsilon - \frac{\tau\pi_h\alpha}{1-\tau} - \pi_h \qquad (7.6)$$

where α is the loan-value ratio. The first term on the right-hand side user cost expression is the homeowner's financing costs if 100% equity financed, and given the tax exempt status of imputed rents. The second term is the tax penalty for a homeowner using debt finance for the fraction α of acquisition costs. Mortgage interest is not deductible under the typical tax arrangements, hence the tax penalty. However, there is an offsetting component (the third term) due to the erosion of the real value of outstanding mortgage debt, which represents an untaxed addition to the household's resources.[11]

It is evident from equation (7.6) that user costs are reduced by the typical tax treatment of homeowners. If we subtract equation (7.6) from equation (7.4) and express as a proportion of the neutral tax user cost measure, we obtain the effective rate of subsidy (S), which is given by:

$$S = \frac{\tau i (1-\alpha) + \dfrac{\tau \pi_h \alpha}{1-\tau}}{i+\upsilon - \pi_h} \tag{7.7}$$

The non-neutral tax treatment lowers the effective price of owner-occupied housing by an amount that is directly related to the owner's marginal income tax rate. Table 7.1 computes S for alternative values of homeowners' marginal income tax rates and loan to value ratios. At each of the chosen loan to value ratios, S declines at the lower marginal income tax rates to the extent that it is less than one half its value at the highest marginal income tax rate. At low marginal tax rates S declines marginally as the loan to value ratio increases, but this pattern is reversed at the highest marginal income tax rate.[12]

Concrete evidence of the distortionary effects of taxation arrangements is presented in Table 7.2, which lists estimates of the user costs of 9908 Australian homeowner households using the 1990 Australian Bureau of Statistics Income and Housing Cost Survey. The households have been ordered into deciles according to household income, and their marginal tax rates have been estimated following the method advocated by Hendershott & Slemrod (1983).[13] We find that mean user cost in the lowest income decile is 1.8 times that typical among households in the highest income decile, a multiple which is generated by a 3.21 percentage point difference in user cost. If the typical household in the lowest income decile were to benefit from a

Table 7.1   The effective rate of subsidy (%) by typical loan to value ratios and marginal income tax rates.[1]

	Marginal income tax rates		
Loan to value ratio	21%	38%	47%
0.25	28	56	72
0.50	26	55	74
0.75	24	54	75

Note

1   These effective rates of subsidy are computed using an interest rate of 10%, a rate of house price appreciation of 5.75% and operating costs that are 2.4% of asset value.

Table 7.2   Mean household income, house value, marginal tax rate, loan-value ratios and user costs by decile of household income inclusive of net imputed rent for all owning households.[1]

Decile	Household income (A\$)[2] (1)	House value (A\$) (2)	Marginal tax rate % (3)	Loan-value ratio % (4)	User cost % (5)
1	12752	97416	23.05	7.34	7.45
2	19952	113175	27.96	7.25	6.78
3	25345	122897	28.91	11.67	6.88
4	30888	129816	29.31	13.75	6.92
5	36654	137569	33.21	15.15	6.52
6	42779	144851	38.12	15.43	5.91
7	50115	156037	40.25	16.75	5.67
8	58929	168986	41.41	16.17	5.51
9	71001	199058	45.40	16.14	4.95
10	120804	359320	48.69	10.63	4.24
All	43209	155483	33.85	12.81	6.18

Notes

1   The sample size is 9908 households. Details on the methods used in computing these measures can be found in Wood (1995).

2   Household income inclusive of net imputed rent.

3.21 percentage point reduction in user cost, their annual user cost would fall from 56.9% (\$7257) of household income to 32.4% (\$4130) of household income, a sizeable reduction in the effective price of housing. We can explore variation in the effective price of housing across the life cycle by grouping households into age groups, using the age of the head of household. In Wood (1995, Table 6.9) households are classified into three age groups (less than 45, 45 to 65 years and over 65 years) and three household types (married couples with and without dependants, and single persons). For each household type and every income decile, the user cost of capital declines as we move from younger to older age categories. This reflects the lower marginal tax rates of younger households.

Investors and rental housing

The variation in the user cost of homeowners' housing capital due to taxation measures is well known. Less well appreciated are the systematic variations in landlord user costs of housing capital due to the tax treatment of their returns. Governments commonly grant tax shelter benefits to investors in rental housing to promote supply. In the USA accelerated depreciation and the low-income housing tax credits are examples (Hendershott & Ling 1984; McClure 2000). In Australia there has been a building write-off allowance since 1987, and passive losses can be deducted from other sources of income. In the UK various tax-efficient vehicles for the promotion of investment in private rental housing have been created (Wood & Kemp 2001). Capital cost allowances are used in Canada to stimulate the construction of rental housing (MacNevin 1997). In all of these countries there is preferential treatment of real estate capital gains as compared to ordinary sources of income such as rents.

In the USA typical project models have been calibrated to explore the effectiveness of tax shelter benefits in lowering the user costs of investors. The approach uses measures of cash flows for a representative rental housing development, to solve for the minimum rental rate at which an investor can meet his/her user cost of capital (see, for example, De Leeuw & Ozanne 1981; Brueggeman *et al.* 1982; Hendershott & Ling 1984; Fisher & Lentz 1986; Follain *et al.* 1987; Hendershott *et al.* 1987; Ling 1992; MacNevin 1997). These studies generally assume that marginal landlords come from the top marginal income tax bracket; in competitive housing markets tax shelter benefits are then passed on to tenants in lower rents as determined by the marginal investors' income tax bracket. The assumptions that these studies make about tax brackets of marginal investors are then critical.[14]

To fix ideas consider the present value function of an investor in rental housing who can deduct mortgage interest, real estate taxes and operating costs from assessable rental income; however, capital gains are tax exempt.[15] The present value function can be expressed (Wood & Tu 2001) as:

$$V = (m - p(0)q) + (p(T)q - m)e^{-kT} + \int_0^T (1-\tau_L)[r(t)q - \upsilon p(t)q - im] \times e^{-kt}dt \qquad (7.8)$$

where τ_L is the marginal income tax rate of the landlord. The value of $R = r(0)/p(0)$ that equates the present value of revenues and costs such that $V = 0$ is the pre-tax real reservation rental rate the project must earn if it is to be an attractive investment. On evaluating the integral in equation (7.8), factoring q and m, re-arranging and solving for R we obtain (Wood & Tu 2001):

$$R = \frac{r(0)}{p(0)} = i + \upsilon - \frac{\pi_h}{(1-\tau_L)} \qquad (7.9)$$

where the right-hand side is the familiar user cost of capital.[16] The assumption that capital gains are tax exempt means that if the expected rate of capital appreciation increases by one percentage point, R can fall by a multiple of one percentage point because of the tax that is avoided on a lower rental rate. With capital gains receiving preferential treatment, investors prefer to receive returns in this form. This preference is stronger the higher the marginal income tax rate of the investor. Thus the investor user cost of capital is inversely related to the marginal income tax rate.

Wood & Watson (2001) use the Australian Bureau of Statistics 1993 Rental Investors Survey to measure the marginal income tax rates of investors. They found that of the sample of 2906 individual investors, only 315 belong to the top marginal income tax bracket. Thus it would appear that rental housing supply is price inelastic at the reservation rental rates of landlords who belong to the top bracket. It is not known whether this finding is due to capital market imperfections (Litzenberger & Sosin 1978), an insufficient number of top bracket investors (Sunley 1987) or institutional impediments to multi-property portfolios (Wood & Tu 2001). Whatever the reason, the implications are profound. In order to attract rental investors from lower tax brackets, market rental rates must rise above the levels necessary to meet the reservation rental rates of investors from the top bracket. The latter become intra-marginal investors earning above normal returns. Only part of their tax savings is passed on to tenants in the form of lower rents.

In Table 7.3 the landlords comprising the Wood & Watson (2001) study are arranged into deciles according to our user cost measure, and mean user cost, property value and marginal tax rate are listed in each decile.[17] The importance of tax preferences in driving variation in user cost is illustrated by the strong inverse relationship between the investor's marginal tax rate and his/her user cost. The latter increases from a mean of 4.3% in the lowest decile to a mean value of 12.1% in the highest user cost decile. There is a correspondingly monotonic increase in mean market rental rates from 5.9% in the lowest decile, to 9.0% in the highest decile (see Wood & Watson 2001, footnote 41). These figures indicate that intra-marginal suppliers in the lowest user cost deciles are making above normal returns, while low tax bracket marginal suppliers in the highest deciles are typically making below normal returns. In the longer run we can anticipate exit of these marginal landlords. This brings us to a particularly worrying aspect of the findings reported in Table 7.3. The column listing mean property values indicates that marginal suppliers are concentrated in low-income rental housing. Any stock losses due to poor returns will then typically occur in this low value segment of the stock. It is significant that Yates & Wulff (2000) find that in Australia between 1986 and 1996 there has been a healthy expansion in the *total* stock of rental housing, yet they observe a contraction in the stock of *low-income* rental housing in that same period.

Table 7.3   Mean property value (Australian dollars), weighted average effective tax rate and user cost by decile of user cost.[1]

Decile	Mean property value A$	Weighted effective marginal tax rate %	User cost[2] %
1	177560	48.2	4.25
2	143466	41.8	6.17
3	142873	37.1	6.91
4	133944	33.3	7.48
5	122050	29.9	7.98
6	125003	26.0	8.43
7	119327	20.6	8.91
8	104543	20.2	9.41
9	94147	15.5	10.07
10	63604	13.9	12.05
All	122654	28.7	8.17

Notes

1   Marginal landlords (those in the highest user cost decile) typically have relatively low effective marginal rates of tax. They are also concentrated at the bottom end of the rental housing market.

2   The user cost estimates are computed with respect to the baseline assumptions that $i = 10.0\%$ and $q = 4.75\%$.

Source: Wood & Watson (2001, table 2).

Tax arbitrage[18]

Typically we think of taxation measures lowering the cost of owner occupation relative to renting in higher income tax brackets. For a given residence the market rent payable by a potential occupant is independent of their marginal tax rate. However, because net imputed rents and capital gains are tax exempt, the cost of purchasing the given residence for owner occupation falls as the marginal tax rate of the purchaser increases. From this perspective the tax system subsidises ownership among high-income individuals.

But there is a sense in which the tax system is biased in favour of renting (Litzenberger & Sosin 1978; Kiefer 1978, 1980; Titman 1982). Above I argued that competitive housing markets will ensure that tax shelter benefits from investment in rental housing will be passed on in the form of lower market rents that reflect the tax bracket of the marginal landlord. In the absence of impediments to investors in rental housing, landlords from the highest income tax bracket can be prepared to invest in rental residences, and offer housing services to low bracket taxpayers at a rent that places home purchase at an after-tax cost disadvantage.

It has been shown by Anstie *et al.* (1983), Gordon *et al.* (1987), Follain & Ling (1988), Hendershott (1988), and Nordvik (2000) that this tax arbitrage process can be analysed using break-even tax rate models. Given a pre-determined demand for housing services, individuals are assumed to choose the tenure that supplies these housing services at least cost. Once appropriate cost equations for the supply of housing in each tenure have been specified, the models can be solved for the marginal income tax rate at which an individual is indifferent between owning and renting, and landlords are just willing to let housing. Equation (7.6) above can be interpreted as the maximum rental rate that a potential occupant would be willing to pay before turning to purchased housing.[19] On the other hand equation (7.9) can be interpreted as the minimum rental rate (the reservation rental rate) that an investor is willing to accept before realising their real estate investment. On setting equation (7.6) equal to equation (7.9) and solving for τ, we derive the break-even tax rate (τ^*) given by[20]

$$\tau^* = \frac{\tau_L \pi_h}{(1-\tau_L)i(1-\alpha)} = \frac{\tau_{max} \pi_h}{(1-\tau_{max})i(1-\alpha)} \qquad (7.10)$$

The break-even tax rate describes the conditions under which there is a mutually advantageous landlord–tenant match, assuming that marginal landlords come from the top tax bracket where the tax rate is τ_{max}. These conditions are that the maximum rental rate a potential occupant is prepared to pay must be equal to (or greater than) the landlord's reservation rental rate. Potential occupants with tax rates less than τ^* will find it financially advantageous to rent rather than own. Their relatively low tax bracket status means that the effective price they must pay to become owner-occupiers is relatively high, while landlords belonging to the top tax bracket can lease housing to them at rents that are financially more attractive.

A particularly important implication of this model is its prediction that the demand for rental housing will be particularly strong in the low value segments of the market, and this is where tenant–landlord matches are most likely. The low value end of the market is of course more affordable to low bracket taxpayers with $\tau < \tau^*$, but in addition their maximum rental rates are greater than those high tax bracket individuals are willing to offer, as equation (7.6) above demonstrates. Provided marginal landlords belong to the highest tax bracket, mutually advantageous landlord–tenant matchings are then most likely at the bottom end of the market.[21] Given the evidence provided in Table 7.3 above we should question the validity of this final hypothesis, since it shows that marginal landlords do not belong to the top tax bracket, and marginal landlords belonging to lower tax brackets are concentrated at the bottom end of the market.

Table 7.4 presents the results when we calibrate the break-even tax rate model using the Australian Bureau of Statistics 1993 Rental Investors Survey. The 1907 properties are arranged into deciles according to landlords' reservation rental rates. Mean break-even tax rates are listed for each decile, and for three loan to value ratios (LVR). At the high LVR of 0.75 the mean break-even tax rate is 77.8%. All Australian taxpayers have marginal tax rates less than 78% (see final column), which implies that renting is relatively less costly than purchase for all taxpayers at this LVR. Even at the lower LVR of 0.5 the mean break-even rate of 38.9% implies that more than three quarters of Australian taxpayers find renting relatively less costly. Only at the low LVR of 0.25 does the relative cost of homeownership become more favourable for a majority of taxpayers. The other notable finding in Table 7.4 is that the break-even tax rate declines as we move to higher reservation rental rate deciles. Yet these higher deciles contain the concentrations of low value rental housing that is affordable to low-income groups (see Table 7.3). Successful tenant–landlord matchings are least likely in these segments, which contradicts the pattern predicted by the break-even model. This unexpected finding arises because marginal landlords come from the lower tax brackets and are concentrated in low value segments. If housing and capital markets were competitive the supply of rental housing would be perfectly elastic at the reservation rental rates of top tax bracket investors. As was pointed out earlier, the presence of low tax bracket investors implies that market imperfections of one form or another impede additional rental investments by top bracket taxpayers.

It is also perplexing to observe that many Australian households find homeownership financially unattractive given the predominance of owner occupation in Australia. It would seem that preferential taxation is not responsible for the high rates of home ownership observed in Australia and countries with similar taxation arrangements. The puzzle may be resolved on recognising that certain costs, such as agency costs, are unique to rental housing. Landlords cannot write perfect rental contracts that cover all pos-

Table 7.4 Mean break-even tax rate and % of taxpayers with marginal tax rate (MTR) less than break-even tax rate (BTR) by decile of the landlord's reservation rental rate (land taxes, transaction costs and agency costs = 0).[1]

Decile	Break-even tax rate % (LVR = 0.25)	Break-even tax rate % (LVR = 0.5)	Break-even tax rate % (LVR = 0.75)	% of Taxpayers with MTR < BTR (LVR = 0.25)[2]	% of Taxpayers with MTR < BTR (LVR = 0.5)[2]	% of Taxpayers with MTR < BTR (LVR = 0.75)[2]
1	59.57	89.36	178.7	100	100	100
2	40.75	61.12	122.2	79.1	100	100
3	34.17	51.25	102.5	41.6	100	100
4	29.42	44.14	88.27	41.6	79.1	100
5	24.11	36.17	72.34	41.6	41.6	100
6	20.96	31.44	62.88	41.6	41.6	100
7	16.58	24.86	49.73	0.55	41.6	100
8	13.11	19.66	39.32	0.55	41.6	79.1
9	10.94	16.41	32.83	0.55	0.55	41.6
10	9.76	14.64	29.29	0.55	0.55	41.6
All	25.93	38.89	77.79	41.7[3]	79.2[3]	100[3]

Notes

1 The break-even tax rates are computed for the baseline case in which the expected rate of inflation is 4.75%.

2 The Medicare levy is ignored for this calculation. LVR is loan-value ratio.

3 At the sample mean break-even tax rate.

Source: Wood (2001), Tables 1A and 1B.

sible contingencies, thus tenants do not face the social marginal cost of their utilisation of the rental housing stock ('the fundamental rental externality'; see Henderson & Ioannides 1983). Agency costs are the resources devoted to screening tenants, negotiating contracts, compiling inventories, conducting property inspections, collecting rents and whatever monitoring or policing actions are called for in managing the rental externality associated with landlord–tenant relationships. We obtain a proxy measure for agency costs by setting them equal to the property management and letting fees landlords pay real estate agents, if the latter are engaged to undertake all monitoring and policing tasks.[22] Our measure of agency costs is incorporated into the break-even model and the results are presented in Table 7.5.[23]

We now find lower break-even tax rates at all LVR employed in the micro-simulations. At the mean break-even tax rates for these LVR only 1% of taxpayers find mutually advantageous tenant–landlord matches. Thus home ownership has a relative cost advantage over renting for most individuals, but taxation factors are not the only explanation. The agency costs that landlords incur as a result of managing the principal/agent relationship are avoided when people rent from themselves as owner-occupiers. This is an important source of owner occupation's relative cost advantage.

A striking finding is the negative break-even rates found in the five highest reservation rental rate deciles. This indicates that mutually advantageous tenant–landlord matches cannot be found, unless there are direct rental subsidies that overcome homeownership's relative cost advantage. It is in these segments that the break-even tax model predicted that landlord–tenant matches would be most common. Critically important here is the observation that marginal landlords in these high reservation rental rate deciles are concentrated in low value segments of the rental market. One possible explanation for this finding is rent clientele effects, an inefficiency in housing market processes that I address in the next section.

Table 7.5 Mean break-even tax rate and % of taxpayers with marginal tax rate (MTR) less than break-even tax rate (BTR) by decile of the landlord's reservation rental rate (inclusive of land taxes and agency costs).[1]

Decile	Break-even tax rate % (LVR = 0.25)	Break-even tax rate % (LVR = 0.5)	Break-even tax rate % (LVR = 0.75)	% of taxpayers with MTR < BTR (LVR = 0.25)[2]	% of taxpayers with MTR < BTR (LVR = 0.5)[2]	% of taxpayers with MTR < BTR (LVR = 0.75)[2]
1	46.25	69.38	138.76	79.1	100	100
2	24.48	36.72	73.45	41.6	41.6	100
3	15.18	22.77	45.53	0.55	41.6	79.1
4	9.06	13.58	27.17	0.55	0.55	41.6
5	3.58	5.37	10.73	0.55	0.55	0.55
6	−1.89	−2.84	−5.67	0	0	0
7	−6.06	−9.09	−18.17	0	0	0
8	−8.71	−13.07	−26.14	0	0	0
9	−13.41	−20.11	−40.23	0	0	0
10	−14.81	−22.11	−44.42	0	0	0
All	5.36	8.04	16.07	0.55[3]	0.55[3]	0.55[3]

Notes

1 The break-even tax rates are computed for the baseline case in which the expected rate of inflation is 4.75%.

2 The Medicare levy is ignored for this calculation. LVR is loan-value ratio.

3 At the sample mean break-even tax rate.

Source Wood (2001), Tables 2A and 2B.

Taxation, inefficiency and market processes

Clientele effects

In the previous section I argued that there appear to be impediments that prevent additional investment by top tax bracket investors in private rental housing. As a consequence lower tax bracket investors, who have higher costs, are attracted into the market by the higher rents required if they are to cover those inflated costs. The costs of supply are therefore higher than would otherwise be the case. The consequences of this inefficiency are particularly severe in low-income rental housing because marginal investors are concentrated in this low value segment.

An explanation for this pattern is important if we are to address the issue from a policy perspective.[24] Wood & Tu (2001) develop a housing segmentation model in which there are two sub-markets X and Y. They make the following assumptions.

- In a market offering rental housing services only, housing is identical in all respects except location. Investors' user costs of capital are as described in equation (7.9).

- The expected rate of property price appreciation is higher in X than Y.

- There are two income tax brackets with marginal rates higher in the top bracket.

- There are capital market imperfections, which are such that in the short run high bracket investors can finance acquisition of rental housing in sub-market X, but they are constrained on attempting to finance the acquisition of all housing in Y.

- Rent levels are sticky in the short run and the housing stock is fixed in the short run.

- Capital and rent values are initially the same and the former are equal to replacement costs.

High bracket investors will compete with low bracket investors to enter sub-market X, but the former gain more from tax exempt capital gains and will be prepared to pay a relatively high premium to acquire rental investments in X. Market values in X begin to rise, while in Y market values fall in order to attract investors through higher market rental rates. Equilibrium requires satisfaction of two arbitrage conditions. Firstly, equalisation of post-tax real returns for high bracket investors ensures that they are indifferent between X and Y. Secondly, market rental rates in Y must rise such that low bracket investors find it just profitable to invest in Y. Wood & Tu (2001) demonstrate that when there is simultaneous satisfaction of these two arbitrage conditions high bracket investors become intra-marginal suppliers while low bracket investors are marginal suppliers in sub-market Y. The latter are deterred from investing in X by the prospect of negative returns.

The model's principal proposition is that we can expect to observe tax-driven investor clienteles in which low (high) tax bracket investors are concentrated in low (high) value segments. This is consistent with the evidence presented in Table 7.3, and demonstrates that there can be supply-side sources of housing market segmentation where market rental rates for identical housing are driven apart by the clustering of tax-driven investor clientele groups. Wood & Tu (2001) estimate a two-equation model using cross-section data on market rental rates and determinants from the Australian Bureau of Statistics 1993 Rental Investors' Survey. The degree to which capital gains are given tax preferential treatment is found to have a statistically significant negative impact on market rental rates, which is consistent with the operation of a clientele effect.

There is also an interesting corollary of this model. In the short run, Tobin's-q will exceed one in the high value segment X, so that we can expect expansion in the higher value stock in the long run. On the other hand, Tobin's-q will be less than one in the low value segment Y and we can expect contraction in this segment.[25] Some part of the flow of resources into segment X would occur even if there were symmetric tax treatment of capital gains and rental income. But the privileged tax status of capital gains amplifies the flow of resources into segment X, and is the source of market inefficiency. One policy response is the introduction of tax preferences targeted on landlords holding low-income rental housing (see Wood *et al.* 2001 and the concluding section below).

Lock-in effects

Capital gains taxation measures can be the source of lock-in effects that cause investors to hold on to rental housing assets and discourage changes in portfolios. The effect arises because of the failure to tax gains as they accrue. By deferring realisation of an investment the present value of a capital gains tax liability is reduced. As a consequence investors end up holding a less preferred set of investments and welfare losses ensue. Gravelle (1994, p. 143) considers these lock-in effects to be the primary argument for reducing capital gains tax if the effect is a powerful one. This is because large welfare gains will be generated relative to revenues forgone, and it is even possible that lowering the tax rate would actually raise revenues through increased realisations.

The magnitude of lock-in effects will reflect the way in which capital gains taxes are applied. For instance the effect will be magnified if:

- the tax is forgiven on death, as in the USA;

- depreciation allowances are recaptured by subtracting allowances from the cost base used to calculate taxable capital gains, as in Australia and the USA;

- capital gains are taxed by the 'top slice' method that applies to increments in ordinary income, as in the UK.

On the other hand churning incentives will reduce the magnitude of lock-in effects (Hendershott & Ling 1984; Gordon *et al.* 1987; Gravelle 1994). Churning incentives are evident when the purchaser of a building can begin depreciation again, based on the sale price of the asset, as in the USA. If the difference in the present value of the tax shelter benefits of depreciation in the hands of the seller and the hands of the purchaser exceed the capital gains tax, then realisation is tax advantaged (Gravelle 1994, p. 135).

However, there are other economic factors that can impact on the size of lock-in effects. To fix ideas consider a real estate investment that has been held for T years. If the investment is realised now, capital gains tax liabilities are given by:

$$\lambda \tau_L \, q[p(T) - p(0)] \tag{7.11}$$

where $0 < \lambda < 1$ is the tax preference with respect to capital gains tax, and all other parameters are as defined above. If the landlord continues to hold the asset for a further n years, the present value of capital gains tax liabilities on gains accrued up to year T are:

$$\lambda \tau_L \, q[p(T) - p(0)]e^{-kn} \tag{7.12}$$

On subtracting (7.12) from (7.11) we obtain a measure of the value of deferring capital gains tax liabilities. This is given by:

$$\lambda \tau_L \, q[p(T) - p(0)](1 - e^{-kn}) \tag{7.13}$$

It is evident from equation (7.13) that the option to defer has a value that is increasing in the rate of capital appreciation, the number of years the investor has held the asset, the expected number of years that the investor expects to continue to hold the asset if the option to defer is chosen, and the rate of inflation (and hence discount rate). We can therefore expect lock-in effects to be particularly significant in inflationary conditions that are accompanied by buoyant property prices. In addition, lock-in effects are typically larger for older investors, because they are likely to have held assets for a longer period.

When an investor is considering switching into a new asset, the rate of return which the new asset yields has to increase by an amount at least equal to the value in equation (7.13), if it is to leave the investor as well-off as holding the existing asset. This approach to the measurement of lock-in effects was originally suggested by Holt & Shelton (1962). Gravelle (1994, Table 6.6) has applied the measure to building structures, but there have not been other applications to real estate where the focus has been on churning incentives. Similarly there have been no attempts to measure the welfare losses from lock-in effects with respect to real estate assets. Typically studies have concentrated on corporate stock (Feldstein *et al.* 1980) or the use of tax return databases where no distinction is drawn between assets (Auten & Clotfelter 1982). This is clearly an area worthy of research.[26]

The demand for housing, over-investment and welfare losses

Clientele and lock-in effects are a relatively recent concern in the real estate literature concerning taxation and efficiency losses. The early literature focused on measurement of the deadweight welfare losses consequent upon using tax expenditures to promote the consumption of owner-occupied housing. In an early study of this kind Laidler (1969) assumes a perfectly elastic long-run supply of housing and a −1.5 price elasticity of demand. Using an approach similar to equation (7.7) above, Laidler calculates the impact of tax subsidies on price, and estimates that the stock of housing in the USA would be 17.1% lower if imputed rent had been taxed. The excess burden or welfare loss triangle corresponding to this subsidised increase in consumption sums to only 0.14 of 1% of the value of the housing stock in the USA. King (1981) estimates that in the UK taxation of imputed rent would result in a 13.7% decline in the long-run consumption of housing services, a figure very similar to that obtained by Laidler (1969). Once again the excess burden is small at only 0.4 of 1% of mean income, and those with the highest incomes are worst hit.

Rosen (1979) uses a cross-section database to estimate jointly the quantity of housing services demanded and tenure choice. If taxation of imputed rent was in operation, this study projects that the incidence of owner occupation would be 4.4% lower. Rosen & Rosen (1980) estimate a time series model of the tenure choice decision for the period 1949–1974. Imputing measures of the relative price term in the absence of tax preferences allows the authors to employ their regression model for the purposes of generating ex-post forecasts of the long-run proportion of home owners. Their regression model indicates that the incidence of owning would fall from 64% to 60%. Using the homeownership rate adjusted for changes in the demographic structure of the population, Hendershott & Shilling (1982) project that the incidence of homeownership would be 59% if property taxes and mortgage interest were not deductible.

The positive impacts of tax subsidies on owner-occupied housing investment that are implied by the above studies raise the possibility that tax induced increases in housing investment have crowded out industrial capital. When capital gains are tax exempt and mortgage interest is deductible, accelerating inflation raises the cost of investment in industrial capital relative to owner-occupied housing (Rosen 1985). Simulation studies based on the typical project approach incorporate this relative cost into investment functions, and show that when inflation increases owner-occupied housing investment rises relative to business investment (Hendershott & Hu 1981). In Mills (1987) a two-sector neoclassical growth model is estimated for the US economy, and employed to estimate the efficient allocation of capital stock. The model estimates imply that the housing stock is 33% higher than is optimal. Wood's (1988a) two-sector neoclassical model permits estimation of inter-sectoral externalities and factor input productivity differentials. When estimated for the Australian economy the model estimates indicate that housing is responsible for the generation of positive externalities that promote growth of the economy. In addition factor inputs appear to be no less productive when deployed in the housing sector rather than in the rest of the economy.[27]

These conflicting results suggest the need for research that identifies the existence and significance of the transmission mechanisms through which positive and negative externalities manifest themselves. The more recent literature has been exploring the links between homeownership on the one hand and health, neighbourhood stability, social involvement and socially desirable behaviours on the other.[28] These examples of potentially positive externality transmission mechanisms are being balanced by a recent spurt of studies into the potentially adverse impacts of an individual's home ownership on the duration of unemployment spells, and the link between regional unemployment rates and the incidence of homeownership (Oswald 1997b; Green & Hendershott 2001a).

Concluding comments

A number of important policy concerns are evident from this overview of taxation and housing markets. In respect of owner occupation a consistent issue raised by commentators has been the inequitable distribution of tax subsidies. Given typical taxation arrangements it has been firmly established that the effective price paid by homeowners varies inversely with their marginal income tax rate. In addition younger low-income homeowners with low net worth face a relatively high effective price.

The belief that typical taxation arrangements encourage expansion of home-ownership at the expense of rental housing and even industrial capital, and is therefore responsible for allocative inefficiencies, has not attracted so much concern in recent years. This is because of a growing number of studies offering empirical support for the idea that encouraging owner occupation yields significant social benefits (Vandell 2000). In addition, there is the view that tax shelter benefits available to high tax bracket landlords are passed on in lower rents, that advantage households with zero or low marginal tax rates (Weicher 2000).

Policy responses to the concerns about the distribution of homeowner tax preferences initially focused on introducing taxation of net imputed rents. However, it has been shown that the resulting increase in tax liabilities can be regressive, with elderly 'asset rich–income poor' households particularly adversely affected (Ling & McGill 1992; Bourassa & Hendershott 1994). Transitional arrangements can be framed to mitigate these concerns, and a 'package' of reforms can be assembled whereby taxation of net imputed rents replaces regressive real estate taxes and transaction taxes, thereby ensuring a progressive redistribution of the tax burden (Wood 1995). But it seems that most policy analysts consider taxation of net imputed rents a politically unrealistic policy reform. Less ambitious measures such as the phased removal of mortgage interest and real estate tax deductions (Bourassa & Grigsby 2000), or the conversion of deductions into tax credits (Green & Vandell 1999) are now seen as more realistic measures. As noted earlier, there is a change in sentiment with respect to homeowner tax concessions, in view of the growing number of studies confirming social benefits from expansion of homeownership. These studies strengthen the case of those who favour retaining tax concessions, but in a form that would extend the benefits further down the income distribution.

A more recent issue has emerged as a result of evidence confirming a growing shortage of low-income rental housing (Malpezzi & Green 1996; Yates & Wulff 2000; Somerville & Holmes 2001), and the role of taxation measures as one of the factors causing this phenomenon (Wood & Tu 2001). It appears as though there are impediments that cause the supply of rental housing to be price inelastic at the reservation rental rates of investors belonging to the top tax bracket. As a consequence market rental rates rise in order to attract low bracket investors, and only part of the tax shelter benefits received by top bracket investors are passed on in the form of lower rents. To the extent that marginal (low bracket) landlords are concentrated in low value segments of the rental housing market, this has particularly severe impacts on affordable rental housing for low-income groups. It turns out that successful tenant–landlord matches are then least likely in the low value segments, and the exit of low-income housing landlords is to be expected. The uncompetitive position of this segment of the private rental housing stock is compounded by relatively high agency and transaction costs for landlords investing in such rental housing (Wood & Watson 2001).

A number of potential policy responses to this issue deserve attention. The first focuses on relaxing any impediments that deter residential rental investment by high tax bracket investors. These impediments could arise due to capital market imperfections, government regulation or fiscal intervention. There is a paucity of evidence here that could guide policy formulation.

A second approach emphasises the use of targeted tax subsidies to sharpen the incentive to invest in low-income rental housing. In the USA the 1986 Tax Reform Act reduced the tax shelter benefits available to rental housing investors, and raised concerns that low-income rental housing investment would decline. A targeted low-income tax credit was introduced to allay these fears, but its administrative complexity and limited scope has caused analysts to question its effectiveness (McClure 2000). However, Wood *et al.*

(2001) show that a low-income tax credit targeted at rental units that are in the lowest quartile by rent, and which is open-ended, lowers the mean King-Fullerton effective marginal tax rate from 61% to 37%.

A third approach is based on the observation that agency costs are relatively high in the low value segment of the private rental housing stock. It is in this segment that we are most likely to observe marginally housed tenants, whose attachment to the labour market is weak and where rent arrears, un-anticipated breaches of lease contracts and other agency problems are most severe. Vertical disintegration, in which privately financed rental housing is managed by social housing agencies who have professional expertise in housing management, could lower agency costs sufficiently to restore the competitive position of this segment of the rental housing stock.

Given signs that access to home ownership is increasingly difficult, particularly for those on low incomes, a strong demand for rental housing that is affordable to low-income groups can be anticipated. Evidence that this segment of rental housing is costly to supply, and contracting in size, is then a serious concern warranting a policy response.

Acknowledgements

The author is grateful for the constructive and helpful comments provided by Christine Whitehead, Kenneth Gibb, Tony O'Sullivan and participants at the workshop held at Glasgow University, 9th and 10th November 2001.

Notes

(1)   The analysis presented in this chapter assumes an Anglo-American fiscal regime in which there is a relatively high reliance on direct taxes levied on income. In other countries such as those in Southern Europe, there is a greater reliance on indirect taxes. The focus on Anglo-American fiscal regimes reflects a bias in the English language literature, and the author's empirical work that has been conducted using Australian and British data.

(2)   An exception is the US low-income housing tax credit introduced in 1987 (McClure 2000).

(3)   Though the early literature emphasised static deadweight welfare losses, more recently there has been an increasing recognition of the positive externalities associated with increases in the size and quality of the housing stock. If sufficiently large these positive externalities can justify a fiscal regime that discriminates in favour of housing. I consider this further later in this chapter.

(4)   These concessions are also enjoyed by owners of second homes that are not rented out (Bourassa & Grigsby 2000, p. 524).

(5)   Thus the notion of equity that I have in mind is that all households pay the same price for a given bundle of housing services. I should acknowledge an alternative view of equity. In a progressive tax system tax burdens are relatively onerous for high-income households. If governments decide to lower the tax burden by introducing tax expenditures, higher income households will benefit more from the reduction in the tax burden. This is 'fair' because it ensures symmetry in the tax system, given that higher income households will contribute proportionately more of their income in tax.

(6)   Defined to include both land and the building structure. The ratio of land to building structures is assumed to be fixed. The capital variable could comprise land and building structures from one or more properties.

(7)   Economic depreciation is ignored.

(8)   The first two terms on the right-hand side of equation (7.1) are the homeowner's initial equity stake and discounted sales proceeds. The third term is the present value of capital gains tax liabilities when gains are taxed as they accrue and at the homeowner's marginal income tax rate. The final term is the present value of after-tax net imputed rents. Transaction costs have been ignored.

(9)   Or as Chinloy (1991, p. 516) defines the term, it is 'the price which an owner occupier must pay to obtain a unit of services, while owning a unit of stock'.

(10)   The chosen benchmark is the tax treatment prevailing in Australia, Canada and New Zealand, where imputed rents and capital gains are tax exempt, but mortgage interest and real estate taxes cannot be deducted. Now that the mortgage interest deduction has been phased out in the UK, the present value function will also be the same in that country as well.

(11)   Under the tax neutral provisions this term disappears because the real value of the interest deduction is also eroded.

(12)   At higher marginal income tax rates the tax benefit from non-taxation of the erosion of the real value of mortgage debt becomes more important relative to the tax penalty associated with debt. Compare the second and fourth components of equation (7.6).

(13)   This method involves calculation of the homeowners' tax liability inclusive and exclusive of their net imputed income. The resulting incremental tax liabilities are expressed as a proportion of net imputed income. The Australian statutory marginal tax rate schedule in 1990 was applied in this calculation. The marginal tax rate estimates obtained by this method can exceed the highest statutory marginal tax rate because we have taken forgone tax rebates into account. Homeowners with a high-income elasticity of demand will, *ceteris paribus*, have larger net imputed rents and higher estimated marginal tax rates. It follows that homeowners with a high-income elasticity of demand will tend to have a lower user cost of capital.

(14)   Narwold (1992) has offered a theoretical rationale for the top marginal income tax bracket assumption.

(15)   The role of inheritance taxes has been ignored. The evidence presented below uses Australian data. In this country estate and inheritance taxes were abolished by all state governments by the early 1980s (see Wood 1992).

(16)   If the investor cannot access depreciation allowances, and capital gains are tax exempt, this user cost expression is the same as that applicable in the USA. In Hendershott & Slemrod (1983), Gordon *et al.* (1987), Follain & Ling (1988) and Narwold (1992) the user cost expression reduces to equation (7.9) under these conditions.

(17)   The user cost measure estimated in Wood & Watson (2001) is in fact more comprehensive than that expressed in equation (7.9). Measurement of landlords' marginal income tax rates uses similar methods to those used in measurement of homeowner marginal income tax rates (see Note 14).

(18)   This section is based on Wood (2001).

(19)   Equation (7.6) is the user cost of capital for homeowners under typical taxation arrangements. If the individual's pre-determined demand for housing can be met at a lower market rental rate, renting is the financially more attractive option.

(20)   In the derivation of equation (7.10) the component in the homeowner's user cost expression representing erosion of the real value of mortgage debt has been omitted to ensure a unique solution. The consequences of its omission are minor in a low inflation environment, as has been typical of the 1990s. The consequences are even less important for individuals in low tax brackets, who are a particular focus of concern here.

(21)   In the absence of rental subsidies, the top end of the market is affordable to high bracket taxpayers only. But given $\tau > \tau^*$ the maximum rental rates they are willing to offer are lower than those which low bracket individuals are prepared to offer for affordable residences. A landlord–tenant matching is then much less likely at the top end of the housing market.

(22)   A wider range of costs than this is relevant. For example, there are rent arrears, vacancies and delays in the payment of direct housing subsidies that are formally transferred to landlords by government agencies on behalf of tenants. Thus the proxy measure is imperfect. I am at present engaged in a programme of research that is seeking to provide more precise and inclusive measures of these costs in different value segments of the housing stock.

(23)   See equations 4 and 5 of Wood (2001) for a derivation of the agency cost version of the break-even model. Land taxes are also included in this version of the model.

(24)   Also critical is identification of the impediments that prevent expansion of the supply of private rental housing by top bracket investors. This question is outside the scope of this chapter, but is an important item on a future research agenda.

(25)   In addition the model implies that current market rental rates should predict future rates of price appreciation. Empirical support for this hypothesis can be found in Capozza & Seguin (1995) and Clark (1995).

(26)   Real estate has an added significance in this respect since transaction costs are generally thought to be large, and will be an additional source of lock-in effects. Indeed real estate's illiquidity can be traced to lock-in effects. Real estate illiquidity is thought to be the source of rent premiums that vary according to investor holding periods. Liu *et al.* (1995) argue that these premiums give rise to 'dividend-like' clientele effects, and Wood & Tu (2001) offer evidence to suggest that these premiums are a further source of supply-side segmentation.

(27)   These two-sector growth models draw on the production function approach to changes in aggregate output deployed by Feder (1982) and Ram (1986) to investigate the relationship between size of the export sector, government sector and economic growth.

(28)   See Rohe *et al.* (2000) and McCarthy *et al.* (2001) for a review of this literature.

8

The Economics of Social Housing

Christine M. E. Whitehead

Introduction: the role of economic analysis in social housing

Some thirty years ago when Duncan Maclennan was first beginning to work in housing economics the concept of social housing was a simple one. In the UK, the objective of housing policy was seen to be 'a separate house for every family that wishes to have one' (Ministry of Reconstruction 1945). The need was for as much housing as possible – anywhere and of any type – as a result not only of wartime destruction and massive under-investment during and immediately after the war but also because of the rapid growth in population and households in the post-war era. The UK government approach to meeting this need was through public ownership and development of large numbers of dwellings, rents set at well below market levels and administrative alloca-tion of the available public sector housing. Public sector provision was seen as the only way forward, not simply on ideological grounds, but also because of limited private sector capacity, the fact that much of the land available for housing was in public hands, and that the slum clearance and redevelopment of urban areas necessary to meet appropriate standards required large-scale direct local authority involvement. As a result the 1960s in particular had seen the longest period of sustained expansion in public housing output ever experienced in the UK. The picture was very similar in much of Europe as a result of massive shortages. Policy was simply a numbers game and public production the easiest means of alleviating that shortage.

Equally there had been very little economic analysis of either the rationale of social housing or the impact of particular policies on housing outcomes. The requirement of a separate home was seen to be obvious, as was the need for subsidy to public provision and the benefits of pooling costs across the existing stock and new development of social housing. Instead, economic analysis in the UK tended to be limited to examining positive economic questions relating to housing and the macroeconomy and to changes in incomes, prices and costs (Whitehead 1974).

Yet the picture was beginning to change. Most importantly, the 1971 Census for the first time showed that the number of dwellings exceeded the number of households in almost every local authority area in the UK. The 1971 White Paper 'Fair Deal for Housing' no longer looked simply to numbers, but spelled out a more complex set of objectives defined as 'a decent home for every family at a price within their means' (Department of the Environment 1971), raising issues of quality and price for the first time. The idea that some dwellings might already be unacceptable led the Department to undertake a survey of difficult-to-let properties – the response to which showed examples in almost all authorities. Nor were demolition and replacement any longer seen as a panacea for the problem of slums. Instead the emphasis moved towards rehabilitation and area improvement – recognising that the idea of a decent home was no longer restricted to the dwelling itself but included the surrounding area (Paris & Blackaby 1979).

It was in this context that Anthony Crosland, the then Secretary of State for the Environment, ordered a full review of housing policy in England, and economics for the first time played a more central role in policy analysis. This marked the beginning of a far more analytic approach to policy evaluation (Department of the Environment 1977).

The link between economic analysis and policy development is not simply about understanding what is happening. If it is to be of any value there must be some capacity to modify government policy as a result of that analysis. It is in this context that Duncan Maclennan has made his most immediate contribution, not just through detailed studies of how policy has operated and how it could be improved but in his preparedness to take a central role in arguing for policy change consistent with these analyses.

Policy change over the last twenty-five years has inherently been incremental, and often seems to have been aimed as much at undoing the problems arising from earlier policies as at developing a proactive approach to changing requirements. Economic analysis, on the other hand, has concentrated not only on assessing particular measures, but also on examining more fundamental issues underlying these policies. Even though politicians are usually pragmatic and better at adding policies than at rationalisation, there is a coherent economic framework that can be applied to the analysis of government intervention in housing and against which policies can be assessed.

In the context of social housing these more fundamental issues include the following.

- Does meeting government objectives necessarily imply a significant social housing sector? Other countries with equivalent commitment to adequate accommodation for all, notably Germany and Switzerland (as well as the USA and Australia where the commitment can be argued to be less), have effectively met social objectives through private provision.

- Does the existence of a social sector necessarily imply public ownership? Again, clearly not in many European countries such as the Netherlands, France and Sweden, where independent social landlords play a major, sometimes core, role in social provision.

- Does the existence of a large social sector necessarily imply below-market rents? Again there are examples, such as in Sweden and the Netherlands, where rents in the social sector are as high or higher than in the market sector.

- Should there be administrative allocation of social housing to ensure that certain groups obtain adequate accommodation, or should there be consumer choice between sectors? Again many European countries, while giving priority to particular groups, provide tenure neutral assistance, so that social objectives can be achieved across the whole stock (Turner & Whitehead 1993; Turner *et al.* 1996; Stephens *et al.* 2002).

These are fundamental policy issues but they are also issues where economic principles can make a relevant contribution. In particular economics can address:

- whether markets can provide housing efficiently as long as people have adequate purchasing power – in which case there may be no need for a specific social housing sector;

- whether there are economic reasons why housing itself should play a proactive role in income redistribution through supply rather than demand subsidies together with administrative allocations to ensure that priority needs are met; and

- whether there are reasons why the social governance of housing might be more cost-effective than private provision – which would suggest a reason for public or at least social ownership to address questions of risk bearing, management and funding.

This chapter concentrates on these three issues by examining the efficiency rationale for government intervention, the use of housing as a means of re-distribution, and the relevance of transactions costs and 'new' institutional economics to the appropriate governance structure for housing provision and management. Addressing these issues helps to provide some insights into the appropriate role for social housing in the twenty-first century.

Efficiency reasons for social housing provision

Mainstream economics provides a well-defined typology of the rationale for government intervention to achieve allocative and productive efficiency in a market system. This concentrates on the situations where prices do not properly reflect social values and where there are factors that inhibit effective adjustment to price incentives. It also suggests that government may intervene in three fundamental ways – regulation, both to define the framework within which individual decisions occur and directly to control price or quantity; taxation or subsidy; and direct provision of relevant goods and services.

Sources of market failure

Housing has many of the characteristics likely to generate market failure and therefore both productive and allocative inefficiency. Equally, all types of government intervention have been applied to its provision, not only in the UK, but across the industrialised world (Charles 1977; Maclennan 1982; Whitehead 1984).

Most fundamentally, housing lies somewhere along the spectrum between private goods, where the market can be expected to work well, and public goods – where the market will generally not provide effectively (Barr 1998). In this context, housing is very clearly a private good, in that the consumption of housing is both rival and excludable and the vast majority of benefits go to the owner or the occupier of the dwelling. Most importantly a house provides very different utility to different people – a flat in the centre of town may be exactly what a young couple wants, while a family spending the same amount of money is likely to choose a house, perhaps with a garden, further out of town. It is this emphasis on the value of choice that lies at the core of libertarian views that housing be privately provided and allocated, with assistance concentrated on income support (Whitehead 1991).

However, the housing market does suffer from significant market failures, at least at the bottom end of the market – and it is these that generate the economic rationale both for intervention and social provision. The most important sources of such failure are seen as arising from externalities of three types: direct, interactive and intergenerational. The majority of direct externalities relate to health in that poor housing can encourage the spread of disease, although generally only at standards well below those prevalent in advanced economies (Burns & Grebler 1977). In this context much of the emphasis has been on a government regulatory framework that applies to all sectors. This helps determine location, density, design, building materials and occupation levels. Social housing provision still has a role because these standards may not be affordable to all, and regulations are difficult to enforce – so direct provision can provide an efficient approach to ensuring compliance. An important current example here is the evidence that many of the most distressed areas in England are made up of private rented housing, which is in far worse condition than the social housing nearby (Smith 1999). More generally, some 30% of unfit housing actually in use is in the private rented sector (Department of Environment, Transport and the Regions 1998).

Interactive externalities occur across the whole spectrum of provision, wherever the use or upkeep of a particular property impacts on the value of another, and vice versa. Thus if I paint my property some of the benefits fall to my next-door neighbours, while if I do not bother, some of the costs are also borne by them – resulting in an incentive to under-maintain and perhaps even to generate slums (Davis & Whinston 1961; Rothenberg 1967). Social housing addresses this issue by internalising the externalities, but whether the incentives are there for optimal investment in maintenance and improvement is far from clear.

Externality inefficiencies are also the major source of more general neighbourhood decline, where there is no incentive for individuals to invest up to the appropriate level across local services and neighbourhood management, nor a capacity to enforce private contracts which attempt to overcome these failures (Davis & Whinston 1961; Galster & Killen 1995). The problems apply just as strongly to the land market, where externalities, both positive and negative, generate a strong case for land use planning and use allocation to ensure optimal locational patterns (Harrison 1977).

Intergenerational externalities arise both because financial markets are themselves imperfect and because the social discount rate is lower than the private rate – individuals die, while society continues into the future. As a result, individual decisions are likely to emphasise more short-term and consumer-oriented expenditures while society, as a whole, requires longer-term solutions (Hirshleifer 1970). This suggests that, left alone, the private market will under-invest in both new development and improvement investment. Social housing is a direct way of generating both higher levels of investment and more fundamental improvement responses.

These problems are exacerbated by both lack of information and asymmetry in that information (Macho-Stadler & Pérez-Castrillo 1997). This means that consumers cannot effectively evaluate the benefits of their own investments nor choose appropriate suppliers. In particular the housing market does not properly reflect the utility of these investments, so that the private owners cannot readily realise their value nor borrow to obtain the required finance. More generally, individuals tend to be risk averse, which again reduces the incentive to invest and supports the case for government intervention to increase the resources for housing investment – in that government decisions should be based on risk neutrality (Arrow & Lind 1970; Arrow 1971).

A further reason for government involvement relates to problems of monopoly power. Traditional forms of market power are not inherently a major failure of housing markets. In particular, economies of scale either in production or management appear to be relatively limited, while in most areas there are large numbers of housing suppliers. There are, however, significant problems associated with interpersonal contracts, particularly in the context of landlord and tenant relationships where there is often asymmetric information, and contracts are not based on equal access to information. These can be addressed either by social ownership, where the objective is to maximise tenant benefits and social value, or by owner occupation, which internalises the contractual arrangements. On the other hand social ownership can generate large-scale administrative failure, if objectives are poorly specified and agency relationships inadequately addressed. In particular social ownership brings with it its own monopoly power in localities where it becomes the main source of lower-income rented housing.

One of the most prevalent market failures relates to the problems of slow adjustment in the housing system – and most importantly the fact that in market systems price can adjust far more rapidly than quantity. Thus in times of sudden reduction in supply, increases in demand or rapid migration, markets will generate adverse distributional outcomes, some of which will impact on the efficient use of resources. Social production and ownership is the most usual way of addressing the problem with respect to new development. In the existing private rented sector rent controls tend to be the immediate response, but in the longer term the results of that control often generate a greater incentive for social provision and allocation (Quigley 1998).

It can be reasonably argued that the most important reason for government intervention and provision is that housing is seen as a merit good – i.e. one where the value to society is higher than for individual members of society. This is based not just on the existence of externalities and distributional concerns, but because of interdependence of utilities – so it is often regarded as paternalism (Musgrave 1959). This argument applies most clearly at the bottom end of the system but can also apply more generally, if the accepted social welfare function includes significantly higher housing aspirations (Hancock 1991).

Thus there is no doubt that housing is subject to significant market failures. These generate lower than optimal levels of housing investment and management as well as distortions in that provision, take inadequate account of the wider benefits of good quality accommodation as well as the wider costs of bad housing and neighbourhoods, make it difficult to address problems of risk and financing to the individual, and do not allow available economies of scale and scope to be realised in order to minimise the costs of production.

Is the existence of market failure enough to support government provision?

The analysis of market failure in housing generates an *a priori* case for government intervention – if not directly for government provision. Two important questions have to be addressed before the practical case is made:

- is the impact of market failure in terms of higher costs, lower benefits, under-investment and inappropriate allocation of housing resources large enough to matter in an anyway imperfect world; and

- will administrative allocation actually overcome the problems of market failure or simply replace them with equally undesirable or even worse problems of administrative failure?

A great deal of work has been done over the last few years examining the costs of poor housing and the benefits of increasing investment (Whitehead 1998; Bratt 2002). These have concentrated on two main aspects – the impact on lifetime opportunities and social exclusion, together with the associated costs to government, society and neighbourhoods of these failures; and on the positive role that housing can play in effective urban regeneration.

There is growing evidence of a relationship between poor housing and poor health. Overcrowding, dampness, cold, poor air quality and housing-related stress all appear to have some relationship with poor health, the probability of accident and particularly the individual's perceptions of problems (Kellet 1989; Anderson *et al.* 1993; Burrows *et al.* 1997; Carr-Hill 1997; Housing Studies, Special Issue 2000). However, except for those in temporary accommodation, the impact is not seen to be very great. The relationship between poor health and the experience of homelessness and living in temporary accommodation is much stronger (Burrows *et al.* 1997; Social Exclusion Unit 1998). However, the existence of a relationship is not enough to determine causality, especially as there is strong evidence to suggest that poverty and indeed inequality affect health and housing experiences (Wilkinson 1996).

Similar analyses have been undertaken with respect to housing and education – where again the strongest evidence of the costs of poor housing relates to those who have experienced homelessness or have been placed in temporary accommodation (McBeath 1997; Stone 1997). The most important problems that have been identified tend to relate not so much to the quality of the home itself – except to some extent in terms of overcrowding – but more to the neighbourhood, and indeed the neighbours. Much the same applies to employment opportunities, where problems relate as much to peer group experience and accessibility to the appropriate labour market as to housing conditions themselves (Hopkins *et al.* 1997).

An issue of considerable current relevance relates to the positive role that housing can play in effective urban regeneration. Early regeneration programmes in the UK concentrated almost entirely on housing investment, in part because subsidy arrangements could be readily put in place and because of its capacity to lever-in private finance. Latterly, regeneration programmes have become more widely based, taking in employment and training opportunities, programmes to reduce antisocial behaviour and improvements in social infrastructure. Even so, housing remains at the core of this more comprehensive approach because it is central to the interests of residents, and housing organisations tend to be relatively well-equipped to take leading roles in the partnerships necessary for success (Murie & Nevin 1997; Social Exclusion Unit 2001).

Thus the evidence on the wider impact of poor quality housing and inadequate investment as well as the benefits of housing-led regeneration points to significant, if not overwhelming, market failure problems that generate costs both to the individuals involved and to the locality and society more widely.

It is far less obvious that social investment in housing will necessarily solve these problems. It is clear that social housing programmes can generate large-scale investment both in new dwellings and in the existing stock – this is evidenced across Europe over the post-war period. It is less clear that the results are achieved at the lowest cost; that they are indeed additional, in that private housing development may be reduced, offsetting social investment; that the design and management of building are the most appropriate; that social housing meets people's aspirations, in terms of the type of housing provided; and that the allocation process enables adequate choice and so maximises the value to the individual. In England it is also clear that the total amount of social provision is not adequate to ensure that defined government objectives, in terms of a decent home for every household at a price within their means, can be achieved. In many areas there is a mismatch between the supply of housing and identified needs, resulting in continuing problems of homelessness and the use of temporary accommodation, even for those for whom the government takes direct responsibility.

Moreover, social provision and allocation policies can, of themselves, generate significant costs. In particular they tend to concentrate problems in specific localities resulting in major problems of social exclusion (Social Exclusion Unit 1998). In this context it has been argued that the problems are, to a significant extent, the effect of administrative rather than market failure. On the other hand, although there are heavy concentrations in some social housing areas, the majority of such problems occur outside these areas, including in particular localities dominated by the private rented sector (Smith 1999). Equally, similar concentrations of problems are found when allocation is left to the market sector – as is obvious from US experience (Housing Studies, Special Issue 2002).

The evidence on market failure reasons for social housing provision thus relates mainly to the potential external costs of bad housing and neighbourhood, and to the social value put on good quality accommodation. Other fundamental aspects of market failure, such as the extent of suboptimality in investment and allocation, have been subject to far less empirical scrutiny.

Housing as a means of redistribution

The principles

The strongest political case for the provision of social housing has never been in terms of efficiency, but rather in terms of a direct and effective means of redistribution and ensuring minimum housing standards. The main strand of the argument is straightforward: low-income households need assistance to purchase the necessities of life. How should this assistance be provided?

One way is in the form of income subsidies, increasing capacity to pay but allowing freedom of choice about what is purchased. Success then depends on the efficiency of the market incentive system to generate the required supply response. Alternatively the subsidy can be given to providers, either private or social, directly to provide additional accommodation and to allocate it on the basis of agreed priorities. This then raises the additional question of how these priorities should be translated into practical decisions – in other words, who should receive the actual subsidy that is affected by both the allocation and pricing principles applied.

A rather different distributional issue relates to the impact of disequilibrium on prices and allocation, especially where there are housing shortages, so that benefits are being redistributed to the private landlord or landowner at the expense of consumers. The immediate problem can be addressed by rent controls in the private sector. However, these may adversely impact on the incentive to expand provision to bring provision back into equilibrium and imposes costs on those not able to access controlled sector housing. Equally it can be alleviated by social provision and rental subsidies for those in priority need. The choice might be argued to depend on the relative efficiency of the two sectors in responding to the incentive to provide as well as on the relative equity of the resultant allocation rules.

The basic argument of principle is usually seen in terms of the relative benefits of bricks and mortar as compared with income subsidies (Hills *et al.* 1990; Galster 1997; Yates & Whitehead 1998). The form of that subsidy may, in turn, impact on the amount of both public and private resources made available and on the relative capacity of the social and private sectors to ensure that provision is forthcoming.

It might not be unreasonable to argue that one of the few lessons politicians appear to have taken from economists is that income subsidies are to be preferred to supply subsidies on the grounds that they provide higher utility to the individual because of the greater choice available. This is taken to apply without modification to the case of housing. However, such an argument is over-simplistic. In principle regulation, taxation, subsidy and direct provision can all address market failures equally effectively. In reality appropriate methods of intervention depend both on the nature of the market and the practical attributes of intervention procedures. It is thus necessary at the same time to address the question of the relative efficiency of different means of intervention to offset market failures (Whitehead 1983). In particular income subsidisation takes no account of the relative capacity of the private and social sectors to provide the additional housing. It is also partial in that it only takes account of the housing market and not of other distortions such as the impact on the labour/leisure choice of recipients (especially where, as in the UK, the form of the income subsidy is particularly inappropriate). Equally, supply subsidies can be used to offset externality and other market failures, that are not directly addressed by choice-based demand subsidies. Supply subsidies are also the most obvious way of reflecting the extent to which housing is a merit good. Lastly, in a second-best world where there are distributional as well as efficiency objectives, it can be shown that transfers in kind of goods with low price elasticities of demand may generate fewer allocative distortions than income transfers (Bös 1983, 1985). Fundamentally, therefore, even though the question being addressed is that of distribution, the most appropriate way to achieve an agreed distributional objective comes down to the relative importance of different market failures on the ground. This can only be answered by empirical evidence.

Within this more general question of income subsidies versus subsidies to provision as well as regulation in the face of shortage lies the role of prices and rents, which determine the extent of assistance provided.

In a well-operating market environment prices reflect resource costs and therefore help to maximise the utility achieved from given housing resources. In practice, especially where there is disequilibrium, capacity to pay can come to dominate these efficiency benefits and make intervention inevitable. In social housing the determination of rents and prices raises significant problems about underlying objectives to help meet socially determined needs – e.g. by making larger housing cheaper so that those with families can pay for adequate accommodation – or to reflect the relative valuation or cost of the housing provided (Maclennan 1986c; Kleinman & Whitehead 1991). The problems of ensuring distributional as well as efficiency objectives are exacerbated when pricing below market levels generates shortages, so that those excluded have to pay far more for their housing in the market sector.

The practice

It is hardly surprising that views about the relative benefits of demand and supply subsidies in different countries depend significantly on the government's ideological stance (Yates & Whitehead 1998). In the USA there is general acceptance that demand-side subsidies are more efficient – in part because there is little weight given to market failure, merit good and social welfare arguments – so that the only criteria for this assessment relate to choice and cost (Galster 1997). Much of the US analysis supporting demand-side subsidies is based on an understanding of how people in receipt of subsidy might have the incentive to move between sub-markets and therefore provide incentives to suppliers to increase investment and remove poor quality units – a version of the filtering theory. In Europe the basis for assessment tends to be wider. The analysis by Yates and Whitehead, for instance, argues for a more agnostic approach, based on an understanding of the factors preventing either form of subsidy effectively achieving their goals, more detailed assessment of the relative weights to be given to the different objectives and empirical evidence on their relative effectiveness.

In practice in the UK and in most of the rest of Europe, although supply-side subsidies continue, increasingly they tend to be targeted. The extent of overall subsidy to housing has been much reduced and the importance of demand-side subsidies has increased (Turner & Whitehead 2002). Thus, supply subsidies have been reduced to the point where in the Netherlands and Sweden, both countries with a strong commitment to housing as a social good, there is now no longer a net financial allocation by government to supply, and in Britain such subsidies are limited to improvement of the social stock, together with a very limited new build programme. Arguably, this reflects the changing impact of market failure in growing economies. The large-scale development programmes have solved the problem of shortage, except in areas of sudden change (as in some parts of Germany in the 1990s).

Increasing national income has generated higher average housing standards and reduced the impact of basic negative externalities, while the worst housing has been cleared or improved with government assistance. Individual demands, across much of the income distribution, are such that basic repairs and improvements are generally undertaken even if the level of investment is below the social optimum. As standards rise, the emphasis on housing as a merit good – as compared for instance with health, where improved technology keeps expanding the range of treatments and preventive medicines which society wishes to ensure are available to all – must inherently decline. Equally, national incomes have generally increased in absolute terms so that even if the actual distribution of income may have worsened so the need is seen to be for broader support to low-income households.

As a result, only three main areas of intervention appear to remain important in terms of current government priorities in Europe:

- ensuring access to adequate housing for those at the bottom of the income scale who are still excluded because of the failure of other programmes;

- addressing the issue of neighbourhood, as the nature of housing services is redefined to take account of local environment and services (where market failure arising from negative externalities tends to dominate), and offsetting problems of adjustment, for instance, addressing the housing consequences of sudden reductions in regional or sub-regional economic viability; and

- maintaining and improving the existing stock, where problems of under-investment arising from inadequate information and risk aversion are prevalent.

At the same time many European countries have been restructuring their social sectors and introducing greater private involvement, especially with respect to funding. In the Netherlands in particular the emphasis has been on ring-fencing the social rented sector and is now moving towards policies that aim to increase the proportion of owner occupation. In Sweden direct subsidies are being concentrated on particular areas of economic decline. In Britain the majority of council housing is being transferred to independent landlords, greater emphasis continues to be placed on shared ownership and other low-income homeownership schemes, and new social sector building is being directly linked to private sector developments (Turner & Whitehead 2002).

In the USA the emphasis remains on providing direct assistance only to those at the bottom end of the income/access scale. Most new programmes are concentrated on increasing individual opportunity, reflecting the emphasis on choice. Equally, new programmes concentrate on offsetting the costs of immobility and discrimination (notably racial discrimination) that tend to exclude households from employment and housing markets. These policies particularly stress physical relocation into more mixed communities and access to owner occupation that is now seen as carrying with it many benefits of access to credit, employment and a healthier lifestyle (Housing Studies, Special Issue 2002).

Thus the general trends across Europe and North America are towards greater concentration of assistance, targeting low-income households and poor neighbourhoods. It is still the case however that the emphasis in Europe remains more on continued intervention in supply, especially in terms of regeneration, while in the USA assistance is concentrated on helping particular individuals to improve their position in the housing system.

Both these approaches raise issues of the relative efficiency of private and social provision and thus the question of market versus administrative failure.

The governance of housing

The principles

Throughout the 1970s the question of market failure, and therefore the case for government intervention, dominated the economic discussion of housing policy. It was not until the early 1980s that economists, led by political reality, started to apply the emerging analysis of comparative governance systems, and particularly that of administrative failure, to the question of housing provision.

The theory of administrative failure is based on an examination of the nature of property rights. Well-defined private property rights give the individual power to use resources to that individual's best possible advantage. They will be used efficiently because that individual will wish to maximise independent individual utility. Private property rights also allow these resources to be transferred in such a way that expected future values are properly capitalised in the price. Thus resources will be put to their highest and best use and inefficiencies will be competed away. If this is the case then government policy should concentrate on liberalising markets and improving contractual frameworks.

Social ownership carries with it problems of ill-defined property rights and an incapacity to capitalise either efficiency or inefficiency. There is therefore no direct incentive to transfer resources to more efficient providers. Inadequately defined interaction between decision makers and those carrying out the policy generates inefficiencies of team production, because information is imperfect and decisions are based on bounded rationality, so that the outcome is not that desired (Hölmstrom 1979, 1982; Macho-Stadler & Pérez-Castrillo 1997). In particular there are inherent problems of agency that are not mediated by market pressures. Thus decision makers use resources to meet their own objectives rather than those of society or individual owners. These problems are exacerbated in situations of risk and uncertainty, perhaps particularly where that risk is political (Williamson 1979). Thus, local authorities and other social providers tend to have a paternalistic view of housing provision and allocation that does not necessarily reflect either individual or society objectives.

Equally, the costs of provision, and especially management and maintenance, tend to be significantly higher than would be the case under profit maximisation. Allocation mechanisms will thus not normally reflect either opportunity cost or value. At the same time rent seeking behaviour tends further to misallocate resources (Posner 1972). These problems are seen to be particularly prevalent in housing because of the complex nature of the good and the different values that this complex mixture of housing attributes generates to those with different preferences.

The more general analysis of transactions costs (Williamson 1975, 1986) stresses the extent to which internalising decisions within organisations can reduce the potential range of contractual failures – arguing for firms rather than markets and for integration where there are incomplete contractual arrangements. This analysis would tend to favour larger scale provision, internalisation of externalities and removing contractual arrangements – for instance through owner occupation rather than landlord/tenant arrangements. On the other hand problems of information and agency within the organisation and in particular the lack of external market pressures to allocate resources tells against social ownership arrangements.

The core of the comparison between different forms of governance lies in three elements.

- Clarity of objectives – if objectives are not transparent, and in particular, if there are multiple objectives, it is impossible to draw up effective contracts and it is extremely difficult to specify incentives and to monitor outcomes effectively.

- The appropriateness of incentive structures especially, where there are trade-offs to be made between risk and maximising values – administrative systems tend to have far less well-defined incentive structures but to have a wider range of monitoring procedures available.

- The framework by which the relevant activity – here the provision of social housing – is linked to the rest of the economy and therefore to overall resource allocation. In market systems this is done through asset capitalisation and realisation; in administrative systems it is achieved mainly through the regulatory framework.

In reality, any governance system is imperfect. It is therefore a matter of analysing the different attributes of the market, regulatory and administrative systems in the context of the particular product to determine the least-cost approach – as such, many of the most relevant factors come back to market and informational failures.

Over the last few years there have been considerable developments in the analysis of ways to reduce the costs of governance failures of all types, notably in the context of finance markets but also in relation to non-profit maximising organisations. These stress appropriate risk sharing procedures and also the use of debt finance and regulatory frameworks in order better to enforce efficiency incentives (Pollack 1985; Hansmann 1996; Allen & Gale 2000). All suggest that there is no single answer, but they also suggest that the form of governance does not have to be directly related to the extent to which social and private objectives differ (Bromwich *et al.* 2002). It is these developments that open up the opportunities for using the whole range of possible approaches – from public ownership and allocation through to private markets with income subsidies – to achieve the social goal of a decent home for every household at a price within their means.

The reality: administrative versus market failure

It was not until after the Conservative government was elected in 1979 that the analysis of administrative failure began to emerge as central to the economic analysis of housing policy in the UK. At that time the sale of council houses through the Right to Buy was included in the Conservative Manifesto as the first intimation of the priority to be given to more general privatisation (see the chapter in this volume by Williams). The reasons housing led this change in policy were mainly political and macroeconomic: ease of immediate cutbacks (85% of the net cuts in the first two years of the Conservative government concentrated on housing); the potential for using the liberalised finance system both to extend owner occupation and to restructure social rented sector assets; and the fact that housing was not high on the political priority list. More fundamentally there was growing emphasis on individuality (as Mrs Thatcher famously said, there is no such thing as society) and the benefits of choice, particularly in housing allocation where its private good nature appeared to have been lost in the actuality of social provision.

Privatisation was therefore seen as improving productive efficiency, making resource allocation far more consumer oriented, and utilising the newly liberalised financial system to introduce private incentives and constraints into production and later into the management and improvement of the existing stock (Whitehead 1984). This style of analysis lay at the heart of decisions to move to compulsory competitive tendering (Baker *et al.* 1992). It also lies at the heart of the private finance initiative that attempts to bring together the benefits of lifetime private contracting and risk bearing with meeting well-defined social objectives. Since 1997 these ideas have become more closely linked with a growing emphasis on models of partnership and consortia that bring together the required range of skills within an appropriate incentive framework. This is in line with the developing analysis of agency relationships and how to minimise the costs of mediating different objectives (Bromwich *et al.* 2002).

However, there is still very little empirical analysis of the outcomes of changing governance structures. The early work by Duncan Maclennan on the relative efficiency of management in the local authority and housing association sectors remains one of the few detailed comparative studies (Centre for Housing Research 1989). In the main, evaluations have examined results on their own terms – for instance, what has been the outcome of introducing private finance into housing association provision (Chaplin *et al.* 1995). This in part reflects political reality – but it is a failure nonetheless.

Moreover, even if administrative failures can be limited by better incentive systems and improved monitoring and enforcement, which would make it more worthwhile both to meet reasonable household demands and to use least-cost methods of production, there remains a fundamental problem. In part, because politically housing is not a priority, public funding will always remain constrained. As a result levels of provision are held below the optimum, and decisions about, for instance, rent increases and permission to borrow, that limit the capacity both to build the new units required or to maintain and improve the existing stock, are made not on the basis of optimal resource allocations but of political expediency.

Conclusions

The analysis in this chapter suggests a practical rationale for observed trends across the industrialised world – but economic principles have had an impact, not only on immediate policy decisions but also on our general understanding of how and when governments should provide social housing. These principles also allow us to make a first attempt at answering the questions about the nature and role of social housing posed at the beginning of this chapter: do we need a significant social sector; should it be publicly owned; should rents be below market levels; and should administrative allocation continue? The answers are not straightforward in either economic or political terms, and in both contexts the appropriate way forward depends on the impact of past policies and the existing strength of organisational, regulatory and market frameworks.

Both economic theory and evidence point to the need for significant housing-specific subsidies to lower income housing to achieve social objectives. Current estimates for England would imply, for instance, that over one third of newly forming households will require some form of assistance (Holmans

2001). Analysis suggests however that social objectives can be achieved without public, or indeed social, ownership. But, if we start from the current situation in the UK, were inappropriate constraints to be removed, both local authorities and housing associations would be likely to have a comparative advantage in providing, or ensuring provision into the longer term, for those in need of secure, subsidised accommodation.

The case for rents below market levels is far less clear, especially in areas where there is a reasonable balance between households and dwellings. The ideal is rather to ensure provision is adequate, and income-related assistance is structured to give suitable incentives as well as reasonable access to housing. This can seem an impossible dream in current conditions, especially if economic activity remains so spatially unbalanced. Yet the economic case for greater consumer choice in an expanding economy where minimum standards of housing can be achieved from a reasonable proportion of basic incomes is strong. This also implies that, while the case for ensuring those with least bargaining power are helped to achieve acceptable housing is overwhelming, that for administrative allocation is much weaker.

The most important implication of the analysis is that, in the twenty-first century, there should be less emphasis on social housing *per se* and far more on managing markets, ensuring adequate investment and enabling different types of providers (public, non-profit and private) to compete on cost and quality, rather than ideological grounds. A role for social housing will remain, but it should only survive if it both meets reasonable aspirations and provides good value for money.

While changes in government policy in most countries can still best be described as knee-jerk responses to particular political pressures, there is evidence of rather slow movement towards a framework that attempts to bring together the better elements of private provision and allocation and link them with wider social objectives. In principle this could produce a social housing system using a range of instruments and relationships chosen on the basis of the relative costs of market and administrative failure.

In practice, what is still the most likely outcome is that little will change, especially during periods when political pressures are low, but that political tensions, either macroeconomic or distributional, will dominate in times of crisis. Housing policy will then remain a cat's cradle of policies addressing specific problems rather than a coherent whole – but at least economics has given us some tools by which we can assess outcomes and suggest improvements.

9

Neighbourhood Dynamics and Housing Markets

George C. Galster

Introduction

The urban neighbourhood has been the subject of intense scrutiny by several academic disciplines since at least the 1920s. Economists came rather late to this field, amassing what could be called a body of work only since the 1960s. Two volumes that Duncan Maclennan wrote and contributed to (Maclennan 1982; Grigsby *et al.* 1987) laid an important foundation for this emerging field of economic study. Their contributions were to: (1) place the analysis of neighbourhood dynamics within the overarching context of metropolitan-wide but segmented housing markets, and (2) demonstrate that standard neoclassical assumptions about supply, demand, and market operations required significant supplementation in the case of housing and neighbourhoods.[1] This essay builds upon these contributions, examining further the nature of neighbourhood, the source and nature of changes therein, and the consequences associated with such changes.

I begin by forwarding an economics-based interpretation of neighbourhood, and consider the many idiosyncrasies associated with the concept. I go on to consider various aspects of the origins and nature of neighbourhood change,[2] and argue that neighbourhood dynamics are rife with social inefficiencies. Lastly, I draw some inferences from the approach adopted for public policies related to neighbourhood regeneration.

Defining neighbourhood

I define neighbourhood as follows:

Neighbourhood is the bundle of spatially based attributes associated with clusters of residences, sometimes in conjunction with other land uses.

This definition owes its intellectual genesis to the work of Lancaster (1966), who originally formulated the notion of complex commodities as multi-dimensional bundles comprised of simpler (albeit sometimes abstract) goods. The spatially based attributes comprising the complex commodity called 'neighbourhood' consist of:

- structural characteristics of residential and non-residential buildings: type, scale, materials, design, state of repair, density, landscaping, etc.;

- infrastructural characteristics: roads, sidewalks, streetscaping, utility services, etc.;

- demographic characteristics of the resident population: age distribution, family composition, racial, ethnic, and religion types, etc.;

- class status characteristics of the resident population: income, occupation and education composition;[3]

- tax/public service package characteristics: the quality of public schools, public administration, parks and recreation, etc. in relation to the local taxes assessed;

- environmental characteristics: degree of land, air, water, and noise pollution, topographical features, views, etc.;

- proximity characteristics: access to major destinations of employment, entertainment, shopping, etc., as influenced by both distance and transportation infrastructure;[4]

- political characteristics: the degree to which local political networks are mobilised, residents exert influence in local affairs through spatially rooted channels or elected representatives;[5]

- social-interactive characteristics: local friend and kin networks, degree of inter-household familiarity, type and quality of inter-personal associations, residents' perceived commonality, participation in locally based voluntary associations, strength of socialisation and social control forces and local social institutions, etc.;[6] and

- sentimental characteristics: residents' sense of identification with place, historical significance of buildings or district, etc.

The unifying feature of these attributes constituting the bundle called neighbourhood is that they are *spatially based*. The characteristics of any attribute can be observed and measured only after a particular *location* has been specified. This is not to say that neighbourhoods are homogeneous on any attribute, merely that a distribution or profile can only be ascertained once a space has been demarcated. Moreover, to say that attributes are spatially based does not mean that they are intrinsically coupled with the geography; some are (infrastructure, topography, buildings), whereas others are associated with individuals who lend their collective attribute to the space purely through aggregation (race, income, life-cycle stage).

I emphasise that while most of the attributes above are usually present to some extent in all neighbourhoods, the quantity and composition of constituent attributes typically vary dramatically across neighbourhoods within a single metropolitan area. This implies that, depending on the attribute package they embody, neighbourhoods can be distinctly categorised by type and/or by quality. This is, of course, a tenet of social area analysis (Greer 1962; Hunter 1974). However, unlike that school of thought, I extend the dimensions over which neighbourhoods can be classified beyond the demographic- and status-related. The extension is necessary if one is to understand neighbourhood change, for key decision makers evaluate more than merely the demographic and status attributes of a space before investing in it.

Commodities are consumed, of course, but in the case of neighbourhood many of the attributes take on a quasi-public good character, with non-excludable, non-rival consumption. Four distinct types of users potentially reap benefits from the consumption of neighbourhood: households, businesses, property owners, and local government.[7] Households consume neighbourhood through the act of occupying a residential unit and using the surrounding private and public spaces, thereby gaining some degree of satisfaction or quality of residential life. Businesses consume neighbourhood through the act of occupying a non-residential structure (store, office, factory), thereby gaining a flow of net revenues or profits associated with that venue. Property owners consume neighbourhood by extracting rents and/or capital gains from the land and buildings owned in that location. Local governments consume neighbourhood by extracting tax revenues, typically from owners, based on the assessed values of residential and non-residential properties.

Idiosyncrasies of neighbourhood

Here I discuss four aspects of spatially based attributes and the idiosyncrasies that result for neighbourhood dynamics. These aspects are: cross-attribute variation in durability, cross-attribute variation in ability to be priced, relativistic evaluations of attributes by consumers, and consumption impacts on attributes.

The spatially based attributes comprising neighbourhood vary in their durability. Some, like certain topographical features, are permanent. Sewer infrastructure and buildings typically last generations. Others, such as tax/public service packages and demographic and status profiles of an area, can change over a year. The area's social interrelationships and public behaviours can sometimes alter even more rapidly. The implication of this observation is as follows. Although some of the key features that define a desirable neighbourhood from the perspective of its many consumers can be counted on to remain constant (and therefore predictable) for extended periods, others cannot. This means that consumers' *predictions* about future changes in these less-durable features, coupled with their aversion to risk and their preferences for these various, non-durable attributes, will play a major role in determining decisions about mobility, financial investments, and psychological investments in neighbourhoods over the long term.[8]

The spatially based attributes comprising neighbourhood vary in their ability to be priced by market mechanisms. In order for potential consumers to make bid offers for a commodity they must have some modicum of information about the quantity and quality of that commodity and what likely benefit they would receive from its consumption. Real estate markets have been shown to meet this criterion for a large number of spatially based attributes. Indeed, this is the foundation of over three decades of empirical work estimating 'hedonic indices'.[9] These studies have shown that attributes like structural size and quality, accessibility, tax/public service packages, demographic and status composition of residents, and pollution can be priced and, in turn, be converted into a measure of household consumers' willingness to pay. However, most social interactive dimensions of neighbourhood cannot be priced well because they are hard *ex ante* for prospective bidders to assess. The idiosyncratic and personalised nature of neighbourhood social interactions means that prospective in-movers will only be able to ascertain how they will 'fit in' after an extended period of residence. One implication is that long-term residents may have considerably different market evaluations ('reservation prices') for their neighbourhood than prospective residents or investors because the former have capitalised (positively or negatively) their assessments of the social interactive dimension. Thus, the former may be highly resistant to external market forces when they assess a positive social environment, and may be more easily out-bid and eventually supplanted by new owners and residents when they assess a negative one. Another implication is that neighbourhoods are particularly prone to forms of insider dealing, with privileged information communicated to preferred buyers and in-movers by current residents, owners, and their market intermediaries.

Even if the market can price attributes comprising neighbourhood, however, their price will typically be based on a comparison of attributes in competing neighbourhoods, not on the intrinsic characteristics of the attribute set.[10] Perhaps the most obvious example is the status dimension. The absolute income levels of households in a particular neighbourhood may rise, but if they are rising at least as quickly in all other neighbourhoods in the metropolitan area there likely will be no change in consumers' evaluations of that neighbourhood's status attribute. Analogous arguments can be made regarding other attributes, such as proximity, school quality, and public safety. The upshot is that, when new neighbourhoods are created through large-scale construction or rehabilitation projects, they can change the relative attractiveness of existing neighbourhoods. And because *relative* evaluations will alter flows of resources across space, *absolute* changes in the existing neighbourhoods will follow (Galster 1987; Grigsby *et al.* 1987).

The spatially based attributes comprising neighbourhood can change by the very act of consuming them. This can occur directly and indirectly. With regard to direct change, as households consume neighbourhood by occupying residences in it, they may simultaneously alter the demographic and/or socio-economic status profile of the neighbourhood if the in-moving households differ systematically from longer-term residents. Analogously, a different type of ownership of homes or stores may emerge if the consumption changes to absentee-owned instead of owner-occupier, for example. Indirectly, changes in the occupancy and/or ownership profiles of a neighbourhood not only changes tautologically its current attributes, but may trigger longer-term changes in a wider variety of attributes. This can occur if the occupancy or ownership changes yield different decisions by current or prospective consumers of the neighbourhood that affect the flows of resources into that space, a topic I discuss in more depth later. Put differently, the monetary and psychic benefits and costs associated with the consumption of a neighbourhood largely originate externally to the consumer in question (Maclennan 1982).

Suffice it to note briefly here the corollary of the foregoing point: attributes of neighbourhood are mutually causal over time. Changes in one attribute may change decisions by one or more type of consumer, which lead, in turn, to changes in other attributes, and so on (Galster 1987; Grigsby *et al.* 1987; Temkin & Rohe 1996).

How neighbourhoods come to be

Although it is tempting to conceive of neighbourhood as a commodity with fixed, clearly defined characteristics, it is more appropriately viewed in a more dynamic perspective. The attributes comprising neighbourhood at any moment are, in fact, the result of past and (typically) current *flows* of households and resources – financial, social-psychological, and time – into and out of the space in question (Galster 1987). Certainly, when a subdivision or estate of homes is newly constructed one might say that a neighbourhood has come into being, though without household occupants it is not yet a fully formed neighbourhood. From that moment on, what attributes that place will possess – what that neighbourhood will *be* – will be shaped by the decisions of current and prospective consumers.

Thus, in a fundamental way, the *consumers* of neighbourhood can be considered the *producers* of neighbourhood as well. Households consume a neighbourhood by choosing to occupy it, thereby producing an attribute to that location related to that household's demographic characteristics, status, civil behaviours, participation in local voluntary associations and social networks, and so forth. Property owners consume a neighbourhood by buying land and/or buildings in it; they subsequently produce the neighbourhood's attributes through their decisions regarding property construction, upkeep, rehabilitation, or abandonment. Business people consume a neighbourhood by operating firms there, thereby producing attributes related to structure types, land use, pollution and accessibility. Local governments consume neighbourhood by extracting property tax revenue and, in turn, produce attributes associated with public services and infrastructure.

The list of producers of importance to any neighbourhood is expansive and diverse. In the first rank are the aforementioned consumers: households, property owners, business people, and local governments. The list of producers also includes, in a secondary but nevertheless important way, those in the real estate brokerage, insurance, and mortgage finance sectors. Within these broad categories of producers further dimensions of variation are manifested. These groups include both those who currently reside, own property, and/or earn income or tax revenues in a given neighbourhood, and those who do not but may under certain circumstances. They include those who perceive a vested financial or social-psychological interest in the area and those who do not. They include those who make decisions using the cold calculus of profit maximisation, those who consider sentiment and personal satisfaction, and still others who are motivated by political pressures.

The mobility, purchasing, and resource allocation decisions related to neighbourhoods (what I will refer to hereafter as 'investing') are inherently fraught with an unusual amount of uncertainty emanating from both within and without. First, the aforementioned dual functions of consumer and producer mean that the decisions by one will affect directly and indirectly the investment outcomes of all in the neighbourhood. Although the neighbourhood as a whole affects the well-being of each consumer/producer, what happens to that neighbourhood is a function of changes in numerous constituent attributes associated with it, each of which has an uncertain future because there is a large number of consumer/producers of different types and motivations controlling it. Second, the flows of resources across all neighbourhoods in a metropolitan area will be influenced by uncertain metro-wide factors related to the regional economy, technological innovation, population and immigration, state and federal government policy, and vagaries of nature (Grigsby *et al.* 1987; Temkin & Rohe 1996), as will be explained below.

This high uncertainty translates into substantial long-term risk because, once made, investments of resources in neighbourhoods are not easily reversible. Many sorts of potential investments have substantial out-of-pocket and psychological transaction costs, costs which consumer/producers are loath to incur on a frequent basis. Other sorts of potential investments, especially structures and infrastructures, have long projected life spans and are spatially fixed. The high uncertainty–high risk nature of neighbourhood investments holds important implications for the characteristics associated with neighbourhood change.

Changes in neighbourhood

Above I argued that neighbourhoods would change (i.e., their attributes would be altered) based on the decisions made by the welter of consumer/producers that influence the ongoing flow of resources to a neighbourhood. These decisions are based heavily on relativistic, inter-neighbourhood comparisons and future expectations embedded within a risk-laden, highly interactive, multi-actor context. In this section I will examine further the nature of neighbourhood dynamics these conditions give rise to.

I find it helpful in understanding why and how an individual neighbourhood changes to think of two overlapping processes at work. One is a macro process that reverberates through the entire system of neighbourhoods in a metropolis, which can best be analysed through a neoclassical, segmented market framework. The other is a series of micro processes describing the nature of adjustments within a neighbourhood and between neighbourhoods within a common market segment. The micro processes can best be modelled with 'complexity models' of non-linear and discontinuous changes.

I begin below describing the macro process and argue that, fundamentally, forces originating outside of neighbourhoods initiate neighbourhood change. I then discuss micro-processes, and show how they result in non-linear, threshold adjustments in individual neighbourhoods. Lastly, I explain why changes in neighbourhood are socially inefficient.

The macro process of neighbourhood change

Consider a quality-segmented model of the metropolitan housing market.[11] It presumes a predominantly private housing market for rental and sales units, wherein suppliers and households are motivated importantly (but not solely) by longer-term rates of return and satisfaction, respectively. Begin by classifying the housing stock in a metropolitan area into 'quality sub-markets', sets of dwelling units that households perceive as closely substitutable, considering all the various attributes of the housing bundle, including spatially based attributes comprising its neighbourhood (see the chapter by Tu in this book for a detailed consideration of the concept of housing sub-markets).[12] Sub-markets can be arrayed from 'lowest' to 'highest' quality levels, with increasingly dissimilar comparisons of quality levels representing decreasing degrees of substitutability.[13] Each sub-market can be modelled as having its own supply and demand functions. It is beyond the scope of this chapter to consider the determinants of these functions; it will suffice here to emphasise only the mechanism of inter-sub-market repercussion, which is crucial for understanding the systemic process of neighbourhood change.

Supply into one sub-market (through new construction and/or net conversion of existing dwellings) will be influenced, among other things, by the relative (risk-adjusted) rate of return that developers and owners can expect to reap in this sub-market compared to others. Demand by households in any one sub-market will be influenced, among other things, by the relative market valuations (sales prices or equivalent capitalised rents) in close-substitute sub-markets. Shocks to either supply or demand in any one sub-market are transmitted sequentially throughout the sub-markets array by housing owners/developers altering their supply decisions in response to a new sub-market's relative pattern of expected rates of return, and by households altering their occupancy decisions in response to new relative market valuations across substitute sub-markets.

This model of segmented metropolitan housing markets can be usefully applied to elucidating the fundamental macro process behind neighbourhood dynamics (Rothenberg *et al.* 1991). Metropolitan housing sub-markets and neighbourhoods are not synonymous, but their relationship is straightforward. A sub-market is more than a neighbourhood or contiguous collection of them. It is comprised of all closely substitutable dwelling units, regardless of their location or propinquity. However, most neighbourhoods in the US and many other nations consist primarily of residences classified (by households, owners, and developers) in the same quality sub-market, for three reasons (Vandell 1995). First, economies of scale in construction lead developers to build homes in a subdivision or units in large rental estates that typically have similar physical characteristics. Second, the American (and, perhaps, other societies') willingness to pay premiums for class homogeneity, often backed up with various exclusionary land use regulations, limits diversity of housing types within small geographic areas (Grigsby *et al.* 1987). Third, because spatially based attributes contribute to a housing unit's quality and, hence, sub-market, units in close proximity will share many common attributes and thus tend to be classified in the same quality sub-market tautologically.

The foregoing suggests first that macro forces strongly affecting a particular housing sub-market will similarly affect the neighbourhoods where such a classification of dwelling is located; the greater the concentration of the given sub-market type in a neighbourhood, the greater the spatial impact there. Second, it suggests that macro forces originally impacting anywhere (either in terms of quality sub-market or geographic location) in the metropolitan area will eventually have some (albeit minimal, perhaps) impact everywhere, as the shock is transmitted in progressively damped severity across sub-markets (and the neighbourhoods where they are predominantly represented) of increasingly dissimilar substitutability.

As illustration, consider the following scenario. Developers speculate by building neighbourhoods comprising a number of high-quality sub-market homes on undeveloped land at the periphery of the given urbanised area (Galster & Rothenberg 1991). Should this increase in supply exceed the increase in demand for the high-quality sub-market (say, due to growth of high-income households in the metropolitan area), there will be a net decline in the market valuations and rate of return associated with such dwellings, at least for some period. Some households who previously would have chosen not to occupy the high-quality sub-market now would do so, as affordability has risen from their perspective.[14] Concomitantly, these declines in actual (and expected) rates of return would provide incentives for owners of pre-existing (especially rental) dwellings in the high-quality sub-market to downgrade the quality of their units to take advantage of comparatively superior rates of return in the somewhat lesser-quality sub-market(s). They typically accomplish this by passive under-maintenance: investing insufficient upkeep to maintain the dwelling in its original sub-market. These adjustments by households and suppliers jointly work toward re-establishing the initial rates of return in the high-quality sub-market but simultaneously reduce those in the lower-quality one(s). There, demand has now fallen (from some erstwhile occupants choosing instead a superior quality sub-market) and supply has risen (from some owners downgrading from higher quality sub-markets), thereby driving down market valuations. An adjustment process on both supply and demand sides of the market ensues analogous to that above, but disequilibrating forces are transmitted still farther down the sub-market quality array. At every step, the magnitude of inter-sub-market repercussion will depend on a host of elasticity-influencing factors implicit in the aggregate profiles of households (e.g. degree of positive social attachments to their neighbourhood, preferences for structural compared to neighbourhood components, risk aversion) and housing suppliers (e.g. cost of converting structures, expectations about duration of altered rates of returns, risk aversion).

As the system as a whole adjusts to eliminate large inter-sub-market differentials in rates of return, the model predicts a series of changes in demographic and physical attributes of neighbourhoods constituting sub-markets. There is a tendency in every sub-market where demand and/or supply has been altered for the least competitive neighbourhoods to evince: (1) an in-migration of households of somewhat lower means than the typical residents who left (called 'income succession'), and (2) a decline in the physical quality of the dwellings; in the extreme, dilapidation and even abandonment may occur in the neighbourhoods where the lowest-quality sub-market predominates. The new construction of high-quality dwellings in excess of household demand for such rendered an array of somewhat lower-quality neighbourhoods *relatively* less attractive to households, and less expensive. This generated altered flows of resources (occupancy patterns by households, financial resources by owners) that ultimately changed *absolutely* the population and housing attributes of these neighbourhoods.[15]

The dominance of external forces of change

What I wish to stress about the scenario described above is that forces originating outside of them triggered alterations to existing neighbourhoods.[16] Although this particular scenario involved speculative new construction as the initial shock, equally powerful macro process dynamics can be produced by such things as metropolitan immigration or emigration, technological changes, new transportation infrastructure, alterations in taxes, utility costs, a wide range of public policies, and shifts in the household income distribution. These forces external to a particular neighbourhood may well lead those controlling resources flowing into it to change their decisions, based on the connections described by the quality sub-market array of the metropolitan housing market. Thus, the most fundamental sorts of neighbourhood change are *externally induced.*[17] This is not to say that, once initiated, change cannot become cumulative or self-fulfilling.

Micro processes of neighbourhood change

Once triggered by macro process, the dynamic of neighbourhood adjustment is often non-linear, even discontinuous: what I call a threshold effect.[18] There are four distinct, not mutually exclusive, mechanisms suggested by theory through which thresholds may be produced: collective socialisation, contagion, gaming, and preference models.[19] The first two rely upon collective actions and social intercourse to create thresholds; the other two involve more atomistic attitudes and behaviours. One can analyse: behaviour of households to move out through collective socialisation, gaming, and preference models; behaviour of households to move in through gaming models; and behaviour of residents, owners, and business people who remain in the neighbourhood through collective socialisation, gaming and contagion models.

Collective socialisation theories focus on the role that social groups exert on shaping an individual's attitudes, values and behaviours (e.g. Levine 1971; Weber 1978). Such an effect can occur to the degree that: (1) the individual comes in social contact with the group, and (2) the group can exert more powerful threats or inducement to conform to its positions than competing groups. These two preconditions may involve the existence of a threshold. Given the importance of interpersonal contact in enforcing conformity, if the individuals constituting the group in question were scattered over urban space, they would be less likely to be able either to convey their positions effectively to others with whom they might come in contact or to exert much pressure to conform. It is only when a group reaches some critical mass of density or power over a predefined area that it is likely to become effective in shaping the behaviours of others. Past this threshold, as more members are recruited, the group's power to sanction non-conformists probably grows nonlinearly. This is especially likely when the position of the group becomes so dominant as to become normative in the area.[20]

The basic tenet of contagion models is that if decision makers live in a community where some of their neighbours exhibit non-conforming behaviours, they will be more likely to adopt these behaviours themselves. In this way, social problems are believed to be contagious, spread through peer influence. Crane (1991) proposes a formal contagion model to explain the incidence and spread of social problems. He contends that the key implication of the contagion model is that there may be critical levels of incidence of social problems in neighbourhoods. He states that if

> 'the incidence of problems stays below a critical point, the frequency or prevalence of the problem tends to gravitate toward some relatively low-level equilibrium. But if the incidence surpasses a critical point, the process will spread explosively. In other words, an epidemic may occur, raising the incidence to an equilibrium at a much higher level' (p. 1227).

Gaming models assume that, in many decisional situations involving neighbourhoods, the costs and benefits of alternative courses of action are uncertain, depending on how many other actors choose various alternatives. The individual's expected payoff of an alternative varies, however, depending on the number or proportion of others who make a decision before the given actor does. Thus, the concept of a threshold amount of observed prior action is central in this type of model. The well-known prisoners' dilemma is the simplest form of gaming model (Schelling 1978), but more sophisticated variants have been developed and applied to neighbourhood change processes (Granovetter 1978; Granovetter & Soong 1986). As illustration, consider the situation of a dilapidated neighbourhood for which the market is signalling potential gains in property values were its owners to improve their properties as a group. But individual owners may believe that they will not earn back the value of their marginal investment if they were to upgrade but no others followed suit. A conservative gaming strategy of behaving to minimise maximum prospective loss, regardless of what others may do, will lead many owners to refrain from upgrading first. Only if a threshold proportion of owners were to upgrade would these sceptics be convinced to upgrade (Taub, Taylor & Dunham 1984).

Preference models claim that actors in a residential environment will respond if the aggregate behaviour of others (or an exogenous event) raises an undesirable neighbourhood attribute above the level they find tolerable. An endogenous process can be triggered once the attribute reaches the critical threshold. The trigger occurs because actors in a neighbourhood are assumed to have different tolerance levels, with the least tolerant responding first. If additional change in the neighbourhood attribute results from the course of action taken in response to the initial event by those with the lowest tolerance level, the new level of the neighbourhood attribute may now be above the tolerance level of some of the less tolerant remaining actors. The process may continue with new rounds of attribute change and actor adjustment until the process is completed. At the extreme, the process may end when all the original actors in a neighbourhood have responded. The theoretical development of preference models has focused on changes in a neighbourhood's racial composition, though extensions to preferences for other sorts of neighbourhood attributes are straightforward.[21]

Uncertainty over the origin of thresholds should not obscure the point that the dynamic of neighbourhood adjustment initiated by macro process is not necessarily swift, smooth, or continuous. Micro processes introduce considerable complexity and uncertainty about adjustments. In some cases, neighbourhoods will be extremely slow to adjust; in other cases they will adjust spasmodically if they began near their threshold point. Macro process may induce a few households to change neighbourhoods, but if the movers' race or class matters significantly to households in either origin or destination neighbourhoods the adjustments associated with micro sorting processes may go far beyond what would have been predicted at the macro level.

Neighbourhood change and social efficiency

The foregoing discussion implies that changes in the flows of resources into neighbourhoods are not likely to produce socially efficient outcomes. At least four reasons come to bear: externalities, gaming, expectations, and inadequate pricing of attributes.

Because the act of consuming neighbourhood can change its attributes directly and indirectly, and such changes affect the decisional calculus of other consumer/producers, the act can be thought of as generating externalities. The choice of a minority to move into an all-white occupied neighbourhood imposes externalities on the bigots there. The choice of a property owner to repair the façade provides external benefits to neighbours. Because such external costs and benefits do not accrue to the decision maker, a sub-optimal amount of the activity is chosen.

The earlier discussion of gaming is also once again relevant here. With lack of certainty about the decisions of other consumers/producers in the neighbourhood, yet dependency of one's payoffs from alternative choices dependent upon such, autonomous decision makers are likely to adopt strategies that do not produce the greatest good for the collective. The unwillingness to renovate dilapidated buildings in an area until other investors do so first is a classic example.

Expectations are, of course, imperfect and prone to major errors. But this in itself does not imply a systematic bias toward inefficient choices. Rather, expectations about the future may prove to be so 'certain' in the view of the decision maker that the resulting choice encourages the expectation to transpire. This is the famous 'self-fulfilling prophecy' phenomenon. An illustration is panic selling of homes. Because of some anticipated neighbourhood change, several homeowners become convinced that property values will fall rapidly. They therefore try to sell their homes quickly, offering a discount. But the rash of 'For Sale' signs and the rumours that these homes are selling cheaply convinces other owners in the neighbourhood that, indeed, values are on the way down. As they join in the attempt to unload their properties, panic ensues and prices do, as some prophesied, drop precipitously. The sorts of prices produced by these self-fulfilling prophecy dynamics are unlikely to allocate resources efficiently. Instead of accurately capitalising the underlying quality (and replacement cost of the dwellings) in the neighbourhood, these artificially-deflated prices encourage purchase by owners with less personal financial means. These owners are likely to invest less in home maintenance and repair activities than their higher-income forebears (Galster 1987), thereby shortening the useful lifetimes of these valuable assets.

Lastly, I explained above how certain attributes of the neighbourhood, especially those associated with the sentimental and social-interactive dimensions, could not be evaluated well by potential consumers/producers not yet located in a given neighbourhood, compared with those located there for some time. This divergence in information creates an agency problem in which inefficient transactions are likely to occur. Owners attempting to sell or rent their properties will have a bias toward disguising any undesirable attributes – and not discounting the price appropriately – of the neighbourhood that may not be known to prospective buyers or renters. This means that the latter group will make inefficient choices: they would have chosen a neighbourhood offering a superior quality of life for the money had they but been fully informed.

Implications for neighbourhood regeneration policy

Space permits only brief reference to some salient neighbourhood policy implications from the foregoing.[22] First, thresholds imply a need for careful targeting of policy. Interventions concentrated on neighbourhoods poised on the brink of incipient, catastrophic decline represent a wiser allocation than spreading scarce public resources more evenly across an array of neighbourhoods. As illustration, my reading of the US empirical work on the effects of concentrated poverty suggests that a variety of social problems escalate when the neighbourhood poverty rate exceeds 20% (Galster, forthcoming).

Second, decision-makers' relativistic comparisons among neighbourhoods raise the spectre of zero-sum interventions. In a stagnant metropolis with little household or income growth, a massive public initiative to raise dramatically the physical quality of one depressed neighbourhood will erode the fortunes of all neighbourhoods over which the regenerated community leapfrogs. Inasmuch as the relative quality of such leapfrogged neighbourhoods have declined, investors and households with means will switch their resources from them into the regenerated area, leading to absolute decline of the former set. Several *caveats* are however in order. The consequences of regeneration of low-quality neighbourhoods will more likely have positive-sum consequences to the degree that there is: (1) an increase (decrease) in the number of households with rising (falling) real incomes in the metropolitan area; (2) a substantial share of subsidised, means-tested housing provided in the regenerated area; (3) social housing providing the dominant form of supply in the leapfrogged neighbourhoods; and (4) a limited number of neighbourhoods leapfrogged because many are regenerated concomitantly.

Summary and conclusion

In this chapter I have attempted to build upon the insights on the economics of neighbourhood provided two decades ago by Duncan Maclennan. I proposed that the urban neighbourhood could be usefully defined as the bundle of spatially based attributes associated with clusters of residences, sometimes in conjunction with other land uses. This bundle of attributes is multidimensional, consisting of everything from structures and topography to demography, public services, and social interactions.

The stock of attributes comprising neighbourhood at any moment is the result of past and current flows of households and resources – financial, social-psychological, and time – into and out of the space in question. Four key users make decisions affecting these flows: households, businesses, property owners, and local government; they thus can be viewed as producers of neighbourhood. However, these same actors play dual roles because they potentially reap benefits from the consumption of this complex commodity called neighbourhood. To understand the factors and processes that influence these production and consumption decisions is to uncover the roots of neighbourhood change.

Multi-dimensional commodities are common, but the neighbourhood offers a variety of significant idiosyncrasies that suggest the following insights into these decisions.

- Different neighbourhood attributes vary in their durability. Investors therefore must take a long-term strategy with durable features, with concomitant reliance upon imperfect and socially influenced expectations. Self-fulfilling prophecies and gaming strategies that result yield inefficient outcomes.

- Social-interactive and sentimental attributes of neighbourhood are not well-priced because of information asymmetries. The resultant agency problem leads to inefficient outcomes.

- Consumers evaluate neighbourhood attributes relatively. This provides the vehicle by which changes elsewhere in the metropolitan area can lead to changes in the given neighbourhood. This implies that the prime origins of change in a particular neighbourhood are located outside that neighbourhood.

- The act of households or property owners consuming neighbourhood attributes typically changes the attributes directly and indirectly. This means that attributes of neighbourhood are mutually causal over time. Because this process generates externalities imposed on other consumers/producers operating in the neighbourhood, inefficient outcomes are manifested.

The foregoing suggests an unmistakable case of market failure. For a variety of reasons inherently associated with the concept of neighbourhood, changes in flows of households and resources across space will produce socially inefficient outcomes. There is thus a *prima facie* case for some sort of collective intervention, whether it comes from informal social processes, non-profit, community-based organisations, or the governmental sector.

Informal social processes might take the form of sanctions and rewards meted out by neighbours that are designed to enforce compliance with collective norms regarding civil behaviour and building upkeep. Community-based organisations might politically organise, establish neighbourhood bonds of mutual solidarity, or foment a positive public image of the neighbourhood. Unfortunately, the foregoing two options operate at too small a spatial scale to affect the macro process producing neighbourhood change.

Governments might offer financial incentives, regulations, and investments of infrastructure and public services, and target them to neighbourhoods at crucial threshold points. In concert, these actions can help alter perceptions of key neighbourhood investors, provide compensatory resource flows, minimise destructive gaming behaviours, internalise externalities, and moderate expectations, thereby defusing self-fulfilling prophecies. On the other hand, massive regeneration efforts may run afoul of zero-sum neighbourhood effects unless particular criteria are met.

Acknowledgments

I am grateful for the insightful suggestions provided on an earlier draft by Glen Bramley, Kenneth Gibb, Ade Kearns, Tony O'Sullivan, and Gavin Wood, that substantially improved this work. Some of the material in this chapter originally appeared in *Urban Studies*, whose permission to reproduce is acknowledged.

Notes

(1) Similar perspectives were also developed in roughly contemporaneous works by Galster (1987), and Rothenberg *et al.* (1991), that expanded the analysis theoretically and empirically.

(2)   For comprehensive reviews of the social scientific literature on neighbourhood, see Hunter (1979), Schwirian (1983), Hallman (1984), and Temkin & Rohe (1996).

(3)   Von Boventer (1978) and Maclennan (1982) have been especially incisive in analysing the implications of this component.

(4)   This was the salient factor determining household location choice in the earliest economists' models (Maclennan 1982).

(5)   For more on this dimension, see Hunter (1979), Schoenberg (1980), and Temkin & Rohe (1996).

(6)   For more on this dimension, see Warren (1975), Schoenberg (1980), Fischer (1982), and Warren & Warren (1977).

(7)   Visitors may also consume neighbourhoods in which they do not reside by the act of working, shopping, or seeking entertainment there. For simplicity I omit them as key consumers when analysing the main determinants of neighbourhood change.

(8(This point has also been stressed by Leven *et al.* (1976); Maclennan (1982).

(9)   For critical reviews of theory and evidence on hedonic indices, see Maclennan (1977b; 1982); Rothenberg *et al.* (1991).

(10)   Although some attributes may have associated with them an absolute minimum threshold value, below which no price will ever be bid, such as the case of air quality.

(11)   This model was originally developed by Rothenberg *et al.* (1991). In housing markets dominated by state production and allocation mechanisms, the model has more circumscribed relevance as a tool for understanding neighbourhood change.

(12)   Maclennan (1982) suggested that 'sub-markets be adopted as a working hypothesis', based on the durability, multi-dimensional complexity, and spatial fixity of housing. He did not specify that quality be the metric for segmentation, however. See Malpezzi (this volume) for how hedonic indices can be employed in market segmentation studies.

(13)   This proposition is true for both demanders and suppliers; owners of existing units find it increasingly costly to modify their dwellings as the quality change implied grows.

(14)   The precise response would be governed by the cross-price elasticity of demand between the sub-markets in question (Rothenberg *et al.* 1991).

(15)   The astute reader will recognise this scenario as producing what often has been labelled 'filtering'. For more complete analyses, see Maclennan (1982) and Galster & Rothenberg (1991).

(16)   A similar position was articulated in Maclennan (1982), Grigsby *et al.* (1987), Galster (1987) and Temkin & Rohe (1996).

(17)   This stands in contrast to some who argue that the internal institutional and social structures of the neighbourhood are central to understanding its trajectory (Schoenberg 1980).

(18)   This was also recognised by Maclennan (1982).

(19) For a review, see Quercia & Galster (2000); for new evidence, see Galster *et al.* (2000). Meen (this volume) discusses a related set of 'complexity models' yielding similar conclusions to those forwarded here.

(20) More modern sociological treatises closely related to collective socialisation also suggest thresholds, such as Wilson's (1987) contention that as a critical mass of middle-class families leave the inner-city, low-income blacks left behind become isolated from the positive role models that the erstwhile dominant class offered. Economists also have developed several mathematical treatises involving collective socialisation effects in which thresholds often emerge as solutions to complex decision problems under certain assumptions (Akerlof 1980; Galster 1987; Brock & Durlauf, forthcoming).

(21) Seminal work in this vein has been produced by Schelling (1971; 1978), Schnare & MacRae (1975), Von Boventer (1978) and Taub *et al.* (1984). Variants are explored by Meen in Chapter 6.

(22) For deeper analyses, see Galster (1987), Grigsby *et al.* (1987), Rothenberg *et al.* (1991), Temkin & Rohe (1996) and Quercia & Galster (2000).

10

Access to Home Ownership in the United States: the Impact of Changing Perspectives on Constraints to Tenure Choice

Joseph Gyourko

Introduction

Access to home ownership is an important social and economic issue in many countries around the world. However, the factors determining that access vary across countries. This chapter reviews and discusses the marked change in emphasis in US research and policy circles on what constitutes the relevant budget constraint facing households making a tenure choice decision.[1]

Specifically, the American focus has shifted from permanent income to (non-human) current wealth as the binding constraint on access to home ownership. This change has had a number of important impacts that have influenced both the academic literature and US public policy surrounding home ownership. Given that Duncan Maclennan has played a prominent role in both the academic and policy worlds, this makes the topic particularly appropriate for inclusion in this volume.

The first impact of the change has been on research into tenure choice generally and has involved a recasting of the driving forces in theoretical models of tenure transition. Rather than permanent income and the relative user costs of ownership and renting driving the decision, a new characterisation has been adopted following the work of Jones (1995), in which current net worth and the asset price of the home drive the transition from renting to owning. This new perspective is commented on more fully below. Empirical work by Jones (1989) and Linneman & Wachter (1989) confirms that current non-human wealth is extremely important in explaining tenure differences across households and that it dominates permanent income as an explanatory factor.

The second prominent impact of the new view of budget constraints in tenure choice has been an important change in how racial differentials in home ownership rates in America are viewed. Recent research using micro data finds that racial differentials in home ownership narrow considerably, or are eliminated altogether for the mean household, in specifications with good household wealth controls. This is particularly relevant in the US context, where large aggregate differences of 25 percentage points in home ownership propensities by race still exist. Building upon this work, Charles & Hurst (forthcoming) recently concluded that it is racial differences in mortgage application propensities that account for the bulk of the black/white difference in home ownership outcomes. Racial differences in income, in family structure, and in intergenerational transfers involving parental wealth help explain the mortgage applications gap. Hence, wealth – this time of parents – again plays a critical role. Naturally, this has important implications for policy makers interested in narrowing the aggregate racial gap in home ownership in the United States.

The third major impact of the new perspective that current wealth is the primary binding constraint on the transition to home ownership has been on our understanding of the affordability of owner occupation. The dominance of wealth over income in empirical tenure choice studies strongly suggests that relaxing down-payment constraints, not policies that help households meet payment-to-income requirements (e.g., via lower interest rates), is what is needed to expand home ownership in America. Very low down-payment loans have proliferated in the United States recently, and the overall home ownership rate has increased. This is not to say that this is good policy, as the default experience for these loans is not yet known and has not been cycle tested. Nevertheless, the availability of low down-payment loans has been influenced by research that has helped change our perspective on what really constrains the transition from renting to home ownership.

The remainder of this chapter is organised as follows. The next section introduces and discusses the new theoretical developments that are associated with the view that current wealth is the key constraint to tenure choice. It includes a brief discussion of the key initial empirical work testing the theory. This is followed by a section focused on the impacts of the new view on our understanding of racial differences in home ownership in the United States. Home ownership affordability issues are raised in the penultimate section. Finally, there is a brief summary and conclusion.

Constraints to tenure choice – theory and empirical evidence

The literature on tenure choice is a long and venerable one because of its importance in housing economics.[2] The traditional model of tenure choice is one in which the rent/own decision is a function of the relative user costs of housing services obtained by owning versus renting and of permanent income, along with life cycle traits that reflect utility-based preferences for owner occupancy.

Rosen (1979) provides an especially clear elucidation of this model in which households pick the tenure mode offering them the greatest utility. Utility from ownership is given by

$$V_o = f(p_o, p_x, y) \tag{10.1}$$

where V_o is the indirect utility function conditional on owning, p_o is the user cost (or price per unit) of housing services associated with ownership, p_x is the price of all other goods (with x being the numeraire good), and y is permanent income. Analogously,

$$V_r = f(p_r, p_x, y) \tag{10.2}$$

where V_r is the indirect utility achieved conditional on renting and p_r is the user cost (or price per unit) of housing services associated with renting.

A household chooses to own if $V_o > V_r$. Empirical implementation of the model typically is done as part of a binary choice modelled in equation (10.3):

$$V^* = V_o - V_r = v(p_o/p_r, y, z) \tag{10.3}$$

in which the price of housing services is put in terms of the numeraire good and z is included to capture household traits that might affect the utility associated with a particular tenure mode independent of the quantity of housing services actually consumed. Equation (10.3) then is expressed as a likelihood function, with a logit or probit model estimated.

Underlying this structure is some uncertainty or imperfection that creates a preference for one tenure mode over another.[3] The lumpiness of housing, incomplete rental markets, and non-neutral taxation have all been offered as candidates for why tenure preferences would arise.[4] For our purposes, it is noteworthy that permanent income is the essential constraint on the tenure decision in this model. With housing being lumpy and its demand essentially determined from a multi-period optimisation of housing consumption, if households are not liquidity constrained, then some threshold level of permanent income is required. Hence, in the absence of liquidity constrained households, higher permanent income is expected to be associated with a higher probability of owning.

Jones (1995) provided a different perspective, arguing that tax non-neutralities in particular do not provide a solid foundation upon which to base a theory of tenure choice.[5] Building on a series of primarily empirical studies indicating that many households were credit constrained,[6] on data showing that a very large fraction of American and Canadian households past a certain age were owners and remained owners even in the face of substantial changes in incomes, interest rates, and the like, and on the theoretical implications of newly developed asset pricing models with illiquid durable goods,[7] he suggested that there was a fundamental preference for ownership. In this view, stable households that are not especially mobile across housing markets are presumed to receive higher utility from ownership (holding constant the amount of housing services across tenure, of course).

Who rents in this world? The answer is primarily younger, less permanently formed households, those households with little wealth available to make a down-payment, and those households with a relatively undiversified portfolio of highly leveraged, illiquid, risky assets. When do these households switch to owner occupancy? They change tenancy when the net change in their utility from switching is non-negative. In an influential paper on asset pricing by Grossman & Laroque (1990), the agent purchases a home only after a threshold amount of a riskless, liquid asset has been accumulated.[8]

Current liquid wealth, not the wealth associated with human capital embedded in permanent income, is the essential constraint to home ownership in this world. The difference in utility between owning and renting can be written as

$$V^{*} = v(w, p_{h}, z) \qquad (10.4)$$

where w is the net wealth of the household, p_{h} is the stock price of housing (not the relative prices of a unit of the service flows), and z captures demographics that reflect how permanently formed and/or mobile the household is. Relative user costs are omitted in the pure form of Jones' (1995) model, as he argues that owned versus rental units are weak substitutes at best.[9] This is a strong assumption that has not been fully accepted by some researchers in the field. Indeed, much subsequent empirical work includes a control for the relative price of owning versus renting. This specification issue has not affected the key finding that, in fact, wealth constraints dominate income constraints in terms of their practical impact.[10]

While there are other interesting conceptual issues underlying the differences in these theoretical perspectives on tenure choice, we now turn to the recent empirical evidence, as it is that which motivates the changing views on race and home ownership and on housing affordability discussed in the introduction. While there were indications from earlier work that wealth constraints might be relevant to the tenure choice or tenure transition process,[11] Jones (1989) and Linneman & Wachter (1989) provided direct evidence that down-payment requirements themselves were not only very important, but dominant factors empirically.[12]

Jones (1989) estimated the probability of owning as a function of household net worth (w), permanent income (y_p, itself estimated), illiquid asset holdings (ia), and a set of demographic controls (z) as in equation (10.5)

$$\Pr(\text{Own}) = g(w, y_p, ia, z) \tag{10.5}$$

Importantly, net worth (w) was specified as a series of dummy variables indicating by how much household net worth was less than or greater than house prices in the relevant market area. Illiquid asset holdings were included to test for the presence of a Grossman & Laroque (1990) and Plaut (1987) effect whereby households need to hedge housing price risk. The models were estimated on Canadian cross-sectional data, focusing on younger households.[13]

Linneman & Wachter (1989) pursued a similar approach using US data,[14] but modelled their constraints based on the Federal National Mortgage Association (FNMA or Fannie Mae) and Federal Home Loan Mortgage Corporation (FHLMC or Freddie Mac) underwriting criteria for conventional loans. That is, they used the fact that these two agencies require mortgage insurance before they purchase any loan on a property with a loan-to-value (LTV) ratio of greater than 80% to guide their specification of the borrower's wealth constraint. This 20% equity down-payment requirement implies that the maximum home purchase price that satisfies the underwriting wealth criterion is five times household net worth. The authors then devised a series of variables to reflect the degree by which a household was wealth constrained. Similar measures were included to capture the extent to which the household was constrained by income-related underwriting requirements of Fannie Mae and Freddie Mac.[15] Linneman & Wachter (1989) then estimated their models using the Federal Reserve Board's 1977 *Survey of Consumer Credit* and its 1983 *Survey of Consumer Finances*. They restricted their sample to recent movers in both cross-sections.

The results from both of these papers strongly indicated that wealth constraints dominated income constraints in terms of influencing tenure status. Stated differently, the negative impact of being wealth constrained on the probability of ownership was far greater than that of being income constrained. A representative result from Linneman & Wachter (1989) is that the probability of ownership was about 32% lower among highly income-constrained households than among unconstrained households *ceteris paribus*, but this pales in significance to the impact of being highly wealth constrained. For example, they report that highly wealth constrained house-holds were 61% less likely to own than otherwise identical unconstrained households. This is an extremely large impact for a country in which just over 60% of all households own. Essentially, if an American household is wealth constrained as determined by standard underwriting criteria, the probability that it owns is quite low in absolute terms – even if it has all or many of the demographic traits such as being well-educated, over 35 years old, and a married head with minor children in the home that are typically associated with owner occupancy.

In every sample examined in either study, the adverse impact of being highly wealth constrained exceeds that of being highly income constrained. Linne-man & Wachter (1989) suggest that this is due to the fact that if a family can-not make the required down-payment on its desired home, its most viable alternative is to rent. However, this is not the case if the family is income constrained, but not wealth constrained. In this situation, the family can reduce its loan-to-value ratio below 80% in order to satisfy the payment-to-income criteria. This explanation that there is another alternative to renting when the household is income constrained, but not wealth constrained, is intuitively appealing.

Other subsequent empirical work has confirmed these initial results.[16] This research has had significant practical consequences; the increase in low down-payment mortgages, some with loan-to-value ratios in excess of 95%, in the mid- to late 1990s in the US is testimony to this.[17] There is a broad (if informal) consensus among leading housing researchers and policy officials that the substantial increase in home ownership rates in the 1990s from 60 to 68% at least partially reflects the easing of underlying wealth constraints.[18]

Thus, it is now clear to all that liquefiable wealth is the critical factor influ-encing access to home ownership – for Americans and Canadians, at least. And, it is equally obvious that this is due to equity-related needs associ-ated with down-payment requirements. This immediately suggests that savings behaviour and savings ability, not merely current income and the level of interest rates, are important factors in determining who can own their residence. Moreover, the savings history of parents, not just younger households, could be important because of the extent of intergenerational transfers. As the next two sections highlight, these factors are crucial to our understanding of racial differences in ownership propensities in the United States and to our understanding of what really drives housing affordability.

Wealth constraints and racial differences in ownership in the United States

Large aggregate racial differences in home ownership propensities have persisted over a long period in the United States. Decennial census data from 1970 showed that 61.2% of households with white heads owned versus 38.3% of households with black heads, so that the percentage of white households owning was about 1.6 times that of black households. By 1990, ownership rates had increased roughly proportionately for both races so that the percentage of white owners was still nearly 1.6 times that of black owners (69.4% versus 44.5%). These differences are of interest for at least three reasons: (a) the tax-favoured status of owner-occupied housing;[19] (b) the important role that home equity plays in the creation and retention of household wealth;[20] and (c) the social benefits that many people attach to owning one's home.[21]

The empirical work discussed in the previous section is relevant to this issue because it raises the possibility that controlling for wealth could substantially narrow the estimated racial difference in the probability of owning. Aggregate-level racial differences in net worth are known to be substantial. Using data from the 1994 wave of the *Michigan Panel Study of Income Dynamics*, Charles & Hurst (forthcoming) calculate that the mean wealth or net worth of black households is $43 365 versus $220 428 for white households. Skewness in the distribution of wealth certainly affects the means, but the wealth differential is large for the median black and white households, too. Specifically, the median black household's net worth is $9435, while that for the median white household is $77 371.[22]

Thus, racial differences in wealth should be controlled for using micro data to see if this might help account for the large aggregate racial difference in the propensity to own. Results in Linneman & Wachter (1989) suggested that this might be very important. In fact, when evaluated at the mean values of the relevant parameters, Linneman & Wachter's (1989) logistic function results indicate that there are no racial differences in ownership rates *ceteris paribus*. That is, once wealth is carefully controlled for, an otherwise typical household with a black head is no less likely to own than an otherwise observationally equivalent household with a white head.

Gyourko, Linneman & Wachter (1999) investigated more fully the possibility that the entire aggregate racial difference in ownership rates is due to racial differences in wealth that allow white people to meet down-payment requirements more easily. Using three cross-sections of the Federal Reserve Board wealth surveys from 1962, 1977, and 1983, they estimated a series of models that allowed them to measure racial differences in ownership probabilities for households away from the mean sample values.

Wealth constraints in their paper were developed following the 'regulatory rule' perspective adopted in Linneman & Wachter (1989). Thus, a household is considered wealth constrained if its net worth is insufficient to fund fully the down-payment implied by standard secondary market agency underwriting criteria for the purchase of loans. Given the 20% equity requirement imposed by Fannie Mae and Freddie Mac before mortgage insurance is needed, this means a household is categorised as constrained if the value of the home typically owned by other households with the same socio-economic trait set is more than five times net worth.[23] In addition, this study included two other sets of variables to help control for the degree of wealth constraint (i.e., whether the household is barely constrained or hugely constrained in terms of its wealth shortfall, with unconstrained households having a zero shortfall) and for the degree of wealth 'cushion' (i.e., for unconstrained households, a measure of how much net worth exceeds the down-payment requirement of the household).[24]

Gyourko, Linneman & Wachter (1999) then estimated binomial logistic functions with all wealth constraint-related variables (and permanent income) interacted with a race dummy. Consistent with previous research, the results showed that wealth constraint status had a huge impact on the probability of owning. For an unconstrained household with a white head and other traits typical of an owner-occupier, the propensity to own was estimated to be 96% in the 1962 cross-section. Changing the wealth constraint status of that household is estimated to reduce the probability of ownership by 51 percentage points to 45%. For the analogous minority-headed household, the impact of being constrained is even larger at 80 percentage points (i.e., the probability of owning drops from 100% to 20%).

However, the racial differences in implied ownership probabilities among unconstrained households are very small. The top panel of Table 10.1 reproduces results from Gyourko, Linneman & Wachter (1999) for the earliest and latest years they studied. Among unconstrained households, minorities are estimated to own at slightly higher propensities than their white counterparts,[25] but the differences are quite small and the probabilities are quite high for all. This is the result implied in Linneman & Wachter (1989) when the regression findings are evaluated at sample means. Stated differently, there are no economically meaningful *ceteris paribus* differences in ownership rates among white and minority households who possess sufficient wealth to meet down-payment and closing cost requirements associated with standard mortgage underwriting criteria.

The bottom panel of Table 10.1 shows this is not the case for wealth-constrained households. Among this group, white households own at much higher rates than observationally equivalent minority households. The difference was 25 percentage points in the 1962 sample and 12 percentage points in the 1983 sample. These are not only large differences, but it is quite relevant to minority households as they are over-represented among constrained households. That is, these differentials apply to about one-third of the white households in the samples and to well over one-half the minority households.

Thus, racial differences in wealth cannot account for all of the racial difference in ownership propensities. Moreover, the fact that many wealth-constrained households own, especially those where the head is white, suggests some type of systematic measurement error exists. Households categorised as constrained tend to have very low measured net worths – barely above zero. This indicates that households with low measured wealth have greater access to down-payment resources than is captured by household wealth in the Federal Reserve Board surveys.

Other research suggests that intergenerational transfers from parents are a logical source of such unmeasured resources.[26] Not only are such transfers

Table 10.1   Predicted ownership probabilities and differential implied probabilities of ownership by race.

	1962	1983
Typical unconstrained head		
Minority head	1.00	0.97
White head	0.96	0.91
Differential implied probability	0.04	0.06
Typical constrained head		
Minority head	0.20	0.17
White head	0.45	0.29
Differential implied probability	−0.25	−0.12

Source: Gyourko, Linneman & Wachter (1999), Table 6. See their paper for the details and definitions of the underlying reference households.

Note: Gyourko, Linneman & Wachter (1999) used a white versus non-white characterisation of race. More detailed racial categories were experimented with (including a black versus non-black breakdown), but none of their essential results were changed.

large, there is no doubt that the parents of young minority households tend to have much lower net worths than the parents of young white households. While Gyourko, Linneman & Wachter (1999) speculate that racial differences in transfers from parents could account for the racial differences in ownership rates among constrained households, the fact is that their results cannot be thoroughly convincing as to the direction of causality because they arise from a cross-sectional analysis.

The recent study by Charles & Hurst (forthcoming) addresses these issues using the University of Michigan's *Panel Survey of Income Dynamics* to follow a sample of black and white renters over time. They analyse the factors causing the racial gap in housing transitions that occurs among their sample of renters. Importantly, they are able to investigate separately racial differences in the likelihood of applying for a mortgage and in the likelihood that a mortgage application is accepted or rejected. While there is a significant racial difference in the probability of having a mortgage application rejected, the authors find that this has very little explanatory power with respect to the much lower transition of black households to owner occupancy. Rather, the bulk of what they term the housing transitions gap is due to the fact that black people are far less likely to apply for mortgages in the first place. Their investigation then shows that differences in income, family structure, and in parental transfers to help with down-payments are the primary reasons for the applications gap. Thus, parental wealth, not just younger household wealth, should be considered when modelling the budget constraint to the tenure choice decision.

Just as the findings in Jones (1989, 1995) and Linneman & Wachter (1989) raised an important policy question regarding what was necessary to expand home ownership rates, those in Charles & Hurst (forthcoming) raise the same issue with respect to black households. There is a huge literature on discrimination in the mortgage market,[27] and while Charles & Hurst (forthcoming) do find evidence that lenders do not treat black and white households equally, it is wealth – either their own or of their parents – that appears to be so constraining for minorities. The evidence is more convincing now because it has shown up in panel data that can be exploited to identify more carefully the direction of causality.

Thus, finding ways of relaxing those constraints should be a priority for those who wish to address the aggregate racial difference in ownership probabilities. While discrimination in the lending market certainly should be stamped out wherever and whenever possible, policy makers and households should understand that that alone will do little to narrow the racial gap in ownership.

Implications for the affordability debate

In the 1980s, the affordability of single-family owner-occupied housing joined traditional issues such as housing quality and racial discrimination as a focus of housing policy debates in the United States. While an ageing population led many to predict rising home ownership rates during the decade, the aggregate ownership rate actually declined by 1 percentage point, marking a reversal of a trend dating back to the end of the Second World War.[28]

While concern over the affordability of owner occupation for lower- and middle-class households led to a national housing bill entitled the National Affordable Housing Act of 1990, the fact was (and still is) that what is meant by housing affordability is not precisely defined. However, as Linneman & Megbolugbe (1992) have noted, how affordability is defined can have important policy consequences.

Prior to the research findings on wealth constraining the transition to owner occupancy, interest rate policy was seen as the key to the affordability issue. This is implicit in the most widely known affordability index in the United States, which is published by the National Association of Realtors (NAR). This index is constructed such that an index value of 100 implies that the median income family qualifies for the median value home. Because interest rates are much more variable than income, changes in the NAR Housing Affordability Index over time primarily reflect changes in interest rates. This is evident in Fig. 10.1, reproduced from Gyourko & Tracy (1999). Whenever long-term mortgage rates are low, the NAR series signals excellent affordability conditions (and vice versa). Given the continued low long-term inter-

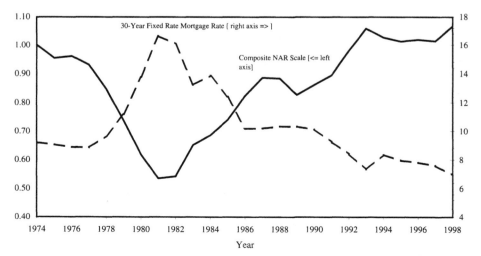

Fig. 10.1 National Association of Realtors (NAR) housing affordability indices. Source: Gyourko & Tracy (1999), Chart 1.

est rates in America, this series suggests that housing is now more affordable than at any time since 1974.

However, various economic changes including a substantial increase in the dispersion of income-by-skill group cast doubt as to whether it is sensible to focus solely on the affordability of the median-priced home. While lower interest rates certainly do reduce the income necessary to purchase a home, they do not directly reduce the down-payment-related requirement. Thus, consistent with the implications of the research cited above, the levels and growth rates of savings and incomes (in addition to house prices and interest rates) are key components of housing affordability.

Two articles by Gyourko & Linneman (1993) and Gyourko & Tracy (1999) try to use the insights of the new view of wealth constraints as the key to tenure choice to move beyond the NAR Housing Affordability Index. Using decennial census and *American Housing Survey* (AHS) data, Gyourko & Linneman (1993) tried to answer a simple question: is a home of a given quality from 10–15 years ago more affordable or less affordable today to a household similarly situated to the one that occupied the home then? To perform their analysis, they constructed unadjusted and quality-adjusted price indices for five types of homes. The latter series were developed using standard hedonic techniques described in their paper.

A first point to note from that research is that real house price appreciation varies significantly over time and across the house price distribution. That is, cheap and expensive homes have fared far differently over time in terms of their price growth. This is illustrated in Table 10.2. These data are for raw, unadjusted prices that do not hold constant the quality of the homes in the

Table 10.2   Real house price appreciation – US national data aggregate and average per annum (in parentheses) figures.

Percentile of the house price distribution	Time period		
	1960–74	1974–81	1981–89
10th	35.1	54.1	−38.1
	(2.2)	(6.4)	(−5.8)
25th	48.8	39.6	−28.7
	(2.9)	(4.9)	(−4.1)
50th	44.5	17.3	−16.8
	(2.7)	(2.3)	(−2.3)
75th	46.5	19.2	−1.5
	(2.8)	(2.5)	(−0.0)
90th	49.2	41.2	−2.0
	(2.9)	(5.1)	(−0.0)

Source: Gyourko & Linneman (1993), Table 4. Calculations made from decennial census and *American Housing Survey* data.

10th, 25th, 50th, 75th, and 90th percentiles of the house price distribution. It is clear that the 1980s witnessed a dramatic reversal in the earlier pattern of consistently positive real house price appreciation in the United States, with the percentage declines being especially large among lower valued homes. In fact, the drops in real value for the cheaper homes at or below the 50th percentile were so large that by 1989 their real prices had reverted to 1974 levels.

The constant quality price series estimated by Gyourko & Linneman (1993) then tell a different story.[29] Table 10.3 reproduces results that compare constant quality and unadjusted price appreciation for the different types of homes. Note that constant quality real price growth is significantly greater than the appreciation in actual (or unadjusted) prices for lower quality bundles.[30] Not only does this indicate that the raw price series may seriously misrepresent the affordability of a specific low- or moderate-quality unit over time, it also suggests that there may have been a serious erosion of housing quality among lower priced homes. Whether this was due to changes in demand fundamentals or to the inability of many lower income households to maintain their homes adequately after expending most of their wealth to purchase them is unknown. At a minimum, it raises the spectre of savings and wealth once again, importantly influencing the ability to own and to protect the equity in one's home.

Table 10.3 also shows that the pattern of actual versus constant quality prices is very different for more expensive and, presumably, higher quality homes. At the upper end of the price distribution, appreciation in the unadjusted series exceeds that for the constant quality series, suggesting that quality improvements can help account for the huge price growth. Consistent with much research in labour economics, Gyourko & Linneman (1993) also showed that real wages of the least-skilled workers (defined as those without a high school degree) had actually declined between 1960–1989. Combined, the constant quality price data and the earnings data suggested that households headed by low-skilled workers could afford to own single-family housing at the end of the 1980s only by having two earners or by reducing the quality of the home consumed (or both). Since there are limits to how far down the quality spectrum one can shift from the 10th or 25th percentile home, it seems likely that this is where the affordability problem has become most serious. These households simply cannot afford to save for a down-payment, and the data are at least suggestive that they may be allowing their housing capital to depreciate if they are able to become owners.

Gyourko & Linneman (1993) concluded that there was not a similar change in affordability conditions for the typical occupant of a home at or above the median quality. Wages and salaries for these earners were stagnant or grow-

Table 10.3 Constant-quality and unadjusted price appreciation: homes and trait bundles from various percentiles of the house price distribution.

	1974 trait bundles			Unadjusted prices		
	1974–1989 (%)	1974–peak (%)	Peak–1989 (%)	1974–1989 (%)	1974–peak (%)	Peak–1989 (%)
10th percentile						
Total appreciation	28.1	54.6	–17.2	–4.7	54.1	–38.1
Avg. annual appreciation	1.7	6.4	–2.3	–0.3	6.4	–5.8
25th percentile						
Total appreciation	13.1	20.2	–5.9	–0.5	39.6	–28.7
Avg. annual appreciation	0.8	4.7	–0.6	–0.0	4.9	–4.1
50th percentile						
Total appreciation	13.7	22.8	–7.5	–2.5	22.6	–20.4
Avg. annual appreciation	0.9	5.3	–0.7	–0.2	4.2	–2.3
75th percentile						
Total appreciation	4.4	29.2	–19.2	17.4	48.3	–20.1
Avg. annual appreciation	0.3	6.6	–1.9	1.1	10.4	–2.0
90th percentile						
Total appreciation	4.4	28.7	–18.9	38.3	41.7	–2.4
Avg. annual appreciation	0.3	6.5	–1.9	2.2	7.2	–0.2

Source: Gyourko & Linneman (1993), Table 6. Calculations made by the authors based on 1974–1989 *American Housing Surveys.*

Note: Calculations also made using trait bundles from 1989. The implications for quality changes are unaffected. See Gyourko & Linneman (1993) for the details.

ing, and the real prices of high quality, constant-quality housing bundles barely rose. Hence, the moderate or high quality home from the mid-1970s still is affordable to these households, even if the higher quality stock that has been built since then is not.

Gyourko & Tracy (1999) further examined the affordability issue by updating the analysis with data from the 1990s and by employing a quantile regression approach in addition to the mean regression approach standard in the literature. The quantile regression approach uses methodology similar to the mean regression approach, but relaxes the restriction that only average trait prices are used to construct the constant-quality price indices. That is, each individual price index (e.g. the one for the 25th percentile home) is constructed using its own trait prices. More specifically, the trait prices for the 25th percentile are selected so that 75% of actual home prices are higher than what one would predict based on the house traits and on the 25th percentile trait prices. In addition, 25% of actual house prices are lower than what one would predict based on the house traits and on the 25th percentile trait prices. Thus, if a trait such as bathrooms tends to contribute relatively more value to high-quality homes than to low-quality homes, then this will show up as differences between the quantile-specific price for bathrooms at the upper and lower ends of the house quality distribution.[31]

Figures 10.2, 10.3, and 10.4 reproduce Gyourko & Tracy's (1999) findings for the raw price series, for the constant quality series using the mean regression approach, and for the constant quality series using the quantile regression

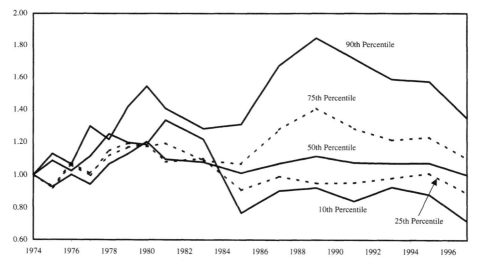

Fig. 10.2 Real house price distribution – unadjusted series. Source: Gyourko & Tracy (1999), Chart 5; underlying data are from the AHS national series.

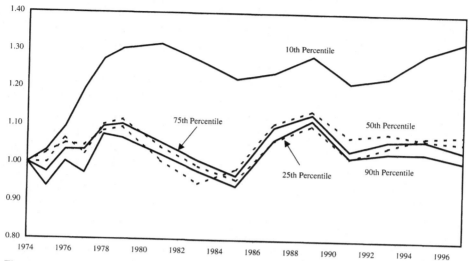

Fig. 10.3   Constant quality house price indices mean regression method. Source: Gyourko & Tracy (1999), Chart 6; series estimated by authors using the AHS national series.

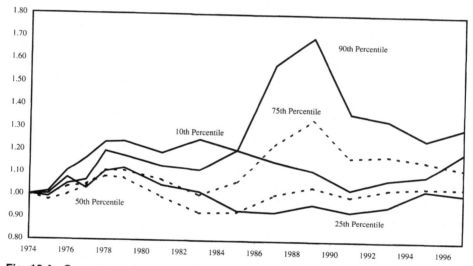

Fig. 10.4   Constant quality price indices quantile regression method. Source: Gyourko & Tracy (1999), Chart 7; series estimated by authors using the AHS national series.

approach. While the latter two approaches share many common features, there are some important differences in results in the upper and lower tails of the price distribution. In the upper tail, the quantile approach suggests there was more rapid real price growth between 1974 and 1997. While the average hedonic measure indicates that the 90th percentile constant quality price was only 1% higher in 1997 than in 1974, the quantile hedonic measure suggests the increase was 31%. Figure 10.2 indicates that the unadjusted series for the 90th percentile home was 35% higher in 1997 than in 1974. The implied increase in quality among higher-end homes looks to be considerably smaller when estimated using the quantile regression approach.

At the bottom of the price distribution, the average hedonic price index (Fig. 10.3) suggests that a constant quality house at the 10th percentile was 33% more expensive in 1997 than in 1974. The quantile specific index plots a similar, but less stark picture, as the analogous appreciation measure was 20%. The fact that the 10th percentile unadjusted series is well below both constant quality series suggests that average quality has worsened at the bottom of the house price distribution, with the magnitude varying by estimation strategy.[32]

In sum this research, and the work discussed above that confirms the importance of wealth constraints, should lead us away from reliance on affordability measures that focus on the median household or which rely exclusively on income or interest rates in their composition. While the NAR's affordability index suggests that home ownership opportunities have improved steadily throughout much of the past two decades, other evidence suggests scepticism is in order in this regard, especially as one moves down from the median home or the median earner. While the quantile regression results of Gyourko & Tracy (1999) indicate the constant quality price of the 10th percentile home did not rise as much as implied by the mean regression approach used in Gyourko & Linneman (1993), both papers conclude real constant quality prices of that lower quality home have risen. And the data from the labour market continues to show a widening dispersion in wages, with low skilled workers performing the worst in absolute and relative terms. It is difficult to imagine that wealth constraints will not continue to be binding for such households. If we care about such households owning, then it must be recognised that series driven by interest rates will not give an accurate picture of the affordability conditions they face.

Summary and conclusion

Much has been learned over the last decade about the constraints involved in the transition from renting to owning. New models and abundant empirical work show that wealth constraints are the critical hurdle facing most households. This new insight from the academic literature has important practical implications for those who believe that expanding home ownership will bring valuable social and economic benefits to new owners. With respect to basic affordability, it is clear that low interest rates alone cannot make ownership affordable, particularly to low wealth households.

It is not at all clear that very low down-payment loans of the type that has proliferated in the United States in the latter half of the 1990s will turn out to be a good idea – financially or socially. Work in a British context (Maclennan *et al.* 1997) strongly suggests that there are costs in a downturn associated with extending low down-payment loans to households in periods of strong economic growth. While the American and British markets are different enough to rule out simple extrapolations, such work is cautionary. However, it is clear that something like this is needed to surmount the most basic of affordability constraints.

In addition, recent research suggests that racial differences in wealth play a large role in accounting for the wide aggregate racial differences in home ownership that exist in the United States. In this case, parental wealth is an important factor, not just that of the younger household wishing to become an owner. At a minimum, policy makers in America should be aware that an end to alleged discrimination in the mortgage market will not substantially narrow the racial gap in home ownership, in the absence of a policy that deals with the very uneven racial distribution of liquid wealth.

Finally, it is clear that future research should not focus so squarely on the median household. Increasing wage dispersion in the labour market, among other factors, has acted to make affordability conditions vary across the income distribution. Different estimation techniques should be used to provide better insight into just how affordability varies across different types of households.

Acknowledgements

I particularly appreciate the comments of Kenneth Gibb, Peter Linneman, and Tony O'Sullivan on previous drafts. Naturally, they are not responsible for any remaining errors.

Notes

(1)   While accessibility to home ownership is an important international issue, this chapter focuses on the US situation and literature. Covering multiple countries is not feasible without a material increase in paper length because key country-specific factors such as mortgage market regulations and racial effects differ so much across nations.

(2)   The literature is voluminous and an exhaustive bibliography will not be attempted here. An excellent understanding of the key issues can be obtained from the following selected articles: Artle & Varaiya (1978), Weiss (1978), Rosen

(1979), Hendershott (1980), Brueckner (1986), Poterba (1991), and Henderson & Ioannides (1983).

(3) See Arnott's (1987) review for the details. With perfect knowledge and complete markets, neutral taxation, divisible housing and other assets, and no transactions costs, households would be indifferent between owning and renting.

(4) Because housing is heavily subsidised under the US tax code, tax non-neutralities are particularly well studied in the American literature. Rosen (1979) is the canonical example of this strand of research. The interested reader should see Follain & Ling (1988) and the citations therein for a review.

(5) Jones (1995) noted that the empirical literature is ambiguous at best regarding the hypothesis that the probability of ownership is decreasing with relative user costs (p_o/p_r). Linneman (1985) also provides strong evidence that the tax sorting implications of the tax-based models are not borne out in reality.

(6) In particular, see Jones (1989), Linneman & Wachter (1989), Haurin (1991), and Duca & Rosenthal (1994).

(7) See Grossman & Laroque (1990).

(8) Households need to hedge housing price risk in these models. See Plaut (1987) for an early version of this insight applied to the tenure transition decision.

(9) This reflects his underlying assumption that there exists a fundamental preference for ownership. In addition, it must be the case that one cannot expect a higher return to owner-occupied versus rental housing (regardless of one's tax bracket). See Jones (1995) for the details.

(10) In Jones (1995), the implied wealth threshold in equation (10.4) is endogenously determined. Other researchers have proposed models with exogenous constraints, typically in the form of down-payment requirements. See Artle & Varaiya (1978), Brueckner (1986), and Engelhardt (1994b).

(11) For example, Dynarski & Sheffrin's (1985) finding that transitory income affects the probability of ownership hints that this complements net worth and that there is more than permanent income to the constraint story. Similarly, Henderson & Ioannides's (1987) conclusion that the steepness of one's permanent income path affects the probability of owning also suggests that permanent income alone is not all that is relevant.

(12) Credit should also be given to Bossons (1978), who Jones (1989, 1995) drew on for inspiration, and who provided the very first empirical evidence of which I am aware that household wealth strongly influenced the choice of tenure mode.

(13) Specifically, the micro data were from Statistics Canada's 1977 and 1984 *Surveys of Consumer Finances* (SCF).

(14) Although they included a user cost measure and therefore did not estimate the pure tenure transition model advocated by Jones in his 1989 or 1995 papers, as I have already indicated, this is not significant for our current purposes.

(15) Fannie Mae and Freddie Mac underwriting requirements stated that annual mortgage payments needed to be no more than 28% of the borrower's annual family income. See Linneman & Wachter (1989) for the details.

(16)   For example, see Duca & Rosenthal (1994) and Gyourko, Linneman & Wachter (1999).

(17)   Low down-payment loans ease the equity or wealth constraint while increasing the severity of the income constraint, as special mortgage insurance or higher interest rates (or both) typically apply on these loans. Hence, the income burden is more severe.

(18)   That said, this is not all due to the spread of low down-payment mortgages. Rising real wages and increased wealth creation during the 1990s also made it easier for households to save for the 20% down-payment on standard mortgages that do not require mortgage insurance or bear a special risk premium.

(19)   Poterba (1991) estimates that tax benefits lower the user cost of owning by about 15% for the highest income (and highest tax bracket) households.

(20)   Recent research by Tracy *et al.* (1999) shows even with the great boom in equities in the US in the 1990s, home equity still constitutes virtually all of household wealth for the vast majority of households, including the median household.

(21)   See Green & White (1997) and DiPasquale & Glaeser (1999). They find that owning one's home is associated with better social outcomes for children and enhanced political and community involvement. That said, Oswald (1997b, 1999) believes there is a downside to this social capital, primarily in terms of higher unemployment.

(22)   See Charles & Hurst (forthcoming) for the details behind their calculations.

(23)   We abstract here from a host of empirical issues such as closing costs and the estimation of the 'desired' home. See Gyourko, Linneman & Wachter (1999) for the details.

(24)   Consistent with the results in Jones (1989) and Linneman & Wachter (1989), this study found non-linear effects associated with the extent to which a household was constrained. Basically, once the household is quite constrained, being constrained by another dollar has little further impact on tenure outcomes. The results for the wealth cushion variables were consistent with Grossman & Laroque (1990) effects, as households with net worths just barely above their implied down-payment requirements had lower probabilities of owning compared to households with more substantial wealth cushions. Thus, the data are consistent with the implication that households prefer not to be cornered in illiquid and risky housing.

(25)   The slightly higher estimated ownership propensities among unconstrained minorities probably reflect sample selection bias. Particularly in 1962, but in later years too, widespread discrimination in labour markets prevented many minorities from amassing enough wealth to be unconstrained. Minority households able to surmount that discrimination probably possess unobserved traits making them disproportionately likely to own.

(26)   Research on intergenerational transfers is part of a broader literature on savings behaviour. See Kotlikoff (1988) for a review. In the housing context, see Engelhardt (1994a, 1994b, 1995) and Engelhardt & Mayer (1994, 1995) for analysis of how savings behaviour interacts with parental gifts and down-payment constraints.

(27)   Examples of recent work include that by Munnell *et al.* (1996) on mortgage acceptance and rejection and by Berkovec *et al.* (1994) on default. Quigley (1996) provides an excellent review of the literature accompanying the debate on whether or not there is discrimination. Lastly, Kain & Quigley (1972a) is the pioneering work on racial differences in ownership and location outcomes.

(28)   In the US, affordability concerns tend to be focused on home ownership. In many other countries, the focus is more on rental affordability (e.g., see Maclennan & Williams 1990a,b, and Maclennan, Gibb & More 1990). In America, rental affordability is often viewed as part of a broader set of welfare-related issues, consideration of which would take us too far afield from the issues of primary concern in this chapter.

(29)   Ten quality bundles were priced via hedonic regressions. Five trait bundles from 1974 were priced going forward, and five 1989 trait bundles were priced going backward in time. Traits controlled for were the number of bathrooms, the number of bedrooms, the number of other rooms, whether the unit was detached, whether there was a garage, whether there was a cellar, the type of heating system, whether there was central air conditioning, neighbourhood quality, overall house quality, whether the home was in the central city of its metropolitan area, and house age entered as a quadratic. The specific bundles themselves were determined by the traits typical of homes in the 10th, 25th, 50th, 75th, and 90th percentiles of the single-family house price distribution in 1974 and 1989, respectively. See Gyourko & Linneman (1993, Appendix Tables 1 and 2) for the details.

(30)   The 1974 and 1989 bundles associated with the lowest quality homes appreciated by 28.1% and 33.2%, respectively, over the 1974–1989 period, while the unadjusted price for the home in the 10th percentile of the price distribution actually declined by 4.7% (in real terms).

(31)   The specification itself was identical to that in Gyourko & Linneman (1993). See Note 29 for the details.

(32)   All that said, one still cannot simply conclude that quality changes must underpin any differences between unadjusted and constant quality price growth rates. The average hedonic method may miss demand-induced price changes, but the quantile hedonic method may price up quality changes in addition to demand-induced price effects. See Gyourko & Tracy (1999) for the details. The average and quantile hedonic methods may provide a way to bound the true unobserved constant quality price index.

11

Planning Regulation and Housing Supply in a Market System

Glen Bramley

Introduction

A basic contention of this chapter is that housing supply matters. Housing supply structures and mechanisms have a number of important economic effects on, among other things, macroeconomic cycles, wealth accumulation, overall welfare and its distribution, economic competitiveness, regional labour market imbalance, urban vitality and environmental performance. A few British-based examples serve to underline this general contention.

- New housing supply is relatively inelastic in Britain, and this exacerbates price volatility across the economic cycle and gross price disparities between regions. These price effects have major implications for the distribution of wealth and probably serve to further destabilise the macroeconomy (Bramley *et al.* 1995; Meen 1996, 1999b).

- Instability of the housing market, resulting partly from inelastic supply, probably exacerbates the technical conservatism of residential construction and its mediocre quality record (e.g. because of reliance on subcontracting, undersupply of training) (Ball 1996a).

- Competitive behaviour in the face of regulation may lead to deadweight costs of developer activities designed to gain planning permission (rent-seeking), and there are dangers of impropriety/corruption in the system; the way in which planning and development control are applied may serve to increase delay and uncertainty (Evans 1991; Cheshire & Leven 1982; School of Planning & Housing 2001).

- Local political control over planning may create systematic biases in land supply for different activities, so affecting overall competitive performance (Lambert & Bramley 2002).

- Mechanisms for infrastructure provision and financing, in an era of public expenditure constraint when most development is privately promoted, may be incoherent and ineffective, giving rise to delays and inequities (Healey *et al.* 1993; Monk & Whitehead 2000; Department of Transport, Local Government and the Regions 2001).

- Planning may be used to support urban renaissance and vitality, but it may also frustrate it (Department of the Environment 1999b; Llewellyn-Davies 1994).

However, it seems that the supply side of the housing market receives limited attention compared with that lavished on the demand side. How can we explain this imbalance? Is it really the case that there are no interesting questions about the supply of housing? Or is it rather that our standard economic toolkit does not help very much with addressing such questions? At a theoretical level, for example, the assumptions of competitive behaviour may assume away the problems. In practice, to address the major issues may involve engaging with messy institutional or political processes, requiring a retreat from the preferred deductive modelling paradigm. Even if we can describe some of these processes, we may not be able to measure them.

In simple terms, housing supply may be decomposed into three main dimensions:

- construction of new dwellings;

- management of existing housing, including issues of ownership, access, pricing and financing; and

- maintenance of housing, including repair and up- (or down-) grading of the stock.

This chapter addresses the first of these dimensions, presenting some empirical work undertaken using English data. The main focus of attention is upon land use regulation and its impact on housing supply and thence on the housing market. However, understanding this impact entails assumptions about both the structure of the industry and the structure of regulation, including its linkage with infrastructure and fiscal issues.

The next section briefly reviews past economic research on new housing supply. This draws out the particular significance of land supply and the key role of land use planning in influencing this process. The third section discusses planning land use regulation in general terms, describing the operation of the British system and drawing out some contrasts with systems in other countries. This section also reviews previous efforts at measuring the economic impact of planning. The following section sets the scene for subsequent empirical analysis, describing the inter-urban panel dataset used and commenting on certain aspects of the study, particularly its geographical framework and its theoretical underpinnings. The fifth section presents the empirical modelling results. The elasticities derived are compared with previous studies, and in the concluding section brief comments are made on the significance of these findings for policy.

Researching housing supply

Econometric models of housing have hitherto followed two traditional approaches: (a) macro and regional time series; (b) hedonic house price models and related urban models. The former have become increasingly sophisticated in their treatment of dynamics and trends over time, including the application of cointegration techniques (Meen 1996, 1998, 1999b; Guissani & Hadjimatheou 1991; Muellbauer & Murphy 1997; Munro & Tu 1997). While the major emphasis has been on cycles in demand and house prices, there have been quite sophisticated models of new building supply and/or investment in this tradition (Tsoukis & Westaway 1991; Ball 1996b). However, up until now this type of research has lacked any data to get a handle on land supply and the influence of planning policy and practice.

The latter type of research, the dominant tradition in US urban economics, typically involves cross-sectional analysis at either individual property level or at small area level. On the whole, most of the thrust of this work has concerned questions about demand, including measuring the demand for different attributes within the housing bundle, and measuring the demand/willingness to pay for environmental benefits (e.g. Michaels & Smith 1990). Cheshire & Sheppard (1989, 1997) explore this approach to measuring some of the benefits of planning regulation, for example, urban open space protection. A good part of this kind of work has been concerned with the emergence or persistence of 'sub-markets' (Schnare & Struyk 1976; Goodman 1981; Adair *et al.* 1996; Maclennan & Tu 1996), and part of the reason for the existence of these may be supply constraints (as recognised by Maclennan 1977b, 1982; Ball & Kirwan 1977). Another tradition within urban economics has been the analysis of housing supply in terms of the intensity of land use (following Muth 1969; see reviews in Bartlett 1991; Bramley *et al.* 1995, Chapters 2 & 8). However, there seems to have been relatively little intra-urban and cross-sectional analysis of new build supply itself.

There is also a significant qualitative research tradition in this field, for example involving key actor interviews and case studies (often with a longitudinal element). Such work may be informed by standard microeconomic theory, by emerging perspectives including public choice and institutional economics, or by perspectives from other disciplines. Examples of work within this tradition include Monk & Whitehead (2000), Rydin (1985, 1986), Short *et al.* (1986) and Barlow (1993). Other work gives insight into the motivation and behaviour of landowners (Adams & May 1992; Adams *et al.* 1999), as well as the planners and housebuilders who tend to be the primary focus. Organisations with a policy interest in the field support work that provides a combination of monitoring data, local case studies and critical commentary (Council for the Protection of Rural England 2001; Bate 1999; Industrial Systems Research 1999; Joseph Rowntree Foundation 1994).

One key challenge is the development of systematic conceptualisation and measurement of planning/regulatory restriction (Bramley 1998; Malpezzi 1996; Needham & Lie 1994). There is clearly potential for more sophisticated theoretical treatment of local planning regulation, possibly involving the techniques of game theory. Some US 'local public choice' literature treats planning ('zoning') as one of the key strategies available to local jurisdictions engaged in 'fiscal competition' for businesses and (some kinds of) residents (Tiebout 1956; Hamilton 1975; Fischel 1990).

One of the paradoxes of researching housing supply is that it cannot actually be separated from demand. Land is not a factor like other factors, and with its spatial fixity and restricted supply, land cost reflects demand-based value; in other words, land cost is endogenous (Anas & Arnott 1993a; Bartlett 1991). Furthermore, with significant lags in the production process (Maclennan 1982), the derived demand for housing land or new construction is subject to expectations and uncertainty about a housing market that is itself highly unstable (Bramley 1989; Bramley *et al.* 1995).

Planning and regulation of land use

The differing nature of planning/regulatory regimes

As stated, the main purpose of this chapter is to look at practical attempts to model empirically the impact of land use regulation, or 'planning' as it is generally known in Britain, on new housing supply and the housing market. As a preliminary to that it is perhaps useful to clarify what these terms mean, and to draw attention to important differences in the nature of land use planning and regulation between Britain and other English-speaking countries.

Land use regulation is a legal or administrative system that prescribes what type of use is permitted on any given parcel of land. 'Use' encompasses both the type of activity accommodated (e.g. housing, industry, retailing) and, to some degree, the type, scale and form of buildings that may accommodate that use. Such regulation comes into play most often when landowners seek to change the use of a piece of land; a change of use constitutes 'development'. There are perhaps two main reasons why this form of regulation comes to be associated with 'planning'. One reason is that a common and natural way to express current or permitted patterns of land use is in the form of a map (i.e. literally, a plan, in the sense of blueprint). A second reason is that decisions about future land uses/developments to be permitted are often made in the context of a forward looking, comprehensive policy procedure and document, also generally known as a plan (but this time emphasising the time dimension and the notion of intentionality).

It should not be forgotten that planning as just defined is not exclusively a public function. However, in general, advanced societies have found it necessary or desirable to interpose a public legal and administrative basis for land use regulation and planning. In the USA and many other countries this primarily takes the form of 'zoning'. Under this approach the territory is divided up into zones within each of which certain types of land use are permitted subject to certain parameters, for example minimum lot sizes and building lines for housing. The essence of this approach is that the landowner has the right to develop within these parameters (and the corresponding right to expect that neighbouring plots will not be developed in a 'nonconforming' fashion). (Cullingworth 1997a provides a transatlantic perspective on the system as it has actually evolved).

This approach contrasts strongly with the British system, under which since 1947 land use rights have been 'nationalised' and there is no automatic presumption in favour of development. Any significant development requires permission from the local planning authority, which has considerable discretion in decision-making (Grant 1992). One of the interesting developments of the 1990s has been an attempt to make the British system more 'plan-led', so that there is a general presumption that there should be operative, site-specific local plans in place, and that a site 'allocated' for a particular use has a presumption in favour of development for that use. This can be seen as a move towards more of a zoning approach, although commentators are quick to qualify any such conclusion (Tewdyr-Jones 1996).

Formally the British approach entails a hierarchical system, ranging from national policy guidance, regional planning guidance (in England), structure plans (for county or sub-regional areas), and local plans. The apparently comprehensive character of this policy framework and forward planning system distinguishes it from that found in many other countries. In principle, local development control decisions should be determined on the basis of a rational comprehensive system that works out the local spatial implications of general policies in a way that is locally sensitive and democratically accountable. The system as it operates in practice falls somewhat short of this ideal. Shortcomings include the tendency for plans to be slow to be completed or updated, so that the currently available plans may not reflect current information or policies (School of Planning & Housing 2001), and hence there remains considerable scope for discretion. Most of the delays that characterise development control decisions, particularly on larger developments, result from the negotiations that such discretion allows. These negotiations are often concerned with infrastructure provision, which increasingly developers are expected to pay for.

Currently the British planning system is under substantial scrutiny and review, reflecting a range of concerns about speed of decision-making, responsiveness to economic needs, and whether it performs its longer term spatial directing role effectively. There are contradictions between some of the desiderata which different commentators and lobbies put forward for planning – more certainty versus more flexibility, more economic responsiveness versus more environmental sustainability, more local democracy and participation versus more rationality and efficiency. Thus it is difficult to predict how the system will evolve in practice. However, the hitherto very different systems of Britain and North America may be converging to some extent. This is particularly apparent now that 'growth controls' and 'smart urban growth' have become important features of the American scene.

The economic impact of planning and regulation

There is broad agreement among economists about the nature and direction of the effects of planning and land use regulation on the housing market, based on economic theory. Planning/regulation that significantly restricts the supply of land for new housing development is likely to reduce supply elasticities, increase land and house prices, and increase housing densities. However, there are theoretical grounds for differences of view about (a) the properties of a notional 'no planning' regime and (b) the welfare interpretation of these impacts. On the first point, for example, there are grounds for doubting whether supply elasticities would be infinitely high in the absence of planning, owing to issues of accessibility, infrastructure availability and uncertainty (see Bramley 1989; Evans 1983; Wiltshaw 1985; Neutze 1987). On the second point, planning/regulation may create positive environmental amenity effects that account for at least some of the apparently higher prices associated with the regime (Cheshire & Sheppard 1989, 1997; Monk *et al.* 1991).

The more important arena for debate is around the empirical magnitude of the various effects postulated. This shifts the emphasis to issues of empirical measurement and modelling, including both understanding and measuring planning regulations themselves, modelling supply responses, and modelling housing market adjustment to these effects over time and space. This applied empirical focus is wholly in the spirit of Maclennan's contributions to housing economics and has informed the present author's contributions, including the empirical work reported later in this chapter. Lack of space prevents a full review of existing empirical literature, but it is useful to highlight the main points emerging so far, drawing on a number of useful reviews including Fischel (1990), Monk *et al.* (1991), Podogzinski & Sass (1991) and School of Planning & Housing (2001).

US studies have mainly employed hedonic house price modelling to examine the effects of zoning and the recent proliferation of growth controls. There is a surprising lack of unanimity across different studies, with some appearing to show that land use controls are not an effective constraint, whilst others argue that they are and that they do push up housing and developed land prices. The impact depends in part on the degree of competition between jurisdictions and the extent to which controls are generalised. Fischel (1990) argues that for political/legal reasons growth controls tend to go 'too far' and create net welfare costs for society in terms of excessive sprawl (leapfrogging beyond areas of control) and increased commuting.

Cheshire & Sheppard (1989, 1997) is the most directly comparable British work, that applies a sophisticated intra-urban model to measure the impact of planning controls and planned amenity provision in a limited number of cities. Their general conclusion is that British planning control, by containing urban extension, tends to increase house prices moderately but has its main (adverse) welfare impact by increasing density. These conclusions are consistent with the qualitative observations of Evans (1991) concerning the type of housing produced under the relatively tight planning regime characteristic of southern England. Also consistent are the findings of Monk *et al.* (1996) from four case studies, showing much higher differentials between housing and agricultural land values in areas of greater planning constraint.

The present author has undertaken a series of cross-sectional studies at an inter-urban scale of analysis with an explicit planning/land supply component providing medium-term simulations of the impact of varying planning policies (Bramley 1993a & b, 1999; Bramley & Watkins 1996a). This work confirms the low supply elasticities found under British conditions, and estimates that system-wide changes in land release would impact on house prices with an elasticity in the range –0.15 to –0.30. The model developed draws explicit attention to the transmission mechanism between planning policies and outcomes, part of the basis for subsequent debate with Evans (1996).

As already noted, one of the central problems in empirical work in this area is that of how one actually measures planning restraint. Bramley (1998) reviews a range of measures, some objective and some subjective, and considers their logical interrelationships and some pitfalls of interpretation. There is an interesting parallel development of measures of restrictiveness in the US, reviewed and tested in Malpezzi (1996). Many of these measures are only effectively available on a cross-sectional basis, limiting the scope for time series or panel models. Yet this leads into another area of potential criticism of most of the models developed to date. By relying on cross-sections, they are vulnerable to a number of problems including the ecological fallacy, inconsistently defined (heterogeneous) areas, and an inability to model dynamic effects (lags and expectations) adequately. Some US work may be better than what has been attainable in Britain, by utilising more consistently-defined metropolitan housing market areas, and/or by recognising the phenomenon of varying degrees of competing jurisdictions. The problem that demand-side adjustments to constraints in one area may be substantially displaced to other surrounding areas, but to differing degrees, means that econometric models applied to sets of such areas may not adequately capture price impacts. This point is picked up again below.

Panel-based models with a time dimension as well as a cross-section dimension to local housing market areas provide one way forward to overcome some at least of the above limitations.

Following Hsiao (1986 ch.1), it can be argued that a panel-based approach should improve the robustness of models in the following ways:

- greatly increasing the number of observations and degrees of freedom;

- discriminating between competing hypotheses which might be consistent with the same 'facts';

- enabling some account to be taken of lags and dynamic effects, subject to the limitations of length and detail of time series; and

- enabling the stripping-out of the effect of certain omitted variables (e.g. fixed area effects).

In addition, one could add the following potential benefits:

- lessening the danger of results being distorted by ecological correlations and spatial autocorrelation; and

- bringing important macroeconomic variables like interest rates into the models.

Hitherto, data availability in Britain has prevented the application of this approach. However, there is now a substantial body of secondary data on the housing market and related variables available on a consistent annual basis for local or sub-regional areas. In particular, data on land available through the planning system is now available for a period of 10 years or so in both England and Scotland. These data do not yet permit investigation of the complex transmission mechanisms between planning policies and land actually made available with planning permission, as examined in Bramley (1993b), Bramley *et al.* (1995) and Bramley & Watkins (1996a) using sample cross-section data. However, they enable us to model the supply of new building on land with planning permission, house prices, and certain related variables including migration.

Panel-based models are beginning to appear in this field. Mayer & Somerville (2000) provide a US example, but even here it should be noted that the measures of land use regulation are only cross-sectional. Leishman & Bramley (forthcoming) provide an early attempt at this approach using data for Scottish districts. The next sections go on to report initial tests of a similar model applied to larger zones in England.

Setting up an inter-urban panel model

Recently, government-funded work has been undertaken to develop a policy model with which to predict internal migration flows within England and Wales. This model, known as MIGMOD, has been developed up to an operational level. Champion *et al.* (1998, 2000) describe the model in detail. It comprises two main sub-models:

- a panel model to predict gross out-migration flows by age and sex for 98 zones in England and Wales, calibrated on 15 years' data for 1983–97; and

- a spatial interaction model to distribute flows across the 98 zones, calibrated cross-sectionally but separately for each origin zone and each age/
  sex group.

These are combined in a user-friendly front-end to predict flows conditional
on assumed values of determinant variables. In order to calibrate this model,
a uniquely large dataset was constructed, including a significant number of
time-varying factors for the first stage model. This dataset is valuable for our
purposes because it includes a wide range of economic, demographic, housing, social and environmental factors that potentially can influence housing
market outcomes.

Part of the motive for examining housing market relationships using this
dataset is to explore the potential for 'endogenising' the housing market
within the migration model. It is generally recognised that both migration
and housing prices and outputs are determined simultaneously within the
same system, and subject to similar influences. Actual or potential migration may be regarded as an important part of the transmission mechanism
which drives the housing market and links the behaviour of different but
proximate geographical areas. It would be possible to incorporate migration
rates as endogenous variables within a simultaneous system designed to
analyse housing supply and price responses. I do not do this here owing to
technical limitations on the basic panel dataset and the complexity of the
full migration model. Basically, this issue of the interaction between migration and housing is on the agenda for the next stages of research, building
on MIGMOD. Nevertheless, the panel models presented do take indirect
account of migration insofar as the key drivers of migration are included as
explanatory variables.

Key variables

For the purposes of this exercise data from one additional source has been
incorporated. This is the annual 'PS3' return made by local planning authorities to central government, recording the stock of land with outstanding
planning permission for new private housing development, measured both
by the number of units capacity and the area in hectares. These data are
available for the 10-year period from 1988 to 1997. There are a considerable
number of missing cells at local authority district level. Rounded values
were entered in missing cells by interpolation, but a count of missing cells
was maintained. When aggregated to the 90 (see below) MIGMOD zones,
this count was used to provide a 'reliability' weighting subsequently incorporated in the analysis. The main measure used in the panel dataset (PLSH)

is the number of housing units capacity, divided by the population in thousands and by a notional average household size of 2.5 to yield a stock measure per 1000 households (or occupied dwellings).

Brief comments on several other key variables in the modelling are also in order. House prices are measured in real terms (discounting general inflation) and standardised using a typology of four 'optimised' housing types developed by the University of Newcastle. The data source is the Nationwide Building Society, one of the larger national mortgage lenders, which has maintained data over a 20-year period. New housing output is measured by private completions as per local authority returns based on building control records. These data are not wholly reliable but they are the best available. This measure (PQPR) is expressed in annual units per 100 existing dwellings (all tenures).

Other economic variables available on a local and time-varying basis include: a measure of gross household income (HHINC, based on Bramley & Smart (1996) and the Office for National Statistics (ONS) sub-national personal income series); three-year change in employment by workplace (EMPGRO); unemployment rate over working age population for males aged 30–44 (ASUNEM). Time-varying housing variables include vacancy rates (PVAC) and social housing completion rates (PQSR). National time series for mortgage interest rates (MGINTR_Z) and real GDP changes (RGDPCH_Z) are included. All time varying factors in the model are entered as levels with a one-year lag. In principle it would be possible to explore more elaborate lags.

Sophisticated techniques have developed in recent years to tackle the inherent econometric problems associated with time series analysis. The relatively short length of the time dimension in our panel dataset largely precludes the more sophisticated approaches involving cointegration. However, as a precautionary measure to deal with time trends in the data we incorporate a simple time trend in the models for levels (TIME_Z). We also test the use of a model constructed wholly in first differences.

The share of new housing built on formerly urban (alias 'brownfield' or 'recycled') land is available currently as a cross-sectional indicator (PNBU), although eventually this measure should be available as an annual series. A general 'urban' composite indicator is constructed using principal components analysis based on a measure of settlement pattern (basically, the density of existing population) and a number of other highly correlated cross-sectional indicators. The URBAN composite variable contains one time-varying component, a measure of international immigration rate, and so the differences in this variable effectively relate to immigration (hence the label IMMIGD). Other important cross-sectional variables utilised in the models include: an indicator of occupational structure weighted by gross migration propensities from the 1991 Census (OCCMIG), which broadly measures high occupational class; share of people with single marital status (SINGLE); share of non-white ethnic population (NONWH); and a composite measuring warmer and drier weather conditions (CLIMATE). London represents an extreme in many aspects of the housing market and to allow for this we also include a London dummy variable in the models, to allow for any simple shift effects not captured in other variables.

A wider range of variables, mainly cross-sectional and relating to housing and environmental conditions, were tested but discarded before the final stage of the modelling. The MIGMOD dataset includes a substantial number of 'regional' variables, measuring the difference between values in closely surrounding zones and the value in a particular origin zone. We retain only one of these, the measure of total population, which provides an indicator representing conurbation locations. This aspect of the model, relating to potential spatial interactions, could be developed further. The final version of the stage 1 MIGMOD model utilised a quadratic functional form (Champion *et al.* (2000), but in this paper we only test a quadratic form for one variable, price, together with a couple of key interaction terms. Otherwise, the models fitted are linear.

Theoretical interpretation

The models reported here constitute a relatively straightforward supply and demand system. Demand is represented by an inverted demand function, with price as the dependent variable and a wide range of determinant variables including new housing supply or its key exogenous determinant, available land. Housing demand is also expected to be influenced by economic conditions (income level and growth, employment/unemployment, interest rates), environmental conditions (e.g. climate), socio-economic profiles (class), demographic factors, proximity to major urban agglomerations, and other sources of housing supply (social housing, vacancies). Part of the way demand variations are expressed is through migration.

Supply is represented as the flow supply of new completions. New flow supply is modelled as a function of a smaller subset of variables, including price and available land. Bramley & Watkins (1996a & b) suggest that this function can be derived formally from models of a 'representative' profit-maximising developer holding a given stock of land and confronting given or expected price and cost levels. Since housing cannot be built without land being available with planning permission, this variable is crucial to the model, and it can be argued that the functional form of the model should reflect this dependence. For example, there is a case for interacting price with land available, or using a log-log formulation (we illustrate the former approach below). It is assumed that price embodies most of the demand-side influences, but there is a case for including other economic variables to capture their impact on developers' costs. This applies particularly to interest rates but may also apply to unemployment, although in the latter case the demand effects may predominate. It is also expected that supply will be influenced by locational characteristics, particularly urban settings and land in former urban use, as these are generally believed to entail greater costs and risks for developers. Private supply may also be influenced by other sources of supply, from the social housing sector and vacancies.

Clearly, price and completions are endogenous within this system. We therefore use two-stage least squares (2SLS) to estimate the structural price and supply equations, having first regressed these on all exogenous variables retained in the model. However, we also report a comprehensive single stage OLS model for comparison. In addition, we explore some variations in functional form in relation to the key variables of price and output.

Geographical units

Comment is also in order on the nature of the geographical zones used in this analysis. These comprise the 90 MIGMOD zones covering England, Wales having been discarded owing to lack of data on land with planning permission (and some other data weaknesses). These zones are the former Health Authority areas for which migration data up to 1997 were available. They are in fact simple aggregations of 366 local authority districts. In 'shire' areas the zones are counties; in provincial metropolitan areas they are normally single metropolitan districts (e.g. Manchester, Bolton). In London they are aggregations of 2–4 contiguous London boroughs.

Previous research using local authority districts has been criticised for utilising a spatial unit that did not consistently represent a meaningful concept of local housing market (or labour market) area (see Bramley 1993a; Evans 1996). The present set-up of 90 zones is to some extent open to the same criticism, although arguably less severely. The zones are certainly not self-contained regions, in the sense that the migration between them is not solely long-distance labour migration, but includes a varying element of housing or environment-led migration (as discussed for example in Gordon 1991).

This issue has some bearing on the interpretation of the inverted demand function. The more self-contained are the zones, the more the feedback effects from land supply and new housebuilding onto market prices should be contained within them, and the less these effects leak out into surrounding areas. Given the hybrid nature of the zones, it is expected that some of the price effects of supply do leak out, and will not be fully captured in a model that treats each zone as though it were independent. Bramley (1993a, 1999) argued that, working with smaller district level units, this effect was so great that it was better to approach price impacts by conducting whole-system simulations, rather than simply reading off the coefficients for district-level effects. Using the larger MIGMOD zones, it may be expected that the price model coefficients will capture more of the supply impact, and the results reported below seem to bear this out. Nevertheless, these measured impacts should still be regarded as giving an incomplete picture of system-wide effects. In the longer term, it is hoped that by integrating these models with a fully interactive migration model, or by incorporating spatial interaction within these housing models, a fuller picture can be obtained.

Despite their limitations, the models reported shed light on a number of policy-relevant issues, as identified earlier, including supply elasticities with respect to price and land availability, and the impact of an emphasis on urban and brownfield land development.

Model results

The demand side

Table 11.1 presents the key regression results for house prices using the panel model set up in the manner described above. This model should as noted above be interpreted as an inverted demand function. The first two columns (model (1)) show the fullest OLS model, incorporating both levels and differences in time-varying variables on the right-hand side (this is effectively the reduced form price equation underlying model (3)). The remaining columns give the structural demand equations resulting from the 2SLS procedure. The key difference from model (1) is that in that case 'supply' is represented by the exogenous land availability indicator (PLSH), while in the remaining cases this role is taken on by the endogenous new completions variable (PRPQPR) as predicted in the first stage reduced form regression. Model (2) is a more parsimonious version including only levels indicators on the right-hand side, while model (3) is a fuller version including both levels and differences for the time-varying explanatory variables. Model (4) is a model set up purely in first differences. This has the advantage of removing possible bias associated with unmeasured fixed area effects, but the disadvantage of not enabling estimation of any cross-sectional variable effects.

All models in levels achieve a reasonable fit to the data, with adjusted r-squared values around 0.85–0.87. This high fit is characteristic of cross-sectional price models in previous research. The first differences model (4) achieves a much lower fit, as expected, because it omits all cross-sectional variables and because it is more vulnerable to errors of measurement. Most of the variables retained in the model are statistically significant. The only exceptions are the urban composite (in the 2SLS models), employment growth (in most models), some of the difference variables in model (1), and the sub-regional interaction term for neighbouring population. The urban variable might have been hypothesised to have a positive effect, reflecting the classic urban economic land rent model, or alternatively a negative effect indicating an aversion to urban environments; in practice neither effect is confirmed. Possibly the variable SINGLE captures the central city effect. Employment growth suffers from some measurement problems associated with sampling error in the annual employment survey; it is possible that the income and unemployment variables adequately capture the underlying effects of employment.

Most of the remaining variables that are statistically significant have effects in the expected direction. House prices are strongly driven by income, higher occupational class and better climate, with negative effects from unemployment and interest rates. The only case where the sign is clearly opposite to that expected is national GDP growth, although this effect is not very strong and will be offset by the stronger income variable. The negative time trend effect is slightly surprising but again this will be offset by the income variable. The positive effect of non-white ethnic population is interesting, suggesting that the positive demand effect of ethnic population concentrations outweighs any negative effects on the demand from the indigenous population.

The most interesting results in the context of our analysis of supply are those relating to the price impacts of the supply variables. In the first OLS model, the amount of land available has a modest negative impact on house prices. In the 2SLS structural levels models, the predicted supply of new housing completions has a more substantial impact on house prices. The coefficient indicates that a 10% increase in output at the mean would lower local house prices by 3.1–3.4% (see Table 11.4). This effect is substantially stronger in the first differences model (4), 8.5% lower prices for a 10% higher output.

Table 11.1 Panel model regressions for house price (90 health authority areas in England annual series 1988–97).

Explanatory variable		(1) OLS		(2) 2SLS levels		(3) 2SLS levels		(4) 2SLS 1st differences	
		Coefficient	t-stat	Coefficient	t-stat	Coefficient	t-stat	Coefficient	t-stat
Constant		122176	7.60	126857	8.68	159798	9.48	-6074	-4.76
*URBAN	Composite dense urban	6067	3.91	-1247	-0.83	-992	-0.67		
*IMMIGD	Difference in urban	15144	1.46			12836	1.22	-15621	-1.50
*HHINC	Household income level	107.9	7.74	147.0	10.55	155.4	13.68	50.0	0.71
	Difference	3.66	0.05			41.9	0.60		
*ASUNEM	Unemployment level	-1551	-5.85	-2471	-9.89	-2339	-8.37	-6299	-9.67
	Difference	832	1.23			727	1.07		
*EMPGRO	Job growth % change	-128.0	-0.54	-43.1	-0.19	-145.1	-0.61	-784	-3.78
*PQSR	Social hsg completions level	2084	1.95						
	Difference	1897	1.87						
*PVAC	Vacancy rate level	-2008	-4.10						
	Difference	-684	-0.90						
*PLSH	Land available with OPP¹ level	-64.4	-2.60						
	Difference	43.5	0.68						
*PRPQPR	Predicted new completions level			-28906	-10.29	-31492	-11.51	-78655	-6.70
	Difference								

		Coeff	t	Coeff	t	Coeff	t		
PNBU	Urban land share	205.8	8.37						
OCCMIG	Occupational class index	25940	6.13	18241	4.19	17722	4.08		
SINGLE	Single marital status	339	1.22	1529	5.66	1430	5.19		
NONWH	Nonwhite ethnic population	131.2	1.55	184.5	2.16	146.3	1.73		
CLIMATE	Composite warmer/drier	2389	3.66	5092	8.18	5028	7.75		
TOPOPN	Neighbouring popn level	182.4	0.26	974	1.36	947	1.36		
MGINTR_Z	Interest rate level	-5201	-7.49	-4128	-10.56	-5920	-8.78		
	Difference	4603	5.42	5381	6.47	5381	6.47	-2531	-5.65
RGDPCH_Z	Real GDP growth %	-2071	-2.60	-563	-1.89	-1611	-2.04		
TIME_Z	Time trend	-7894	-14.69	-7861	-23.44	9042	-16.86		
LONDONDU	London dummy	-3388	-1.61	-9118	-3.90	9755	-4.26		
Adj r-squared		0.866		0.853		0.861			
F		194.9		298.8		248.2			
N		719		719		719			
HPRICE	Dep. variable mean value	76930		76930		76930			

Note: * indicates local time-varying factors; all level variables with 1 year lag; _Z indicates national time series; all regressions weighted by population and reliability index.

¹ OPP = outline planning permission.

It is difficult to compare this result directly with previous studies, because of differences in exactly what is being measured on the supply side. The elasticity of price feedback with respect to output of –0.33 above is well above the –0.041 for secondhand sales and –0.191 for new sales found in Bramley (1993a & b). It is rather more similar to the result yielded by cross-sectional price regression equations at district level in the second study by Bramley & Watkins (1996a ch.6). It is also rather stronger than the results obtained by Leishman & Bramley (forthcoming) applying a panel 2SLS model to Scottish districts, which yielded an elasticity of house prices with respect to predicted completions of –0.225. The significance of the size of zones for this measure of feedback was discussed above, where it was suggested that the larger MIGMOD zones would be expected to capture a greater degree of feedback, and these findings appear consistent with that view.

The supply model

We can now turn to the supply model results that are summarised in Table 11.2. These are of greatest interest in the context of this chapter. It should be remembered that supply here is defined as the annual flow of new private housing units.

As with house prices, we compare an OLS formulation (model (1)) with several 2SLS equations. There is some evidence to support a model involving an interaction between price and land availability, together with a quadratic term in price, so we include both this version (2B) and a simpler linear form (2A) of the structural equation. The interaction of price (or more strictly, gross development profit) with land availability featured in the previous work by this author (Bramley 1993a & b; Bramley & Watkins 1996a & b). The rationale is simply that houses cannot be built without land with planning permission, so that the effect of price may be expected to work in conjunction with land supply rather than independently. The data appear to support this formulation in the new panel model (comparing (2B) with (2A)), as it did in the previous cross-sectional models.

The overall fit of the supply models is poorer than that of the price models, with about half the variance in output levels being explained. This is consistent with all previous comparable work. Supply is more difficult to model, perhaps because there are more unique local factors making for a lumpiness in annual output rates not related to the broad, systematic variables included in the model. There are also some grounds for doubt about the accuracy of the recording of the timing of housing completions, imparting greater random error. Mention has already been made of the weaknesses in the measurement of the key driver of land supply, and of the reliability weighting incorporated in the regressions. The fit is particularly poor for the first differences model (4), although some of the key variables remain significant.

The model results broadly do show that both price and land availability have a positive impact on the level of housebuilding output. However, price is negative and not significant in the OLS model (1), while land supply is negative and insignificant in the first differences model (4). The first finding probably reflects the inappropriateness of OLS when price is clearly endogenous and strongly related to a number of other variables included in this model. The second finding may reflect data weaknesses in the context of a poorly fitting model. It may also reflect a spurious negative correlation effect, because increased completions would, for any given level of new planning permissions, tend to deplete the existing stock of completions more quickly.

Looking at the 2SLS models in levels, when price and land are entered separately as linear variables, as in models (2A) and (3), both are significant and positive, but the land effect is much more robust in its significance. When entered as an interaction term (model (2B)), this improves the overall model fit and the combined variable is positive and robust in terms of its significance. The squared price terms appear to have a negative effect, but this is not statistically significant. Thus, there is some support, but not robust evidence, for the argument that the price-supply function weakens or bends backwards at higher price levels (as discussed in Pryce 1999). It is interesting to note that in model (2B) the separate land term has a negative effect, although this is of marginal statistical significance. This suggests that allocating more land in a situation where prices are low could have a low or even negative impact on output. Model (3) confirms the broad magnitude and significance of both price and land effects when a wider range of explanatory variables, including difference terms, are included. It is noteworthy that both the level and change in land supply have positive effects of a similar order of magnitude.

What are the implications of these findings for housing supply elasticities? Calculating values at the mean and allowing for the net effects with any interactions, the supply elasticities revealed by this model are shown in Table 11.3. The price elasticities from the 2SLS levels models lie in the range 0.36–0.38. The first differences model (4) yields a higher figure of 0.585, although the shortcomings of this model should be remembered. The elasticities of supply with respect to land available with planning permission lie in the range 0.25–0.31, except in the case of the first differences model where it is as noted negative and insignificant.

Table 11.2 Panel model regressions for new private housing completions (percent of total housing stock; 90 health authority areas in England annual series 1988–97).

Explanatory variable		(1) OLS Coefficient	t-stat	(2A) 2SLS Coefficient	t-stat	(2B)2SLS interaction Coefficient	t-stat	(3) 2SLS levels Coefficient	t-stat	(4) 2SLS 1st differences Coefficient	t-stat
Constant		1.873	4.16	0.444	2.03	1.293	5.99	0.271	0.66	-3.74E-2	-4.35
*HPRICE	House price level	-1.12E-6	-1.14	3.94E-6	5.42			4.16E-6	2.99	6.34E-6	2.97
	Difference	-1.70E-6	-1.25								
*HPRICE_Q	House price squared					-2.31E-7	-0.53				
*HPRICE x PLSH	Price x land interaction					1.20E-7	6.02				
*PLSH	Land available OPP[1] level	6.88E-3	10.97	5.78E-3	10.63	-2.38E-3	-1.59	6.56E-3	12.23		
	Difference	5.71E-3	3.49					5.15E-3	3.18	-1.13E-3	-0.86
*PQSR	New social hsg comps level	2.29E-2	0.85	-7.34E-2	-3.23	-5.50E-2	-2.47	-2.08E-2	-0.75		
	Difference	2.64E-2	1.02					4.48E-4	0.02	7.83E-2	3.54
*URBAN	Composite dense urban	-7.91E-2	-2.00	-9.87E-2	-4.08	-8.76E-2	-2.96	-0.104	-3.44		
*IMMIG	Difference	5.31E-2	0.20								
*HHINC	Household income level	2.14E-3	5.83								
	Difference	2.51E-4	0.14								
*EMPGRO	Job growth % change	9.52E-4	0.16								
*ASUNEM	Unemployment level	-1.23E-2	-1.78			-5.79E-3	-1.15	5.91E-4	0.10		
	Difference	-1.45E-2	-0.84					-1.14E-2	-0.72		

Planning Regulation and Housing Supply in a Market System   213

*PVAC	Vacancy rate level	-1.13E-2	-0.91	1.04E-2	0.81	8.60E-3	0.70	4.61E-3	0.34		
	Difference	4.28E-3	0.22					6.53E-3	0.33	6.96E-3	0.46
PNBU	Share of former urban land	-8.16E-4	-1.25	-2.54E-3	-4.08	-2.31E-3	-3.36	-1.93E-3	-2.69		
OCCMIG	Occupational class index	-0.404	-3.69								
SINGLE	Single marital status	1.93E-2	2.75								
NONWH	Nonwhite ethnic population	-1.38E-3	-0.65								
CLIMATE	Composite warmer/drier	1.76E-2	1.05								
TOPOPN_Y	Neighbouring population	-6.54E-3	-0.37			-8.54E-3	-0.50	-1.89E-2	-1.08		
MGINTR_Z	Interest rate level	-5.09E-2	-2.53	-4.11E-3	-0.46	-3.37E-2	-5.04	-4.26E-3	-0.30		
	Difference	6.15E-2	2.70			2.81E-2	1.92			-3.18E-2	-5.62
TIME_Z	Time trend	-5.08E-2	-3.06	9.33E-4	0.08	-2.03E-2	-2.24	1.22E-2	0.74		
LONDONDU	London dummy	-0.20	-3.76	-0.154	-3.28	-4.77E-2	-1.01	-0.129	-2.83		
Adj r-squared		0.519		0.439		0.511		0.498		0.049	
F		30.8		63.6		63.5		45.6		8.45	
N		719		719		719		719		719	
PQPR	Dep. variable mean value	0.8756		0.8756		0.8756		0.8756		0.8756	

Note: * indicates local time-varying factors; levels variables with 1 year lag; _Z indicates national time series; all regressions weighted by population and reliability index; price terms are based on predicted price from reduced form in 2SLS models.

[1] OPP = outline planning permission.

Table 11.3 Elasticities of supply (private completions) from different models (evaluated at mean).

Model	Price elasticity of supply	Land elasticity of supply	Urban land elasticity of supply
(1) OLS	−0.102	0.300	−0.062
(2A) 2SLS simple	0.362	0.252	−0.194
(2B) 2SLS interactive	0.365	0.308	−0.149
(3) 2SLS levels and differences	0.381	0.286	−0.147
(4) 2SLS 1st differences	0.585	−0.049	n/a

It is clear that the main message of this new model is that housing supply elasticities in England in this period are relatively low. For example, the estimates in Table 11.3 are well below the results reported in Bramley (1993a) which were of the order of 0.8–1.1, based on cross-sectional analysis at district level for 1988. However, this new low estimate is more comparable to recent national and regional results from Meen (1998), and also to other cross-sectional estimates (unpublished) for the 1990s from this author, and the Scottish results from Leishman & Bramley (forthcoming). These elasticities are markedly lower than those reported in US literature. Low supply elasticities imply that demand shocks are more likely to generate larger price fluctuations rather than output responses. They also imply that it will be difficult to achieve large increases in owner occupation (Meen 1998). A further implication is that any demand-side subsidies would tend to be capitalised into house prices (this may be of contemporary significance in the context of policies to subsidise access for key workers).

One hypothesis that may go some way to explaining the apparently falling supply elasticities might be that there are increasingly important variations on the cost side of the development equation, upon which we do not have systematic data. The brownfield land variable (PNBU) attempts to pick up one aspect of this. But there is an increasingly significant phenomenon of planning agreements being used to secure the provision and financing of large elements of infrastructure, and also other costly elements such as 'affordable housing'. These onerous requirements are most prominent on large developments on greenfield sites in the south of England. This means that the relationship between price and 'gross development profit' becomes increasingly tenuous. Pending the collection of systematic data on planning agreement costs, this remains speculation.

The land supply elasticities are also surprisingly low. This may reflect in part the measurement inadequacies mentioned above. However, more substantively, it indicates that just allocating extra land for housing and giving it planning permission is not sufficient to ensure that it will all be built upon in the short to medium term. The lower values for this parameter than in previous research (typically around a half) may be in part a reflection of the larger geographical units in this study; the 'steering' effect of land allocations may be stronger at the lower district scale than at the broader MIGMOD zone scale.

It is possible to combine these estimates of land supply elasticity of output with the estimates of supply-price feedback derived from the price model, as shown in Table 11.4. The implied price impact of a 10% increase in land availability would be of the order of −0.8% to −1.0%. This elasticity of price with respect to land supply of around −0.1 is rather below the range of estimates (−0.15 to −0.30) presented in Bramley (1999), but the latter were based on whole system simulations of general increases/reductions rather than single-zone scenarios.

A number of other variables in the supply model are also of policy relevance. The share of former urban land (brownfield land) within the supply (PNBU) has a consistently negative effect on output. Table 11.3 shows that the elasticities are of the order of −0.15 to −0.19. This is consistent with the widespread assumption that brownfield sites are likely to be more costly, difficult or risky to develop. The government is seeking to increase the share of brownfield land in housing provision; this evidence suggests that this policy will carry some cost in terms of reduced output from a given land stock, with some feedback effect on to house prices. For example a 10% increase in the urban land share would reduce output by 1.49% at the mean. Combining this elasticity of −0.149 with the −0.33 elasticity of price with respect to output would give a price impact of +0.49%. Another way of looking at the urban land share effect is to regard it as a cost mark-up. The 10% rise in urban land share has the same impact on output as a 3.91% fall in prices (model (3)), equivalent to £2955 for an average housing unit. This could be a measure of the marginal cost effect of brownfield land, although as such it looks rather on the high side.

Table 11.4   Elasticities of local price feedback (evaluated at mean).

Model	Supply-price feedback	Impact of 10% more land
(1) OLS		−0.30%
(2A) 2SLS simple	−0.309	−0.78%
(2B) 2SLS interactive	−0.309	−0.95%
(3) 2SLS levels & differences	−0.337	−0.96%
(4) 2SLS 1st differences	−0.849	−0.59%*

* derived from reduced form.

Also consistent with this evidence is the significant negative coefficient on the URBAN composite variable; output is lower, other things being equal, in more urban settings. The London dummy effect is also negative, which can be seen as part of the same general story.

Lastly, the time trend variable is significantly negative in all the models. This can perhaps be related to the general policy concern being voiced by the housebuilding industry at the moment that the overall level of housebuilding output in England is at record low levels in the late 1990s, despite the buoyant economic climate and high or rising prices.

Conclusions

The supply side of housing has been relatively neglected in housing economics, despite presenting a range of important analytical and policy challenges. Neither of the dominant traditions in econometric work has got fully to grips with the key supply constraints associated with land use regulation. Ways forward for research may involve more micromodelling of supply, more incorporation of insights and measures from qualitative/institutional work, more incorporation of spatial interaction perspectives, and the combining of time and cross-sectional dimensions. This chapter exemplifies the latter approach by exploring the application of a panel model to analyse the impact of the amount and type of available land on new housing supply and market price outcomes in England.

Planning regulation has survived the wave of deregulation in Britain since 1980, while in the US there is a pronounced move towards more interventionist urban growth controls. The policy issues to which these interventions respond – environmental, fiscal, social and urban – are sufficiently important that simple calls for getting rid of all regulation are unlikely to be acted upon. What are needed are more intelligent, well-informed and well-implemented policies, and urban economics has a role in providing the information and intelligence required.

Economists agree about the general nature of the impact of planning regulation on housing supply and markets. What is unclear is the relative magnitude of different effects, some of which are potentially contradictory. Existing empirical work provides some indications of the likely effects, but the magnitude and interpretation of these results varies. Thus there is a need for better-specified models.

Results of the initial application of the inter-urban panel model in England support a number of propositions. Firstly, the price elasticity of new build supply is low in this country, and may be getting lower. Secondly, land availability through planning is a strong driver (or steerer) of development. Thirdly, greater supply does reduce house prices, although the local impact of this is quite moderate. Fourthly, increasing the emphasis on urban and brownfield land does carry a significant output penalty, with a modest consequent impact on house prices.

Acknowledgements

This chapter draws heavily on data generated within a research project commissioned by the Department of Transport, Local Government and the Regions (DTLR, formerly DETR) concerned with modelling migration flows in England. The author was a member of this research team but would like to acknowledge the permission given by DTLR for use of these data, as well as the help and encouragement of other members of the research team, particularly Tony Champion, Stewart Fotheringham and Stamatis Kalogirou of the University of Newcastle, and other colleagues at Universities of Newcastle and Leeds.

Particular thanks are due to the Nationwide Building Society for permission to use house price data derived from their lending records.

The author would also like to acknowledge support and encouragement provided by Duncan Maclennan for earlier efforts in this area.

Responsibility for the conclusions and interpretations drawn, as well as any errors or omissions, remain the responsibility of the author.

12

Economics and Housing Planning

Tony O'Sullivan[1]

Introduction

There has long been a general presumption in the UK that local authorities have a role in the planning of housing provision.[2] This role encompasses all tenures, including housing directly provided by local authorities, social housing provided through non-profit making organisations, and housing supplied solely through private markets for rent or to own. This state of affairs is in marked contrast to the situation in the USA where such a role for municipal government is not considered at all feasible or appropriate.

Maclennan (1991) provides a succinct case for the need for local strategic housing planning – although, as he notes, this does not necessarily imply municipal government should have the responsibility for undertaking it. The case is essentially that:

- *in efficiency terms*, local housing markets are so pervasively beset with problems of market failure, arising from long product life, slow supply adjustment, information imperfections and external effects, that markets operating without a socially determined 'game plan' to orient them are bound to be sub-optimal; and

- *in equity terms*, the product 'housing' looms so large in the welfare of all households that the consequences of local housing markets getting it wrong are socially (not to mention politically) unacceptable.

Almost by default it has come to be seen as a local authority responsibility in the UK. Among other things, this has involved an implicit assumption that local authorities are actually capable of doing the sort of planning envisaged. Taking their responsibility at face value, local authorities are as a consequence confronted with a demanding set of analytical tasks.

Effectively, local authorities are expected to make a credible forecast of demand for housing for their areas of jurisdiction over a 3–5 year planning horizon. This forecast should nest within a 10–15 year forecast of the overall infrastructure and land requirements (commercial and industrial as well as residential) of the regional economy in which an authority operates. By making allowance for future trends in income growth and distribution, consumer preferences and market supply adjustments (the latter heavily influenced by land use planning), authorities are expected to establish the required volume and location of subsidised social renting accommodation. At the same time, they must monitor physical and social obsolescence of existing housing, and encourage, fund or take (where they own the housing) appropriate offsetting action. In principle, to deliver against these expectations involves the application of a considerable amount of economics in local housing contexts, covering (among other things) articulation of new and second-hand market structure and evolution, preference measurement, demand forecasting and tenure choice estimation.

In this chapter I consider how well local authorities dispense the housing planning function. The next section describes how this responsibility on authorities evolved over the greater part of the twentieth century, and the current position. Thereafter, I present evidence that demonstrates a gulf between the requirements and reality of local authority housing planning. This conclusion is reinforced by consideration of the contribution made by land use planning (also a local authority responsibility) to housing plans. The penultimate section considers reasons for the gap between requirement and reality. It looks at the economic toolkit implicitly required to effect housing planning and compares this with available economic tools. It also considers the behavioural incentives and disincentives that face local authorities in this area. The evidence available raises questions concerning the application of the rational comprehensive planning model to housing. The final section offers some concluding thoughts.

The policy and institutional framework

The emphasis of housing policy in the UK has changed markedly over time as a consequence of both change in perceptions of the nature of housing problems, and the actual and perceived success or failure of specific policy initiatives. (Galster & Daniell 1996, show this has been true for the US also, and demonstrate the role social science has played there in a housing planning/policy making context.)

In general, one consequence of this evolution has been that planning expectations on UK local authorities have steadily increased over time.[3] In the years immediately preceding World War II, local authorities had two principal sets of responsibility: provision and management of houses to let, and improvement of private sector stock condition. The latter included slum clearance and grant-aided improvement, both of individual dwellings and area improvement schemes. Severe shortages of housing developed during the war years. For the two decades following the war there was consequently a need for more house building virtually everywhere. Over this period

'catching up with shortages took much longer than expected because the number of households increased faster than anyone had foreseen. Where to build was a matter of equity between people living in different parts of an authority's area rather than anything to do with the economics of housing markets'.[4]

Shortages eased after the mid-1960s. The 1970s then saw the emergence of the idea of a

'comprehensive housing service covering potential as well as existing consumers, with local authorities taking the broadest view of their statutory housing functions'.

(Smith 1989, p. 61)

An early signal from central government that local authority focus should broaden and deepen from a singular emphasis on building as many 'social renting' units as possible came from Scotland. The Scottish Housing Advisory Committee published a report in 1972 on the need for a comprehensive approach to area housing needs assessment (Scottish Housing Advisory Committee 1972). This body noted:

'The approach we are recommending goes well beyond the assessment of the need for local authority housing. In our view, the responsibilities of local authorities should extend far beyond providing for the needs of those who are actually housed by them: they should be looking at the totality of needs – hidden needs, needs which are not being met, and needs which may arise in the future... This includes needs of those who do not wish or cannot be housed in the public sector. The provision of a council house is one way of meeting a need; it is not the only way. The implication is that local authorities should make an assessment of the need for other types of housing provision. In practical terms this involves, in particular, ensuring that sufficient suitable land is allocated for private building ...'

(Scottish Housing Advisory Committee 1972, pp. 7, 12)

In England, central government introduced a new system of local authority 'housing investment programmes' from 1978/9 onwards. This framework quickly became linked to the idea of a strategic housing responsibility for local authorities that was to be based on comprehensive local housing plans (Department of the Environment 1977; Smith 1989). Impressive official guidance on how to do the required analysis subsequently emerged (Department of the Environment 1980), and was not updated until quite recently (Bramley *et al.* 2000).

In Scotland, the 1977 Green Paper on Scottish Housing Policy (Scottish Office 1977) proposed that housing plans prepared by Scottish local authorities would form a continuing, informed database on Scottish housing. Although it would be 2001 before such plans (or 'local housing strategies') became a statutory responsibility on authorities in Scotland, from 1977 housing capital allocations to authorities were to be based on locally-prepared and detailed triennial plans covering all sectors (Maclennan 1989). This was supported by the publication in 1977 of detailed guidance to assist officials of local authorities engaged in preparing comprehensive assessments of housing needs in their areas (Scottish Development Department 1977). Guidance on how to analyse local housing markets has not subsequently been officially updated, although in the early 1990s Scottish Homes[5] developed an approach jointly with Glasgow University, and subsequently published it (Maclennan *et al.* 1998a). More generally, there has been a continuing stream of commentary and contribution from academic and other sources (see, for example, Audit Commission 1992; Van Zilj 1993; Maclennan 1991; Fordham & Brook 1995; DETR 1997; Hawtin 1996; Wood & Preston 1997; Goss & Blackaby 1998).

In the 1980s council house building was cut back to virtually nothing. New social provision was henceforth to be predominantly made through housing associations –voluntary sector institutions that develop housing through combining public sector capital grant with private loans. The reduced provider role for local authorities was rationalised as part of a further shift by local authorities (under government pressure) into a 'strategic' housing role. Subsequent developments in policy such as encouragement to transfer remaining authority-owned stock to other landlords and to secure social housing from planning gain arising from private residential development have further increased the pressure on authorities to develop this strategic role.

These policy developments have been accompanied by a changing operating context that has in the last decade been increasingly complicating the task. Market provision now accounts for around four-fifths of all housing in the UK. Moreover, from a general position of national and local shortage, the housing situation has developed into one where there is a complex and shifting pattern of areas of high and low demand for housing relative to supply.

The current position is that there is a statutory responsibility on UK local authorities, within a framework of policy set by central government, to prepare and submit housing plans, or 'local housing strategies' with a 3–5 year timeframe, on a regular basis. Moreover (Bramley *et al.* 2000), there is general agreement among practitioners, experts and published guidance that the main and essential elements of a local housing strategy are:

- a broad vision for the area covered by a local authority and its housing;

- consultation with local 'stakeholders' including private sector organisations on trends, problems, issues and appropriate ways of addressing them;

- sound, up-to-date information on the local housing system; full tenure coverage and understanding of its key dimensions, including interactions between tenures;

- clear priorities for tackling specific problems that have been identified through analysis, and clear, appropriate objectives based on these priorities;

- development and appraisal of options to achieve these objectives; and

- a clear implementation framework for the selected options.

Housing plans in practice

Two studies that span the 1990s experience of local authority housing plan production allow us to investigate the analytical quality of housing plans produced in the UK. The first was a study by Varady (1996) that has the advantage of giving a view from totally outside the British framework.[6] Varady took a case study approach focused on four British cities: Glasgow and Dundee in Scotland, and Birmingham and York in England. The housing plans of these four cities, identified as best practice examples on the basis of official and academic advice, were variously produced between 1990 and 1993. Varady evaluated the plans against seven criteria:

- quality of 'mission statements';

- extent to which plans got beyond a focus on purely low-income housing;

- approach(es) to measuring housing problems;

- methods of establishing priorities;

- extent of private sector and consumer consultation;

- coverage of implementation issues (e.g. co-ordination between housing and planning agencies); and

- degree to which neighbourhood geography figured in the plans.

For all that Varady commends the British system relative to the situation in America, he produced some rather trenchant criticisms of what were, after all, best practice examples.

On the scope of these plans, he noted that all four plans discussed shelter (low-income housing) needs, but were less than adequate in addressing the middle-income section of the market (a criticism still being made with respect to Glasgow by Robertson (1998), and with considerably more venom).

With regard to analytical content, Varady used a housing plan for Dundee produced by Grant *et al.* (1976), a plan produced with much central government support, and the basis for the guidance produced in 1977, as a benchmark. He noted that none of the plans considered achieved the analytical comprehensiveness of the 1976 Dundee plan, and that for all four there was in fact little connection between housing market analysis and the remainder of the plan. With respect to the establishment of priorities and the selection of options, in none was there any indication whatsoever of how the priorities reflected in the plans were developed.

Varady noted that all four plans discussed at length what policies each authority intended to implement but both the Scottish city housing plans suffered from lack of co-ordination with development (land use) planning. On issues of neighbourhood, or the internal structure of urban markets, performance was again patchy. Only the Birmingham plan paid any real attention to geographic housing issues. Glasgow and York had little in the way of any neighbourhood focus, while it was noted that

'the Dundee Housing Plan is not a geographically oriented document'

(Varady 1996, p. 281)

How had the situation changed by the end of the 1990s? For the answer to this we turn to a study by Blackaby (2000), which provides an evaluation of the extent to which local authority housing assessments in England and Scotland, conducted at the end of the 1990s, cover private sector housing issues.[7] In this study, Blackaby considered the work done by or on behalf of 34 local authorities that responded to a more general invitation to authorities to participate.

Blackaby (2000) asserts local housing strategies should include:

- coverage of the private housing market;

- attention to interaction between tenures;

- consideration of the scope for the private market to meet housing need;

- identification of potential improvements to the efficiency and effectiveness of the private housing market; and

- evidence of involvement of private agencies in the housing requirements assessment process.

Blackaby found that relatively few of the assessments contained information on the private market. Where present, discussion was superficial. None of the assessments contained any analysis of the characteristics of the key players in the local housing market. Many included some price and rent statistics, but these were generally restricted to single point in time averages.

Further, Blackaby concluded little or no attention had been given to questions of tenure interaction. With respect to the potential role of the private market in meeting housing need, he noted analysis might be expected to cover the extent to which households require subsidy and in what degree, the extent of households in mortgage difficulties, and the tightness of the private rental system. Again, limited coverage of these topics was evident.

In terms of analysis of the structure and operation of the local housing market from an efficiency point of view, Blackaby found again that this was largely absent. Indeed, in most cases local authorities had not even seen private housing organisations as relevant sources of intelligence in constructing local assessments. Examples of good practice were very much the exception to the rule, with only one assessment attempting a systematic review of the current state of the housing market, and only one attempting a detailed analysis of supply/demand balances across all tenures in any detail.

Echoing the findings of Varady in another way, Blackaby also found little evidence of concrete policy conclusions arising from the assessments undertaken, or of any actual policy adjustments made on the basis of the assessments. The final conclusion drawn from the study was that:

> 'Most reports included in this review fall short of the comprehensive approach to assessment envisaged by much of the official guidance ... Only a minority of documents sought to draw out the relationship between demand and supply across all tenures or to discuss in any depth the current state of the housing market.'

> (Blackaby 2000, p. 34)

The land use planning system and housing planning

An important complementary process to housing planning in the UK is the land use 'planning system'. This is also a responsibility of local government. Since 1947, local authorities have been obliged to prepare plans for the use and development of land. The context for and priority accorded to the planning system have changed markedly since its introduction, but the basic legislative principles underlying the operation of the system have remained unchanged (Davies 1998). There is not enough space here for a full discussion of the planning system and its relationship with housing planning. However, it is important to note that, historically, the most sophisticated analysis of various dimensions of local housing markets have actually tended to arise through the planning system *per se* rather than through plans produced by housing departments. Household number forecasting, housing market boundary identification and tenure choice issues are often addressed by local authority land use planners rather than by their housing planning colleagues. Even so it is widely felt that the economic content of land use planning is very limited (Cullingworth 1997b).

Briefly, it needs to be noted here that for the most part future household numbers are established on the basis of demographic projection, with few attempts to allow for economic influences (and none that would be considered successful).[8] In terms of the geographic boundaries of private housing markets, it has been argued that land use planning policies should not only reflect the functional boundaries of local housing markets, but also the existence of any underlying sub-market structures (Jones & Watkins 1999). However, only the most sophisticated of Structure Plans attempt to broach the issue, even in a cursory fashion (School of Planning and Housing 2001; Jones 2002). Maclennan & Tu (1996) note the paucity of understanding of the structure and functioning of major UK housing markets.[9] Lastly, with respect to estimating current and future market demand, the School of Planning and Housing (2001) recently concluded that little attention has ever been paid by planners in Scotland to house prices as a source of evidence – a conclusion that is borne out in an English context by the work of Monk (2000b) and Monk & Whitehead (2000).[10]

The roots of the problem

Overall, then, it would appear that the conclusion drawn by Maclennan *et al.* (1994), to the effect that housing plans lack content, method and credibility, still holds true. In particular, housing plans or local housing strategies are silent or superficial in their treatment of private housing issues, and in their use of economic analysis to understand past trends, present circumstances or future prospects. If after so many years the analytical basis of housing planning remains so patently underdeveloped, it is reasonable to ask why.

The approach to housing strategy development taken and promoted in the UK is one of comprehensive rational planning (More 2002). This approach emphasises extensive use of analytical tools, and promotes the role of forecasting as a basis for plan development. Accepting the validity of this approach to housing planning for the moment, one can note that practical analytical tools to assist housing planners largely remain to be developed. Addressing the matter explicitly in terms of time and space, Table 12.1 suggests some questions where economics might be expected to furnish answers.

In other words, therefore, those charged with the development of local housing strategies might look to economists to:

- provide methods for isolating the functional boundaries of local housing markets at a point in time and for tracking the way in which they change over time. This would involve accounting for the key determinants of

Table 12.1 Economic aspects of housing markets.

	Present conditions	Future prospects
Housing market identification	A What are the current boundaries of the local housing market and what factors determine them?	B How are these boundaries adjusting over time and what factors are driving this? Are there cycles and/or trends evident within the local housing system? What is the trajectory of local demand, given regional and national employment trends?
Internal system structure	C What is the structure of housing supply and demand within the system? How do the various housing sectors interact at the margin? What is the spatial structure of supply and demand across the various sector price distributions? What is the nature of the local supply system in terms of capacity and ability to read and respond to demand signals? Do sub-systems or sub-markets exist and if so why? What problems are failure of the market and non-market sectors to equilibrate causing?	D Are overall trends likely to generate specific rubbing points at the margins between sectors, or in specific localities? Is the supply base within the system adequate to emergent demand conditions?

these boundaries (the structure and evolution of local labour markets) and the impact on them of significant policy positions taken by local authorities (particularly with respect to the spatial structure of planning permissions);

- construct models of household formation and housing demand within given geographies that are also underpinned by satisfactory representations of labour markets (effectively building in sensible approaches to migration forecasting), and which allow for search, income and price dynamics (Maclennan 1986a);

- map the structure of the housing industry across and within local housing markets, providing meaningful representations of likely decisions regarding supply from new and existing supply sources under different market conditions and prospects;

- develop typologies of demand and supply that permit the reduction of the overall complexity of a 'local housing market' into meaningful but more homogeneous groupings of spatially referenced demand and supply;

- establish methods for identifying, tracking and forecasting spatially referenced sub-market emergence and resolution (this does not simply refer to private market housing, but encompasses the patterns of behaviour that occur in the social rented sector);

- develop methods for identifying local market failures, their underlying causes and appropriate solutions;

- create policy simulation models that using a credible behavioural base allow the examination of 'what-if' scenarios that support deeper understanding of the economic consequences of specific policy positions; and

- provide techniques for evaluating alternative options for achieving specific objectives, and more generally for setting priorities and allocating resources across programmes of expenditure.

Against this list, one can note firstly (Table 12.1 A) that while there are sophisticated conceptual representations of the scale of urban housing markets (DiPasquale & Wheaton 1996) these do not translate into ready frameworks for practical application in specific housing planning contexts. One searches in vain in the literature for applied studies on the overall scale and functional boundaries of local housing markets in the UK (Jones 2002). As a consequence, while most accept that functional housing market areas are more appropriate than formal administrative areas for assessing the scale of housing demand and supply imbalances, we cannot satisfactorily identify them. Nor do there exist compelling forecasting models of housing demand based on functional geographies. More broadly (Table 12.1 B), there is a lack of any explicit dynamic analysis of local housing markets that would allow housing planners to separate function from dysfunction in observing their operation. Long-run trends, steady-state operation of housing markets as individual households move through their life cycles and the impacts of one-off shocks are all likely to manifest in superficially similar behaviour,[11] but the tools to filter the evidence remain to be developed.

Practical analysis of the internal structure of local housing markets (Table 12.1 C) is hardly more firmly founded, although there is more of it around (Jones *et al.* 2001b). To understand the operation of a local housing market one must be able to decompose it into more substitutable from less substitutable housing 'products'. One must also be able to establish whether specific sub-markets exist, and where they do, to map their spatial structure. Efforts to characterise the internal structure of local housing markets include work by Maclennan attempting to define 'product groups' based on the attribute structure of existing stock within Scottish cities (see Maclennan *et al.* 1994). Most UK studies attempt to identify spatial sub-markets using a hedonic approach, which raises considerable well-known conceptual problems.[12]

There is little in the way of analysis of household behavioural responses to administered systems of housing supply. There is also a dearth of understanding of market housing supply issues, from the question of how best to characterise regional, local market or intra-market supply structures, to the development of meaningful representations of the behaviour of supply agents under different market conditions.

Finally, there is the question of intra-market dynamics (Table 12.1 D). There has been a substantial US-based model-building effort since the 1970s (particularly at the National Bureau of Economic Research, and the Urban Institute – see Rothenberg *et al.* (1991) for a review of these models). Work following the lead of these contributions in a UK context includes that of Ballas & Clarke (1999), and the demand forecasting work of Gibb *et al.* (2000). Such models can be used to simulate the allocation of households to housing stock. The Gibb *et al.* study forecasts demand for both social renting and owner occupation in Glasgow City to 2009, based on a disaggregation of demand into three areas, and as it breaks down between net migration into the city, new household-based demand, and moves between the three areas by tenure and house type (see Chapter 2 for a fuller discussion). There is no doubting the value of such work, or that key issues can be addressed using it. However, the geographies for the work are still dominated by formal areas rather than functional; the explanatory variables used remain constrained by what is available rather than what is relevant, and the quality of forecasts (where they exist) for some key explanatory variables remains extremely low.

The foregoing does not add up to a complete analytical toolkit for the housing planner concerned to get a defensible handle on the state of affairs in a local housing market, existing housing needs, or immediate prospects for the housing system.

If, however, housing planners had a suitable, comprehensive toolkit of techniques for characterising, investigating and understanding the local housing market, would that then solve the problem? Unfortunately, even with more tools available, there is a strong likelihood they would remain unused.[13] A second key inhibitor is behavioural rather than technical. Housing plans are likely to remain weak in terms of both analytical rigour and economic content largely because of the incentive structures facing organisations and individuals involved in housing planning.[14]

Economists concerned with the theory of economic planning have long been clear that a central aspect of any planning problem is ensuring it is in the interests of agents in the economy to behave as the centre requires them to behave (Heal 1973). Equally, public sector economic theorists have long recognised the issue of appropriate incentives (Niskanen 1994), as in a practical sense do successful practitioners of strategic management (Simpson 1998). Strategic planning of local housing markets clearly has a number of more or less self-evident benefits, but these seldom accrue directly to those individuals and organisations to which the costs of such planning falls. Goodlad (1993) maintains that the benefits of good housing planning include:

- maximisation of the effectiveness of public expenditure on a long-lasting good, with an ability to address problem causes rather than symptoms;

- contributions to 'the democratic process' as explicit statements of priorities and objectives can be disagreed with and challenged;

- a feedback mechanism whereby outcomes can be evaluated and future policies made more effective; and

- a clear guide to action, ensuring resources are devoted to programmes in line with priorities.

Goodlad concludes that, given these advantages, it is surprising to encounter resistance and difficult to understand failure to engage in comprehensive rational planning. But is it really?

Firstly, the amount of resource a local authority is willing to devote to comprehensive planning will be conditioned by the extent to which that influences subsequent resource allocation. The early history of housing planning in Britain was blighted by disillusionment caused by lack of a link between plans and resources. In the English context, Bramley *et al.* (1999) argue an upswell of interest *circa* 1990 had much to do with a central government shift in resource allocation, from one based predominantly on a 'top down' statistical formula (the 'General Needs Index') to one more driven by the quality of authorities' strategy and performance (Bramley *et al.* 1999). But as we have seen, the quality of plans produced subsequent to this change was still poor. In the Scottish context, while the allocation criteria were never very explicit, it was known throughout the 1990s that the quality of housing plans played some substantial part in final allocations of permission to spend on housing. Again, however, the comprehensiveness of plans fell considerably short of the ideal.

While plans might influence the allocation of some resources, they might not be perceived by local authorities to influence resource allocation enough (in terms of either the total size of the cake or its distribution among authorities) to be worth the associated costs. Blackaby (2000) reports that in some cases authorities may have been unwilling to undertake a comprehensive assessment because even with a better understanding of problems there would be few means available to put them right.

A second point is that central government has been consistently unwilling to insist that authorities use any available resources specifically for strategic planning purposes, and any approaches by authorities for additional resources for such purposes have been rejected. This position must have sent confusing signals to authorities regarding the importance of strategic planning for housing.

More generally, while there is no study evidence available to corroborate it, anecdotal evidence suggests that most authorities do not have recruitment policies geared to attracting quality research staff or strategic thinkers. Nor do they have promotion, reward and training systems providing a sound underpinning to support progressive improvement in strategic information availability or the comprehensive assessment of housing requirements. The evidence on plan quality certainly supports this conclusion. As Simpson (1998) notes:

> 'if you want "A" but reward "B", chances are pretty small you are going to get "A". Employees are very smart – they pay attention to what gets rewarded, not to what gets said.'

> (Simpson 1998, p. 626)

The issues raised above suggest that mindsets towards housing planning in the UK need to be changed. In fact,

> 'the real difficulty may be that housing planning as set out in the mid 1970s may now lack credibility and have the wrong emphases. In the advice about housing planning (there was) a presumption that the local authority was in control, that needs estimates could be made convincingly ...and that fixed plans would hold over a number of years ... The 'plan' emphasised a set of figures, clear investor roles and read as if change and uncertainty were minor considerations.'

> (Maclennan 1991, p. 191)

Thus, housing planning as a process has been under-emphasised relative to housing planning as production of a set of numbers and a document. In addition, it has been wrongly presented as something that is comparatively straightforward to do.

Conclusions

The rhetoric and the reality of housing planning in the UK differ, and have done so for a very long period of time. Some may ask whether local authorities should continue to have the role that has been assigned them in such an unquestioning way. The equity/efficiency case for some form of housing strategy development at the local scale remains a strong one (and not just in the UK). In the absence of any other obvious agency to perform this role, municipal government would appear to remain the best candidate for its delivery, but a new and robust consensus is required about the precise nature of the role, the competencies needed, and the tools and incentive systems both necessary and available to support its delivery.

For the future, the development of sound housing planning processes needs more emphasis, and plans produced at a point in time must be understood as contingent on unknown and currently unknowable future events. Modesty is in order. This is not to embrace defeat, nor to suggest that the apathy towards planning for local housing markets evident in the US is a superior model. As Maclennan so nicely (and characteristically) put it,

> 'there is no reason why we should restrict our planning to an optimistic disembowelling of sheep in the top floors of housing departments. For if there are clear objectives, an assessment of the best opening strategic moves and a continuing capacity to observe and react to change, then organisations, with bounded rationality, may best cope with the unfolding future.'
>
> (Maclennan 1991, pp. 191–2)

Acknowledgements

I am grateful for the comments provided on an earlier draft by David Donnison, Glen Bramley, George Galster, Alan Holmans, Alison More, Christine Whitehead, and Gillian Young.

Notes

(1)   The views expressed in this chapter are those of the author writing in a personal capacity, and should not be taken to represent the views of Communities Scotland.

(2)   Within the UK, central government has exercised control of local authority functions through a number of territorially-based departments. For the most part this chapter deals with the situation in Scotland and England. In England, the Department of Transport, Local Government and the Regions oversees the activities of English-based authorities. In Scotland this responsibility falls to the Scottish Development Department. The different parts of the country have broadly kept in step over time regarding what has been expected of local government in housing planning terms.

(3)   I am grateful to Alan Holmans for advice on this section, as it relates to England.

(4)   Quoted from private correspondence with Alan Holmans.

(5)   A national 'quasi-autonomous non-governmental organisation' (or 'quango') set up in 1989.

(6)   Varady is an American academic who produced his study on a sabbatical visit, with a primary objective of drawing useful lessons for American housing planning systems.

(7)   The work by Blackaby complements an earlier study by Evans *et al.* (1999) looking at the private sector coverage of Welsh housing strategies and operational plans.

(8)   See DoE (1999a) for the details of the latest English national projections available at time of writing; for discussion of different aspects of these numbers and their sub-national breakdown, see Breheny (1999), Jones & Watkins (1999); for the role of economic factors in household formation, see Bramley & Lancaster (1998) and Bramley *et al.* (1997). Business Strategies Limited (1998) offer an interesting economic-based alternative approach to household numbers forecasting, as does the work of Peterson *et al.* (1998), which has attracted some fierce criticism from Wilcox (1998). An alternative approach that projects owner occupancy rates for England to 2016 is provided by Meen (1998). However, in doing so, Meen eschews modelling the propensity for households to form from a given population on the basis of economic considerations, essentially because of data limitations.

(9)   In an interesting series of papers (Jones *et al.* 2000; 2001a; 2001b), analysis of price and owner-occupier movement dynamics is explored as the basis for understanding the underlying structure of the Glasgow housing market. This builds on work done much earlier but not subsequently capitalised on by authors such as Hancock & Maclennan (1989) and Maclennan *et al.* (1987).

(10)   Barlow *et al.* (1994) in a survey of all local planning authorities in England and Wales found the working relationship between planning and housing departments to be variable. In many cases there was very little liaison. A later study by Bramley *et al.* (1999) on the basis of a postal survey estimated that between 1991 and 1998 some 350 housing needs surveys had been carried

out in England by local authorities. Half of these had been developed as a joint exercise between planning and housing departments. This latter study was an assessment of the state of the art in local housing needs assessment as applied to estimating social/affordable housing need at the local authority level (rather than explicitly focusing on overall models of the housing system generally). Bramley *et al.* give a cogent description of how the housing and planning departments might come together for this purpose. The study findings do not however suggest it is a good representation of what actually happens. While this review found much to applaud in the work being done by individual local authorities, it still concluded that in conducting housing analysis it is typically the case that:

- estimates of social renting at a point in time, or projected forward, are not typically integrated with supply data, either in total or disaggregated by property size, or geographic areas;
- employment and income data tends to be used as descriptive 'decoration' rather than constituting a part of the overall analysis; and
- analysis tends to be fixed at the local authority level, ignoring the issues of broader functional markets or internal sub-market structures (Bramley *et al.* 1999).

(11)   For example, movement of young households from rural areas to urban, and the reverse movement of middle-aged households, is equally compatible with a steady state symbiotic operation of urban/rural housing markets, closure of dominant industry employment in a rural area and increased commuting as local prices adjust to reflect this, or urban growth increasing the pressure on surrounding settlements. The only study I have come across which shows even a dim awareness of these types of issues is that by Nevin *et al.* (2001).

(12)   Rothenberg *et al.* (1991) using US data have developed the notion of 'quality sub-markets' as an alternative to using a spatial approach, which addresses some of the problems involved in using the hedonic method, but its applicability has not been explored in the UK context.

(13)   A friend and colleague has argued the point forcibly as follows: 'There is a more basic failure to use economics as a framework for thinking about housing planning issues (even down to just recognising the basics of supply and demand), a failure to think of housing as a system and a general absence of strategic thinking...Housing planning could improve a lot if planners had a more sophisticated conceptual framework, never mind operational models' (A. More, private correspondence). The key question, of course, is what prevents this from happening?

(14)   One may of course fairly apply this reasoning to the prior problem. That is, the incentive structure facing economists may well have militated against their applying themselves to the production of useful tools for supporting housing planning.

13

The Right to Buy in Britain

Nick Williams

Introduction

The most contentious and arguably the most significant housing policy in Britain over the last twenty years has been the right to buy public sector housing for sitting tenants (the 'Right to Buy'). Successive Acts of Parliament have given tenants a statutory Right to Buy the dwelling they are renting from a public sector landlord at considerable discounts off the market price. Since the statutory Right to Buy was introduced by the first Thatcher (Conservative) government in 1980 over two million tenants have bought their homes, and this has been a major element in increasing owner occupation in Britain from 55% to 68% of private households over the same period. Local authority-owned housing has fallen from 25% of the total stock to less than 17%, although large-scale transfer to other landlords has also made a contribution to this shrinkage.

The introduction of the statutory Right to Buy in 1980 was ideologically driven as part of a wider objective by Margaret Thatcher to reduce collectivist provision across a broad range of goods and services. In the late 1970s, public sector housing was seen as a high priority for this process by the Conservative Party, given the large numbers of council tenants who traditionally supported the Labour Party, and the electoral attractiveness of a policy which (it was perceived) could be used to induce council tenants to switch their votes. A statutory Right to Buy was therefore viewed in prospect not only as a potentially effective mechanism for extending market forces on a large scale but also a political weapon to obtain the power to do so (although see Williams *et al.* (1987) for evidence that the electoral gain for the Conservatives was limited). Legislation followed swiftly after the Conservatives' victory in the 1979 General Election.

The reaction from academics and housing professionals to the introduction of a statutory Right to Buy was largely hostile and was itself at least partly ideological, founded upon a deeply-held attachment to council housing and unverified assumptions about the long-term effects of the legislation. It could be fairly said that both the policy itself and the initial resistance to it were not founded upon either robust evidence or a rational and comprehensive assessment of the likely consequences. More recently, the relationship between policy, evidence and research has become more coherent with the introduction of a modernised Right to Buy in Scotland that attempts to rationalise housing subsidies across tenures.

No attempt is made here to provide a history of the Right to Buy. Comprehensive accounts can be found elsewhere (see Forrest & Murie 1988; Jones & Murie 1999; Williams 1993; Wilson 1999). The focus of attention in this chapter is the relationship between policy and research, especially the extent to which the latter has influenced the former. It will be argued that most of the academic research on the Right to Buy has been reactive, and that until the recent legislation in Scotland most of the policy changes that have occurred have been driven by factors other than a rational analysis of the likely wider effects of those changes.

The following sections examine the policy objectives behind successive Acts of Parliament and show how a drive to expand owner occupation (as well as to reduce public expenditure) lay behind them. The details of the relevant Acts are described and the research findings on the consequences of the Acts are summarised. In particular, I show that this research was used by Conservative governments simply to increase the attractiveness of the Right to Buy as sales flagged after an initial rush of purchases. Lastly, an assessment is made of the contribution that academic research has made to the development of policy in this area, including consideration of the recent legislation in Scotland to modernise the Right to Buy.

Policy objectives

The most important objective of the Right to Buy for the first Thatcher government was, without question, to increase the number of owner-occupiers in Britain. Theoretical arguments could have been used to justify the policy in terms of removing imperfections in housing markets and increasing labour mobility (see for example Hughes & McCormick 1981; and Minford *et al.* 1988), but the overwhelming weight of the government's argument for the Right to Buy was ideological. In moving the second reading of the 1980 legislation Michael Heseltine stated the objectives as follows:

'...first, to give people what they want, and, secondly, to reverse the trend of ever-increasing dominance of the State over the life of the individual. There is in this country a deeply ingrained desire for homeownership. The Government believe that this spirit should be fostered'.

(Official Report 15 January 1980, cols 1444–5)

In terms of this single objective, the policy was a huge success. The impact of the 1980 legislation was immediate. Sales were rapid, rising to a peak of over 220000 in 1982. Sales then halved by 1985 as pent-up demand was satisfied, and (as will be seen) the government introduced further legislation to boost purchases. The capital receipts from sales were used to reduce public expenditure and Conservative governments forced local authorities to use these receipts to pay off debt.[1]

Critics of the policy and indeed neutral observers pointed out however that there could be wider and undesirable consequences of large-scale sales. These were defined in the House of Commons Environment Committee's Second Report for Session 1980–81, which was devoted to council house sales (Environment Committee 1981). The possible consequences included the impact of sales on meeting need for rented housing through loss of quality rented stock in specific localities, impacts on the mainstream housing market through an increase in supply, effects on public finances and the wider economy, and distributional effects between individuals. The Committee criticised the government for being unable to provide robust information on these issues and recommended a programme of research and monitoring to obtain it. Monitoring was to record information on purchasers and dwellings bought, and research was to cover the effects of sales on relets, management and maintenance costs of the remaining stock, and the distribution of income and wealth.

The evidence base for the 1980 legislation

The 1980 Housing Act (and in Scotland the 1980 Tenants' Rights Act) were not passed in a complete absence of data on the likely pattern of sales or possible consequences of those sales; discretionary sales to sitting tenants had been possible for many years and had occurred on a significant scale in some local authorities. The evidence from the period of discretionary sales indicated that it was mainly the better houses with gardens on the most desirable estates that were bought, and that purchasers were drawn disproportionately from middle-aged tenants in work with skilled occupations (see Bassett 1980; Beazley 1980; Forrest & Murie 1976; Malpass 1980; Murie

1975; National Council of Social Service 1980; Richmond 1980; Truesdale 1980). This evidence was indicative rather than definitive however, since discretionary sales by some local authorities were selective. Birmingham and Leeds, for instance, did not offer flats for sale under voluntary arrangements. It was thus difficult to extrapolate from the evidence to the likely effects of a statutory and more extensive Right to Buy.

The government was influenced however, by strongly-put arguments that a statutory Right to Buy would be directly harmful in two specific ways. First, that it would damage housing opportunities for older people by reducing the supply of sheltered housing. Second, that sales in rural areas would be harmful because of high external demand for holiday and retirement homes, and because of the already smaller proportion of stock in such areas in the rented sector. No systematic evidence was available at the time to substantiate these claims but lobby groups put them forcefully, and the legislation was consequently amended in two ways. First, sheltered housing was exempted, and second, in certain circumstances tenants of council dwellings in rural areas could be denied some of the purchase rights granted automatically to other tenants (see Williams & Sewel (1987) for a fuller discussion). The legislation had been changed, but as a result of political pressure skilfully applied, not substantive evidence.

Subsequent research on the statutory Right to Buy

Given the political prominence of the Right to Buy and the fears that had been expressed concerning the consequences of its statutory nature, there was an obvious need and an opportunity for research to contribute to the policy process by monitoring the pattern of sales, and in the longer term by investigating the wider consequences. Detailed guidance on what this research should address had already been given in the Environment Committee's Second Report as noted above, but not all of these recommendations were followed in the subsequent work that has been undertaken.

Research has been undertaken both in-house by government (see Foulis 1983; Kerr 1988; Lynn 1991; MacNee 1993; Scottish Homes 1996) and also by academics. The most significant academic contributions have been made by Forrest & Murie (1984a, 1984b, 1988, 1990a), with evidence from Scotland by Williams *et al.* (1984, 1986, 1987, 1988); Williams & Twine (1992, 1993, 1994); Pawson *et al.* (1997); and Pawson & Watkins (1999).

The research that has been done has generated evidence on the following topics:

- the pattern of sales in terms of dwelling type and location;

- the socio-economic characteristics of purchasers and non-purchasers;

- implications of sales for the role of public sector housing within the housing system; and

- effects of resold dwellings on the mainstream private housing market.

Notably absent, however, has been research on the specific and quantitative effects of sales on relets in particular localities and on consequent ability to meet the need for affordable rented housing, as defined by the Environment Committee. In the early period after 1980 this was for the simple reason that the consequences would take time to emerge, since those purchasing their council dwelling would probably stay in it for some period thereafter; but as time went by the absence of this research became less excusable. Undoubtedly lack of work here can be linked to lack of funding by government, and the fact that it is a difficult area to research involving long time-scales and a complex multivariate situation, in which loss of relets through Right to Buy sales is only one influence on opportunities to rent. Given the importance of the issue however, it is particularly regrettable that no body of substantive work has been undertaken.

Evidence on some aspects of the wider consequences of sales for the housing system and for the housing opportunities of different types of household was, however, emerging during the later 1980s. Research was revealing not only a non-random pattern of sales by dwelling type, but also by tenant characteristics. In fact, the pattern of Right to Buy sales was very similar to the discretionary pre-1980 sales. Sales have been predominantly of houses on the more popular estates, and to middle-aged tenants in work with no dependent children. Sales to non-working households, lone parents and those in non-skilled low paid employment have been conspicuous by their absence. There have also been geographic variations. Sales have been significantly higher as a proportion of the public sector stock in rural areas than urban areas (but have not been high enough to trigger the reduction of purchase rights built in to the 1980 legislation to protect rural stock). There have also been higher sales in the more prosperous parts of the country, especially the south of England, and lower sales in the less prosperous industrial north of England and the deprived parts of urban Scotland.

These non-random patterns of sales have certainly had consequences for the housing system as a whole, and for households' opportunities within the system, but these cannot be evaluated in isolation from other changes occurring to housing at the same time. The selective loss of properties and tenants from the public sector noted above would have had limited significance if the properties sold were being replaced, and similar households were becoming tenants to those exiting through the Right to Buy. Nevertheless, neither of these things has occurred, leading to a general 'residualisation' of the public sector in which it has shrunk in size and housed an increasing proportion of poorer and benefit-dependent tenants. This in turn led some commentators to argue that the role of public sector housing has changed to that of a safety net for only the poorest households as in the United States. This has not been a generally accepted view (see Clapham & Maclennan 1983; Forrest & Murie 1990b; Malpass 1983; and Williams *et al.* 1986), but we can say that the housing opportunities of those households who need or prefer to rent have been reduced since 1980 and that the Right to Buy has made a contribution to this process. To reiterate the point made earlier, however, there has unfortunately been no published research on the actual extent to which the Right to Buy has reduced opportunities to rent in specific locations, especially in rural areas where fears on this have been most vociferously expressed since the first legislation in 1980.

Sales to sitting tenants not only affect the rented sector; they also increase the supply of housing for sale should the Right to Buy purchaser decide to resell. Evidence is now available on the role resold dwellings play in the housing market, and in particular whether they continue to increase access to owner occupation for low-income households, or widen choice for those already able to enter, or within the tenure. This evidence comes from England (Forrest & Murie 1990a) and Scotland (Williams & Twine 1992, 1993, 1994; Pawson *et al.* 1997; Pawson & Watkins 1999).

Resale purchasers are generally younger than tenant purchasers, and about 25% said that resale purchase was their only route into owner occupation. Perhaps more significantly, most said that the resold dwellings widened their choice of property to buy mainly because equivalent dwellings in the mainstream market were more expensive. This most commonly meant being able to buy a larger house rather than a smaller flat. As well as being younger, resale purchasers tend to be in non-manual or skilled occupations and hence differ significantly from those households seeking rented accommodation, who throughout the 1990s have been increasingly drawn from non-working benefit-dependent households. The evidence also indicates that very few resold council dwellings are being used as second or holiday homes, one of the major fears of those who were concerned about the effects on opportunities to rent in rural areas.

The relationship between policy and research

Much of the reaction to the evidence that has been assembled over time has been limited to the initial impact of sales rather than to the longer-term strategic effects; those with strong ideological positions, for or against, have been able to select evidence to suit their position. Government used little of the research evidence accumulated in the 1980s and 1990s in a strategic way to reassess the role of the Right to Buy in the wider housing system. The only policy responses that can be related to research are the greater incentives to purchase that were introduced in the 1984 and 1986 Acts.

The Housing and Building Control Act 1984 reduced the residency qualification for Right to Buy from three to two years, with a minimum discount of 32% and the maximum discount increased from 50 to 60% in order to boost sales. Forrest & Murie (1988) estimated that these changes increased the number of eligible tenants by over 250 000.

Accumulating evidence both from government in-house research and academics also confirmed that the overwhelming number of sales had been of houses rather than flats. Up to 1986 over 80% of sales were houses. The government's response to this was to legislate further to make purchase more attractive to flat dwellers. The Housing and Planning Act 1986 increased the minimum discount for flats to 44%, with the discount increasing thereafter by 2% per annum up to a maximum of 70% after 15 years.

Sales rose in response to both Acts and by 1989 had recovered to almost 200 000. Flats also constituted a larger proportion of sales, rising to 25% in 1990, but houses still made up the overwhelming majority. (The boost to sales was ultimately short-lived, however, and sales fell sharply again in 1990 to 135 000, partly as a result of recession in the economy and high interest rates. Sales since 1990 have fallen further and have bottomed-out at between 50 000 and 70 000 per year.)[2]

Yet research has also revealed significant effects on the housing system and information regarding losers and gainers from the Right to Buy, that were ignored by policy makers. Purchasers have been allowed to buy good quality dwellings at large discounts and many have made large capital gains on resale. The losers have been those on low incomes who cannot attain home-ownership even through the Right to Buy, and for whom affordable renting is the only avenue to acceptable housing. Their housing choices have been dramatically reduced as the public sector has shrunk in size and quality. Since it is the wealthier tenants who have bought, sales have been highly regressive. In the late 1980s and early 1990s council tenants had rents 35 to

40% less than market values but could receive discounts on purchase of 50% or more (see Hills 1991; Maclennan *et al.* 1991a). The wealthier tenant who exercised the Right to Buy would thus receive a larger housing subsidy than the poorer tenant who had to remain as a tenant. Moreover, the redistribution of housing choice implicit in the Right to Buy policy has been random and unintended. Sales receipts have not been used to reinvest in housing, and the conclusion must be drawn that during the 1980s and 1990s British housing policy including the Right to Buy failed to cohere across tenures. Subsidies remained unrelated to income and households' true housing preferences were obscured because of the unequal subsidy treatment of the tenures. Sales to sitting tenants are not inherently good or bad but in the absence of a strategic context can have adverse and unintended consequences. As configured by 1980s legislation, they represented an additional subsidy to a selected group of homeowners and led to distortion within the housing market. Within a broader and integrated package of policies it is conceivable that the Right to Buy could play a valuable role. The experience of the 1980s and 1990s was unfortunately different.

The modernised or strategic Right to Buy in Scotland

Maclennan had raised many of these points and potential concerns in a 1977 discussion paper. It is worth quoting directly from this paper:

> 'Raised in isolation from a particular context of national housing policy and national economic constraints, the council house sales issue is a red herring. Before deciding whether or not properties should be sold there must be a clear statement of government policy for the growth of owner occupation and policy towards the level and distribution of public sector housing subsidy.'

> (Maclennan 1977a, p. 2)

and further:

> '...it is only within a dramatically revised system of housing subsidy, which is sectorally neutral and income or wealth related, that council house sales can play a useful role in housing policy'.

> (Maclennan 1977a, p. 13)

It was precisely these conditions that were absent when the Right to Buy policy was introduced and extended from 1980 onwards.

Devolution of power to Scotland and the establishment of the Scottish Parliament in 1999, with housing as a devolved function, provided the opportunity for more rational arrangements for the Right to Buy to be established north of the border. In 2001 legislation was passed by the Scottish Parliament that attempts to place the Right to Buy in a more strategic and rational context as described by Maclennan.[3] Moreover, this legislation in contrast to previous Housing Acts was based on a review of all the existing published research relevant to the Right to Buy in Scotland. Additional research and statistical modelling of likely future levels of Right to Buy sales based on different levels of discount was undertaken by civil service-based research professionals. This review and research was published during the consultation process to which the legislation was subject (Maclennan *et al.* 2000). On the basis of the analysis and reaction to it, the Executive concluded that the Right to Buy should be retained in Scotland but rebalanced so that it would be a strategical rather than an ideological policy instrument. Four issues were central to this rebalancing process.

(1) What was the subsidy attached to the existing Right to Buy and was it tenure neutral? Did it give tenants of public sector housing a large subsidy on purchase in the form of the discount on the market price not shared by other households with similar incomes but in a different tenure?

(2) Was it logical that some tenants should have the Right to Buy and others should not? This was an issue particularly because Right to Buy status of tenants of housing associations,[4] by 1999, varied according to a range of factors. Housing associations with 'charitable status'[5] had since 1980 been exempt from the Right to Buy. Those without charitable status could find their housing subject to the Right to Buy, depending on the subsidy regime under which a property had been developed, or the form of tenancy agreement held by the tenant.[6]

(3) Would extending the Right to Buy to non-charitable housing associations threaten their financial viability through loss of stock and therefore net rental income?

(4) What were the local consequences of Right to Buy and would it be possible to balance community and individual interests in specific localities, especially in areas where Right to Buy sales had decreased the availability of affordable rented housing?

The modernised Right to Buy as incorporated in the Housing (Scotland) Act 2001 has the following features. To equalise inter-tenure subsidies at the mean (Maclennan *et al.* 2000), the discounts on purchase have been reduced; they start after five years at 20% rising annually by 1% to a maximum of 35%, with an absolute financial cap at £15 000. This compares with the prior conditions, of a two-year qualifying period with a maximum discount of 60% after 30 years (70% after 15 years for flats) and no cap, and is thus a significant reduction in the attractiveness of the Right to Buy for new tenants (existing tenants have a preserved Right to Buy under the previous conditions).

The modernised Right to Buy was extended to tenants of non-charitable housing associations who at the time of the passing of the Act did not have it, but suspended for ten years, unless an association chooses to opt in at an earlier date. This was designed to protect associations financially and give them time to adjust to the new arrangements. In terms of balancing individual purchaser interests with those of local communities needing affordable housing to rent, the legislation allowed for Right to Buy to be suspended for up to five years (with the facility for subsequent renewal) in areas designated as 'pressured'. Pressured areas can be designated by local authorities, with ministers' approval, where it can be shown by authorities that there is an unsatisfied demand for rented housing and that the continuation of Right to Buy sales would be likely to exacerbate the shortage.

Perhaps most significantly from the point of view of the relationship between policy and research, Scottish ministers have a duty under the 2001 legislation to publish within four years of the Act coming into force, and at regular intervals thereafter, evidence on the effects of the Right to Buy in Scotland on local housing systems.

The modernised Right to Buy represents a significant improvement on its previous form. It has not been without its critics, however. Concerns have centred on housing association financial viability implications, despite the measures built into the legislation to allow time for adjustment (Scottish Federation of Housing Associations 2000). Worries continue to be voiced about the effects of the new legislation on the supply of affordable rented housing in specific localities, as well as the demotivating effects it will have on housing association committee members who offer their services on a voluntary basis. There are also concerns about the effectiveness of the safeguards introduced in the form of pressured areas in that it is not yet clear what sort of evidence will be required by the Scottish Executive to approve applications for pressured area status. It was noted above that a large gap in the available research evidence is the impact the Right to Buy has had on the supply of rented accommodation at local level. This evidence will continue to be difficult and expensive to acquire.

The jury will be out in Scotland for some time as to whether the modernised Right to Buy will have the effects its creators hope for. Only time and evidence can answer the questions that have been raised. Nevertheless, what is fair to say is that there has been an explicit attempt to use research to guide the development of Right to Buy into a more strategic policy instrument, focused on issues of housing equity and efficiency in local housing contexts. Moreover, it is likely the situation in Scotland will be judged to be preferable to that in England and Wales even by critics of the modernised Right to Buy, in that there are no major proposals to change the Right to Buy south of the border.[7]

Conclusions

The history of the Right to Buy in Britain is not a happy one for those who believe that housing policy should be rational, based on evidence and with the objectives of maximising housing choice and quality in as fair a manner as possible. It began life as an ideological instrument to expand homeownership, which could be used as an electoral weapon, and rapidly became the single most effective revenue raiser for a government intent on swingeing cuts in public expenditure and personal taxation. The accumulating evidence on the Right to Buy was cherry-picked by the Thatcher governments and used to expand its effectiveness as a consumer policy and revenue raiser divorced from any concern for or interest in the wider consequences flowing from it.

It is not as if there was no evidence that could have been used to place the Right to Buy within a more rational and strategic context, even in 1980. Most of the research done on the Right to Buy has been quality work. Unfortunately, it has also been selective and left at least one important gap. Much of the work instigated by academics related to the pattern of sales by property and household and confirmed that the best properties were more likely to be bought by more prosperous households. The possible adverse consequences of these patterns were often averred in terms of reduced opportunities to rent in the social rented sector, but the follow-up research to test these predictions has never been done. It was not until 1990 that the first evidence of the impact of Right to Buy resales on the wider owner occupier market was published by Forrest & Murie, and there is still a lack of hard evidence on the effects of Right to Buy sales on opportunities to rent in the social rented sector although this was flagged up by the Environment Committee as desirable in 1981.

Government can be criticised for not funding this research, but academics can also be criticised for not arguing for it to be done. Not until the reform of the Right to Buy in Scotland was all the research evidence available taken seriously (and indeed further work done on prediction of the effects of sales on the rented stock) and used to reconstruct policy.[8] Politicians through their control of funding have a major influence on what research is done, but academics have a duty to define gaps in knowledge and attempt to fill them even when the results might cast doubt on their own ideological predilections.

Notes

(1)   Between 1980/81 and 1985/86, housing privatisation (mostly Right to Buy sales) yielded over £9 billion, more than half of all privatisation proceeds of £16.4 billion (Forrest & Murie 1988). This was immensely useful to a government that also had as an overriding objective the reduction of personal taxation and the shrinkage of the public sector. The cash raised from council house sales could have been used in various ways including investment in the housing stock, but in fact was mainly used to reduce the taxation burden (see Murie 1989).

(2)   It should be noted that the 1986 Act was not primarily concerned with the Right to Buy, but with a more comprehensive approach to the privatisation of public sector housing involving block sales to developers for onward sale and large-scale transfers to housing associations (private not-for-profit landlords in receipt of public subsidy whose major objective is the development and management of quality housing for low income households). The declining level of Right to Buy sales after 1990 is an indication that the government had also made a shrewd assessment in 1986 that, in terms of their primary objective to reduce the size of the public housing sector, additional mechanisms would be required.

(3)   It is not irrelevant to this that the First Minister in Scotland had employed Maclennan in 1999 as a special adviser with a particular responsibility for the proposed Scottish housing legislation!

(4)   Not-for-profit landlords – see Note 2.

(5)   A legal status, which circumscribes the operations of housing associations that seek it, but carries certain tax advantages.

(6)   It should also be noted that where an association acquired stock through transfer of property from another landlord (usually a local authority) and tenants held the Right to Buy under the transferring landlord, that right was preserved under the receiving landlord.

(7)   There has however been some recent change in England, in that maximum discounts have been introduced which vary regionally, being highest in London (£38 000) and lowest in the Northeast (£22 000). More change may be in prospect.

(8)   It is tempting to say that Maclennan's employment as an adviser to the First Minister was crucial, but it must also be said that the housing minister responsible for the Bill, Wendy Alexander, was committed to a reformed Right to Buy and without her enthusiasm it probably would not have happened.

14

The Political Economy of Housing Research

David Donnison & Mark Stephens

Introduction

In this essay we ask: what has shaped the evolution of housing research in Britain; how do we choose and formulate the questions to be studied? And what can today's housing researchers learn from this discussion that may help them in the years to come? We deal with work by economists but do not confine ourselves to their discipline. Our more fundamental purpose is to remind our colleagues who think of themselves as analysts of housing problems and policies that we should occasionally step back and recall that we are applied social scientists for whom our own profession is also a proper subject for study.

We start by looking briefly at the evolution of housing research since World War II, focusing mainly on the first and last decades of that period, and making liberal use of hindsight. After this brief review we pause to note developments that have changed the power structures within which researchers operate in Britain and the academic context for their work. These developments help to explain changes in the scale and character of the research done in this field. We conclude by drawing a few lessons from our discussion for housing researchers looking to the future.

The quantity of research done by academics on housing and the variety of questions they explore have both increased, but there has also been an increase in the competing enterprises doing such research. The comparative advantages remaining to academics working within this wider industry are their opportunities – and obligations – to gain a broad understanding of the workings of their society, and to speak uncensored truth to power and to the public at large. Since Duncan Maclennan has been a leading exemplar of that philosophy this book is a fitting setting for our argument.

Our chapter, we must stress, is not a literature review. Although many authors are mentioned, they are chosen, not to introduce specific works, but to represent themes, trends and disciplines that play a part in the story. Readers can readily look up their works if they wish to explore them. We give references only to a few of them, that for various reasons should be noted, or call for special comment.

Housing research resumes after World War II

Housing research during the interwar period focused particularly on bad housing in urban slums and rural areas, and the effect this had on the health of those who lived there (see works by R.C.K. Ensor, W.G. Savage, Seebohm Rowntree, Marian Bowley, J.M. Mackintosh, and Margaret Bondfield). That emphasis reflected both the human situation and the political assumptions of the time. Housing conditions were indeed so bad that they often threatened people's health. The government department responsible for housing was the Ministry of Health.

After World War II, there was no time and little need for research. The problems were critical but simple: the main obstacles to progress were the urgent need to repair war damage, shortages of building materials and skilled labour, and the precarious state of Britain's post-war economy. For several years the government felt compelled to restrict output to 200 000 houses a year and to channel most of that building through local authorities.

Research took off again during the late 1950s and 1960s, based mainly in university departments of social administration, and funded to a great extent by the Joseph Rowntree Trust (now the Joseph Rowntree Foundation). Most of those who played leading roles in the new wave of research (Lewis Waddilove, Rowntree's director, and academics such as J.B. Cullingworth, David Donnison, Adela Nevitt, John Greve and Lionel Needleman) were motivated by concerns about the needs of working-class people and the development of a welfare state that would meet those needs. First, housing scarcity and then, slum conditions were the problems to be tackled. Later, attention turned to private rents and homelessness, particularly in London (reported on by the Milner Holland Committee in 1965), and then to urban renewal and the small minorities left homeless.

These researchers hoped that the right to a decent home at affordable cost would become as universally assured as the right to free education and medical care.[1] Whether they were members of the Labour Party or not, most of them were spiritually embedded in the intellectual wing of the Labour movement, led by Richard Titmuss, head of the LSE's Social Administration Department.[2] When Labour lost power in 1951 these links with the Party were strengthened. For thirteen years its leaders had to do without civil service advisers and they naturally turned to the universities for help – many of them being former academics themselves (Attlee, Dalton, Gaitskell, Crossman and Crosland were among the more distinguished examples).

The British housing research agenda of the time therefore reflected the housing problems of the time, viewed through a specific social, political and cultural perspective. A few researchers (Donnison, Greve and later Roger Duclaud-Williams) did their best to learn what was going on in other countries of Europe, West and East. In Western Europe, under similar political systems and faced with similar problems, the basic priorities of researchers and policy makers were much the same as ours.

In countries of the Soviet bloc, where the Communist Party and the state were all-powerful, more attention was being paid to sheer volume of output, and therefore to research on building methods and materials. Engineering and architecture were the dominant disciplines in the big research institutes where most of that research was done. Working on a study for the United Nations in the early 1960s, one of the authors of this chapter was going from one European capital to another to consult the ministries responsible for policies in this field. In Moscow the top official in the Ministry of Construction of the Soviet Union's Russian Republic began his speech of welcome by saying: 'In the Soviet Union we have solved the housing problem. We have learnt how to stick the big panels together.' He was not joking. Like most of his colleagues sitting round his boardroom table he was an engineer.

From the United States, a country relatively unscarred by war and with an altogether different political tradition, there came a cold blast of economic and philosophical reasoning from forerunners of Milton Friedman and Charles Murray. Richard Muth was prominent among them, but even Robert Nozick, in his famous philosophical defence of anarchy, chose rent control as a prime example of the evils of state intervention (Nozick 1974, pp. 270–271). If British academics tended to treat housing as an arena in which to advance the development of the welfare state, many Americans treated it as an arena in which to attack the pretensions of government: LSE social administration versus Chicago economics.

In Australia, where an American plenitude of land and owner-occupied housing was combined with a European respect for the capacity of the state, there came a creatively different research agenda, placing housing firmly in an urban and economic framework. (Hugh Stretton was – and still is – the guru of this tradition: see, as examples, Stretton 1971, 1974, 1978; but there were many others such as Max Neutze, Ian Manning, Leone Sandercock, Patricia Apps and Patrick Troy.)

Academics have recently made criticism of the state for its crippling divisions between separate, 'top-down', bureaucratic 'silos', an art form of conference speeches. Their own silos have been just as damaging. The institutions and disciplines that at this time provided a base for housing research also restricted the questions the researchers asked. It was difficult to bring the perspectives of social and urban policy together in Britain owing to accidents of academic history. Here, the study of social policy originated in the training of social workers, and recruited from students of sociology and psychology. Meanwhile the study of urban policy originated in the training of town planners, and recruited from students of geography and economics. These two kinds of department usually operated not merely in different disciplines but in different faculties. It is no accident that some of the most distinguished work that broke out of these disciplinary pigeon-holes took place outside the academy (Michael Young's team at the Institute of Community Studies, including Peter Willmott and Peter Marris, were outstanding examples).

As for building and transport, which in countries of the Soviet bloc were researched along with housing and architecture in the great state institutes, these, in Britain, were mainly studied outside the universities in places like the Building Research Station and the Transport and Road Research Laboratory, which recruited scientists, engineers and mathematicians for the purpose. Neither the academics working in social policy departments nor those in the urban studies field had much to do with them. We were, and still are, divided by C.P. Snow's 'two cultures'.

Meanwhile, at this time, no one provided any training for housing managers. Most of them worked for the lower tier of district authorities that had no tradition of training for staff with such modest status – people who had probably worked their way up after years spent as clerks or rent collectors.

Recent research on housing

By the end of the twentieth century the housing research field had grown considerably. Tables 14.1 and 14.2 show the results of a bibliographical

Table 14.1 Analysis of housing articles published 1990–2001 (numbers).

	1990	1991	1992	1993	1994	1995	1996	1997	1998	1999	2000	2001	Total
Social rented housing/sector	1	0	0	0	3	3	5	1	0	1	2	2	18
Social housing	14	13	23	26	62	65	90	50	68	87	89	94	681
Homelessness	70	69	68	44	65	75	76	74	115	88	91	95	930
Owner occupation or home ownership	19	26	28	20	37	33	33	27	40	35	59	48	405
Housing + economics/economy	10	11	7	9	30	25	35	25	38	72	77	88	427
Housing + land/planning	15	14	25	27	37	59	81	70	90	83	103	113	717
Housing + gender	4	1	7	1	0	5	8	9	4	10	12	9	70
Housing + old people/elderly	9	8	2	7	14	3	7	6	8	5	5	8	82
Housing + ethnic minorities/race	3	9	7	3	5	3	15	16	20	20	24	26	151
Housing + disability/disabilities	0	0	0	0	1	3	1	0	0	4	0	3	12
Housing + labour market/ mobility	10	9	5	7	9	21	20	14	25	25	30	37	212
Housing + health	6	6	6	6	15	18	19	8	12	25	37	40	198
Housing + fuel poverty	0	0	0	2	0	0	0	0	0	0	0	0	2
Housing + construction industry	2	3	3	1	7	8	12	9	8	13	11	9	86
Housing + design	6	2	5	4	13	13	5	7	5	7	14	24	105
Housing + careers/pathways	0	3	1	0	0	0	1	0	0	0	1	2	8
(Social rented) housing + private finance	0	1	0	1	1	2	0	0	0	0	0	0	5
Private rented sector/ private landlords	4	3	1	1	1	0	1	0	1	0	1	4	17
Housing + affordability	3	2	6	8	5	2	3	4	4	4	4	3	48
Housing + area regeneration	0	0	0	0	0	0	0	0	0	1	2	0	3
Housing + regeneration	1	1	1	0	2	3	2	3	0	3	4	3	23
Housing + subsidies	13	13	8	8	0	3	4	1	11	12	22	22	117
Housing + public expenditure	0	0	0	3	1	5	1	3	0	5	3	3	24
Total	190	194	203	178	308	349	419	327	449	500	591	633	4341

Table 14.2 Analysis of housing articles published 1990–2001 (percentages).

	1990	1991	1992	1993	1994	1995	1996	1997	1998	1999	2000	2001	Total
Social rented housing/sector	1	0	0	0	1	1	1	0	0	0	0	0	0
Social housing	7	7	11	15	20	19	21	15	15	17	15	15	16
Homelessness	37	36	33	25	21	21	18	23	26	18	15	15	21
Owner occupation or home ownership	10	13	14	11	12	9	8	8	9	7	10	8	9
Housing + economics/ economy	5	6	3	5	10	7	8	8	8	14	13	14	10
Housing + land/planning	8	7	12	15	12	17	19	21	20	17	17	18	17
Housing + gender	2	1	3	1	0	1	2	3	1	2	2	1	2
Housing + old people/elderly	5	4	1	4	5	1	2	2	2	1	1	1	2
Housing + ethnic minorities/race	2	5	3	2	2	1	4	5	4	4	4	4	3
Housing + disability/disabilities	0	0	0	0	0	1	0	0	0	1	0	0	0
Housing + labour market/ mobility	5	5	2	4	3	6	5	4	6	5	5	6	5
Housing + health	3	3	3	3	5	5	5	2	3	5	6	6	5
Housing + fuel poverty	0	0	0	1	0	0	0	0	0	0	0	0	0
Housing + construction industry	1	2	1	1	2	2	3	3	2	3	2	1	2
Housing + design	3	1	2	2	4	4	1	2	1	1	2	4	2
Housing + careers/pathways	0	2	0	0	0	0	0	0	0	0	0	0	0
(Social rented) housing + private finance	0	1	0	1	0	1	0	0	0	0	0	0	0
Private rented sector/ private landlords	2	2	0	1	0	0	0	0	0	0	0	1	0
Housing + affordability	2	1	3	4	2	1	1	1	1	1	1	0	1
Housing + area regeneration	0	0	0	0	0	0	0	0	0	0	0	0	0
Housing + regeneration	1	1	0	0	1	1	0	1	0	1	1	0	1
Housing + subsidies	7	7	4	4	0	1	1	0	2	2	4	3	3
Housing + public expenditure	0	0	0	2	0	1	0	1	0	1	1	0	1
Total	100	100	100	100	100	100	100	100	100	100	100	100	100

('BIDS') search for articles on 18 housing-related topics published in social science journals between 1990 and 2001.[3] The tables do not include every article on housing published during the period, and the same article may be counted more than once. Nevertheless, the results are interesting.

The volume of published work exploded in the 1990s, rising nearly every year to climb from fewer than 200 entries in 1990 to more than 600 in 2001.[4] At the same time, as we shall see, housing research has addressed at least some of the silo problems evident in the 1960s and 1970s.

Does this imply that all is now well in the world of housing research? The long-familiar emphasis on social housing and homelessness has continued. Articles on homelessness account for more than one-fifth of those found in our BIDS search – more than 900 over a dozen years – while social housing accounts for nearly 700. There is much more work than there used to be on various aspects of home ownership and its influence on the wider society – especially its economy. Much of this work was prompted by the disruptive impact of the housing market on the economy in the UK and Scandinavia following financial deregulation during the 1980s and 1990s. John Muellbauer's work on this theme has been particularly revealing and influential (see Muellbauer & Murphy 1997). So has that of Geoff Meen on the treatment of house prices in econometric models (Meen 1993).

Articles on housing and the economy have found their way beyond the housing journals into mainstream economics journals, with a more recent emphasis on the impacts of the European single currency appearing in both.[5] The application of economic principles to the study of housing finance has been a persistent theme since the 1980s, with the two Duke of Edinburgh enquiries reflecting these principles. The distinguished work by John Hills on the interaction of housing subsidies, taxation and social security benefits has now spanned almost two decades. Work co-ordinated by Duncan Maclennan in the early 1990s applied survey techniques to the new world of housing finance deregulation, equity withdrawal and negative equity (Maclennan *et al.* 1997). The influence of housing on savings, investment, consumption, labour mobility and labour costs also has been researched, although not as thoroughly as it should have been, notwithstanding Andrew Oswald's (1996, 1999) interesting, if controversial, work on unemployment and tenure (recently challenged by Coulson & Fisher 2002).

Given the problems British society perceives itself facing, there are other, perhaps bigger gaps in the coverage of recent housing research work. There has been relatively little work on housing and health (although the number of articles devoted to this theme grew considerably in the second half of the

1990s). There have been surprisingly few articles about the elderly and people with disabilities.[6] The huge importance for housing policy of predictable demographic growth among the oldest people, the rising profile of disability rights and recent legislation on this subject in the UK and the USA all suggest that more work is needed in these fields.

The private rental sector remains under-researched. There has been very little research on the house building industry, and still less on aesthetics and what people want their housing and the neighbourhood in which it stands to look and 'feel' like.[7] Moreover, with building design and technology on the brink of major changes, social scientists have a part to play in projects now being launched by environmental pioneers to create structures that leave a minimal footprint on the planet.

Housing careers, the ways in which people first set up home and then move in the course of their lives through housing of different kinds, the capacity of different kinds of cities to welcome newcomers and give them scope for 'successful' careers, though not wholly neglected, are important, under-researched themes. So are the careers of houses – the ways in which they are used, extended or subdivided, re-equipped, repaired or neglected over their lives (not surprisingly perhaps: both themes are difficult to research).

While there is therefore a much greater volume of housing-related research being undertaken and published, there is still nothing like complete coverage of the issues that currently matter. Some issues have remained mainstays of the research industry; others have emerged, but many important questions remain consistently unexplored. Some would say that the increase in the volume of research work conducted in the academy has been accompanied by a reduction in the real impact this work makes on society. While these developments reflect the changing interests of housing researchers, they are also shaped by political, cultural, technical and other factors, to which we now turn.

A changing environment for research

Our analysis of changes in the environment in which research has been done starts with the British political setting for research, and then deals with changes in academic resources and priorities. We focus particularly on the 1970s and 1980s – the decades between the two periods examined in previous sections of this chapter, but more recent developments are also briefly covered.

Political changes

In 1979 an ice age descended for those raised in the years of hope: academics who believed they had a part to play in carrying housing and urban policies forward in liberal directions, in collaboration with colleagues who worked for the state. Funding for research in most of the social sciences was reduced. The Centre for Environmental Studies, having rashly grown too dependent on government, had the rug pulled from under it and closed. The Central Housing Advisory Committee, which had a distinguished record of research-based public inquiries into housing going back to the 1930s, was abolished, along with similar Advisory Committees in education and other fields.

The new government had a very simple housing policy: selling council houses, reducing rent controls, relaxing many town planning restrictions – in short, abandoning the field. Chicago, for the time being, had won. This attempt to extricate the state from any obligation to provide housing had been tried before by Conservative governments, first in the 1930s, then again in the 1950s. But because many people in an unequal society cannot pay for a home that they and their fellow citizens regard as tolerable, only the state can resolve the basic market failure. So, when British governments try to extricate themselves from doing anything about housing, they are always compelled to take up the burden again – usually after scandals and disasters that help to unseat the party in power.

Meanwhile, other things were happening to British governance and civil society. The important parts played in policy development by small, independent, London-based groups such as the Fabian Society and – in an earlier generation – the Charity Organisation Society and Toynbee Hall (a middle-class settlement in London's East End) had long been noted by students of policy development.[8] It was inevitable that the deliberate creation of such groups – 'think tanks' as they came to be called in Britain – would follow. The term 'think tank' originated in the United States to describe research institutes that offered distinguished scholars opportunities for developing and discussing their ideas. In Britain it was given a different meaning, describing research groups of a more partisan kind that have distinctive policy agendas. Here we shall adopt the British meaning but make that clear by escorting the phrase with inverted commas.

Viewed from the outside, a 'think tank' looks much like a small institute for research in the applied social sciences. But while there is no clear-cut boundary between institutes and 'think-tanks' there are important distinctions between those at the opposite ends of this spectrum. Researchers in an institute strive to publish their work in the best peer-reviewed journals, and measure their success by the respect they win from colleagues working worldwide in their discipline. Researchers in a 'think tank' measure their success by the number of their proposals – probably first published in pamphlets and in-house journals – that are taken up by the government, and the numbers in their team who are appointed as policy advisers to prestigious ministers. In the heyday of Margaret Thatcher's regime it was said that the Institute of Economic Affairs had ties made for its staff showing the numbers of times their proposals had been incorporated in legislation. Although we have been assured that this tale is apocryphal, it nicely illustrates the distinction we are making.

'Think tanks' have many advantages – particularly for bright, young, childless people who can do without security, for a change of political fashion may consign promising projects to the dustbin and compel those responsible for them to look for other jobs. Being unconfined by academic constraints, they can speculate more freely. But their ideas do not have to be put under the harrow of critical review by their peers; nor do they have the daily encounters with life's harsher realities that the Charity Organisation Society and Toynbee Hall gained from their social work.

Thus, disastrous mistakes can be made. The poll tax, 'back to basics' (John Major's slogan for a while) and the privatising of British Rail all seem to have originated at least partly in 'think tanks'. Their need to remain constantly accessible to power compels them to base themselves in London, dimming their view of more distant parts of the country, and that too may lead to serious errors. Some have argued that supply-side assumptions about the causes of long-term unemployment, unsuited to Scotland, Northern Ireland, the former coalfields and the North of England, are an example of such errors.

When it comes to assessing the influence that housing researchers exert on events we shall have to take the growth of 'think tanks' into account. If exerting a direct influence on government is a researcher's main aim, an academic appointment may no longer be the best place to start from. There may at the moment be an oversupply of 'think tanks' in London, but if Scotland, Wales and Northern Ireland are to develop policies suited to their needs they cannot rely on research based in SW 1 and WC 2: they need their own 'think tanks'.

The influence of such bodies may have grown, and that of academics been reduced, by the growing importance of radio and television as arenas for public debate and political education, and their producers' obligations to demonstrate political 'balance'. They are tempted to stage cock-fights between speakers who will provide crisp, contentious sound-bites of a predictable kind – an art form for which partisan policy advisers are better suited than serious academics. Meanwhile the increasing complexity of the analyses expected of scholars in some disciplines and the pressures on them to address, not the laity, but the small, specialised audiences that read the most prestigious peer-reviewed journals, means that they are less likely than their predecessors to be invited to contribute to broadcast discussions. The economists to be heard on the BBC's *Today* programme – most influential of daily commentaries on the news – usually work for consultancies, stockbrokers and banks, not for universities. Its political science, too, is now more often contributed by journalists and polling agencies than by academics.

There are more fundamental questions to be asked about the erosion of Britain's capacity for staging serious public debates about domestic policy. The Royal Commissions, Committees of Inquiry and Advisory Committees we used to rely on for much of this have mostly been abolished. Academics played their parts in these as members, researchers and witnesses. But governments have come to regard the pressure groups, the social scientists and the spokesmen of the public service professions who used to fill their lists of witnesses as a problem rather than a solution. The growing vigour of Select Committees of the House of Commons has gone some way to fill this gap. But politicians' reports do not attract the attention that was given to a major inquiry like that of the Milner Holland Committee on London Housing or its counterparts dealing with education, health, transport or the personal social services; neither do they generate the same amount of research.

Meanwhile the newspaper and publishing industries have changed in ways that tend to stifle academic contributions to debate. Twenty years ago, many of these appeared in *New Society*, an excellent weekly magazine of the social sciences, in Pelican Books, or in Penguin Specials, which could be got into print within weeks of delivering a typescript. All these have folded or withered. Shorter contributions to debate used to be welcome in the centre pages of *The Times* and the *Guardian*, but these and other broadsheet papers now rely mainly on a familiar cast of feature writers whose views become so predictable to regular readers that many give up reading them.

Thus changes in government, governance and society in the 1970s and 1980s brought competing 'firms' into the research 'industry' in which academics operate, and obstructed the channels through which they were accustomed to communicate their findings to a wider public.

Change in the academy

We turn next to changes in the academic environment itself.

Urban studies emerged in the 1970s as a strong suit in British hands, bringing housing and planning research into a broader exploration of the evolution of human settlements, their economies, their social structure, their governance and politics. That development owed a lot to a talented group of scholars, many of them originally geographers (Brian Robson, David Eversley, Peter Hall, Ray Pahl, Nicholas Deakin, Doreen Massey and later Duncan Maclennan) who had escaped from the disciplinary and political allegiances that provided both the inspiration for, and the shackles constraining, much of their predecessors' work. These people got deeply involved in political and practical affairs – an experience providing the sharpest compulsions to shake off disciplinary blinkers, for you cannot talk sense about policy from within the confines of one discipline.

American scholars also emerged as a major influence in the urban studies field. The Centre for Environmental Studies and Glasgow's Department of Social and Economic Research played major parts in forging links with them through conferencing, collaborative research and in the columns of the journal *Urban Studies*. Manchester, the LSE, Birmingham, the Oxford Polytechnic and other academic centres did their best to ensure that Britain could hold its own in this growing field. But the Americans, thanks partly to faster adoption of the computer and to a more specialised and focused research tradition, pulled ahead in work of the sort that required rigorous analysis of big datasets. Meanwhile it became increasingly clear, as the best researchers had always known, that housing studies could never be a self-contained specialism.

The computer arrived, enormously enhancing the capacity of researchers to analyse large amounts of data. That increased the power of mathematical methods and the people and disciplines that could use them. ('It were all fields when I were a lad' commented a well-known planner. 'Now it's all Forrester and Meadows' – Jay Forrester, and Dennis and Donella Meadows.) This also gave a stronger hand to the units – many of them in the larger public authorities – that could recruit these people and pay for the increasingly expensive machines they needed. Meanwhile, the run-down of the atomic energy research programme encouraged able physicists and applied mathematicians to move, first into transport research and then into the broader urban studies field.

Lots of training courses for housing managers sprang up in universities and polytechnics during the 1980s, together with smaller initiatives designed to help tenant activists who were gaining more responsibilities for managing the new, community-based housing associations (Trafford Hall in Cheshire, set up by Anne Power and her supporters, was the biggest centre of this kind). Like academics of every kind, the teachers responsible for these courses were increasingly expected to do some research, which led to more work of the sort that would contribute to their teaching. (Anne Power, Robina Goodlad, Suzie Scott and others led the way in studies of housing management, community-based ways of working, the renewal of run-down estates, dealings with difficult tenants and similar issues.)

While these were beneficial developments, mixed consequences flowed from attempts to change management practices within British higher education that, unlike the American system, relied mainly on the state for funds. As the system grew larger and more expensive it was to be expected that the old informal procedures for assessing the performance of academic institutions – relying essentially on gossip among scholars who knew each other and the departments they presided over – would become increasingly inadequate. Laurie Taylor's weekly column in the *Times Higher Education Supplement*, tracing the slide into chaos and corruption of one mythical sociology department, cut wincingly close to the bone in some quarters. It was to be expected that more rigorous and bureaucratic procedures for assessing teaching and research would be introduced. These, when they came, powerfully reinforced incentives to do research and to publish it in learned journals while reducing the priority accorded to other ways of using the knowledge gained from academic work – in public debate and journalism, policy advice and voluntary work, evening class teaching and so on.

Another change affecting the work of academic policy analysts evolved more gradually. Until the 1950s, university teachers who fulfilled their contracts – to teach, administer and do research – found that after working for three or four years on a particular problem, they knew more about some aspects of it than anyone else. If they communicated their findings in the right ways, politicians and civil servants had to listen to them.[9]

By the 1970s all this had changed. The growth of the social sciences and their masters' degrees in universities all over the country, the recruitment of many of our best graduates to new research units in central government and the larger local authorities, and the computers and databanks acquired by these units, together meant that academics could no longer claim to know more than the civil service about anything much. If we were indeed ahead of the game for a few months, the distribution of research summaries and the data now available on worldwide web sites mean that among ministers' advisers there are people who know more than we do about most things.

Recent developments

In recent years several further trends have emerged that may tend to reinforce cautious orthodoxy, and to make it harder to do independent and innovative housing research in Britain. We note three of these.

First, growing pressure on academics to raise their own salaries from research grants and contracts has compelled them to pay growing attention to their funders' wishes. While much of the research done in this way is perfectly straightforward, the agenda is set by the funder who may also shape the form and timing of publications. Meanwhile, government agencies funding research are expected to find internal 'customers' to whose needs the work should be 'relevant'. The Rothschild Report (Rothschild 1971) on the management of publicly funded research and development work was the originator of the doctrine that 'customers' must be found for every project, who should be prepared to find from their research budgets the funds required for each 'R and D task'. 'Customers' are chosen, not because they suffer from the problems to be researched, but because they control a budget.[10] Meanwhile groups with no money to spend on research are of course excluded from the customer role.

Second, in recent years interests that once had conflicting views about housing policy have tended to converge within a Blair-style 'big tent', reformulating potentially difficult social conflicts as technical problems. That convergence among organisations speaking for different groups in the housing world exerts a smoothing influence upon research agendas and publications that may eventually tend to 'dumb down' the whole industry in which we are involved. Where genuine conflicts of interest or ideology exist we should be trying to articulate and discuss them frankly, not ignore them.

Third, Economic and Social Research Council (ESRC) research programmes may be having unfortunate effects. It is entirely sensible that the ESRC, on which so much of the best research depends, should have priorities that are widely understood. These help researchers in different universities to join forces, to focus their efforts more effectively, and to learn from each other. But when these programmes expand to engross two-thirds of the ESRC's research funds, leaving only one-third for responsive-mode funding, questions must be asked about the influences that select and shape priorities, the role of the state in that process, and the power of the senior academics who, in

effect, wield patronage within the Council's committees. With so much research being done on homelessness, no one can claim that the poorest people
are neglected, but more subtle influences may be at work. We should ask ourselves how often we have felt slightly bewildered by the research questions
of eccentric younger colleagues – questions that later proved prescient and
productive. Would such people get funded today – by committee members
who may not for many years have had opportunities to do really innovative
research of their own?

The significance of these changes

What has the upshot of all this been? While housing research has in the
main become better grounded in a broad interdisciplinary framework, more
rigorous in some respects, more data-driven, and there is more of it about,
academics have given contributions to public debate a lower priority. They
should remember that the only comparative advantage now remaining to
them is their independence and their capacity – if they hold on to it – to speak
truth to power. Officials should also speak truth to power and have more
opportunities for doing so, but academics still have greater scope for picking
the questions they study, for consulting whomever they wish, and – if they
negotiate well-judged funding contracts – for publishing their findings. We
return below to the implications of all that.

The housing research industry

We work in an industry, closely linked as customer and supplier to other
industries – those that send us students, pay us to teach them, and employ
them thereafter; that fund our research and give us access to the sources it
depends on; that publish our books and journals, and buy them. Housing
research is also related to other academic industries – the race relations industry, the gender studies industry, the disability industry, and so on – whose
practitioners occasionally contribute to our journals and our teaching. What
we can do depends on the perceptions and priorities of people in all these
industries and our capacity to turn their attention to new issues – to create
and market new products.

The options for research on housing are now potentially limitless. The
subject was once a fairly distinctive field, posing a limited number of major
questions. Now, every policy problem can be seen to have a housing component. Hospital waiting lists? – can nurses be recruited in areas where housing
costs are too high for them? Support for university students? – should they

be living more cheaply at home, now that we have improved their parents' housing so much and set up universities in every major town? Ozone layer depletion? – can we arrest its destruction without reducing the spread of suburbs and the growth of commuter traffic? Inflation? – can we control it without tighter regulation of the mortgage market? In many parts of Britain the basic shortages of tolerable housing that used to dictate research priorities are a thing of the past – although we have cut back output so far that in some places old-fashioned shortages are re-emerging as a problem. But there is now no limit to the things that housing researchers could usefully study, which is a happy but bewildering position to be in. We offer a few suggestions that may help those grappling with this dilemma.

Lessons for housing researchers

While we may be compelled to take on a good deal of pot-boiling work to keep ourselves and our colleagues employed, we should never forget that our independence and integrity are the only comparative advantages left to us. So we should beware of being used by those who sponsor research simply to give the illusion of action, to delay decisions, or to gain support for decisions already made. If we do not from time to time ask questions that the state and other corporate bodies would not pose and produce findings that they would not publish, then we would do better to work in a consultancy or a government research unit. The mass of work done among homeless people in recent years suggests that no researcher should be prepared to do any more until a major programme of action to help them creates a new situation that may be worth studying.

The most important thing that academics can do is to extend general understanding of our society, the way cities and regions work, and the opportunities they offer to different kinds of people. That kind of research, sometimes done by people who have little interest in specific policy issues, is not likely to be done by the state or the private sector. Policy-focused research of the kinds that government needs has to be embedded in the broader understanding of society that we should be trying to provide.

Meanwhile, outside the academy, society needs a properly informed 'political class' with access to meeting places where people can debate public policy issues, together with 'think tanks', independent of the civil service, where people can shape innovative ideas into a form that governments can use. Academics can play an active part in developing and informing this political class.

Policy discussion must not be confined to the middle-class. We should always remember – what the state too often forgets – that the people who experience a problem are the best single source of evidence about it. We should not only interview them as subjects of our research; we should consult them before going firm on the questions to be researched, consult them again about our conclusions for policy and practice when they are still at a draft stage, and insist that they be invited to play an active part in conferences at which we present our findings. It can be done.[11]

We should bear in mind that the growth of the 'welfare state' that spread government influence into many fields of housing, health care, employment and other matters hitherto dominated by the private sector and charitable bodies did not bring class conflict to an end. It transferred many of the conflicts that used to divide landlord and tenant, employer and worker, middle-class and working-class to the counters of the public services where they may be more fairly managed but continue to this day. Every time we launch a research project on social rented housing after consulting its owners while failing to consult those who live in it, every time we set up a new course for housing managers without providing any education for those who are to be 'managed', we are taking sides in those conflicts. Social exclusion is a process. If we are not among the includers then we shall find ourselves among the excluders.

Despite the emphasis placed on 'relevant' research for which 'customers' can be found, we should remember that even in policy-oriented research, the most important output of a study is often the education of the people who do it. They will bring what they have learnt to bear in due course, by publishing learned papers, offering policy prescriptions, teaching their students, doing voluntary work, or contributing in various ways to public debate. Specified outputs and deadlines for such studies should be required; but the longer-term aim of the work is to contribute to a national intellectual and political resource capable of mounting intelligent discussion in public gatherings and through the media, and raising the general level of public debate. That includes creating effective 'think tanks' that feed ideas to governments.

When it comes to communicating research findings, the influence of researchers usually depends in practice not on the authority and rigour of their conclusions or the elegance of their arguments, but on the 'stories' they tell about society's problems, the moral meanings of these stories, and the timeliness and vividness of the tale. Like proverbs, the messages conveyed by these stories often conflict. It is the politicians' job to decide which story is most relevant to the situations they have to deal with.

Some stories may be demonstrably wrong, but it is not enough to prove that a Charles Murray (1984) has made a lot of errors and leave your readers discussing the same problems in the light of the same moral values. Another and more reliable story, formulating the problems in new ways and giving them different moral meanings, has to be equally vividly presented.[12]

Stories about our society and the way in which it works can be presented with algebra and in figures as well as in prose. The Treasury's model of the British economy is one such story. Note the characters that play a part in it: incomes and taxes, savings and investment, imports and exports ... all of them obviously important. But health, happiness, security, solidarity, education, respect for authority ... none of these appear in the cast, and they may be more important for the nation's welfare. There are researchers who are developing new descriptions of social welfare, how it is created and how different countries can be compared, who are bringing these characters on stage (see, for example, Marmot & Wilkinson (eds.) 1999; Doyal & Gough 1991).

Priorities for Scotland

Since many of our readers will be in Scotland it is appropriate to illustrate some of the practical conclusions to which these arguments lead by offering some thoughts about this country. In this field as in any other, Scottish researchers could doubtless do better, and we have suggested gaps in their agenda that they may want to fill. But they have a more creditable record of research and teaching in the housing and urban studies fields than their colleagues in most parts of the world. Urgent at this point in Scotland's history is the development of lively and well-informed political debate that involves people from all classes in all parts of the country, and the creation of two or three Scottish 'think tanks' to help to form links between the academy, the state and a wider public.

The Institute of Contemporary Scotland is trying to create arenas for better-informed public discussion. It brings different kinds of people together to debate urgent issues, sometimes at short notice, in different parts of Scotland. Other bodies are doing likewise: the Church of Scotland and its Committees are among them. Meanwhile the Scottish Parliament is endeavouring to work in a more open, participative, accountable fashion than its Westminster counterpart. The Scottish Council Foundation, recently declared to be the '"think tank" to watch' in an appraisal of all those operating in the UK,[13] is making an impressive attempt to fill the second role. Housing researchers should be contributing as opportunities arise to discussions in both these arenas.

In conclusion

We conclude by drawing together some of the most important of the points touched upon in a wide-ranging discussion.

Academic researchers interested in the housing field will find that it offers them ways into every kind of issue, not the more clearly defined research agendas their predecessors had. However, their monopoly of intellectual inquiry has long gone. They will find many other researchers working alongside them in consultancies, voluntary agencies, pressure groups, 'think tanks' and the research units of central and local government. Any comparative advantages the academics may retain now arise, not from superior knowledge, intelligence or data but from the scope they have for choosing their own research questions and publishing their own uncensored findings.

They should use that privilege to gain a broad understanding of society and the place of housing within it. Such studies will provide a sounder framework for, and a wiser understanding of, the more sharply focused, policy-oriented research that they and others will also do. Competing research groups based in the state, the voluntary and private sectors have less opportunity to do this broader, scene-setting kind of work.

Researchers should always remember that the people who experience a problem are usually the most important source of evidence about it. Such people should be involved, not only as passive informants, but in formulating research questions, discussing findings and recommendations, and contributing to public discussion of the issue.

Academic researchers should take whatever opportunities they may have for contributing to – and learning from – public education and policy discussions. In doing so they will help to build the penumbra of intelligent and well-informed citizens that every department of government needs if it is to work effectively. They will find that in the longer run their own influence in these discussions depends on helping people to see their society in new ways by offering them stories with moral meanings that clarify the character of its problems and suggest better ways of addressing them.

Acknowledgement

We thank Tony O'Sullivan for helpful editorial advice. We are also grateful to Emily Lynch for processing the BIDS search presented in the tables.

Notes

(1) The Housing (Homeless Persons) Act of 1977 for a while came close to providing that assurance, at least for married couples, households with children and elderly people.

(2) An account of the teaching provided in Departments of Social Administration throughout Britain can be found in Donnison (1961). Most of the research going on in these Departments took place at the LSE.

(3) We could have gone further back in time but feared the record would be increasingly incomplete for earlier years.

(4) Housing journals now attract more and more work – in humblingly good English – from other countries, particularly the Netherlands and Scandinavia, besides a steady flow from the USA and Australia. Authors from the Far East appear fairly often, but there are fewer writing from, or about, third world countries and the former Soviet bloc, although contributions from both are growing.

(5) For example, Maclennan *et al.* (1998b); Memery (2001).

(6) Although again the small number dealing with ethnic minorities grew in the second half of the 1990s.

(7) Despite studies made in earlier years by Pearl Jephcott, Kevin Lynch, and Barbara Adams' team at the Department of the Environment, applied social scientists have generally dismissed aesthetics as 'unresearchable', or – worse still – condemned such work as 'environmental determinism'. The Sunday newspaper supplements and women's magazines however have never hesitated to write about aesthetics, and, at the end of the day, it was often what the buildings and their surroundings looked and smelled like that most discredited public housing and municipal socialism.

(8) Hall *et al.* (1975). See also Donnison (2000).

(9) 'We pay no attention to the books you people write,' said a senior housing official to one of the authors in the early 1960s. 'No-one in government has time to read books. But if you write an article for *The Times* or the *Guardian* I have to read that because the Minister will have seen it before he gets to the office in the morning, and I have to have the answers for him.'

(10) To be fair to him, Rothschild made it clear that he was not talking about the social sciences – but the government did not hesitate to apply his doctrines in this field too. 'I was only trying to tell them how we did it in Shell,' he said when his recommendations were criticised. These are sensible doctrines for technological research of the kind that a big oil company needs, where problems and solutions can be clearly specified.

(11) The study reported in Bannister *et al.* (1993) was handled in this way.

(12) Marris (1997) provides a revealing analysis of these processes from which much of our own version is taken.

(13) *Prospect*/Nirex awards; *Prospect*, November 2001 p. 7.

15

Policy and Academia: an Assessment

Richard Best

Introduction

To what extent can academics play a part in national policy-making? This chapter considers the extent to which published research from academic institutions, and the input of individuals from the academic community, can influence government ministers, civil servants and others responsible for formulating social policy. It concludes that the contribution of research can be of considerable importance in determining changes to policy. But the transmission and translation of the findings from research require special skills either on the part of the academics themselves (for which they are seldom trained or supported) or through the use of skilled intermediaries. The chapter ends with suggestions for enhancing the policy-making role of academia.

Separate worlds?

This chapter concentrates on social policy, with particular reference to housing issues, and on the academics, and the research studies undertaken outside government, that seek to address social policy questions.

Those who approach policy issues from an academic perspective, and those whose job it is to make policy decisions, sometimes appear to inhabit different worlds.

To policy-makers, academics always seem to look back at what has gone before. Researchers usually appear to be in no hurry and, after assembling the evidence, seem loath to come to firm conclusions about the changes to current policy that would make a difference.

By contrast, government ministers face constant pressures, scrutiny and criticism. They must keep looking ahead (not least with an eye on the potential popularity of any changes they might announce). They are in a hurry – after all they may not occupy their posts for very long – and they are likely to have clear and firm opinions. While academics may be comfortable with the conclusion that 'more research is needed', policy-makers must take decisions and must take them quickly.

When the Joseph Rowntree Foundation presents findings from research it has commissioned, the response from politicians often goes much like this: 'You have drawn our attention to shortcomings and problems which have resulted from previous policies. But you have said very little about what would work in the future. We have to take decisions now, in the real world, with all its financial and political constraints. And we need clear guidance. We do not want to hear from those who can criticise but cannot do.'

Mutual interests

While policy-makers may accuse academics of an inability to make up their minds – 'the paralysis of analysis' – academics may be justified in criticising politicians for acting before all the facts are known – 'jumping to conclusions' or 'shooting from the hip'. But despite the apparent divide, those within both groups who want to change the world for the better must grudgingly admit that they need each other.

Even though the primary concern of politicians may appear to be the gaining or retaining of power – which means taking decisions on the basis of their electoral popularity – most recognise that they need a knowledge base on which to take decisions. They need to understand the origins, the causes, the dimensions of whatever social problems come within their remit and they need to get advance warning if their proposed policy changes may lead to failure. Even when politicians appear disdainful of academia, most are hungry for the information that will give them an edge, keep them in the vanguard of new thinking and justify the decisions they want to take.

Academics may see politicians as operating on a superficial plane, pandering to the electorate rather than going where the evidence points. But it takes a different temperament to move beyond the comfort zone of clear evidence. Politics involves risk-taking and a career in the public eye that can be swiftly terminated by the democratic process or by the judgement of superiors. The academic life seldom brings fame or fortune (and it can be as insecure as politics for those not yet in its senior echelons), but it has other attractions.

While politicians are constantly required to face in several directions and must often avoid the slings and arrows not just of opposing parties but of their ambitious colleagues, those who make a career in academia can find it easier to retain their integrity.

From searching to changing

The Joseph Rowntree Foundation commissions and supports a very large amount of academic research activity.[1] It does so not because it wishes to sustain the academic community but because it believes its underlying mission is most likely to be fulfilled by putting high quality research into the hands of key policy-makers and practitioners.

At the beginning of the twentieth century, Joseph Rowntree set aside substantial resources to 'search out the underlying causes' of social problems. He believed that if only the truth could be discovered about the root causes of poverty and disadvantage, the right policies could be put in place to overcome these social evils. He had seen the ways in which disease and death had resulted from outbreaks of cholera and typhoid; and he had seen how public health legislation had treated the problems at source and conquered them. Could not the power of science lead to policy changes that would vanquish social ills just as they could overcome physical ills?

At the Foundation that Rowntree created, the emphasis today remains on trying to secure policy change through funding academics to discover those 'underlying causes'. But, standing between the government machine and the research community, we have had to face much frustration: sometimes academia cannot shed light on the issue because the evidence is absent or the policy question cannot be answered by a research project. Sometimes research does indeed provide grounds for believing – if not on the basis of certainty, at least on probability – that existing or proposed political action will be positively harmful, and yet politicians brush the evidence aside. Sometimes the position is reversed and it is the inability of researchers to operate within tight timescales – or to respond positively to the politician's need to move from knowledge to action – that means the chance to effect change is lost.

However, despite the frustrations that can arise from the lack of connectivity between the output of academia and the demands of policy-makers, I remain convinced of the key role for research in improving social policy. Unless policy is grounded in knowledge and understanding it runs the risk of doing more harm than good.

Improving the connections between research outputs and policy-making may in general require the presence of some additional ingredients to close the gap between what the researcher produces and what the policy-maker needs. But before exploring this further, this chapter considers how academics themselves may sometimes directly engage in policy formulation.

Crossing the divide

Occasionally there are politicians who have been trained as researchers and understand the disciplines involved. There are also academics that walk freely within the policy-maker's world, with a clear understanding of what it takes to convert research into a policy-making tool. As an academic with much experience of both sides of the line, most recently as Special Adviser to Scotland's First Minister, Professor Duncan Maclennan is an example of someone who has bridged the gap. His work in helping politicians who need information and insights has demonstrated to other academics that the policy-makers value what they possess.

What are the pros and cons of those with research skills leaving their ivory towers for a career outside academia where policy-relevant insights can directly influence decision-makers?

Academics in Parliament

As a relatively frequent visitor to the Eastern European countries, I have noted how often leading academics have gone the whole hog and become government ministers. This can have the disadvantage of the individuals 'going native' and forgetting the academic rigour which they should be bringing to their position of power: they can become so caught up in the cut-and-thrust of the political system that their ability to exercise any academic discipline can desert them.

Academics in the UK enter national politics less frequently, but it does occur. A good example is the Liberal Democrat MP Steve Webb, who was also Professor of Social Policy at the University of Bath.[2] There are severe difficulties in the UK – even at the local level – of becoming a politician during or after a successful academic career (even if the back-stabbing and naked ambition of party politics is acceptable!). Nevertheless a Parliamentarian with real academic expertise can contribute to the processes of scrutiny, for example through Select Committees where political point scoring is not so endemic, as well as through their input to the legislative processes.

Moreover by retaining links to the world of academia they can act as a bridge in translating and transmitting the politicians' needs to their colleagues in the research community.

Recent reforms to the House of Lords have led to the appointment of a number of academics as independent ('cross-bench') members, including the Vice Chancellor of Edinburgh University, Professor Stewart Sutherland, and the Director of the Royal Institution of Great Britain, Professor Susan Greenfield, as well as Professor Sir Robert May of Oxford, and Sir Claus Moser. There are proposals for more appointments to the Lords by an Independent Commission set up for the purpose – so the United Kingdom Parliament could in future see more academics with their hands rather nearer to the levers of power.

Think tanks

A half-way house for some of those with research knowledge and an interest in policy lies in engagement with the think tanks that stimulate government thinking from the outside, or in working as an adviser to government on the inside. There is a good deal of crossover between these two: people from think tanks often move into government advisory posts. For example, Geoff Mulgan, the founder Director of DEMOS, moved to the No. 10 Policy Unit after Labour's 1997 election victory and now heads the Cabinet Office's Policy and Innovation Unit. (Rather more commonly, the think tank director goes on to become a Member of Parliament (or, no doubt, a Member of the Scottish Parliament). Thus David Willetts moved from the Centre for Policy Studies (CPS) to become an MP and then a prominent member of the Cabinet.)

The think tanks – such as the Fabian Society, the John Smith Institute, the Scottish Council Foundation, the Institute of Economic Affairs, and the Adam Smith Institute – can be the custodians of a particular ideology, acting as a ginger group for a mainstream party. They can feed that party – whether in opposition or in power – with new ideas (or re-packaged old ones). Or they can be stalking horses for a political party to test out a bold plan and gauge public and media reactions before the party decides whether to absorb it into the mainstream or reject it. When their patron is in power – as with the CPS in the days of Mrs Thatcher's premiership or as with the Institute for Public and Policy Research (IPPR) today – the think tank will be fêted by those who want to influence government, or those who want to know where government policy may be heading.

The problem for academics in becoming too entangled with the think tanks of their choosing is that each has an agenda. Impartiality and independence of thought may not sit well with the vision of the think tank: evidence is needed to support their case, to justify their philosophy, not to expose weaknesses or query their premises. Moreover, to capture the attention of the news media, they are sometimes tempted to be deliberately provocative, expressing opinions that could never be justified by evidence or objective analysis. No academic can be entirely free from their own prejudices and, indeed, value judgements; but for many the approach of the think tank will run counter to their professional training and their instincts. It may better suit the temperament of the committed campaigner than the dispassionate researcher.

Government advisers

The academic who becomes an official adviser moves to the heart of government where sometimes – but not always – there is a hunger for knowledge on which to base new policy.

There are risks for any adviser of being seen thereafter as partisan and politically aligned. But in reality the value to those they advise is not (as it is with the think tanks) in public pronouncements, but in private guidance: for this, the important qualities are the retention of an independent mind, a willingness to present research evidence fearlessly, the exercise of critical faculties and the ability to see more than one side to an argument.

Career civil servants can feel disempowered by the presence of such advisers. But they can be disarmed by charm and tact, and by the adviser working within the conventions and sensitivities of the system; in-house advisers from academia can then be immensely important – and without the necessity of compromising their intellectual integrity.

To fulfil this role effectively, some direct involvement in non-academic institutions concerned with policy implementation can be an undoubted advantage. Duncan Maclennan's career demonstrates this clearly. Prior to appointment as a Special Adviser to Scotland's First Minister in 1999 he served on the Board of Scottish Homes. Combining an academic career with public service in the housing world has helped many to balance the evidence and insights gained from knowledge of research findings, against the political practicalities required to get things done.

By serving in capacities outside the university, academics not only contribute directly to policy-making (or implementation) in the real world but they also lose the naivety that those confined to ivory towers can display. Those on the boards of housing associations have found out, for example, how powerful can be the influence of central government over organisations dependent on a flow of grants and subsidies. Those who serve on local authorities soon discover that the ideal solution may simply be unobtainable because of its cost or electoral fallout. Experience on a health trust or other quango can teach the ability to compromise and concede some ground – not least to accommodate the ambitions and idiosyncrasies of the other personalities involved – and yet to avoid making concessions that really count.

Duncan Maclennan exemplifies many of the qualities that lead to academics being drawn into the heart of government policy. He is secure in his research knowledge; he is highly skilled in synthesising and bringing together the key points from a body of available research; he can present his material to busy political masters in an engaging and accessible style. But one essential step in gaining the confidence of ministers probably lies in gaining experience within statutory or voluntary bodies where different skills can be honed.

Shakers, not movers

What of those who cannot or do not want to move on from their academic base, but who still wish to play a direct, active role in translating research insights into policy or practice change?

For some, opportunities may arise from the invitations to contribute periodically to policy-making task forces, working parties and committees. For example, in England, the Cabinet Office's Social Exclusion Unit has called on individual academics – many of whom have been supported in their research by the Joseph Rowntree Foundation – to sit on policy action teams and to help with particular pieces of ongoing work.

Another example is the House of Commons Select Committee: many of these have drawn on academics as their advisers in their role of scrutinising the work of government departments. Professor Christine Whitehead, for example, has been a key adviser to the Environment Committee. In collaboration with the clerks to these committees, external academics can prove highly influential. In Scotland, similar input to the new Scrutiny Committees, even if on a relatively time-limited basis while a particular topic is under investigation, can provide the chance to make very productive use of knowledge gained from previous research. Reputation is the key to invitations to contribute to policy in these one-off advisory capacities.

Making the connections

Most of the input from academia to the world of policy-making will, of course, come not from direct action by academics, but from policy-makers assimilating the actual work done within the academic base. What are the key factors that will determine the extent of this works influence on policy? Some of the main ingredients must be:

- who pays for the research;

- how it is presented, publicised and disseminated;

- the quality, relevance and timeliness of its content; and

- partnership and persistence in taking forward its messages.

Pipers and paymasters

Who pays for research will directly affect its potential for influencing policy. Most social policy research in universities involves an external financial input, particularly where it is applied rather than theoretical. But external funders are likely to influence what is produced (even where they say – and perhaps believe – that their involvement is entirely dispassionate). Whether research is delivered under contract and must accord with the precise requirements of those who commission it, or whether it is initiated by researchers seeking funds from a research council or a foundation, the source of funding will exert an influence.

Undertaking research for government departments can bring the satisfaction of reaching directly into the policy machine. Where government wants to find out whether, for example, some pilot scheme has proved a success, a great deal depends on what the research unearths. Moreover, the relationship between researchers and senior civil servants, through the execution of completed work, can lead to more direct opportunities to input to the policy process. Thus, academics with a proven track record in concluding work for government departments may get drawn into those governmental task forces, working parties or ministerial sounding boards. When confidence and trust is built up through the contractual process, it can lead to invitations to participate more directly in policy processes.

The downside from 'accepting the king's shilling' and undertaking research that is paid for by the public purse is that the political priorities of the pay-masters can bring tensions and frustrations for conscientious academics. Ministers are unlikely to sanction research which may prove their policies were ill-conceived; when seeking a justification for a course of action to which they are already committed, they see research as the route to proving their point or vindicating their actions; and all too often the evaluations of projects they have set in hand will either be ignored or kept out of the public eye if they produce the 'wrong' result.

Although the funds available from charitable foundations can be stretched much further if their support for research projects goes alongside match-ing contributions from government departments, at the Joseph Rowntree Foundation we have generally eschewed joint funding: the constraints and compromises inherent in sponsoring work alongside a government partner – which must take account of political expediencies – has proved too restrict-ing for us.

For very different reasons, the Foundation has found it difficult to co-fund re-search with the Economic and Social Research Council (ESRC). The ESRC's aims are to 'identify, support and sponsor the highest quality of social science that Britain can produce'; this may or may not connect to policy change. The very factors that give much-needed security to academics – guaranteed sup-port over a relatively long period, without severe pressures to produce speci-fied outputs within tightly defined schedules, and the opportunity for a more reflective, less narrowly focused, approach – may produce results that lack the immediacy and relevance that the policy-makers demand. The purpose of ESRC funding may be more directed to ensuring a corpus of research capac-ity, and backdrop of knowledge and data, than to achieving policy-relevant outputs of immediate and direct use to decision-takers.

And what of the role of foundations, charitable trusts, that support academic research? Confusingly, no two are alike. Each has its own special interests, perhaps relating to the wishes of its founder or the interests of its current trustees. Some have neither the inclination nor the resources to do more than send cheques to worthy academics to get on with the work they have proposed; others interest themselves deeply – with staff to pursue their engagement – in every stage of each research project. The attribute they are likely to have in common is that they stand outside the imperatives of politics, where popularity must be courted, and of business, where research must contribute to the organisation's profitability. Their independence is their common feature but sometimes it seems that the decisions that flow from it are whimsical or simply mysterious.

The Joseph Rowntree Foundation is typical in some ways and distinct in others. It, perhaps more than most, reacts against the notion of simple grant-making: we have rejected 'cheque-book charity', where the objective is accomplished when the grant is made, in favour of a partnership with the academic body concerned.

A partnership in which one side supplies all the money and another does the majority of the work can seem lop-sided. The onus on every foundation is to avoid an abuse of this potentially powerful position: we have to ensure that, even in subtle ways, we are not choosing and guiding research that will confirm any prejudices and unproven opinions which individually or collectively we hold. The value of research we support is undermined if it is not always searching for truth. While we may be helped by the integrity of the Quaker tradition we inherit, we must constantly guard against suggesting, let alone coercing, researchers to follow a particular path that appeals to our own sensibilities.

The essential fact remains – who funds the research will affect how it subsequently influences policy-making and policy-makers.

Presentation and dissemination

Turning to the ways in which academics can themselves help determine whether their work affects policy, a key component is its presentation.

If the intention is to influence policy-makers – national or local politicians, civil servants, and the decision-takers in quangos, voluntary bodies and the business sector – and to reach those who themselves exert influence on policy – the think tanks and the news-media – the academic community must avoid simply talking to itself. Rewards – of money as well as prestige – often flow from impressing fellow academics and from contributing to academic journals. Incentives are lacking to present material in the formats that appeal to those with policy responsibilities. This seems perverse if academia – funded by the wider public for the public good – is to be properly encouraged to be as valuable to the processes of public policy as it could be. There must be a danger that, if outputs from research appear to be intended for other academics and are not accessible to those who genuinely want to understand more and learn from the work done, research based in universities will come to be regarded as irrelevant and self-indulgent; ultimately, this must affect the perceptions of funders and will threaten the support available from governmental and independent sources.

If the subject covered by research is intended to reach the desks of policy-makers, it must use everyday language, be free from jargon, equations and initials (even if referenced at the back), and from elaborate references to its methodology. Technical appendices can contain the items that interrupt the flow of the 'story'. Academics must remember that their readers are more used to gaining information from newspapers and magazines and the only lengthy texts they read are likely to be the works of world-renowned authors.

Academic texts are an essential part of the process: short reports and summaries only have a *raison d'être* if there is a full report behind them. But if the only source of reference is a full-length academic book, or an article in a journal unknown to most decision-takers, the chances of policy change will be slim.

Unfortunately few funders want to pay for editing, literary criticism and investment in the appearance of the work undertaken by researchers. There may be very little cash available for publicising and disseminating the contents of research reports, e.g. through a public launch, articles in newspapers and magazines, specialist seminars, direct presentations for government departments, and the rest, yet with fierce competition for the attention of busy people who have already far more to absorb – now on the internet as well as through the pile of documents that come in the post – important research is likely to go unnoticed without investment in its presentation and dissemination.[3]

An illustration of such investment and the benefits that flow from it comes from the dissemination work that supported a programme of research conducted at the beginning of the 1990s on aspects of housing finance. A series of reports – several based on a survey of 10 000 households in six conurbations with accompanying case studies – were produced for the Joseph Rowntree Foundation and were then incorporated into a well-designed report from the Inquiry into British Housing which received extensive publicity (Housing Research Findings no.19 1990; Maclennan *et al.* 1990). Work with the news media, a public launch at a major conference, presentations to government ministers, all enhanced the research. Ten years later, the Inquiry's secretary could claim a number of policy changes – including the abolition of mortgage interest tax relief – that were initiated or assisted by this research programme (Best 2002).

Quality and timeliness

Although it might be hoped that the quality of the research would be of central importance in determining its impact, brilliant work sometimes remains unacknowledged and second-rate research sometimes proves highly influential. Undoubtedly all researchers will strive for quality (and this chapter is not the place to define it). But topicality and timeliness may prove more potent in the mix when it comes to determining the impact.

Funders can be part of the process of looking ahead to assess the likely topicality and wider interest that will greet a research report. Certainly, it can be galling for us to publish useful analysis just *after* new legislation is enacted on that same subject – with little prospect of further change for many years thereafter. But work done in parallel with a consultative process, perhaps emerging after a Green Paper that seeks an input to the formulation of new policy, can be disproportionately valuable. Thus, a report from Duncan Maclennan on neighbourhood renewal in 2000 was published to coincide with the final stages of the government's preparation of a National Strategy for Neighbourhood Renewal, with presentations accordingly to the key civil servants in the Cabinet Office (Maclennan 2000).

Seldom will timing be perfect. Unpredictable events in the wider world are sure to intervene. For example, the Joseph Rowntree Foundation's *Income and Wealth Inquiry* report, demonstrating how the gap between richer and poorer had widened dramatically in the 1980s, came out at an important moment in the electoral cycle and attracted extensive media interest (Sir Peter Barclay 1995; Hills 1995). Some credit for its timeliness might be attributable to the JRF's forward planning. But much more important to getting substantial coverage was the coincidence of national revulsion in the press over the high salaries which 'fat cats' in the newly-privatised utilities were awarding themselves. It was luck as much as good judgement that meant this major programme (based on research undertaken over several years in over twenty separate academic institutions) caught the public imagination.

But even if luck is sure to play a part, it remains important to consider the timeliness of the research before it begins and to choose the moment for its dissemination. Sometimes the window of opportunity will be much longer than in other cases: work on the outcomes for children of divorce and separation and of the relative success of different ways of moderating the impact of negative effects, is likely to be almost as valid whenever it emerges (for example, Rodgers & Pryor 1998). But research into the effectiveness of, say, policy for rent restructuring in social housing will need to conclude in time to meet a government deadline to review that policy. Or insights and evidence that could influence public spending decisions may be necessary before a government concludes one of its comprehensive spending reviews.

Persistence and partnership

Whether research missed the boat first time round, or whether it was simply ahead of its time, it often requires its messages to be repeated – sometimes over several years – before the penny drops or before the moment is right. But the researcher may well have moved on; funds have been available for other priorities and not for following through and repeatedly revisiting earlier work.

While this characteristic of the research process highlights the importance of getting the timing right first time, it also highlights the theme of the rest of this chapter: this is that researchers may need partners. It may not be sensible to expect research outputs to translate into policy change on their own. Rather it may be wise to conceive of research as but a part of a broader process in the development of policy and practice. Academics keen to see their work used to real purpose may find that a successful outcome requires partnership with an agency for which policy change is a fundamental goal.

Partner organisations can bring to the table a capacity for persistence. Staying with the subject of the research project long after the work is done presents the chance to draw down the evidence at the moment when the work has become most relevant and topical. The partner organisation can pull the pieces together from research evidence accumulated over some years and deliver it when the policy-making world is ready. (This process is being helped by the accessibility of a back catalogue of related research projects on the websites of intermediary bodies of this kind. See, for example, the Joseph Rowntree Foundation's website, www.jrf.org.uk, which holds summaries of nearly 1000 reports including a large number by Duncan Maclennan: Maclennan 1993a, 1994; Maclennan & Meen 1993; Maclennan *et al.* 1991b, c, d.)

However, intermediary agencies dedicated to policy change are thin on the ground. Some – like the Policy Studies Institute and the Family Policy Studies Centre – have been unable to sustain their independent existence through shortages of funding. The weakness or absence of these partners makes it harder for the research community to turn academic work into policy change.

In the absence of such agencies able to enhance presentation and dissemination, and to ensure the timeliness of the intervention in the policy arena and to be persistent in this quest, could academia itself rise to the challenge? Might there be ways in which universities – possibly through specialist dedicated units – could acquire the necessary skills in-house, obtain the required financial resources, and act as the engine for using valuable research to make its impact on social policy?

In conclusion

It may be neither fair nor realistic to expect the research community's academic expertise, analytical skills and intelligence not only to provide high quality research outputs but also to be proficient in the techniques of policy development. Funding for research – often short-term, project-by-project with little capacity for taking a continuing line over a sustained period – does not help. And the mechanisms for rewarding researchers – bestowing prestige and promotion on the basis of the impression made, not least through academic journals, on fellow academics and not on those in the world outside – may be inimical to academia being influential in policy circles (other than through individuals making the transition on a personal basis in the ways I have discussed). It might then be argued that only by the use of intermediary bodies that can add the extra expertise and resources to make research relevant, accessible and topical, will the output of academia be likely to achieve its fullest potential in securing policy change.

But it is hard to find intermediary agencies that have the capability of acting as supportive partners of this kind in the social policy field. Could it be that the universities themselves might be the best places for such complementary skills to be acquired, alongside colleagues who can deliver research of the highest quality? I throw back this challenge to academia – and perhaps to Professor Duncan Maclennan who has shown us all how influential the skills of the academic can be in supporting policy change at the highest levels.

Notes

(1) Currently, over £8 million per annum.
(2) Webb resigned from his academic post in 1997 after the general election, but was subsequently made a Visiting Professor at the University.
(3) The Joseph Rowntree Foundation publishes summaries of research reports using a standard format known as FINDINGS. This approach has been copied by a large number of organisations (including many overseas). The discipline of compressing the contents of a lengthy document onto four sides of A4 can

also concentrate the author's mind on what exactly has been discovered. This technique – perfected by the Foundation's Director of Communications, the late Roland Hirst, in 1990 – can help the busy policy maker or practitioner to get to grips with research outputs. It may also stimulate an interest in reading a longer text. Accessibility and readability – preferably with a length in the region of 15 000 words rather than 150 000 words – remains critical for the main report too. At the JRF we would add that the way the document itself is presented will also make a difference; the layout and print style do matter, preferably with the use of colour and an attractive cover (and with a synopsis of the contents on the back).

References

Abraham, J.M. & Hendershott, P.H. (1996) Bubbles in metropolitan housing markets. *Journal of Housing Research*, **7**, 191–207.

Adair, A.S., Berry, J. & McGreal, W.S. (1996) Hedonic modelling, housing submarkets and residential valuation. *Journal of Property Research*, **13 (1)**, 67–84.

Adair, A., McGreal, S., Smyth, A., Cooper, J. & Ryley, T. (2000) House prices and accessibility: The testing of relationships within the Belfast urban area. *Housing Studies*, **15 (5)**, 699–716.

Adams, D. & May, H. (1992) The role of landowners in the preparation of statutory local plans. *Town Planning Review*, **63 (3)**, 297–321.

Adams, D., Disberry, A., Hutchinson, N. & Munjoma, T. (1999) *Do Landowners Constrain Urban Redevelopment?* Aberdeen papers in Land Economy. University of Aberdeen, Dept. of Land Economy, Aberdeen.

Akerlof, G. (1980) A theory of social custom, of which unemployment may be one consequence. *Quarterly Journal of Economics*, **94**, 749–75.

Allen, F. & Gale, D. (2000) *Comparing Financial Systems*. The MIT Press, Cambridge, Mass.

Allen, M.T., Springer, T.M. & Waller, N.G. (1995) Implicit pricing across residential submarkets. *Journal of Real Estate and Financial Economics*, **11 (2)**, 137–51.

Alonso, W. (1964) *Location and Land Use: Toward a General Theory of Land Rent*. Harvard University Press, Cambridge, Mass.

Ambrose, B.W. & Nourse, H.O. (1993) Factors influencing capitalization rates. *Journal of Real Estate Research*, **8 (2)**, 221–237.

Amemiya, T. (1980) Selection of regressors. *International Economic Review*, **21**, 331–54.

Anas, A. & Arnott, R. (1991) Dynamic housing market equilibrium with taste heterogeneity, idiosyncratic perfect foresight and stock conversions. *Journal of Housing Economics*, **1**, 2–32.

Anas, A. & Arnott, R. (1993a) Technological progress in a model of the housing-land cycle. *Journal of Urban Economics*, **34**, 186–206.

Anas, A. & Arnott, R. (1993b) A fall in construction costs can raise housing rents. *Economic Letters*, **41**, 221–24.

Anas, A. & Arnott, R. (1993c) Development and testing of the Chicago prototype housing market model. *Journal of Housing Research*, **4**, 73–129.

Anas, A. & Arnott, R. (1994) The Chicago prototype housing market model with tenure choice and its policy implications. *Journal of Housing Research*, **5**, 23–90.

Anas, A. & Arnott, R. (1997) Taxes and allowances in a dynamic equilibrium model of urban housing with a size-quality hierarchy. *Regional Science and Urban Economics*, **27**, 547–80.

Anas, A. & Eum, S.J. (1984) Hedonic analysis of a housing market in disequilibrium. *Journal of Urban Economics*, **15**, 87–106.

Anas, A., Arnott, R. & Small, K.A. (1998) Urban spatial structure. *Journal of Economic Literature*, **XXXVI**, 1426–64.

Anderson, I., Kemp, P.A. & Quilgars, D. (1993) *Single Homeless People*. HMSO, London.

Angel, S. (2000) *Housing Policy Matters: A Global Analysis*. Oxford University Press. Oxford.

Angel, S., Mayo, S.K. & Stephens, W. (1993) The housing indicators program: A report on progress and plans for the future. *Netherlands Journal of Housing and the Built Environment*, **8 (1)**, 13–47.

Anglin, P.M. & Ramazan, G. (1996) Semiparametric estimation of a hedonic price function. *Journal of Applied Econometrics*, **11 (6)**, 633–48.

Annez, P. & Wheaton, W.C. (1984) Economic development and the housing sector: a cross-national model. *Economic Development and Cultural Change*, **32 (4)**, 749–66.

Anstie, R., Findlay, C. & Harper, I. (1983) The impact of inflation and taxation on tenure choice and the redistribution effects of home-mortgage interest rate regulation. *The Economic Record*, June, 105–110.

Arnott, R. (1987) Economic Theory and Housing. In: *Handbook of Regional and Urban Economics* (ed. E. Mills), Vol. 2, chap. 24. North Holland, Amsterdam.

Arnott, R., Davidson, R. & Pines, D. (1983) Housing quality, maintenance and rehabilitation. *Review of Economic Studies*, **50**, 467–94.

Arrow, K. (1971) *Essays in the Theory of Risk Bearing*. North Holland, Amsterdam.

Arrow, K.J. & Lind, R.C. (1970) Uncertainty and the evaluation of public investments. *American Economic Review*, June, 364–378.

Artle, R. & Varaiya, P. (1978) Life Cycle Consumption and Homeownership. *Journal of Economic Theory*, **18**, 35–58.

Atkinson, A.B. & King, M.A. (1980) Housing policy, taxation and reform. *Midland Bank Review*, Spring, 7–16.

Attanasio, O.P. & Weber, G. (1994) The U.K. consumption boom of the late 1980s: Aggregate implications of microeconomic evidence. *Economic Journal*, **104**, 1269–1302.

Audit Commission (1992) *Developing Local Authority Housing Strategies*. HMSO, London.

Auten, G.E. & Clotfelter, C. (1982) Permanent vs. transitory tax effects and the realisation of capital gains. *Quarterly Journal of Economics*, **97**, 613–632.

Awan, K., Odling-Smee, J. & Whitehead, C.M.E. (1982) Household attributes and the demand for private rental housing. *Economica*, **49**, 183–200.

Bailey, M.J., Muth, R.F. & Nourse, H.O. (1963) A regression method for real estate price index construction. *Journal of the American Statistical Association*, **58**, 933–42.

Bajic, V. (1985) Housing-market segmentation and demand for housing attributes: some empirical findings. *Journal of American Real Estate and Urban Economics Association*, **13**, 58–75.

Baker, R., Challen, P., Maclennan, D., Reid, V. & Whitehead, C.M.E. (1992) *The Scope for Competitive Tendering of Housing Management.* HMSO, London.

Ball, M. (1973) Recent empirical work on the determinants of relative house prices. *Urban Studies*, **10**, 213–33.

Ball, M. (1996a) *Housing and Construction: a troubled relationship?* Policy Press, Bristol.

Ball, M. (1996b) *Investing in New Housing: lessons for the future.* Policy Press, Bristol.

Ball, M. & Kirwan, R. (1977) Accessibility and supply constraints in urban housing markets. *Urban Studies*, **14**, 11–32.

Ball, M. & Wood, A. (1999) Housing investment: Long run international trends and volatility. *Housing Studies*, **14**, 185–210.

Ballas, D. & Clarke, G. (1999) *Regional Versus Local Multipliers of Economic Change? A micro-simulation approach.* Paper presented to the 39th European Regional Science Association Congress, University College Dublin, Dublin, Ireland, 23–27 August.

Bannister, J., Dell, M., Donnison, D., Fitzpatrick, S. & Taylor, R. (1993) *Homeless Young People in Scotland.* HMSO, Edinburgh.

Barclay, Sir Peter (chair) (1995) *Income and Wealth.* Vol. 1 of Report of the Inquiry Group, Joseph Rowntree Foundation, York.

Barkham, R. (1992) Regional variations in entrepreneurship: some evidence from the United Kingdom. *Entrepreneurship & Regional Development*, **4**, 225–244.

Barlow, J. (1993) Controlling the housing land market: some examples from Europe. *Urban Studies*, **30 (7)**, 1129–50.

Barlow, J., Cocks, R. & Parker, M. (1994) *Planning for Affordable Housing.* HMSO, London.

Barr, N. (1998) *The Economics of the Welfare State.* Oxford University Press, Oxford.

Bartik, T. J., Butler, J.S. & Liu, J. (1992) Maximum score estimates of the determinants of residential mobility: implications for the value of residential attachment and neighborhood amenities. *Journal of Urban Economics*, **32 (2)**, 233–56.

Bartlett, W. (1991) *Housing Supply Elasticities: a review.* Housing Finance, York.

Bassett, K. (1980) Council house sales in Bristol 1960–79. *Policy and Politics*, **8**, 324–33.

Basu, S. & Thibodeau, T.G. (1998) Analysis of spatial autocorrelation in house prices. *Journal of Real Estate Finance and Economics*, **17 (1)**, 61–85.

Bate, R. (1999) *A Guide to Land Use and Housing.* Overview Paper for Joseph Rowntree Foundation, RESC Programme.

Beazley, M. (1980) *The sale of council houses in a rural area: a case study of South Oxfordshire*. Working paper 44, Oxford Polytechnic Department of Town Planning, Oxford.

Berg, L. (1994) Household savings and debts: The recent experience of the Nordic countries. *Oxford Review of Economic Policy*, **10**, 42–53.

Berg, L. & Bergstrom, R. (1995) Housing and financial wealth, financial deregulation and consumption – the Swedish case. *Scandinavian Journal of Economics*, **97**, 421–39.

Berkovec, J.A., Canner, G.B., Gabriel, S.A., & Hannan, T.H. (November 1994) *Discrimination, default, and loss in FHA mortgage lending*. Federal Reserve Board of Governors Working Paper.

Berry, B.J.L. & Bednarz, R. (1975) A hedonic model of prices and assessments for single family homes in Chicago: Does the assessor follow the market or the market follow the assessor? *Land Economics*, **51**, 21–40.

Berry, B.J.L., Chung, K.S., & Waddell, P. (1995) Widening gaps: the behaviour of submarket housing prices indexes in the Dallas area, 1979–1993. *Urban Geography*, **16** (8), 722–33.

Best, R. (2002) *Inquiry into British Housing 1984–1991: What has happened since*. Joseph Rowntree Foundation, York.

Black, J., de Meza, D. & Jeffreys, D. (1996) House prices, the supply of collateral and the enterprise economy. *Economic Journal*, **106**, 60–75.

Blackaby, D.H. & Manning, D.N. (1992) Regional earnings and unemployment – A simultaneous approach. *Oxford Bulletin of Economics and Statistics*, **54**, 481–502.

Blackaby, R. (2000) *Understanding Local Housing Markets: Their role in local housing strategies*. Chartered Institute of Housing/Council of Mortgage Lenders, Coventry and London.

Blomquist, G. & Worley, L. (1982) Specifying the demand for housing characteristics: The exogeneity issue. In: *The Economics of Urban Amenities* (ed. D.B. Diamond & G. Tolley). Academic Press, London.

Boelhouwer, P.J. (2000) Convergence in European mortgage systems before and after EMU. *Journal of Housing and the Built Environment*, **15**, 11–28.

Boelhouwer, P. & Van der Heijden, H. (1993) Housing systems in Europe – A research project. *Scandinavian Housing Planning Research*, **10** (1), 37–42.

Bös, D. (1983) Public pricing with distributional objectives. *Public Sector Economics* (ed. J. Finsinger). Macmillan, London.

Bös, D. (1985) Public sector pricing. In: *Handbook of Public Economics* (ed. A.J. Anerbach & M. Feldstein). North Holland, Amsterdam.

Bossons, J. (1978) Housing demand and household wealth: Evidence for homeowners. In: *Urban Housing Markets: Recent Directions in Research and Policy* (ed. L. B. Bourne and J. R. Hitchcock). University of Toronto Press, Toronto.

Bourassa, S.C. & Grigsby, W.G. (2000) Income tax concessions for owner-occupied housing. *Housing Policy Debate*, **11** (3), 521–46.

Bourassa, S.C. & Hendershott, P.H. (1994) On the equity effects of taxing imputed rent: Evidence from Australia. *Housing Policy Debate*, **5** (1), 73–95.

Bourassa, S.C., Hamelink, F., Hoesli, M. & MacGregor, B.D. (1999) Defining housing submarkets. *Journal of Housing Economics*, **8**, 160–183.

Bover, O., Muellbauer, J. & Murphy, A. (1989) Housing, wages and U.K. labour markets. *Oxford Bulletin of Economics and Statistics*, **51**, 97–136.

Bowden, R.J. (1978) *The Econometrics of Disequilibrium*. North Holland, Amsterdam.

Box, G.E.P. & Cox, D. (1964) An analysis of transformations. *Journal of the American Statistical Association*, Society Series B, **26**, 211–52.

Boyle, M.A. & Kiel, K.A. (2001) A survey of house price hedonic studies of the impact of environmental externalities. *Journal of Real Estate Literature*, **9** (2), 117–44.

Bramley, G. (1989) *Land supply, planning and private housebuilding: a review*. SAUS Working Paper 81. School for Advanced Urban Studies, Bristol.

Bramley, G. (1993a) The impact of land use planning and tax subsidies on the supply and price of housing in Britain. *Urban Studies*, **30**, 5–30.

Bramley, G. (1993b) Land use planning and the housing market in Britain: the impact on housebuilding and house prices. *Environment and Planning A*, **25**, 1021–51.

Bramley, G. (1998) Measuring planning: indicators of planning restraint and its impact on the housing market. *Environment and Planning B: Planning & Design*, **25**, 31–57.

Bramley, G. (1999) Housing market adjustment and land-supply constraints. *Environment and Planning A*, **31**, 1169–88.

Bramley, G. & Lancaster, S. (1998) Household formation: A suitable case for policy? *Housing Finance*, **38**, 20–29.

Bramley, G. & Smart, G. (1996) Modelling local income distributions in Britain. *Regional Studies*, **30**, (3), 239–55.

Bramley, G. & Watkins, C. (1996a) *Steering the Housing Market: new building and the changing planning system*. The Policy Press, Bristol.

Bramley, G. & Watkins, C. (1996b) *Modelling the relationship between land availability, the land-use planning system and the supply of new housing*. Paper presented at RICS 'Cutting Edge' Conference, University of the West of England, Bristol, 20–21 Sept.

Bramley, G., Bartlett, W., & Lambert, C. (1995) *Planning, the Market and Private Housebuilding*. UCL Press, London.

Bramley, G., Munro, M. & Lancaster, S. (1997) *Economic Influences on Household Formation: A Literature Review*. Department of Environment, Transport and the Regions, London.

Bramley, G., Pawson, H., Satsangi, M. & Third, H. (1999) *Local housing needs assessment: a review of current practice and the need for guidance*. Research Paper No. 73, School of Planning and Housing, Edinburgh College of Art/Heriot-Watt University, Edinburgh.

Bramley, G., Pawson, H. & Parker, J. (2000) *Local housing needs assessment: a guide to good practice*. Department of Environment, Transport and the Regions, London.

Bratt, R.G. (2002) Housing and Family Well-being. *Housing Studies*, **17** (1), 13–26.

Breheny, M. (1999) People, households and houses: The basis to the 'great housing debate' in England. *Town Planning Review*, **70**, 275–93.

Britton, E. & Whitley, J. (1997) Comparing the monetary transmission mechanism in France, Germany and the United Kingdom: Some issues and results. *Bank of England Quarterly Bulletin*, **May**, 152–62.

Brock, W. & Durlauf, S. (forthcoming) Interactions-based models. In: *Handbook of Econometrics* (ed. J. Heckman & E. Learner), vol. 5. North Holland, Amsterdam.

Bromwich, M., Harrison, A. Travers, A. & Whitehead, C.M.E. (2002) *An economic analysis of PFI*. LSE London Discussion Paper, forthcoming, LSE, London.

Brown, J., Song, H. & McGillvray, A. (1997) Forecasting U.K. house prices: A time varying coefficient approach. *Economic Modelling*, **14**, 529–48.

Brueckner, J. K. (1986) The down payment constraint and housing tenure choice: A simplified exposition. *Regional Science and Urban Economics*, **16 (4)**, 519–25.

Brueggemann, W.B., Fisher, J.D. & Stern, J.J. (1982) Rental housing and the Economic Recovery Tax Act of 1981. *Public Finance Quarterly*, **10 (2)**, 222–41.

Buchel, S. & Hoesli, M. (1995) A hedonic analysis of rent and rental revenue in the subsidised and unsubsidised housing sectors in Geneva. *Urban Studies*, **32 (7)**, 1199–1213.

Burgess, J.F. Jr. & Harmon, O.R. (1982) Specification tests in hedonic models. *Journal of Real Estate Finance and Economics*, **4 (4)**, 375–93.

Burns, L. & Grebler, L. (1977) *The Housing of Nations*. Macmillan, London.

Burrows, R., Pleace, N. & Quilgar, D. (1997) *Homelessness and Social Policy*. Routledge, London.

Business Strategies Limited (1998) *A Critique of the Official Population and Household Projections for Scotland*. Business Strategies Limited, London.

Butler, R.V. (1982) The specification of hedonic indexes for urban housing. *Land Economics*, **58 (1)**, 96–108.

Cameron, G. & Muellbauer, J. (2000) *Earnings, unemployment and housing: evidence from a panel of British regions*. CEPR Discussion Paper No. 2404.

Can, A. (1992) Specification and estimation of hedonic housing price models. *Regional Science and Urban Economics*, **22(3)**, 453–75.

Capozza, D. & Seguin, P.J. (1995) *Expectations, efficiency and euphoria in the housing market*. National Bureau of Economic Research, Working Paper No. 5179.

Capozza, D.R., Green, R.K. & Hendershott, P.H. (1996) Taxes, mortgage borrowing and residential land prices. In: *Economic Effects of Fundamental Tax Reform* (ed. H. Aaron & W. Gale). The Brookings Institute, Washington, D.C.

Capozza, D.R., Green, R.K. & Hendershott, P.H. (1997) *Income taxes and house prices*. CULER Working Paper.

Carr-Hill, R. (1997) *Impact of housing conditions upon health status*. Paper presented at seminar on The Wider Impacts of Housing, Scottish Homes.

Case, B. & Quigley, J.M. (1991) The dynamics of real estate prices. *Review of Economics and Statistics*, **22 (1)**, 50–8.

Case, K.E. & Shiller, R.J. (1987) Prices of single family homes since 1970: New indexes for four cities. *New England Economic Review*, September/October, 45–56.

Case, K.E. & Shiller, R.J. (1989) The efficiency of the market for single family homes. *American Economic Review*, **79**, 125–37.

Case, K.E. & Shiller, R.J. (1990) Forecasting prices and excess returns in the housing market. *AREUEA Journal*, **18**, 253–73.

Case, K.E., Quigley, J.M. & Shiller, R.J. (2001) *Stock market wealth, housing wealth, spending and consumption*. Unpublished.

Cassel, E. & Mendelsohn, R. (1985) The choice of functional forms for hedonic price equations: comment. *Journal of Urban Economics*, **18**, 135–42.

Centre for Housing Research (1989) *The Nature and Effectiveness of Housing Management in England*. HMSO, London.

Chambers, D. (1992) The racial housing price differential and racially transitional neighborhoods. *Journal of Urban Economics*, **32(2)**, 214–32.

Chambers, D. & Simonson, J. (1989) *Mobility, transactions costs, and tenure choice*. Paper presented at the Seventeenth Midyear Meeting of The American Real Estate and Urban Economics Association, May.

Champion, A.J., Fotheringham, S., Boyle, P., Rees, P., & Stilwell, J. (1998b) *The determinants of migration flows in England: a review of existing data and evidence*. Report to DETR. DETR, London.

Champion, A.J., Coombes, M., Fotheringham, S. *et al.* (2000) *Development of a migration model*. Final report, prepared for the Department of the Environment, Transport and the Regions (DETR), under Contract RADS 5/9/22, University of Newcastle upon Tyne, Newcastle.

Chan, S. (2001) Spatial lock-in: Do falling house prices constrain residential mobility? *Journal of Urban Economics*, **49**, 567–86.

Chaplin, R., Jones, M., Martin, S. *et al.* (1995) *Rents and Risks: Investing in Housing Associations*. Joseph Rowntree Foundation, York.

Charles, K. & Hurst, E. (forthcoming) The Transition to Home Ownership and the Black-White Wealth Gap. *Review of Economics and Statistics*.

Charles, S. (1977) *Housing Economics*. Macmillan, London.

Cheshire, P. & Leven, C. (1982) *On the costs and economic consequences of the British land use planning system*. Discussion paper in Urban and Regional Economics, Series C, no. 11, University of Reading.

Cheshire, P. & Sheppard, S. (1989) British planning policy and access to housing: some empirical estimates. *Urban Studies*, **26**, 469–85.

Cheshire, P. & Sheppard, S. (1995) On the price of land and the value of amenity. *Econometrica*, **62**, 247–67.

Cheshire, P. & Sheppard, S. (1997) *The welfare economics of land use regulation*. Research Papers in Environmental and Spatial Analysis No. 42. Department of Geography, London School of Economics.

Chinloy, P. (1991) Risk and the user cost of housing services. *AREUEA Journal*, **19 (4)**, 516–31.

Cho, M. (1996) House price dynamics: A survey of theoretical and empirical issues. *Journal of Housing Research*, 7, 145–72.

Chowhan, J. & Prud'homme, M. (2000) *City Comparisons of Shelter Costs in Canada: A Hedonic Approach*. Statistics Canada, Ottawa.

Christensen, L.R., Jorgenson, D.W. & Lau, L.J. (1973) Transcendental logarithmic production frontiers. *Review of Economics and Statistics*, **55**, 28–45.

Clapham, D. (1996) Housing and the economy: Broadening comparative housing research. *Urban Studies*, **33**, 631–48.

Clapham, D. & Maclennan, D. (1983) Residualization of council housing: a non-issue. *Housing Review*, **32**, 9–10.

Clapp, J.M. & Giaccotto, C. (1998a) Price indices based on the hedonic repeat-sale method: Application to the housing market. *Journal of Real Estate Finance and Economics*, **16 (1)**, 5–26.

Clapp, J.M. & Giaccotto, C. (1998b) Residential hedonic models: A rational expectations approach to age effects. *Journal of Urban Economics*, **44 (3)**, 415–37.

Clapp, J.M., Giaccotto, C. & Tirtiroglu, D. (1991) Housing price indices: Based on all transactions compared to repeat subsamples. *AREUEA Journal*, **19 (3)**, 270–85.

Clark, W.A.V. (ed.) (1982a) *Modelling housing market search*. Croom Helm, London.

Clark, W.A.V. (1982b) Recent research on migration and mobility. *Progress and Planning*, **18**, 1–56.

Clark, W.A.V. (1993) Search and choice in urban housing markets. In: *Behavior and Environment: Psychological and Geographical Approaches* (eds T. Gärling & R. G. Golledge). Elsevier, Amsterdam.

Clark, Todd E. (1995) Rents and prices of housing across areas of the United States: A cross-section examination of the present value model. *Regional Science and Urban Economics*, **25**, 237–47.

Cliff, A.D., Haggett, P., Ord, J.K., Bassett, K.A. & Davies, R.B. (1975) *Elements of spatial structure*. Cambridge University Press, Cambridge, England.

Colwell, P.F. & Dilmore, G. (1999) Who was first? An examination of an early hedonic study. *Land Economics*, **75 (4)**, 620–6.

Coulson, N.E. & Fisher, L.M. (2002) Tenure choice and labour market outcomes. *Housing Studies*, **17 (1)**, 35–49.

Council for the Protection of Rural England (2001) *Sprawl Patrol: first year report*. CPRE, London.

Court, A.T. (1939) Hedonic price indexes with automotive examples. *The Dynamics of Automobile Demand*. General Motors Corporation, New York.

Crane, J. (1991) The epidemic theory of ghettos and neighbourhood effects on dropping out and teenage childbearing. *American Journal of Sociology*, **96**, 1226–59.

Cressy, R. (1996) Are business startups debt-rationed? *Economic Journal*, **106**, 1253–70.

Cullingworth, J.B. (1997a) *Planning in the U.S.A.: Policies, Issues and Processes*. Routledge, London & New York.

Cullingworth, J.B. (1997b) British land-use planning: A failure to cope with change? *Urban Studies*, **34**, 945–60.

Cunningham, D.F. & Hendershott, P.H. (1984) Pricing FHA Mortgage Default Insurance. *Housing Finance Review*, **3**, 373–92.

Dale-Johnston, D. (1982) An alternative approach to housing market segmentation using hedonic price data. *Journal of Urban Economics*, **11**, 311–32.

Davies, H.W.E. (1998) Continuity and change: the evolution of the British Planning System, 1947–97. *Town Planning Review*, **69**, 135–52.

Davis, O.A. & Whinston, A.B. (1961) The economics of urban renewal. *Law and Contemporary Problems*, **26 (1)**, 163–77.

De Borger, B. (1986) Estimating the benefits of public housing programs: A characteristics approach. *Journal of Regional Science*, **26**, 761–73.

De Leeuw, F. & Ozanne, L. (1981) Housing. In: *How Taxes Affect Economic Behaviour* (eds H. J. Aaron & J. A. Pechman). Brookings Institute, Washington, DC.

De Leeuw, F. & Struyck, R. (1975) *The Web of Urban Housing*. The Urban Institute, Washington, DC.

Department of Environment (1971) *Fair Deal for Housing*, **Cmnd 4728**, HMSO, London.

Department of the Environment (1977) *Housing Policy: a consultative document.* **Cmnd 6851**, HMSO, London.

Department of the Environment (1980) *Housing Requirements: a guide to information and techniques*. HMSO, London.

Department of Environment, Transport and the Regions (1997) *An Economic Model of the Need and Demand for Social Housing*. DETR, HMSO, London.

Department of Environment, Transport and the Regions (1998) *The 1996 House Condition Survey*. HMSO, London.

Department of Environment, Transport and the Regions (1999a) *Projections of Households in England to 2021*. DETR, HMSO, London.

Department of Environment, Transport and the Regions (1999b) *Towards an urban renaissance.* Final report of the Urban Task Force under the chairmanship of Lord Rogers of Riverside. HMSO, London.

Department of Transport, Local Government and the Regions (2001) *Reforming planning obligations: delivering fundamental change*. Consultation paper.

Des Rosiers, F. & Theriault, M. (1996) Rental amenities and the stability of hedonic prices: A comparative analysis of five market segments. *Journal of Real Estate Research*, **12 (1)**, 17–36.

Diamond, D.B. Jr. & Smith, B. (1985) Simultaneity in the Market for Housing Characteristics. *Journal of Urban Economics*, **17**, 280–92.

DiPasquale, D. & Glaeser, E. (1999) Incentives and social capital: Are homeowners better citizens? *Journal of Urban Economics*, **45 (2)**, 354–84.

DiPasquale, D. & Wheaton, W. (1994) Housing market dynamics and the future of house prices. *Journal of Urban Economics*, **35**, 1–27.

DiPasquale, D. & Wheaton, W. (1996) *Urban Economics and Real Estate Markets*. Prentice Hall, Englewood Cliffs, NJ.

Din, A., Hoesli, M. & Bender, A. (2001) Environmental values and real estate prices. *Urban Studies*, **38 (100)**, 1989–2000.

Dobson, J. (2000) *Strategic approaches*. Joseph Rowntree Foundation, Search No 34, winter 2000/2001, 8–11.

Donnison, D. (1961) The teaching of social administration. *British Journal of Sociology*, **12 (3)**, 202–23.

Donnison, D. (2000) The Academic Contribution to Social Reform. *Social Policy and Administration*, **34 (1)**, 26–43.

Doyal, L. & Gough, I. (1991) *A Theory of Human Need*. Macmillan, London.

Dreiman, M. & Follain, J.R. (2000) *Drawing Inferences about Housing Supply Elasticity from House Price Responses to Income Shocks.* (Unpublished).

Dubin, R.A. (1992) Spatial autocorrelation and neighborhood quality. *Regional Science and Urban Economics*, **22** (3), 433–52.

Dubin, R.A. (1998) Predicting house prices using multiple listings data. *Journal of Real Estate Finance and Economics*, **17** (1), 35–59.

Duca, J.V. & Rosenthal, S.S. (1994) Borrowing constraints and access to owner-occupied housing. *Regional Science and Urban Economics*, **24**, 301–22.

Dynarski, M. (1986) Residential attachment and housing demand. *Urban Studies*, **23**, 11–20.

Dynarski, M. & Sheffrin, S.M. (1985) Housing purchases and transitory income: A study with panel data. *The Review of Economics and Statistics*, **67**, 195–205.

Edel, M. & Sclar, E. (1974) Taxes, spending and property values: Supply adjustment in a Tiebout-Oates Model. *Journal of Political Economy*, **82**, 941–54.

Engelhardt, G.V. (1994a) Tax subsidies to saving for home purchase: Evidence from Canadian RHOSPs. *National Tax Journal*, **47** (2), 363–88.

Engelhardt, G.V. (1994b) House prices and the decision to save for down payments. *Journal of Urban Economics*, **36** (2), 209–37.

Engelhardt, G.V. (1995) *House prices and home owner saving behavior.* National Bureau of Economic Research Working Paper, no. 5183.

Engelhardt, G.V. & Mayer, C.J. (1994) Gifts for home purchase and housing market behavior. *New England Economic Review* (May-June), 47–58.

Engelhardt, G.V. & Mayer, C.J. (1995) *Intergenerational transfers, borrowing constraints, and saving behavior: Evidence from the housing market.* Federal Reserve Bank of Boston Working Paper, no. 95–11.

Englund, P. & Ioannides, Y. (1997) House price dynamics: An international empirical perspective. *Journal of Housing Economics*, **6**, 119–36.

Englund, P., Quigley, J.M. & Redfearn, C.L. (1998) Improved price indexes for real estate: Measuring the course of Swedish housing prices. *Journal of Urban Economics*, **44** (2), 171–96.

Environment Committee (1981) *Council house sales.* Second Report HC 366-I, HC 535 I-xi (1979–80), HMSO, London.

Epple, D. (1987) Hedonic prices and implicit markets: Estimating the demand and supply functions for differentiated products. *Journal of Political Economy*, **95**, 59–80.

Ermisch, J. (1984) *Housing Finance: Who Gains?* Policy Studies Institute, London.

Ermisch, J.F., Findlay, J. & Gibb, K. (1996) The price elasticity of housing demand in Britain: Issues of sample selection. *Journal of Housing Economics*, **5** (1), 64–86.

Evans, A. (1973) *Economics of Residential Location.* Macmillan, London.

Evans, A.W. (1983) The determination of the price of land. *Urban Studies*, **20**, 119–29.

Evans, A.W. (1991) Rabbit hutches on postage stamps: planning, development and political economy. *Urban Studies*, **28** (6), 853–70.

Evans, A.W. (1996) The impact of land use planning and tax subsidies on the supply and price of housing in Britain. *Urban Studies*, **33**, 581–6.

Evans, A., Stevens, S. & Williams, P. (1999) *Making Best Use of the Private Sector? A review of Welsh local authority housing strategies and operational plans.* Council of Mortgage Lenders, London.

Fair, R.C. & Jaffee, D.M. (1972) Methods of estimation for markets in disequilibrium. *Econometrica,* **40,** 497–514.

Feder, G. (1982) On exports and economic growth. *Journal of Development Economics,* **12,** 59–73.

Feldstein, M., Slemrod, J. & Yitzhaki, S. (1980) The effects of taxation on the selling of corporate stock and the realisation of capital gains. *Quarterly Journal of Economics,* **94 (4),** 777–91.

Fischel, W. (1990) *Do Growth Controls Matter? A review of empirical evidence on the effectiveness and efficiency of local government land use regulation.* Lincoln Institute of Land Policy Working Paper, Lincoln Institute, Boston.

Fischer, C.S. (1982) *To Dwell Among Friends.* University of Chicago Press, Chicago.

Fisher, F. & Shell, K. (1971) Taste and quality change in the pure theory of the true cost of living index. In: *Price Indexes and Quality Change* (ed. Zvi Griliches), Harvard University Press.

Fisher, J.D. & Lentz, G.H. (1986) Tax reform and the value of real estate income property. *AREUEA Journal,* **14 (2),** 287–315.

Flood, J. (1997) Urban and housing indicators. *Urban Studies,* **34 (10),** 1597–1620.

Follain, J.R. (1982) Does inflation affect real behavior? The Case of Housing. *Southern Economic Journal,* **48 (3),** 570–82.

Follain, J.R. & Jimenez, E. (1985a) Estimating the demand for housing characteristics: A survey and critique. *Regional Science and Urban Economics,* **15 (1),** 77–107.

Follain, J.R. & Jimenez, E. (1985b) The demand for housing characteristics in developing countries. *Urban Studies,* **22 (5),** 421–32.

Follain, J.R. & Ling, D.C. (1988) Another look at tenure choice, inflation, and taxes. *Journal of the American Real Estate and Urban Economics Association,* **16 (3),** 207–29.

Follain, J.R. & Malpezzi, S. (1980a) *Dissecting Housing Value and Rent.* The Urban Institute, Washington, D.C.

Follain, J.R. & Malpezzi, S. (1980b) Estimates of housing inflation for thirty-nine SMSAs: An alternative to the consumer price index. *Annals of Regional Science,* 41–56.

Follain, J.R. & Malpezzi, S. (1981a) Another look at racial differences in housing prices. *Urban Studies,* **18 (2),** 195–203.

Follain, J.R. & Malpezzi, S. (1981b) Are occupants accurate appraisers? *Review of Public Data Use,* **9 (1),** 47–55.

Follain, J.R. & Malpezzi, S. (1981c) The flight to the suburbs: Insight from an analysis of central city versus suburban housing costs. *Journal of Urban Economics,* **9 (3),** 381–98.

Follain, J.R. & Ozanne, L. with Alberger, V. (1979) *Place to Place Indexes of the Price of Housing.* Urban Institute, Washington, D.C.

Follain, J.R., Hendershott, P.H. & Ling, D.C. (1987) Understanding the real estate provisions of tax reform: Motivation and impact. *National Tax Journal*, **3**, 363–72.

Fordham, R. & Brook, R. (1995) *A Methodology for Assessing Housing Need*. Planning Negotiators and National Housing and Town Planning Council, London.

Forrest, R. & Murie, A. (1976) *Social segregation, housing need and the sale of council houses.* Research memorandum 53, Centre for Urban and Regional Studies, University of Birmingham.

Forrest, R. & Murie, A. (1984a) *Right to Buy? Issues of need, equity and polarisation in the sale of council houses.* Working Paper 39, School for Advanced Urban Studies, University of Bristol.

Forrest, R. & Murie, A. (1984b) *Monitoring the Right to Buy 1980–1982.* Working Paper 40, School for Advanced Urban Studies, University of Bristol.

Forrest, R. & Murie, A. (1988) *Selling the Welfare State: the Privatisation of Public Housing.* Routledge, London.

Forrest, R. & Murie, A. (1990a) *Moving the Housing Market.* Avebury, Aldershot.

Forrest, R. & Murie, A. (1990b) *Residualisation and council housing: a statistical update.* Working Paper 91, School for Advanced Urban Studies, University of Bristol.

Foulis, M.B. (1983) *Council House Sales in Scotland.* HMSO, Edinburgh.

Freeman, A.M. (1979) Hedonic prices, property values and measuring environmental benefits: A survey of the issues. *Scandinavian Journal of Economics*, **81 (2)**, 154–73.

Friedman, J. & Weinberg, D.H. (1981) The demand for rental housing: Evidence from the housing allowance demand experiment. *Journal of Urban Economics*, **9 (3)**, 311–31.

Fujita, M. (1987) *Urban Economic Theory.* Cambridge University Press, Cambridge.

Gabriel, S.A. (1984) A note on housing market segmentation in an Israeli development town. *Urban Studies*, **21**, 189–94.

Galster, G.C. (1987) *Homeowners and Neighborhood Reinvestment.* Duke University Press, Durham, NC.

Galster, G.C. (1992) Research on discrimination in housing and mortgage markets: Assessment and future directions. *Housing Policy Debate*, **3 (2)**, 639–84.

Galster, G. (1996) William Grigsby and the analysis of housing submarkets and filtering. *Urban Studies*, **33 (10)**, 1797–1806.

Galster, G. (1997) Comparing demand-side and supply-side housing policies; submarket and spatial perspectives. *Housing Studies*, **12 (4)**, 561–77.

Galster, G.C. (forthcoming) The effects of MTO on sending and receiving neighborhoods. In: *Choosing a better life? A Social Experiment in Leaving Poverty Behind* (eds J. Goering, T. Richardson & J. Feins). Urban Institute Press, Washington, DC.

Galster, G.C. & Daniell, J. (1996) Housing. In: *Reality and Research: Social Science and U.S. Urban Policy Since 1960* (ed. G.C. Galster), 85–112. Urban Institute Press, Washington, DC.

Galster, G.C. & Killen, S. (1995) The geography of metropolitan opportunity – a reconnaissance and conceptual framework. *Housing Policy Debate,* **6 (1),** 7–43.

Galster, G.C. & Rothenberg, J. (1991) Filtering in urban housing: a graphical analysis of a quality-segmented market. *Journal of Planning Education and Research,* **11,** 37–50.

Galster, G.C., Quercia, R.G., & Cortes, A. (2000) Identifying neighborhood thresholds: an empirical exploration. *Housing Policy Debate,* **11 (3),** 701–32.

Garrod, G. & Willis, K.G. (1992a) The environmental economic impact of woodland: A two-stage hedonic price model of the amenity value of forestry in Britain. *Applied Economics,* **24 (7),** 715–28.

Garrod, G. & Willis, K.G. (1992b) Valuing goods characteristics: An application of the hedonic price method to environmental attributes. *Journal of Environmental Management,* **34 (1),** 59–76.

Gatzlaff, D.H. & Haurin, D.R. (1997) Sample selection bias and repeat-sales index estimates. *Journal of Real Estate Finance and Economics,* **14,** 33–50.

Gatzlaff, D.H. & Tirtiroglu, D. (1995) Real estate market efficiency: Issues and evidence. *Journal of Real Estate Literature,* **3,** 157–92.

Gatzlaff, D.H., Green, R.K. & Ling, D.L. (1998) Revisiting cross-tenure differences in housing maintenance. *Land Economics,* **74 (3),** 328–42.

Genesove, D. & Mayer, C. J. (2001) Loss aversion and seller behavior: Evidence from the housing market. *Quarterly Journal of Economics,* **116 (4),** 1233–60.

Gibb, K. (1989) *Housing Economics and the Urban Public Sector.* Centre for Housing Research Discussion Paper 26. University of Glasgow.

Gibb, K. & MacKay, D. (2001) *The demand for housing in Scotland: new estimates from the Scottish House Condition Survey.* University of Glasgow, Department of Urban Studies Discussion Paper.

Gibb, K., Meen, G. & Mackay, D. (2000) *The Demand for Social Rented Housing in Glasgow: Citywide Needs and Demand.* Glasgow City Council/Scottish Homes, Glasgow.

Gillen, K., Thibodeau, T. & Wachter, S. (2001) Anisotropic autocorrelation in house prices. *Journal of Real Estate Finance and Economics,* **23 (1),** 5–30.

Gilley, O.W. & Kelley Pace, R. (1995) Improving hedonic estimation with an inequality restricted estimator. *Review of Economics and Statistics,* **77 (4),** 609–21.

Goldberger, A.S. (1968) The interpretation and estimation of Cobb-Douglas functions. *Econometrica,* **35,** 464–72.

Goodlad, R. (1993) *The Housing Authority as Enabler.* Longman/Chartered Institute of Housing, Essex and Coventry.

Goodman, A.C. (1981) Housing submarkets within urban areas: definitions and evidence. *Journal of Regional Science,* **21,** 175–85.

Goodman, A.C. (1998) Andrew Court and the invention of hedonic price analysis. *Journal of Urban Economics,* **44 (2),** 291–8.

Goodman, A.C. & Thibodeau, T.G. (1995) Age-related heteroskedasticity in hedonic house price equations. *Journal of Housing Research,* **6 (1),** 25–42.

Goodman, A.C. & Thibodeau, T.G. (1998) Housing market segmentation. *Journal of Housing Economics,* **7,** 121–43.

Goodman, J.L. Jr. & Ittner, J.B. (1992) The accuracy of home owners' estimates of House Value. *Journal of Housing Economics*, **2(4)**, 339–57.

Gordon, I. (1990) Housing and labour market constraints on migration across the North-South divide. In: *Housing and the National Economy* (ed. J. Ermisch). Avebury.

Gordon, I. (1991) Multi-stream migration modelling. In: *Migration models; macro and micro approaches* (ed. J. Stillwell & P. Congdon). Belhaven, London.

Gordon, R.H., Hines, J.R. (Jr), & Summers, L.H. (1987) Notes on the tax treatment of structures. In: *The Effects of Taxation on Capital Accumulation* (ed. M. Feldstein). Chicago University Press, Chicago.

Goss, S. & Blackaby, B. (1998) *Designing Local Housing Strategies*. Local Government Association/Chartered Institute of Housing, Coventry and London.

Granovetter, M. (1978) Threshold models of collective behavior. *American Journal of Sociology*, **83**, 1420–43.

Granovetter, M. & Soong, R. (1986) Threshold models of diversity: Chinese restaurants, residential segregation, and the spiral of silence. *Journal of Sociology*, **18**, 69–104.

Grant, M. (1992) Planning law and the British land use planning system. *Town Planning Review*, **63 (1)**, 3–12.

Grant, R.A., Thomson, B.W., Bible, J.K. & Randall, J.N. (1976) *Local Housing Needs and Strategies: A case study of the Dundee sub-region*. Scottish Development Department, Edinburgh.

Gravelle, J.G. (1994) *The Economic Effects of Taxing Capital Income*. MIT Press, Cambridge, Mass.

Green, R.K. & Hendershott, P.H. (2001a) Homeownership and unemployment in the U.S. *Urban Studies*, **38 (9)**, 1509–20.

Green, R.K. & Hendershott, P.H. (2001b) *Homeownership and the duration of unemployment: a test of the Oswald hypothesis*. Paper presented at the AREUEA Annual Meeting, January 2002.

Green, R.K. & Malpezzi, S. (2001) *A Primer on U.S. Housing Markets and Policies*. The Urban Institute Press for the American Real Estate and Urban Economics Association.

Green, R.K. & Vandell, K.D. (1999) Giving households credit: How changes in the U.S. Tax Code could promote homeownership. *Regional Science and Urban Economics*, **29**, 419–44.

Green, R.K. & White, M.J. (1997) Measuring the benefits of homeowning: Effects on children. *Journal of Urban Economics*, **41 (3)**, 441–61.

Greer, S. (1962) *The Emerging City: Myth and Reality*. Free Press, New York.

Grey, A., Hepworth, N., & Odling-Smee, J. (1981) *Housing rents, costs and subsidies: a discussion document* (2nd edn). The Chartered Institute of Public Finance and Accountancy, London.

Grigsby, W. (1963) *Housing Markets and Public Policy*. University of Pennsylvania Press, Philadelphia.

Grigsby, W., Baratz, G., Galster, G.C., & Maclennan, D. (1987) *The Dynamics of Neighborhood Change and Decline*. Pergamon, London, Progress in Planning series no. 28.

Griliches, Z. (1961) Hedonic price indexes for automobiles: An econometric analysis quality change. In: *The price statistics of the Federal Government*, General Series, **73**, 137–96. NBER, New York.

Gross, D.J. (1986) *Designing a suitable project: integration of a demand module into a supply side planning model*. World Bank, Water Supply and Urban Development Department Discussion Paper No. UDD-103.

Grossman, S. & Laroque, G. (1990) Asset pricing and optimal portfolio choice in the presence of illiquid durable consumption goods. *Econometrica*, **58**, 25–51.

Guisanni, B. & Hadjimatheou, G. (1991) Modelling regional house prices in the United Kingdom. *Papers in Regional Science*, **70**, 201–19.

Gyourko, J. & Linneman, P. (1993) The affordability of the American dream: An examination of the last 30 years. *Journal of Housing Research*, **4** (1), 39–72.

Gyourko, J. & Tracy, J. (1999) A look at real housing prices and incomes: Some implications for housing affordability and quality. *Economic Policy Review*, **5** (3), 63–77.

Gyourko, J., Linneman, P. & Wachter, S. (1999) Analyzing the relationships among race, wealth, and home ownership in America. *Journal of Housing Economics*, **8** (2), 63–89.

Haas, G.C. (1922) *Sales prices as a basis for farm land appraisal*. Technical Bulletin 9, University of Minnesota Agricultural Experiment Station, St. Paul, Minnesota.

Haavio, M. & Kauppi, H. (2001) *Housing markets, borrowing constraints and labor mobility*. Paper presented at the Sixth Nordic Conference on Local Public Finance, Helsinki, November 2001.

Hall, P., Land, H., Parker, R. & Webb, A. (1975) *Change, Choice and Conflict in Social Policy*. Heinemann, London.

Hall, S., Psaradakis, Z. & Sola, M. (1997) Switching error-correction models of house prices in the United Kingdom. *Economic Modelling*, **14**, 517–28.

Hall, S., Lazarova, S. & Urga, G. (1999) A principal components analysis of common stochastic trends in heterogeneous panel data: Some Monte Carlo evidence. *Oxford Bulletin of Economics and Statistics*, **Special Issue 61**, 749–67.

Hallman, H.W. (1984) *Neighborhoods: Their Place in Urban Life*. SAGE Publications, Beverly Hills, California.

Halvorsen, R. & Palmquist, R. (1980) The interpretation of dummy variables in semilogarithmic regressions. *American Economic Review*, **70**, 474–5.

Halvorsen, R. & Pollakowski, H. (1981) Choice of functional form for hedonic price functions. *Journal of Urban Economics*, **10**, 37–49.

Hamilton, B. (1975) Zoning and property taxation in a system of local government. *Urban Studies*, **12**, 205–11.

Hancock, K. (1991) *The economic principles of affordability*. Paper given at Housing Studies Association Conference, York.

Hancock, K. & Maclennan, D. (1989) *House price monitoring systems and housing planning in Scotland: a feasibility study*. Report for the Scottish Office, Centre for Housing Research, Glasgow University.

Hansmann, H. (1996) *The Ownership of Enterprise*. Harvard University Press, Cambridge, Mass.

Harrison, A.J. (1977) *Economics and Land Use Planning*. Policy Journals, Newbury.

Harsman, B. & Quigley, J.M. (1991) *Housing Markets and Housing Institutions: An International Comparison*. Kluwer, Boston.

Haurin, D.R. (1991) Income variability, homeownership and housing demand. *Journal of Housing Economics*, **1**, 60–74.

Haurin, D.R., Hendershott, P. & Wachter, S. (1997) Borrowing constraints and the tenure choice of young households. *Journal of Housing Research*, **8**, 137–54.

Hausman, J.A. (1978) Specification tests in econometrics. *Econometrica*, **46**, 1251–72.

Hawtin, M. (1996) Assessing housing needs. In: *Needs Assessments in Public Policy* (ed. J. Percy-Smith), 98–116. Open University Press, Buckingham.

Heal, G.M. (1973) *The Theory of Economic Planning*. North Holland, Amsterdam.

Healey, P., Purdue, M. & Ennis, F. (1993) *Gains from Planning? Dealing with the impacts of development*. Joseph Rowntree Foundation, York.

Hendershott, P.H. (1980) Real user costs and the demand for single family housing. *Brookings Papers on Economic Activity*, 401–42.

Hendershott, P.H. (1988) Home ownership and real house prices: Sources of change, 1965–1985. *Housing Finance Review*, **7**, 1–18.

Hendershott, P.H. & Hu, S.C. (1981) Inflation and extraordinary returns on owner-occupied housing: Some implications for capital allocation and productivity growth. *Journal of Macroeconomics*, **3** (**2**), 177–203.

Hendershott, P.H. & Ling, D.C. (1984) Prospective changes in tax law and the value of depreciable real estate. *AREUEA Journal*, **12** (**3**), 297–317.

Hendershott, P.H. & Shilling, J.D. (1982) Capital allocation and the economic recovery Tax Act of 1981. *Public Finance Quarterly*, **10** (**2**), 242–73.

Hendershott, P.H. & Slemrod, J. (1983) Taxes and the User Cost of Capital for Owner-Occupied Housing. *American Real Estate and Urban Economics Association Journal*, **10** (**4**), 375–93.

Hendershott, P.H., Follain, J.R. & Ling, D.C. (1987) Effects on real estate. In: *Tax Reform and the US Economy* (ed. J.A. Pechman), 71–102. Brookings Institute, Washington, DC.

Henderson, J.V. (1985) *Economic Theory and the Cities*. Academic Press, New York.

Henderson, J.V. & Ioannides, Y. (1983) A model of housing tenure choice. *American Economic Review*, **73**, 98–113.

Henderson, J.V. & Ioannides, Y. (1987) Owner-occupancy: Investment vs. consumption demand. *Journal of Urban Economics*, **21**, 228–41.

Henley, A. (1998) Residential mobility, housing equity and the labour market. *Economic Journal*, **108**, 414–27.

Hicks, J.R. (1939) *Value and Capital*. Clarendon Press, Oxford.

Hicks, J.R. (1960) Linear Theory. *Economic Journal*, **70**, 671–709.

Hill, R.C., Sirmans, C.F. & Knight, J.R. (1999) A random walk down Main Street? *Regional Science and Urban Economics*, **29** (**1**), 89–103.

Hills, J. (1991) *Unravelling Housing Finance: Subsidies, Benefits and Taxation*. Clarendon Press, Oxford.

Hills, J. (1995) *Inquiry into Incomes and Wealth, vol. 2: A summary of the evidence.* Joseph Rowntree Foundation, York.

Hills, J. (2000) *Reinventing Social Housing Finance.* IPPR, London.

Hills, J., Hubert, F., Tomann, H. & Whitehead, C. (1990) Shifting subsidies from bricks and mortar to people. *Housing Studies*, **5**, 147–67.

Hirsch, F. (1976) *Social Limits to Growth.* Harvard University Press, Cambridge, Mass.

Hirshleifer, J. (1970) *Investment, Interest and Capital.* Prentice Hall, Englewood Cliffs, NJ.

Hocking, R.R. (1976) The analysis and selection of variables in linear regression. *Biometrics*, **32**, 1–49.

Hoffman, J. & Kurz, C. (2002) *Rent Indices for Housing in West Germany: 1985 to 1998.* European Central Bank Working Paper No. 116.

Holmans, A. (1996) A decline in young owner-occupiers in the 1990s. *Housing Finance*, **29**, 13–20.

Holmans, A. (2001) *Housing Demand and Need in England 1996–2016.* Town and Country Planning Association, London.

Hölmstrom, B. (1979) Moral hazard and observability. *Bell Journal of Economics*, **10**, 74–91.

Hölmstrom, B. (1982) Moral hazard in teams. *Bell Journal of Economics*, **13**, 324–40.

Holt, C.C. & Shelton, J.P. (1962) The lock-in effect of the Capital Gains Tax. *National Tax Journal*, **XV, (4)**, 337–52.

Hopkins, C. Benjamin, C. & Carter, A. (1997) *Regeneration: Some Legal and Practical Issues.* Lawrence Graham, BURA.

Hort, K. (1997) On price formation and quantity adjustment in Swedish housing markets. *Economic Studies Number 34.* University of Uppsala, Sweden.

Housing Research Findings no. 19 (1990) *Survey of 10,000 households in six conurbations.* Nov. 1990, Joseph Rowntree Foundation, York.

Housing Studies (2000) Special issue: Housing and Health. *Housing Studies*, **15**, 3.

Housing Studies (2002) Special Issue: Opportunity, Deprivation and the Housing Nexus: Trans-Atlantic Perspectives. *Housing Studies*, **17, 1.**

Hoyt, Homer (1939) *The Structure and Growth of Residential Neighborhoods in American Cities.* Federal Housing Administration, Washington, D.C.

Hsiao, C. (1986) *Analysis of Panel Data.* Econometric Society Monographs. Cambridge University Press, Cambridge.

Hughes, G.A. & McCormick, B. (1981) Do council house policies reduce migration between regions? *Economic Journal*, **91**, 919–39.

Hughes, G.A. & McCormick, B. (1985) Migration intentions in the UK. Which households want to migrate and which succeed? *Economic Journal*, **95 (Suppl.)**, 113–23.

Hughes, G.A. & McCormick, B. (1987) Housing markets, unemployment and labour market flexibility in the U.K. *European Economic Review*, **31**, 615–45.

Hughes, G.A. & McCormick, B. (1990) Housing and labour market mobility. In: *Housing and the National Economy* (ed. J. Ermisch). Avebury, Aldershot.

Hughes, G.A. & McCormick, B. (2000) *Housing Policy and Labour Market Performance*. DETR, London.

Hunter, A. (1974) *Symbolic Communities*. University of Chicago Press, Chicago, IL.

Hunter, A. (1979) The urban neighborhood: its analytical and social contexts. *Urban Affairs Quarterly*, **14** (3), 267–88.

Industrial Systems Research (1999) *Political barriers to housebuilding in Britain: a critical case study of protectionism and its industrial-commercial effects*. ISR Business and Political-Legal Environment Reports, ISR, Manchester.

Ingram, G. (1979) Simulation and econometric approaches to modelling urban areas. In: *Current Issues in Urban Economics* (eds M. Straszheim & P. Mieszkowski). Johns Hopkins University Press, Baltimore.

Jaffe, A.J. (1996) On the role of transaction costs and property rights in housing markets. *Housing Studies*, **11** (3), 425–35.

Jones, C. (2002) The definition of housing market areas and strategic planning. *Urban Studies*, **34**, (Forthcoming).

Jones, C. & Murie, A. (1999) *Reviewing the Right to Buy*. University of Birmingham Press.

Jones, C. & Watkins, C. (1999) Planning and the Housing System. In: *Planning Beyond 2000* (ed. P. Allmendinger & M. Chapman), 89–104. Wiley, Chichester.

Jones, C., Leishman, C. & Watkins, C. (2000) *Structural change in local urban housing markets*. Paper presented at the American Real Estate Society Conference, Santa Barbara, California, March.

Jones, C., Leishman, C. & Watkins, C. (2001a) *Migration Linkages Between Urban Housing Submarkets: Theory and Evidence*. (Unpublished).

Jones, C., Leishman, C. & Watkins, C. (2001b) *Housing market processes, urban housing sub markets and planning policy*. Paper presented at Royal Institute of Chartered Surveyors 'Cutting Edge' Conference, Oxford, U.K., September.

Jones, L.D. (1989) Current wealth and tenure choice. *AREUEA Journal*, **17** (1), 7–40.

Jones, L.D. (1995) Testing the central prediction of housing tenure transition models. *Journal of Urban Economics*, **38**, 50–73.

Joseph Rowntree Foundation (1994) *Inquiry into planning for housing*. Report. Joseph Rowntree Foundation, York.

Jud, G.D. & Seaks, T.G. (1994) Sample selection bias in estimating housing sales prices. *Journal of Real Estate Research*, **9**(3), 289–98.

Kain, J. & Agpar, W. (1985) *Housing and Neighborhood Dynamics*. Harvard University Press, Cambridge, Massachusetts.

Kain, J.F. & Quigley, J. (1972a) Housing market discrimination, homeownership, and savings behavior. *American Economic Review*, **62** (3), 263–77.

Kain, J.F. & Quigley, J.M. (1972b) Note on owners' estimates of housing value. *Journal of the American Statistical Association*, **67**, 803–6.

Kaufman, D. & Quigley, J. (1987) The consumption benefits of investment in infrastructure: The evaluation of sites and services programs in underdeveloped countries. *Journal of Development Economics*, **25**, 263–84.

Keeble, D. & Walker, S. (1994) New firms, small firms and dead firms: Spatial patterns and determinants in the United Kingdom. *Regional Studies*, **28**, 411–28.

Kellet, J. (1989) Health and housing. *Journal of Psychosomatic Research*, **33**, 255–68.

Kennedy, P.E. (1981) Estimation with correctly interpreted dummy variables in semi logarithmic equations. *American Economic Review*, **71**, 801.

Kerr, M. (1988) *The Right to Buy: a National Survey of Tenants and Buyers of Council Houses*. HMSO, London.

Kiefer, D.M. (1978) The equity of alternative policies for the Australian homeowner. *The Economic Record*, **54**, 127–39.

Kiefer, D.M. (1980) The interaction of inflation and the U.S. income tax subsidies of housing. *National Tax Journal*, **34 (4)**, 433–45.

King, A.T. (1975) The demand for housing: Integrating the roles of journey-to-work, neighborhood quality, and prices. In: *Household Production and Consumption* (ed. N. Terlecky). NBER.

King, A.T. (1977) Estimating property tax capitalization: A critical comment. *Journal of Political Economy*, **85 (2)**, 425–31.

King, M.A. (1981) An econometric model of tenure choice and demand for housing as a joint decision. *Journal of Public Economics*, **14**, 137–59.

King, M. (1990) Discussion of J. Muellbauer and A. Murphy; is the U.K. balance of payments sustainable? *Economic Policy*, **11**, 383–87.

Kleinman, M.P. & Whitehead, C.M.E. (1991) *Setting a Rent Structure: A Handbook for Social Landlords*. Scottish Homes, Glasgow.

Knight, J.R., Dombrow J. & Sirmans, C.F. (1995) A varying parameters approach to constructing house price indexes. *Real Estate Economics*, **23 (2)**, 187–205.

Knight, J.R., Carter Hill, R. & Sirmans, C.F. (1992) Biased prediction of housing values. *AREUEA Journal*, **20 (3)**, 427–56.

Koskela, E. & Viren, M. (1992) Inflation, capital markets and household saving in the Nordic countries. *Scandinavian Journal of Economics*, **94**, 215–27.

Kotlikoff, L. (1988) Intergenerational transfers and savings. *Journal of Economic Perspectives*, **2**, 41–58.

Laidler, D. (1969) Income tax incentives for owner-occupied housing. In: *Taxation of Income from Capital* (eds A.C. Harberger & M. J. Bailey), 50–76. Brookings Institute, Washington, D.C.

Lambert, C. & Bramley, G. (2002) Managing urban development: Land use planning and city competitiveness. In: *Urban Competitiveness: Policies for dynamic cities* (ed. I. Begg). Policy Press, Bristol.

Lancaster, K. (1966) A new approach to consumer theory. *Journal of Political Economy*, **74**, 132–57.

Lancaster, K. (1971) *Consumer Demand: A New Approach*. Columbia University Press, New York.

Leamer, E.E. (1978) *Specification Searches: Ad Hoc Inference With Nonexperimental Data*. Wiley, New York.

Leishman, C. & Bramley, G. (forthcoming) A Local Housing Market Model with Spatial Interaction and Land Use Planning Controls. Under review, *Environment and Planning, A*.

Leven, C., Little, J., Nourse, H., & Reed, R. (1976) *Neighborhood Change: The Dynamics of Urban Decay.* Praeger, New York.

Levine, D.N. (Ed.) (1971) *George Simmel: On Individuality and Social Forms.* University of Chicago Press, Chicago.

Ling, D.C. (1992) Real estate values, Federal income taxation and the importance of local market conditions. *Journal of the American Real Estate and Urban Economic Association,* **20 (1),** 122–39.

Ling, D.C. & McGill, G.A. (1992) Measuring the size and distributional effects on homeowner tax preferences. *Journal of Housing Research,* **3 (2),** 273–304.

Linneman, P. (1981) The demand for residence site characteristics. *Journal of Urban Economics,* **9,** 129–48.

Linneman, P. (1985) An economic analysis of the homeownership decision. *Journal of Urban Economics,* **17 (2),** 230–46.

Linneman, P. & Megbolugbe, I.F. (1992) Housing affordability: Myth or reality? *Urban Studies,* **29 (1),** 369–92.

Linneman, P. & Wachter, S. (1989) The impacts of borrowing constraints on homeownership. *AREUEA Journal,* **17 (4),** 389–402.

Litzenberger, R.H. & Sosin, H.B. (1978) Taxation and the incidence of homeownership across income groups. *Journal of Finance,* **XXXIII (3),** 947–61.

Liu, C.H., Grisson, T.V. & Hartzell, D.J. (1995) Superior real estate investment performance: Enigma or illusion? A critical review of the literature. In: *Alternative ideas in real estate investment* (eds A.L. Schwartz, Jr. & D.D. Kaplin). Kluwer, Boston.

Llewellyn-Davies (1994) *Providing more homes in urban areas.* Report to Joseph Rowntree Foundation. SAUS Publications (now the Policy Press), Bristol.

Lowry, I. (1960) Filtering and housing standards: A conceptual analysis. *Land Economics,* **36,** 362–70.

Lusht, K.M. (1976) The use of design stratification in mass appraisal. *Assessors Journal,* March, 47–57.

Lynn, P. (1991) *The Right to Buy: a National Follow-up Survey of Tenants of Council Homes in England.* HMSO, London.

Macho-Stadler, I. & Pérez-Castrillo, D. (1997) *An Introduction to the Economics of Information.* Oxford University Press, Oxford.

Maclennan, D. (1977a) *The economics of selling council houses in the Scottish housing system.* Occasional Paper 77–104, Department of Political Economy, University of Aberdeen.

Maclennan, D. (1977b) Some thoughts on the nature and purpose of house price studies. *Urban Studies,* **14,** 39–71.

Maclennan, D. (1982) *Housing Economics: An Applied Approach.* Longmans, London and New York.

Maclennan, D. (1989) Housing in Scotland, 1977–87. In: *Guide to Housing,* 3rd edn. (ed. M. E. H. Smith), 671–704. The Housing Centre Trust, London.

Maclennan, D. (1986a) *The Demand for Housing: economic perspectives and planning practices.* Scottish Development Department, Edinburgh.

Maclennan, D. (1986b) The rents of public housing in Britain. In: *Papers for the Duke of Edinburgh's Inquiry into British Housing* (ed. R. Best). NFHA, London.

Maclennan, D. (1986c) The pricing of public housing in the United Kingdom. *Inquiry into British Housing: Supplement.* National Federation of Housing Associations, London.

Maclennan, D. (1991) Extending the strategic role. In: *The Housing Service of the Future* (eds D. Donnison & D. Maclennan), 185–211. Institute of Housing and Longman, Coventry and Harlow.

Maclennan, D. (1993a) *Housing policy and economic recovery: housing and the economy – what next?* Housing policy and economic recovery, Briefings 2. Joseph Rowntree Foundation, York.

Maclennan, D. (1993b) Spillovers, Expectations and Residents Benefits in a Housing Revitalisation Programme: Glasgow 1977–1987. *Tidjschrift voor Economische en Sociale Geografie,* **84,** 294–303.

Maclennan, D. (1994) *A competitive U.K. economy: the challenges for housing policy.* Housing Research Summary, Joseph Rowntree Foundation, York.

Maclennan, D. (2000) *Changing places, engaging people.* Joseph Rowntree Foundation, York.

Maclennan, D. (2002) *Recognising place and managing territory.* (Unpublished paper).

Maclennan, D. & Gibb, K. (1993) Housing Indicators and Research for Policy from the Perspective of Applied Economics. *Netherlands Journal of Housing and the Built Environment,* **8(1),** 49–60.

Maclennan, D. & Gibb, K. (1994) *Modelling metropolitan housing systems and seeking new micro foundations: big ideas in a cold climate?* Paper presented to the seminar 'Housing Policy and Research Priorities'. Centre for Housing Research, Glasgow University, Glasgow, 22–24 March.

Maclennan, D. & Meen, G. (1993) *Housing markets and national economic performance in OECD countries: lessons for the UK.* Housing Policy and Economic Recovery, Briefings 3. Joseph Rowntree Foundation, York.

Maclennan, D. & O'Sullivan, A.J. (1987) Housing Policy in the United Kingdom: Efficient or Equitable? In: *Housing Markets and Policies under Fiscal Austerity* (ed. W. van Vliet). Greenwood Press, Westport.

Maclennan, D. & Tu, Y. (1996) Economic perspectives on the structure of local housing markets. *Housing Studies,* **11,** 387–406.

Maclennan, D. & Williams, R. (1990a) *Affordable Housing in Europe.* Joseph Rowntree Foundation, York.

Maclennan, D. & Williams, R. (1990b) *Housing Subsidies and the Market: An International Perspective.* Joseph Rowntree Foundation, York.

Maclennan, D. & Wood, G.A. (1982a) Information acquisition: Patterns and strategies. In: *Modelling Housing Market Search* (ed. W. A. V. Clark), 134–59. Croom Helm, London.

Maclennan D. & Wood, G.A. (1982b) *The Pricing of Public Housing: Principles and Implementation.* Northern Ireland Housing Executive.

Maclennan, D., Munro, M. & Wood, G.A. (1987) Housing choice and the structure of urban housing markets. In: *Between State and Market Housing in the Post-industrial Era* (eds B. Turner, J. Kemeny & L. Lundquist), 26–52. Almquist and Hicksell International, Gothenburg.

Maclennan, D., Gibb, K., & More, E.A. (1990) *Paying for Britain's Housing*. Joseph Rowntree Foundation, York.

Maclennan, D., Gibb, K. & More, E.A. (1991a) *Fairer Subsidies, Faster Growth*. Joseph Rowntree Foundation, York.

Maclennan, D., More, E.A. & Gibb, K.D. (1991b) *Subsidising home-ownership*. Housing Research Findings No 35, May 1991. Joseph Rowntree Foundation, York.

Maclennan, D., More, E.A. & Gibb, K.D. (1991c) *Subsidising the independent rented sector*. Housing Research Findings No 37, May 1991. Joseph Rowntree Foundation, York.

Maclennan, D., More, E.A. & Gibb, K.D. (1991d) *Inconsistent rent-setting for council housing*. Housing Research Findings No 36, May 1991. Joseph Rowntree Foundation, York.

Maclennan, D., More, A. & Munro, M. (1994) *Analysing local housing systems: new wine, new bottles or new tastes?* Paper presented to the seminar 'Housing Policy and Research Priorities'. Centre for Housing Research and Urban Studies, Glasgow University, Glasgow, 22–24 March.

Maclennan, D., Meen, G., Stephens, M. & Gibb, K. (1997) *Fixed Commitments, Uncertain Incomes: Sustainable Owner Occupation and the Economy*. Joseph Rowntree Foundation, York.

Maclennan, D., More, A., O'Sullivan, A. & Young, G. (1998a) *Local Housing Systems Analysis: best practice guide*. Scottish Homes, Edinburgh.

Maclennan, D., Muellbauer, J. & Stephens, M. (1998b) Asymmetries in housing and financial market institutions and EMU. *Oxford Review of Economic Policy*, **14**, 54–80.

Maclennan, D., O'Sullivan, A. & Macintyre, C. (2000) *Evolving the Right to Buy: Evidence for Scotland*. Scottish Executive, Edinburgh.

MacNee, K. (1993) *The Right to Buy in Scotland: an Assessment of the Impact of the First Decade of the Right to Buy*. Scottish Office Central Research Unit, Edinburgh.

MacNevin, A.S. (1997) Tax Effects on Rental Housing in Halifax, Nova Scotia. *Canadian Tax Journal*, **45, (1)**, 87–113.

Maddala, G.S. (1983) *Limited Dependent and Qualitative Variables in Econometrics*. Cambridge University Press.

Malatesta, P.H. & Hess, E. (1986) Discount mortgage financing and housing prices. *Housing Finance Review*, **5**, 25–41.

Malpass, P. (1980) Council house sales in Yeovil District. *Policy and Politics*, **8**, 308–15.

Malpass, P. (1983) Residualization and the restructuring of housing tenure. *Housing Review*, **32**, 44–45.

Malpezzi, S. (1990) Urban housing and financial markets: some international comparisons. *Urban Studies*, **27 (6)**, 971–1022.

Malpezzi, S. (1996) Housing prices, externalities and regulation in U.S. metropolitan areas. *Journal of Housing Research*, **7 (2)**, 209–41.

Malpezzi, S. (1998) Welfare analysis of rent control with side payments: A natural experiment in Cairo, Egypt. *Regional Science and Urban Economics*, **28 (6)**, 773–96.

Malpezzi, S. (1999) A simple error correction model of house prices. *Journal of Housing Economics*, **8**, 27–62.

Malpezzi, S. (2000) Housing. In: *Designing Household Survey Questionnaires for Developing Countries: Lessons from Fifteen Years of the Living Standards Measurement Study* (eds M. Grosh & P. Glewwe). Oxford University Press.

Malpezzi, S. & Green, R.K. (1996) What has happened to the bottom of the U.S. housing market? *Urban Studies*, **33 (10)**, 1807–20.

Malpezzi, S. & Mayo, S.K. (1987) The demand for housing in developing countries. *Economic Development and Cultural Change*, **35 (4)**, 687–721.

Malpezzi, S. & Mayo, S.K. (1994) *A Model Design for a Developing Country Housing Market Study*. University of Wisconsin-Madison, Center for Urban Land Economics Research Working Paper.

Malpezzi, S. & Mayo, S.K. (1997) Housing and urban development indicators: A good idea whose time has returned. *Real Estate Economics*, **25 (1)**, 1–11.

Malpezzi, S., Ozanne, L. & Thibodeau, T. (1980) *Characteristic Prices of Housing in 59 SMSAs*. The Urban Institute, Washington, DC.

Malpezzi, S., Ozanne, L. & Thibodeau, T. (1987) Microeconomic estimates of housing depreciation. *Land Economics*, **63(4)**, 373–85.

Malpezzi, S., Chun, G. & Green, R. (1998) New place-to-place housing price indexes for U.S. metropolitan areas, and their determinants: An application of housing indicators. *Real Estate Economics*, **26 (2)**, 235–75.

Mankiw, N.G. & Weil, D.N. (1989) Baby boom, baby bust and the housing market. *Regional Science and Urban Economics*, **19**, 235–58.

Marmot, M. & Wilkinson, R. (eds) (1999) *Social Determinants of Health*. University Press, Oxford.

Marris, P. (1997) *Witnesses, Engineers, and Story Tellers*. University of Maryland, Urban Studies and Planning Program.

Mason, C. & Quigley, J.M. (1996) Non-parametric housing prices. *Housing Studies*, **11 (3)**, 373–85.

Mayer, C. & Somerville, T. (2000) Land use regulation and new construction. *Regional Science and Urban Economics*, **30**, 639–62.

Mayo, S.K. (1981) Theory and estimation in the economics of housing demand. *Journal of Urban Economics*, **10**, 95–116.

Mayo, S.K. & Gross, D.J. (1987) Sites and services and subsidies: The economics of low cost housing in developing countries. *World Bank Economic Review*, **1 (2)**, 301–35.

McBeath, J. (1997) *Learning, school and neighbourhood*. Paper presented at seminar on 'The Wider Impacts of Housing', Scottish Homes.

McCarthy, G., Van Zandt, S. & Rohe, W. (2001) T*he economic benefits and costs of homeownership; a critical assessment of the research*. Research Institute for Housing America, Working Paper No. 01–02.

McClure, K. (2000) The low-income housing tax credit as an aid to housing finance: How well has it worked? *Housing Policy Debate*, **11 (1)**, 91–114.

McDonald, J. (1997) *Fundamentals of Urban Economics*. Prentice-Hall, Upper Saddle River, NJ.

McFadden, D. (1978) Modelling the choice of residential location. In: *Planning Models* (ed. A. Karlquist), 75–96. North Holland, Amsterdam.

Meen, G.P. (1990) The removal of mortgage market constraints and the implications for econometric modelling of U.K. house prices. *Oxford Bulletin of Economics and Statistics*, **52**, 1–24.

Meen, G. (1993) *The treatment of house prices in macroeconomic models: a comparison exercise*. DOE Occasional Paper, Housing and Urban Monitoring Analysis.

Meen, G.P. (1996) Ten propositions in U.K. housing macroeconomics: An overview of the eighties and early nineties. *Urban Studies*, **33**, 425–44.

Meen, G.P. (1998) Modelling sustainable home-ownership: Demographics or economics? *Urban Studies*, **35**, 1919–34.

Meen, G.P. (1999a) *Models of housing in London and the South East*. Paper presented at Citywide seminar, April, Glasgow Clyde Port Authority.

Meen, G.P. (1999b) Regional house prices and the ripple effect: A new interpretation. *Housing Studies*, **14**, 733–53.

Meen, G.P. (2000) Housing cycles and efficiency. *Scottish Journal of Political Economy*, **47**, 114–40.

Meen, G.P. (2001) *Modelling spatial housing markets: Theory, analysis and policy*. Kluwer Academic Publishers, Boston.

Meen, G.P. & Andrew, M. (1998) On the aggregate housing market implications of labour market change. *Scottish Journal of Political Economy*, **45**, 393–419.

Meen, G.P. & Andrew, M. (1999) S*patial structure and social exclusion*. Discussion Papers in Urban and Regional Economics 140: Department of Economics, University of Reading.

Meen, G.P., Gibb, K., Mackay, D. & White, M. (2001) *The Economic Role of New Housing*. NHBC, London.

Meese, R. & Wallace, N. (1991) Nonparametric estimation of dynamic hedonic price models and the construction of residential house price indices. *Journal of American Real Estate and Urban Economics Association*, **19**, 308–32.

Meese, R.A. & Wallace, N.E. (1994) Testing the present value relation for housing prices: Should I leave my house in San Francisco? *Journal of Urban Economics*, **35**, 245–66.

Memery, C. (2001) The housing system and the Celtic Tiger: the state response to a housing crisis of affordability and access. *European Journal of Housing Policy*, **1 (1)**, 79–104.

Michaels, R. & Smith, V.K. (1990) Market segmentation and valuing amenities with hedonic models: the case of hazardous waste sites. *Journal of Urban Economics*, **28**, 223–42.

Miles, D. (1997) A household level study of the determinants of incomes and consumption. *Economic Journal*, **107**, 1–25.

Mills, E. (1967) An aggregative model of resource allocation in a metropolitan area. *American Economic Review*, **57**, 197–210.

Mills, E. (1972) *Studies in the Structure of the Urban Economy.* Johns Hopkins University Press, Baltimore.

Mills, E.S. (1987) Has the United States over-invested in housing? *Journal of the American Real Estate and Urban Economics Association,* **15 (1),** 601–16.

Mills, E.S. & Simenauer, R. (1996) New hedonic estimates of regional constant quality housing prices. *Journal of Urban Economics,* **39 (2),** 209–15.

Minford, P., Ashton, P. & Peel, M. (1988) The effects of housing distortions on unemployment. *Oxford Economic Papers,* **40,** 322–45.

Ministry of Reconstruction (1945) *Housing.* **Cd 6609,** HMSO, London.

Monk, S. (2000a) The 'key worker' problem: The link between employment and housing. In: *Restructuring Housing Systems* (eds S. Monk & C. M. E. Whitehead). Joseph Rowntree Foundation, York.

Monk, S. (2000b) The use of price in planning for housing. In: *Restructuring Housing Systems* (eds S. Monk & C. M.E. Whitehead), 198–207. Joseph Rowntree Foundation, York.

Monk, S. & Whitehead, C.M.E. (2000) *The use of housing and land prices as a planning tool: a summary document.* Cambridge Housing and Planning Research, Research Report 1, Cambridge.

Monk, S., Pearce, B. & Whitehead, C. (1991) *Planning, land supply and house prices: a literature review.* Monograph 21. Department of Land Economy, University of Cambridge. Granta Publications, London & Cambridge.

Monk, S., Pearce, B., & Whitehead, C.M.E. (1996) Land-use planning, land supply, and house prices. *Environment & Planning A,* **28,** 495–511.

More, A. (2002) Planning and Strategy. In: *Introduction to Management,* 2nd edn. (ed. D. Boddy). (Forthcoming, Pearson).

Moulton, B.R. (1995) Inter-area indexes of the cost of shelter using hedonic quality adjustment techniques. *Journal of Econometrics,* **68 (1),** 181–204.

Mozolin, M. (1994) The geography of housing values in the transformation to a market economy – A case study of Moscow. *Urban Geography,* **15 (2),** 107–27.

Muellbauer, J. (1990) The housing market and the U.K. economy: Problems and opportunities. In: *Housing and the National Economy* (ed. J. Ermisch). Avebury, Aldershot.

Muellbauer, J. & Murphy, A. (1990) Is the U.K. balance of payments sustainable? *Economic Policy,* **11,** 347–82.

Muellbauer, J. & Murphy, A. (1997) Booms and busts in the U.K. housing market. *Economic Journal,* **107,** 1701–27.

Munnell, A.H., Tootell, G.M.B., Browne, L.E., & McEneaney, J. (1996) Mortgage Lending in Boston: Interpreting HMDA Data. *American Economic Review,* **86 (1),** 25–53.

Munro, M. & Tu, Y. (1997) *U.K. House Price Dynamics: past and future trends.* CML Research Report, Council of Mortgage Lenders, London.

Murie, A. (1975) *The sale of council houses.* Occasional Paper 35, Centre for Urban and Regional Studies, University of Birmingham.

Murie, A. (1989) *Lost opportunities? Council house sales and housing policy in Britain 1979–89.* Working Paper 80, School for Advanced Urban Studies, University of Bristol.

Murie, A. & Nevin, B. (1997) *Beyond a Half Way Housing Policy.* NHF, London.

Murray, C. (1984) *Losing Ground: America's Social Policy, 1950–1980.* Basic Books, New York.

Musgrave, R.A. (1959) *The Theory of Public Finance.* McGraw-Hill, New York.

Muth, R. (1969) *Cities and Housing.* University of Chicago Press, Chicago.

Muth, R. (1985) Models of land-use, housing and rent: An evaluation. *Journal of Regional Science,* **25**, 593–606.

Narwold, A. (1992) The distribution of the benefits of tax arbitrage in the housing market. *Journal of Urban Economics,* **32**, 367–76.

National Council of Social Service (1980) *Rural Housing in East Hampshire.* NCSS.

Needham, B. & Lie, R. (1994) The public regulation of property supply and its effects on private prices, risks and returns. *Journal of Property Research,* **11**, 199–213.

Nelson, J.P. (1982a) Estimating demand for product characteristics: Comment. *Journal of Consumer Research,* **9 (2)**, 219–20.

Nelson, J.P. (1982b) Highway noise and property values: A survey of recent evidence. *Journal of Transport Economics and Policy,* **16**, 117–38.

Neutze, M. (1987) The supply of land for a particular use. *Urban Studies,* **24**, 379–88.

Nevin, B., Lee, P., Murie, A., Goodson, L. & Phillimore, J. (2001) *The West Midlands Housing Markets: Changing Demand, Decentralisation and Urban Regeneration.* Centre for Urban and Regional Studies, University of Birmingham.

Niskanen, W.A. (1994) *Bureaucracy and Public Economics.* Edward Elgar, Aldershot.

Nordvik, V. (2000) Tenure flexibility and the supply of private rental housing. *Regional Science and Urban Economics,* **30**, 59–76.

Nourse, H.O. (1963) The effect of public housing on property values in St Louis. *Land Economics,* **39**, 434–41.

Nozick, R. (1974) *Anarchy, State, and Utopia.* Basil Blackwell, Oxford.

Oates, W. (1981) On local finance and the Tiebout Model. *American Economic Review,* **71 (2)**, 93–8.

Ohta, M. & Griliches, Z. (1975) Automobile prices revisited: Extensions of the hedonic price hypothesis. In: *Household Production and Consumption, Studies in Income and Wealth.* Vol. 40 (ed. N. E. Terleckyj). [325–398.] University of Chicago Press, for the National Bureau of Economic Research, Chicago.

Olsen, E.O. (1968) A competitive theory of the housing market. *American Economic Review,* **58**, 612–22.

Olsen, E.O. (1972) An econometric analysis of rent control. *Journal of Political Economy,* **80**, 1081–1100.

Olsen, E.O. (1987) The demand and supply of housing services: A critical review of the empirical literature. In: *Handbook of Regional and Urban Economics* (ed. E.S. Mills), Vol. 2, Elsevier.

Olsen, E.O. & Barton, D.M. (1983) The benefits and costs of public housing in New York City. *Journal of Public Economics,* **20**, 299–332.

O'Sullivan, A. (1984) Misconceptions in the current housing subsidy debate. *Policy and Politics,* **12**, 119–44.

O'Sullivan, A. (1987) *The Definition and Measurement of Housing Subsidies for the U.K., 1977.* Unpublished doctoral thesis, University of Sussex.

Oswald, A.J. (1996) *A conjecture on the explanation for high unemployment in the industrialised nations.* University of Warwick Working Paper.

Oswald, A.J. (1997a) Thoughts on NAIRU. Correspondence to *Journal of Economic Perspectives,* **11,** 227–28.

Oswald, A.J. (1997b) *The missing piece of the unemployment puzzle.* An inaugural lecture. Unpublished.

Oswald, A.J. (1999) *The housing market and Europe's unemployment*: a non-technical paper. University of Warwick Working Paper.

Ozanne, L. & Malpezzi, S. (1985) The efficacy of hedonic estimation with the annual housing survey: Evidence from the demand experiment. *Journal of Economic and Social Measurement,* **13 (2),** 153–72.

Pace, R.K. (1993) Nonparametric methods with applications to hedonic models. *Journal of Real Estate Finance and Economics,* **7 (3),** 185–204.

Pace, R.K. & Gilley, O.W. (1990) Estimation employing a priori information within mass appraisal and hedonic pricing models. *Journal of Real Estate Finance and Economics,* **3 (1),** 55–72.

Pace, R.K. & Gilley, O.W. (1997) Using the spatial configuration of the data to improve estimation. *Journal of Real Estate Finance and Economics,* **14 (3),** 333–40.

Palm, R. (1978) Spatial segmentation of the urban housing market. *Economic Geography,* **54,** 210–21.

Paris, C. & Blackaby, B. (1979) *Not Much Improvement,* Heinemann, London.

Pasha, H.A. & Butts, M.S. (1996) Demand for housing attributes in developing countries: A case study of Pakistan. *Urban Studies,* **33 (7),** 1141–54.

Pawson, H. & Watkins, C. (1999) Resale of former public sector homes in rural Scotland. *Scottish Geographical Magazine,* **114,** 157–63.

Pawson, H., Watkins, C. & Morgan, J. (1997) *Right to Buy Resales in Scotland.* Scottish Office, Edinburgh.

Pesaran, M.H. & Smith, R. (1995) Estimating long-run relationships from dynamic heterogeneous panels. *Journal of Econometrics,* **68,** 79–113.

Peterson, A.W.A., Pratten, C.F. & Tatch, J. (1998) *An Economic Model of Demand and Need for Social Housing.* DETR, London.

Phillips, R.S. (1988) Unraveling the rent-value puzzle: An empirical investigation. *Urban Studies,* **25,** 487–96.

Plaut, S.E. (1987) The timing of housing tenure transition. *Journal of Urban Economics,* **21,** 312–22.

Podogzinski, H.U. & Sass, T.R. (1991) Measuring the effects of municipal zoning regulations: a survey. *Urban Studies,* **28,** 597–621.

Pollak, R. (1985) A transaction cost approach to families and households. *Journal of Economic Literature,* **23,** 581–608.

Posner, R.A. (1972) The appropriate scope of regulation in the cable television industry. *The Bell Journal of Economics and Management Science,* **3,** 98–129.

Potepan, M.J. (1989) Interest rates, income, and home improvement decisions. *Journal of Urban Economics,* **25,** 282–94.

Poterba, J. (1991) House price dynamics: The role of tax policy and demography. *Brookings Papers on Economic Activity*, 143–99.

Priemus, H. (1992) Housing indicators: An instrument in international housing policy? *Netherlands Journal of Housing and the Built Environment*, **7 (3)**, 217–38.

Pryce, G. (1999) Construction elasticities and land availability: a two-stage least squares model of housing supply using the variable elasticity approach. *Urban Studies*, **36 (13)**, 2283–2304.

Quercia, R.G. & Galster, G.C. (2000) Threshold effects and neighborhood change. *Journal of Planning Education and Research*, **20**, 146–63.

Quigley, J.M. (1979) What have we learned about urban housing markets? In: *Current Issues in Urban Economics* (eds M. Straszheim & P. Mieskowski). The Johns Hopkins University Press, Baltimore.

Quigley, J.M. (1982a) Nonlinear budget constraints and consumer demand: An application to public programs for residential housing. *Journal of Urban Economics*, **12**, 177–201.

Quigley, J.M. (1982b) Estimates of a more general model for consumer choice in the housing market. In: *The Urban Economy and Housing* (ed. R. Grieson), 125–40. Heath/Lexington, Lexington, Mass.

Quigley, J.M. (1987) Interest rate variations, income, and home improvement decisions. *Review of Economics and Statistics*, **69 (4)**, 636–43.

Quigley, J.M. (1995) A simple hybrid model for estimating real estate price indexes. *Journal of Housing Economics*, **4 (1)**, 1–12.

Quigley, J.M. (1996) Mortgage performance and housing market discrimination. *Cityscope: A Journal of Policy Development and Research*, **2 (1)**, 59–64.

Quigley, J.M. (ed.) (1998) *The Economics of Housing Markets*. Edward Elgar, Cheltenham.

Quigley, J.M. (2002) Homeowner mobility and mortgage interest rates: New evidence from the 1990s. *Real Estate Economics*. Forthcoming.

Ram, R. (1986) Government size and economic growth: A new framework and some evidence from cross-section and time-series data. *American Economic Review*, **76**, 191–203.

Richmond, P. (1980) The sale of council houses in Worcester. *Policy and Politics*, **8**, 316–17.

Robertson, D.S. (1998) Pulling in opposite directions: the failure of post war planning to regenerate Glasgow. *Planning Perspectives*, **13**, 53–67.

Robinson, R. (1979) *Housing Economics and Public Policy*. Macmillan, Basingstoke.

Robinson, R. (1981) Housing tax expenditure, subsidies and the distribution of income. *The Manchester School*, **49**, 91–110.

Rodgers, B. & Pryor, J. (1998) *Divorce and Separation: the outcomes for children*. Joseph Rowntree Foundation, York.

Rohe, W., McCarthy, G. & Van Zandt, S. (2000) *The social benefits and costs of homeownership; a critical assessment of the research*. Research Institute for Housing America, Working Paper No. 01–01.

Rosen, H.S. (1979) Housing decisions and the U.S. income tax: An econometric analysis. *Journal of Public Economics*, **11**, 1–23.

Rosen, H.S. (1985) Housing subsidies: Effects on decisions, efficiency, and equity. In: *Handbook of Public Economics* (eds A.T. Aurbach & M.S. Feldstein), vol. 1, 375–420. Holland, New York.

Rosen, H.S. & Rosen, K.T. (1980) Federal taxes and homeownership: Evidence from Time Series. *Journal of Political Economy*, **88 (1)**, 59–75.

Rosen, H.S., Rosen, K.T. & Holtz-Eakin, D. (1984) Housing tenure, uncertainty, and taxation. *Review of Economics and Statistics*, **66 (3)**, 405–16.

Rosen, S. (1974) Hedonic prices and implicit markets: product differentiation in pure competition. *Journal of Political Economy*, **82**, 34–55.

Rothenberg, J. (1967) *Economic Evaluation of Urban Renewal*. Brookings Institute, Washington, DC.

Rothenberg, J., Galster, G., Butler, R., & Pitkin, J. (1991) *The Maze of Urban Housing Markets: Theory, Practice and Evidence*. University of Chicago Press, Chicago.

Rothschild, N.M.V. (1971) The organisation and management of government R&D. *A Framework for Government Research and Development* (The Rothschild Report), **Cmnd.4814**, HMSO, London.

Rouwendal, J. (1992) The hedonic price function as an envelope of bid functions: An exercise in applied economic theory. *Netherlands Journal of Housing and the Built Environment*, **7(1)**, 59–80.

Royal Commission on Environmental Pollution (1994) *Transport and the Environment*. Eighteenth Report. **Cmnd. 2674**, HMSO, London.

Rydin, Y. (1985) *Residential Development and the Planning System*. Pergamon, Oxford.

Rydin, Y. (1986) *Housing Land Policy*. Gower, Aldershot.

Satsangi, M. (1991) *Fair's Fair? A Measurement of Subsidies to Tenants of Glasgow's Housing Associations*. University of Glasgow, Centre for Housing Research. Unpublished.

Schelling, T.C. (1971) Dynamic models of segregation. *Journal of Mathematical Sociology*, **1**, 143–86.

Schelling, T.C. (1978) *Micromotives and Macrobehavior*. Norton, New York.

Schnare, A.B. & MacRae, C.D. (1975) *A model of neighborhood change*. The Urban Institute, Contract Report no. 225–4, Washington, DC.

Schnare, A. & Struyk, R.J. (1976) Segmentation in urban housing markets. *Journal of Urban Economics*, **3**, 146–66.

Schoenberg, S. (1980) *Neighborhoods that Work*. Rutgers University Press, New Brunswick, NJ.

School of Planning & Housing (Edinburgh College of Art) in association with the Department of Building Engineering and Surveying, Heriot-Watt University (2001) *The Role of the Planning System in the Provision of Housing*. Scottish Executive, Edinburgh.

Schwirian, K.P. (1983) Models of neighborhood change. *Annual Review of Sociology*, **9**, 83–102.

Scottish Development Department (1977) *Assessing Housing Needs: a manual of guidance*. Scottish Housing Handbook no. 1, HMSO, Edinburgh.

Scottish Federation of Housing Associations (2000) *Financial Impact of Extending Right to Buy to Housing Associations*. SFHA, Edinburgh.

Scottish Homes (1996) *Sales of Public Sector Dwellings in Scotland 1980–95*. Edinburgh.

Scottish Housing Advisory Committee (1972) *Planning for housing needs: pointers towards a comprehensive approach*. HMSO, Edinburgh.

Scottish Office (1977) *Scottish Housing: a consultative document*. **Cmnd 6852**, HMSO, Edinburgh.

Sheppard, S. (1999) Hedonic analysis of housing markets. In: *Handbook of Regional and Urban Economics* (eds P. C. Chesire & E. S. Mills), Vol.3. Elsevier.

Shilling, J.D., Sirmans, C.F. & Dombrow, J.F. (1991) Measuring depreciation in single family rental and owner-occupied housing. *Journal of Housing Economics*, **1(4)**, 368–83.

Short, J., Fleming, S., & Witt, S. (1986) *Housebuilding, Planning and Community Action*. Routledge, London.

Short, K., Garner, T., Johnson, D. & Doyle, P. (1999) *Experimental poverty measures: 1990 to 1997*. Census Report, 60–205, June.

Simpson, D.G. (1998) Why most strategic planning is a waste of time and what you can do about it – Part II. *Long Range Planning*, **31**, 623–27.

Smith, G.R. (1999) *Area-based initiatives: the rationale and options for area targeting*. LSE Case Paper no. 25, London School of Economics, Centre for the Study of Social Exclusion, London.

Smith, L., Rosen, K. & Fallis, G. (1988) Recent developments in economic models of housing markets. *Journal of Economic Literature*, **XXVI**, 29–64.

Smith, M.E.H. (ed.) (1989) *Guide to Housing*, 3rd edn. The Housing Centre Trust, London.

Social Exclusion Unit (1998) *Bringing People Together: A National Strategy for Neighbourhood Renewal*. HMSO, London.

Social Exclusion Unit (2001) *A New Commitment to Neighbourhood Renewal: National Strategy Action Plan*. January, Cabinet Office, London.

Soderberg, B. & Janssen, C. (2001) Estimating distance gradients for apartment properties. *Urban Studies*, **38 (1)**, 61–79.

Solow, R. (1973) On equilibrium models of urban location. In: *Essays in Modern Economics* (eds M. Parkin & A. Nobay). Longmans, London.

Somerville, C.T. & Holmes, C. (2001) Dynamics of the affordable housing stock: Microdata analysis of filtering. *Journal of Housing Research*, **12 (1)**, 115–40.

Stein, J. (1993) Prices and trading volume in the housing market: A model with downpayment effects. *Quarterly Journal of Economics*, **110**, 379–406.

Stephens, M. (2000) Convergence in European mortgage systems before and after EMU. *Journal of Housing and the Built Environment*, **15**, 29–52.

Stephens, M., Burns, N. & Mackey, L. (2002) *Social market or safety net?* Policy Press, Bristol.

Stone, E. (1997) *All About Homelessness*. Shelter, London.

Strassman, P.W. (1991) Housing market interventions and mobility: An international comparison. *Urban Studies*, **28**, 759–71.

Straszheim, M. (1974) Hedonic estimation of housing prices: a further comment. *Review of Economics and Statistics*, **56(3)**, 404–6.

Straszheim, M. (1975) *An Econometric Analysis of the Urban Housing Market*. NBER, New York.

Straszheim, M. (1987) The theory of urban residential location. In: *Handbook of Regional and Urban Economics. Volume II Urban Economics* (ed. E. Mills). Elsevier Science, BV.

Stretton, H. (1971) *Ideas for Australian Cities*. Georgian House, Melbourne.

Stretton, H. (1974) *Housing and Government*. Australian Broadcasting Corporation, Boyer Lectures.

Stretton, H. (1978) *Urban Planning in Rich and Poor Countries*. Oxford University Press, Oxford.

Struyk, R. (with Malpezzi, S. & Wann, F.) (1980) *The Performance Funding System Inflation Factor: Analysis of Predictive Ability of Candidate Series and Models*. Urban Institute Working Paper 1436–02.

Suits, D.B. (1984) Dummy variables: mechanics vs. interpretation. *Review of Economics and Statistics*, **66**, 177–80.

Suits, D.B., Mason, A. & Chan, L. (1978) Spline Functions Fitted by Standard Regression Methods. *Review of Economics and Statistics*, **60**, 132–9.

Sunley, E.M. (1987) Comment on Gordon, R.H., Hines J.R. (Jr), & Summers, L.H. In: *The Effects of Taxation on Capital Accumulation* (ed. M. Feldstein), 254–57. Chicago University Press, Chicago.

Sweeney, J. (1974) A Commodity Hierarchy Model of the Rental Housing Market. *Journal of Urban Economics*, **1**, 288–323.

Taub, R.D., Taylor, G. & Dunham, J. (1984) *Paths of Neighborhood Change*. University of Chicago Press, Chicago.

Temkin, K. & Rohe, W. (1996) Neighborhood change and urban policy. *Journal of Planning Education and Research*, **15,** 159–70.

Tewdyr-Jones, M. (1996) *British Planning Policy in Transition: planning in the 1990s*. UCL Press, London.

Thibodeau, T.G. (2002) *Marking Single-Family Property Values to Market Using Hedonic House Price Equations*. Presidential Address to the American Real Estate and Urban Economics Association, Atlanta, January 5.

Thomas, A. (1993) The influence of wages and house prices on British interregional migration decisions. *Applied Economics*, **25**, 1261–68.

Tiebout, C. (1956) A pure theory of local expenditures. *Journal of Political Economy*, **64 (5)**, 416–24.

Titman, S. D. (1982) The effect of anticipated inflation on housing market equilibrium. *Journal of Finance*, **37,** 827–42.

Tiwari, P. & Hasegawa, H. (2000) House price dynamics in Mumbai, 1989–1995. *Review of Urban and Regional Development Studies*, **12(2)**, 149–63.

Tracy, J., Schneider, H., & Chan, S. (1999) Are stocks overtaking real estate in household portfolios? *Current Issues in Economics and Finance*, **5 (5)**, 1–6.

Triplett, J.E. (1974) *Consumer Demand and Characteristics of Consumption Goods*. BLS Working Paper No. 22.

Truesdale, D. (1980) House sales and owner occupation in Stevenage New Town. *Policy and Politics*, **8**, 318–23.

Tsoukis, C. & Westaway, P. (1991) A forward-looking model of housing construction in the U.K. *Econometric Modelling*, **11**, 266–78.

Tu, Y. (1997) The local housing submarket structure and its properties. *Urban Studies*, **34 (2)**, 337–53.

Tu, Y. & Goldfinch, J. (1996) A two stage housing choice forecasting model. *Urban Studies*, **33 (3)**, 517–37.

Turner, B. (1997) Housing cooperatives in Sweden: The effects of financial deregulation. *Journal of Real Estate Finance and Economics*, **15 (2)**, 193–217.

Turner, B. & Whitehead, C.M.E. (1993) *Housing Finance in the 1990s*. Research Report SB:56, The National Swedish Institute for Building Research, Gavle.

Turner, B. & Whitehead, C.M.E. (2002) Reducing housing subsidy: Swedish housing policy in an international context. *Urban Studies*, **39 (2)**, 201–17.

Turner, B., Whitehead, C.M.E. & Jakobsson, J. (1996) *Comparative Housing Finance*. Swedish Government Housing Commission, Bosdstadspolitik 2000, Expertrapporter, SOU.

Vandell, K.D. (1995) Market factors affecting spatial heterogeneity among urban neighborhoods. *Housing Policy Debate*, **6 (1)**, 103–39.

Vandell, K.D. (2000) Comment on Steven C. Bourassa and William G. Grigsby's 'Income Tax Concessions for Owner-Occupied Housing'. *Housing Policy Debate*, **11 (3)**, 561–74.

Van Zilj, V. (1993) *A Guide to Local Housing Needs Assessments*. Institute of Housing, Coventry.

Varady, D.P. (1996) Local Housing Plans: Learning from Great Britain. *Housing Policy Debate*, **7**, 253–92.

Venti, F. & Wise, D.A. (1984) Moving and housing expenditure: Transaction costs and disequilibrium. *Journal of Public Economics*, **23**, 207–43.

Von Boventer, E. (1978) Bandwagon effects and product cycles in urban dynamics. *Urban Studies*, **15**, 261–72.

Wallace, H.A. (1926) Comparative farmland values in Iowa. *Journal of Land and Public Utility Economics*, **2**, 385–92.

Wang, F.T. & Zorn, P.M. (1997) Estimating house price growth with repeat sales data: What's the aim of the game? *Journal of Housing Economics*, **6**, 93–118.

Warren, D. (1975) *Black Neighborhoods: An Assessment of Community Power*. University of Michigan Press, Ann Arbor, MI.

Warren, R. & Warren, D. (1977) *The Neighborhood Organizer's Handbook*. Notre Dame University Press, South Bend, IN.

Watkins, C. (1998) The definition and identification of housing submarkets. *Discussion Paper* 98-10, Centre for Property Research, Department of Land Economy, University of Aberdeen, Scotland.

Watts, H. (1964) *An Introduction to the Theory of Binary Variables (Or, All About Dummies)*. University of Wisconsin. Unpublished.

Weber, M. (1978) *Economy and Society*. University of California Press, Berkeley, California.

Weibull, W.J. (1983) A dynamic model of trade frictions and disequilibrium in the housing market. *Scandinavian Journal of Economics*, **85**, 373–92.

Weibull, W.J. (1984) A stock flow approach to general equilibrium with trade frictions. *Applied Mathematics and Computation*, **14**, 251–76.

Weicher, J.C. (2000) Comment on Steven C. Bourassa and William G. Grigsby's 'Income Tax Concessions for Owner-Occupied Housing'. *Housing Policy Debate*, **11** (3), 547–59.

Weinberg, D.J., Friedman, J. & Mayo, S.K. (1981) Intraurban residential mobility: The role of transactions costs, market imperfections, and household disequilibrium. *Journal of Urban Economics*, **9** (3), 332–48.

Weiss, Y. (1978) Capital gains, discriminatory taxes, and the choice between renting and owning a house. *Journal of Public Economics*, **10** (1), 45–55.

Wheaton, W. (1974) A Comparative Static Analysis of Urban Spatial Structure. *Journal of Economic Theory*, **9**, 223–37.

Wheaton, W. & DiPasquale, D. (1996) *Urban Economics and Real Estate Markets*. Prentice Hall, Englewood Cliffs, NJ.

Whitehead, C.M.E. (1974) *The U.K. Housing Market: An Econometric Model*. Gower, Aldershot.

Whitehead, C.M.E. (1983) The rationale of government interventions. In: *Urban Land Policies: Issues and Opportunities* (ed. H. Dunkerley). Oxford University Press, Oxford.

Whitehead, C.M.E. (1984) Privatisation and housing. In: *Privatisation and the Welfare State* (eds J. Le Grand & R. Robinson). Allen & Unwin, London.

Whitehead, C.M.E. (1991) From need to affordability: an analysis of U.K. housing objectives. *Housing Studies*, **28** (6), 871–87.

Whitehead, C.M.E. (1993) Privatising housing: An assessment of U.K. experience. *Housing Policy Debate*, **4** (1), 104–39.

Whitehead, C.M.E. (1998) *The Benefits of Better Homes*. Shelter, London.

Whitehead, C.M.E. (1999) Urban Housing Markets: Theory and Policy. In: *Handbook of Regional and Urban Economics* (eds P. Chesire & E.S. Mills), Vol. 3. Elsevier.

Whitehead, C. & Odling-Smee, J. (1975) Long-run equilibrium in urban housing. *Urban Studies*, **12**, 315–18.

Wilcox, S. (1998) The numbers game. *Inside Housing*, February, 17–18.

Wilkinson, R. (1996) *Unhealthy Societies: Afflictions of Inequality*. Routledge, London.

Williams, N.J. (1993) Homeownership and the Sale of Public Sector Housing in Great Britain. In: *Ownership, Control and the Future of Housing Policy* (ed. R. Allen Hays), Ch.5. Greenwood Press, Westport.

Williams, N.J. & Sewel, J.B. (1987) *Council house sales in the rural environment*. In: *Rural Housing in Scotland* (eds B.D. MacGregor, D.S. Robertson & M. Shucksmith), Chap. 7. Aberdeen University Press, Aberdeen.

Williams, N.J. & Twine, F.E. (1992) Increasing access or widening choice: the role of resold public sector dwellings in the housing market. *Environment and Planning A*, **24**, 1585–98.

Williams, N.J. & Twine, F.E. (1993) Moving on and trading up: the experience of households who resell public sector dwellings. *Housing Studies*, **8**, 60–69.

Williams, N.J., Sewel, J.B. & Twine, F.E. (1984) The sale of council houses – some empirical evidence. *Urban Studies*, **21**, 439–50.

Williams, N.J., Sewel, J.B. & Twine, F.E. (1986) Council house sales and residualisation. *Journal of Social Policy*, **15**, 273–92.

Williams, N.J., Sewel, J.B. & Twine, F.E. (1987) Council house sales and the electorate: voting behaviour and ideological implications. *Housing Studies*, **2**, 274–82.

Williams, N.J., Sewel, J.B. & Twine, F.E. (1988) Council house sales: an analysis of the factors associated with purchase and implications for the future of public sector housing. *Tijdschrift voor Economische en Sociale Geografie*, **79**, 39–49.

Williams, N.J. & Twine, F.E. (1994) Locals, incomers and second homes: the role of resold public sector dwellings in rural Scotland. *Scandinavian Housing and Planning Research*, **11**, 193–209.

Williamson, O. (1975) *Markets and Hierarchies: Analysis and antitrust implications: A study in the economics of internal organisation*. The Free Press, New York.

Williamson, O.E. (1979) Transaction costs economics: the governance of contractual relations. *Journal of Law and Economics*, **22**, 233–61.

Williamson, O. (1985) *The Economic Institutions of Capitalism: Firms, markets and relational contracting*. The Free Press, New York.

Williamson, O. (1986) *Economic Organisation*. Wheatsheaf Books, Brighton.

Willis, K.G. & Cameron, S.J. (1993) Costs and benefits of housing subsidies in the Newcastle area: A comparison of alternative subsidy definitions across tenure sectors and income definitions. In: *Housing Finance and Subsidies in Britain*, (eds D. Maclennan, & K. Gibb). Avebury, Aldershot.

Willis, K.G. & Nicholson, M. (1991) Costs and benefits of housing subsidies to tenants from voluntary and involuntary rent control: A comparison between tenures and income groups. *Applied Economics*, **23 (6)**, 1103–15.

Wilson, W. J. (1987) *The Truly Disadvantaged*. University of Chicago Press, Chicago IL.

Wilson, W. (1999) *The Right to Buy*. House of Commons Research Paper 99/36.

Wiltshaw, D.G. (1985) The supply of land. *Urban Studies*, **22**, 49–56.

Witte, A.D., Sumka, H. & Erekson, J. (1979) An estimate of a structural hedonic price model of the housing market: An application of Rosen's Theory of Implicit Markets. *Econometrica*, **47**, 1151–72.

Wood, G.A. (1988a) *The role of housing in economic growth*. Working Paper No.21, Murdoch University.

Wood, G.A. (1988b) Housing tax expenditures in OECD countries: Economic impacts and prospects for reform. *Policy and Politics*, **16 (4)**, 235–50.

Wood, G.A. (1992) How do Australian State and Local Governments tax residential housing? *Australian Tax Forum*, **9 (4)**, 441–72.

Wood, G.A. (1995) *The taxation of owner occupied housing in Australia: affordability and distributional issues*. PhD dissertation, Murdoch University.

Wood, G.A. (1996) The contribution of selling costs and local and state government taxes to home buyers' user-cost of capital. *Australian Economic Papers*, **35 (66)**, 60–73.

Wood, G.A. (2001) Are there tax arbitrage opportunities in private rental housing markets? *Journal of Housing Economics*, **10 (1)**, 1–20.

Wood, G.A. & Kemp, P.A. (2001) *The taxation of British landlords: an international comparison*. Paper presented at Tenth Annual International Real Estate Conference (AREUEA). Cancun, Mexico, 6–8 May.

Wood, G.A. & Maclennan, D. (1982) Search adjustment in local housing markets. In: *Modelling Housing Market Search* (ed. W.A.V. Clark), 54–80. Croom Helm, London.

Wood, G.A. & Watson, R. (2001) Marginal suppliers, taxation and rental housing: Evidence from microdata. *Journal of Housing Research*, **12 (1)**, 91–114.

Wood, G.A. & Tu, Y. (2001) *Are there rent clientele groups among investors in rental housing?* Paper accepted for presentation at 10th Annual International Real Estate Conference, May 6–8, 2001, Cancun, Mexico.

Wood, G.A., Watson, R. & Flatau, P. (2001) Tax preferences, effective marginal tax rates and the incentive to invest in residential rental housing. School of Economics Working Paper, presented at 30th Annual Conference of Australia Economists, Perth, September 23–26.

Wood, P.W. & Preston, J. (1997) *Assessing Housing Need: a guidance manual*. Scottish Office Development Department, Edinburgh.

Yates, J. & Flood, J. (1987) *Housing Subsidies Study*. Housing Research Council, Project Series No.160.

Yates, J. & Whitehead, C.M.E. (1998) In defence of greater agnosticism: a response to Galster's 'Comparing demand-side and supply-side subsidies.' *Housing Studies*, **13 (3)**, 415–23.

Yates, J. & Wulff, M. (2000) Whither low cost private rental housing? *Urban Policy and Research*, **18 (1)**, 45–64.

Zodrow, G. (1983) *Local Provision of Public Services: The Tiebout Model After Twenty-Five Years*. Academic Press, NY.

Index

Abraham, J.M. 76
academic environment *see* universities
access-space model *see* trade-off model
Adair, A. 54, 84, 195
Adam Smith Institute 272
Adams, D. 196
adjustment costs 59–60
administrative costs 58–9
administrative failure 13, 140, 148, 150–1
adverse selection 103
aesthetics 255
affordability 15, 42, 173, 182–8, 239
aggregation 104–6
Agpar, W. 31
Allen, F. 150
allocation of social and public housing 137,
    148, 152
allowances 31
Alonso, W. 22, 23, 84
Ambrose, B.W. 77
Amemiya, T. 79
Anas, A. 23, 26, 30, 31, 76, 196
Andrew, M. 32, 105
Angel, S. 86
Anglin, P.M. 86
Anstie, R. 119
appraisal of housing 85
Apps, Patricia 251
arbitrage, taxation 12, 118–22
Arnott, R. 22, 23, 26, 30, 31, 196
Arrow, K.J. 140
asset pricing models 175
asymmetric information 140
Atkinson, A.B. 3
Attanasio, O.P. 93
Australia
    legal and administrative costs 59

research on housing in 251
search costs 58
social and public housing 137
taxation in 112, 114–15, 116, 117, 120, 122,
    128
Austrian economics 2
Auten, G.E. 127
Awan, K. 74, 85

Baker, R. 150
Ball, M. 83, 95, 97, 193, 195
Ballas, D. 229
Baratz, G. 22, 29
Barclay, Peter 279
Barkham, R. 98
Barlow, J. 196
Barr, N. 138
Bartik, T.J. 60
Bartlett, W. 195, 196
Barton, D.M. 85
Bassett, K. 237
Basu, S. 86
Bate, R. 196
Beazley, M. 237
Bednarz, R. 85
Bender, A. 84
Berg, L. 94
Bergstrom, R. 94
Berry, B.J. L. 54, 85
Berry, J. 54
Best, R. 278
bidding 39, 40
Black, J. 98
Blackaby, B. 136, 221
Blackaby, D.H. 94
Blackaby, R. 224–5, 231
Boelhouwer, P.J. 93